THE ULTIMATE STAR WARS AND PHILOSOPHY

The Blackwell Philosophy and Pop Culture Series
Series editor William Irwin

A spoonful of sugar helps the medicine go down, and a healthy helping of popular culture clears the cobwebs from Kant. Philosophy has had a public relations problem for a few centuries now. This series aims to change that, showing that philosophy is relevant to your life – and not just for answering the big questions like "To be or not to be?" but for answering the little questions: "To watch or not to watch *South Park*?" Thinking deeply about TV, movies, and music doesn't make you a "complete idiot." In fact, it might make you a philosopher, someone who believes the unexamined life is not worth living and the unexamined cartoon is not worth watching.

Already published in the series:

24 and Philosophy: The World According to Jack
Edited by Jennifer Hart Weed, Richard Brian Davis, and Ronald Weed

30 Rock and Philosophy: We Want to Go to There
Edited by J. Jeremy Wisnewski

Alice in Wonderland and Philosophy: Curiouser and Curiouser
Edited by Richard Brian Davis

Arrested Development and Philosophy: They've Made a Huge Mistake
Edited by Kristopher Phillips and J. Jeremy Wisnewski

Avatar and Philosophy: Learning to See
Edited by George A. Dunn

The Avengers and Philosophy: Earth's Mightiest Thinkers
Edited by Mark D. White

Batman and Philosophy: The Dark Knight of the Soul
Edited by Mark D. White and Robert Arp

Battlestar Galactica and Philosophy: Knowledge Here Begins Out There
Edited by Jason T. Eberl

The Big Bang Theory and Philosophy: Rock, Paper, Scissors, Aristotle, Locke
Edited by Dean Kowalski

The Big Lebowski and Philosophy: Keeping Your Mind Limber with Abiding Wisdom
Edited by Peter S. Fosl

BioShock and Philosophy: Irrational Game, Rational Book
Edited by Luke Cuddy

Black Sabbath and Philosophy: Mastering Reality
Edited by William Irwin

The Daily Show and Philosophy: Moments of Zen in the Art of Fake News
Edited by Jason Holt

Downton Abbey and Philosophy: The Truth Is Neither Here nor There
Edited by Mark D. White

Dungeons & Dragons and Philosophy: Read and Gain Advantage on All Wisdom Checks
Edited by Christopher Robichaud

Ender's Game and Philosophy: The Logic Gate is Down
Edited by Kevin S. Decker

Family Guy and Philosophy: A Cure for the Petarded
Edited by J. Jeremy Wisnewski

Final Fantasy and Philosophy: The Ultimate Walkthrough
Edited by Jason P. Blahuta and Michel S. Beaulieu

Game of Thrones and Philosophy: Logic Cuts Deeper Than Swords
Edited by Henry Jacoby

The Girl With the Dragon Tattoo and Philosophy: Everything Is Fire
Edited by Eric Bronson

Green Lantern and Philosophy: No Evil Shall Escape This Book
Edited by Jane Dryden and Mark D. White

Heroes and Philosophy: Buy the Book, Save the World
Edited by David Kyle Johnson

The Hobbit and Philosophy: For When You've Lost Your Dwarves, Your Wizard, and Your Way
Edited by Gregory Bassham and Eric Bronson

House and Philosophy: Everybody Lies
Edited by Henry Jacoby

The Hunger Games and Philosophy: A Critique of Pure Treason
Edited by George Dunn and Nicolas Michaud

Inception and Philosophy: Because It's Never Just a Dream
Edited by David Johnson

Iron Man and Philosophy: Facing the Stark Reality
Edited by Mark D. White

Lost and Philosophy: The Island Has Its Reasons
Edited by Sharon M. Kaye

Mad Men and Philosophy: Nothing Is as It Seems
Edited by James South and Rod Carveth

Metallica and Philosophy: A Crash Course in Brain Surgery
Edited by William Irwin

The Office and Philosophy: Scenes from the Unfinished Life
Edited by J. Jeremy Wisnewski

Sons of Anarchy and Philosophy: Brains Before Bullets
Edited by George A. Dunn and Jason T. Eberl

South Park and Philosophy: You Know, I Learned Something Today
Edited by Robert Arp

Spider-Man and Philosophy: The Web of Inquiry
Edited by Jonathan Sanford

Superman and Philosophy: What Would the Man of Steel Do?
Edited by Mark D. White

Supernatural and Philosophy: Metaphysics and Monsters ... for Idjits
Edited by Galen Foresman

Terminator and Philosophy: I'll Be Back, Therefore I Am
Edited by Richard Brown and Kevin Decker

True Blood and Philosophy: We Wanna Think Bad Things with You
Edited by George Dunn and Rebecca Housel

Twilight and Philosophy: Vampires, Vegetarians, and the Pursuit of Immortality
Edited by Rebecca Housel and J. Jeremy Wisnewski

The Ultimate Daily Show and Philosophy: More Moments of Zen, More Moments of Indecision Theory
Edited by Jason Holt

The Ultimate Harry Potter and Philosophy: Hogwarts for Muggles
Edited by Gregory Bassham

The Ultimate Lost and Philosophy: Think Together, Die Alone
Edited by Sharon Kaye

The Ultimate South Park and Philosophy: Respect My Philosophah!
Edited by Robert Arp and Kevin S. Decker

The Ultimate Star Wars and Philosophy: You Must Unlearn What You Have Learned
Edited by Jason T. Eberl and Kevin S. Decker

Veronica Mars and Philosophy
Edited by George A. Dunn

The Walking Dead and Philosophy: Shotgun. Machete. Reason.
Edited by Christopher Robichaud

Watchmen and Philosophy: A Rorschach Test
Edited by Mark D. White

X-Men and Philosophy: Astonishing Insight and Uncanny Argument in the Mutant X-Verse
Edited by Rebecca Housel and J. Jeremy Wisnewski

THE ULTIMATE STAR WARS AND PHILOSOPHY

YOU MUST UNLEARN WHAT YOU HAVE LEARNED

Edited by
Jason T. Eberl
and
Kevin S. Decker

WILEY Blackwell

Library of Congress Cataloging-in-Publication Data

   The ultimate Star Wars and philosophy : you must unlearn what you have learned / Edited by Jason T. Eberl and Kevin S. Decker.
     pages cm – (Blackwell philosophy and popculture series)
     Includes index.
     ISBN 978-1-119-03806-1 (pbk.)
   1. Star Wars films.   2. Philosophy in motion pictures.   3. Philosophy in literature.   I. Eberl, Jason T., editor.   II. Decker, Kevin S., editor.   III. Series: Blackwell philosophy and popculture series.
   PN1995.9.S695U46 2015
   791.43′75–dc23   2015012933

A catalogue record for this book is available from the British Library.

Set in 10.5/13pt SabonLTStd by Aptara Inc., New Delhi, India

1   2016

Contents

From the Journal of the Whills ...

Acknowledgments: Legacy of the Force   ix

Introduction: "The Circle Is Now Complete"   1

I   The Philosophical Menace   **5**

1   The Platonic Paradox of Darth Plagueis: How Could a
Sith Lord Be Wise?   7
Terrance MacMullan

2   "You Are Asking Me to Be Rational": Stoic Philosophy
and the Jedi Order   20
Matt Hummel

3   The Jedi Knights of Faith: Anakin, Luke, and Søren
(Kierkegaard)   31
William A. Lindenmuth

4   Anakin and Achilles: Scars of Nihilism   42
Don Adams

5   Dark Times: The End of the Republic and the Beginning of
Chinese Philosophy   53
Kevin S. Decker

II Attack of the Morals 65

6 Chasing Kevin Smith: Was It Immoral for the Rebel
Alliance to Destroy Death Star II? 67
Charles C. Camosy

7 The Ballad of Boba Fett: Mercenary Agency and
Amoralism in War 79
David LaRocca

8 How Guilty Is Jar Jar Binks? 90
Nicolas Michaud

9 "Know the Dark Side": A Theodicy of the Force 100
Jason T. Eberl

III Revenge of the Alliance 115

10 "Like My Father before Me": Loss and Redemption of
Fatherhood in *Star Wars* 117
Charles Taliaferro and Annika Beck

11 The Friends of a Jedi: Friendship, Family, and Civic Duty
in a Galaxy at War 127
Greg Littmann

12 Light Side, Dark Side, and Switching Sides: Loyalty and
Betrayal in *Star Wars* 136
Daniel Malloy

13 Guardians and Tyrants in the Republics of *Star Wars* and
Plato 148
Adam Barkman and Kyle Alkema

IV A New Hermeneutic 159

14 Pregnant Padmé and Slave Leia: *Star Wars'* Female
Role Models 161
Cole Bowman

15 Docile Bodies and a Viscous Force: Fear of the Flesh in
Return of the Jedi 172
Jennifer L. McMahon

16 Of Battle Droids and Zillo Beasts: Moral Status in the *Star Wars* Galaxy 183
James M. Okapal

V Metaphysics Strikes Back **193**

17 Why the Force Must Have a Dark Side 195
George A. Dunn

18 What Is It Like to Be a Jedi? A Life in the Force 208
Marek McGann

19 "Never Tell Me the Odds": An Inquiry Concerning Jedi Understanding 219
Andrew Zimmerman Jones

VI Return of the Non-Human **229**

20 Mindless Philosophers and Overweight Globs of Grease: Are Droids Capable of Thought? 231
Dan Burkett

21 Can Chewie Speak? Wittgenstein and the Philosophy of Language 240
Rhiannon Grant and Myfanwy Reynolds

22 Can the Zillo Beast Strike Back? Cloning, De-extinction, and the Species Problem 250
Leonard Finkelman

VII The Fandom Awakens **261**

23 "In That Time … " in a Galaxy Far, Far Away: Epic Myth-Understandings and Myth-Appropriation in *Star Wars* 263
John Thompson

24 *Star Wars*, Emotions, and the Paradox of Fiction 274
Lance Belluomini

25 The Mind of Blue Snaggletooth: The Intentional Stance,
Vintage *Star Wars* Action Figures, and the Origins of
Religion   287
Dennis Knepp

26 Gospel, Gossip, and Ghent: How Should We Understand
the New *Star Wars*?   296
Roy T. Cook and Nathan Kellen

Contributors: Troopers of the 501st Legion   308

Index   317

Acknowledgments
Legacy of the Force

The *Star Wars* saga has inspired us to explore questions of metaphysics, morality, politics, and the seven forms of lightsaber combat, from our earliest years as younglings, through our apprenticeship as padawan philosophers, to becoming Socratic Knights and, perhaps one day, Masters of Reason – and hopefully not Dark Lords of any sort! For this tremendous influence on our intellectual formation, we owe an incalculable debt of gratitude to Grand Master George Lucas and all of his creative collaborators, as well as the authors and artists who've expanded the saga from the *Dawn of the Jedi* more than 36,000 years before the Battle of Yavin (BBY) through the continuing *Legacy* of the Skywalker family over 130 years after the Battle of Yavin (ABY).

They say it takes an Ewok village to destroy a Death Star, but it takes much more to assemble a book like this. First of all, this book wouldn't exist without the contributions of the authors, and we recommend that their wisdom should be preserved in a Holocron for future generations. Tackling a Death Star also requires leadership of the likes of Admiral Ackbar or General Crix Madine. In our case, we benefited extensively from the experience of editorial Grand Moff Bill Irwin. It's also essential to have some Bothan spies who can smuggle out the Death Star plans. For this project, we depended on the "insiders" at John Wiley & Sons, Liam Cooper and Allison Kostka, to guide us to our target.

Our widows to *Star Wars*, Suzanne and Jennifer, have patiently endured years of our debating the taxation of trade routes in the Outer

Rim territories, the romantic wooing skills of future Sith Lords, what sort of crystal powers a purple lightsaber, why AT-ATs don't explode when they're standing but do after they're brought down, and whether the Sarlaac looks better with or without its beak. Finally, passing on the *Star Wars* legacy to our children, Kennedy, Ethan, Jack, and August, has been a source of tremendous joy for us as we engaged in mock lightsaber duels and taught them the crucial importance of remembering that HAN SHOT FIRST!

Introduction
"The Circle Is Now Complete"

Star Wars has always inspired probing questions:

January 31, 1997: Lucasfilm/20th Century Fox releases the "Special Edition" of *Episode IV: A New Hope*, igniting a firestorm of controversy over the question, "Who shot first – Han or Greedo?"

May 19, 1999: Lucasfilm/20th Century Fox releases *Episode I: The Phantom Menace*, creating deep public concern centered on the question, "Why is Jar Jar even in this movie?"

May 19, 2005: Lucasfilm/20th Century Fox releases *Episode III: Revenge of the Sith* with its implied violent deaths of younglings and Anakin's gory immolation scene, raising the question in the minds of parents, "Is *Star Wars* still for kids?"

April 25, 2014: StarWars.com announces that the "Expanded Universe" of *Star Wars* outside of the films, radio, and television series is noncanonical, inviting dozens of novel and comic writers to ask the question, "What did I ever do to George?"

November 28, 2014: Lucasfilm releases the trailer for *Episode VII: The Force Awakens*, prompting aspiring Jedi Knights to question, "Does lightsaber design adhere to *any* safety standards?"

The Ultimate Star Wars and Philosophy: You Must Unlearn What You Have Learned, First Edition. Edited by Jason T. Eberl and Kevin S. Decker.
© 2016 John Wiley & Sons, Ltd. Published 2016 by John Wiley & Sons, Ltd.

Beyond fan speculation, and sometimes fan angst, *Star Wars* has also inspired philosophical questions. Here are some examples (in the order Lucas intended):

Episode I: Does having a "destiny" foretold by prophecy rob a person of freedom?

Episode II: How does fear motivate the transformation of democracy into tyranny?

Episode III: Is the difference between good and evil merely a "point of view"?

Episode IV: Is wisdom truly a matter of trusting one's feelings?

Episode V: Do we all have a "dark side" that we must confront within ourselves?

Episode VI: Is it possible to redeem a life spent causing so much evil and suffering?

Episode VII: Is having a beard essential to being a Jedi Master?

Clearly, much of the world has by now got *Star Wars* under its skin. The cultural significance of phrases like "Luke, I am your father," "I've got a bad feeling about this," and "Do or do not, there is no try" aren't merely pop culture clichés. They've penetrated academia, and there are hundreds of scholarly articles and books examining the deeper meaning of George Lucas's fantastical creation. One of these, *Star Wars and Philosophy: More Powerful than You Can Possibly Imagine* (Open Court, 2005), was put together by the valiant editors of the volume you're currently reading and came to Lucas's attention. This may have inspired him to ask a question of his own: "What other deep cultural connections could be made with *Star Wars*?" In turn, this question led him to commission a series of books relating themes in *Star Wars* with history, political science, and religion. In 2007, The History Channel premiered a documentary, *Star Wars: The Legacy Revealed*, which included interviews with scholars commenting on the saga's historical and mythological roots and connections. As much as *Star Wars* presents us with thoughtful examples of philosophical Stoicism (with the Jedi's calm detachment even when being chased by large gooberfish), or raises questions about the mysterious Force (is it an energy field or a bunch of midi-chlorians?) or the power of both hate and forgiveness (as the Emperor and Luke battle for Vader's soul), it also urges us to understand our own historical, religious, and political circumstances. *Star Wars* endures because we see ourselves in its myriad facets.

Of course, a lot has happened since the original *Star Wars and Philosophy* was published just before the release of *Episode III*, not the least of which are the excitement and enthusiasm generated by the knowledge that director J.J. Abrams is kicking off a new trilogy of films set some years after *Episode VI*, and that there are likely to be other films (a Boba Fett spinoff?) as well. As philosophers, the contributors of the various essays in the pages that follow can't speculate on the deeper meaning of what's yet to come. Indeed, as the German thinker G.W.F. Hegel claimed, philosophy only captures *its own time* in thought – so maybe this won't be the "ultimate" volume on *Star Wars* and philosophy after the next trilogy is over! Still, the brilliant chapters you're about to read contribute in novel ways to the critical appreciation of the *Star Wars* saga so far for fans and philosophers alike.

We've been able to delve into subjects that the original *Star Wars and Philosophy* missed, subjects prompted by not only the six feature films to date but also the *Clone Wars* television series and stories from the Expanded Universe. This book also includes new takes on familiar topics like the nature of the Force – does it *have* to have a dark side? – and whether the minds of droids are similar to our own. Feminist authors critically look at how women are portrayed (in elaborate headgear or in gold bikinis) and treated (choked by their husband or chained to a giant slug) in the films. There's even a chapter on Boba Fett, our favorite bounty hunter, and his moral code (or lack thereof). Ties of family and friendship are important in the *Star Wars* galaxy, so several philosophers examine the moral psychology behind the relationships between characters from slaves to princesses. One chapter even answers the age-old question, "Can Chewie speak?"

We also examine the philosophical significance behind the impact of *Star Wars* on the real world as an important artifact of pop culture. Kevin Smith's charge – voiced by slacker Randal in the film *Clerks* – that the Rebellion is actually a terrorist organization comes up for debate. Other chapters engage with the legacy of Joseph Campbell to examine the dark side of the saga's mythological foundation, or offer a framework for understanding what's "canonical" in *Star Wars* – giving fans good reason to assert once and for all that Han shot first.

It turns out that the philosophical questions that inspired us to collect some of the brightest minds in the galaxy in *Star Wars and Philosophy* were only the beginning. With the volume you hold in your hands, the circle is now complete, and those who were once learners may start on the path toward becoming philosophical masters. May the Force be with you!

Episode I

THE PHILOSOPHICAL MENACE

The Platonic Paradox of Darth Plagueis: How Could a Sith Lord Be Wise?

Terrance MacMullan

"Did you ever hear the tragedy of Darth Plagueis the Wise?" When Anakin's friend and mentor Chancellor Palpatine casually asks him this question as they enjoy a Mon Calamari ballet on Coruscant, you can almost hear Anakin wonder to himself, "How could a *Sith* be *wise*?" Believed extinct for a thousand years, the Sith had a terrifying reputation as malicious agents of irrepressible evil. From a certain point of view, particularly that of a Jedi, the idea of a *wise Sith* is quite odd, if not outright impossible.

Another sage who would've been confounded by the idea of a wise Sith was Plato of Athens (429–347 BCE). As a Sith, Plagueis was a devotee of the Dark Side of the Force, which grants enormous powers to those brave enough to become living conduits for passions like hatred and anger. Such a person would be the exact opposite of what Plato would call "wise." For Plato, wisdom is a virtue that is inextricably bound to humility and justice: it is found in the soul of the person who has learned to subdue their spirit and appetite through the exercise of reason. "Plagueis the Wise Lord of the Sith" therefore would present an insurmountable paradox to Plato: if Plagueis is a master of using, rather than calming, his spirit and indulging his appetites, how could he possibly be wise? How is it that he was able to live for well over a century without suffering the self-destruction that Plato foresees for anyone who does not rein in spirit and appetite?

The Ultimate Star Wars and Philosophy: You Must Unlearn What You Have Learned, First Edition. Edited by Jason T. Eberl and Kevin S. Decker.
© 2016 John Wiley & Sons, Ltd. Published 2016 by John Wiley & Sons, Ltd.

This paradox opens horizons for reflection on the themes of ethics, wisdom, and freedom. It also raises the possibility that Plato's ideal of wisdom is too narrow, and that a different philosophy of life might better explain the existence of a wise Dark Lord of the Sith.

Respect for the Difference between Knowledge and Wisdom

No philosopher is more tightly linked with wisdom than Plato. Indeed, when we think of *philosophy* as meaning "the love of wisdom" (*philo* means "love of," and *sophia* is usually translated as "wisdom"), where wisdom is the virtue associated with rationality, moderation, and moral goodness, we are in fact using a definition developed by Plato. Like most philosophers of the ancient world, Plato distinguished knowledge (or *gnosis* in Greek) from wisdom. Knowledge is the straightforward matter of experienced information about the world: once Han Solo gets close enough to a mysterious, large object in space and registers the effect of a tractor beam, he *knows* that the Death Star is no moon. However, wisdom is a subtler thing: on board the *Millennium Falcon*, Obi-Wan doesn't know what the thing is either, but he's wise enough to exhort Han to turn the Falcon around before they're seized by a tractor beam. Plato quotes his master Socrates in the *Apology* as saying that "the wisest of you ... is he who has realized ... that in respect of wisdom he is really worthless."[1] This ideal of wisdom rests on the virtue of humility: in the face of a universe of immense possibilities, the wisdom of a mortal creature is worth little or nothing. This is why Plato would have approved of Dexter Jettster's gentle scolding of Obi-Wan in *Attack of the Clones*: it was unwise to think that the knowledge contained in the Jedi Archives could ever be totally comprehensive. Unlike Jedi archivist Jocasta Nu, who somewhat proudly proclaims, "If an item does not appear in our records, it does not exist," a truly wise Jedi would know she could not know all there is to know!

Before Plato, *sophia* had very different meanings. Friedrich Nietzsche (1844–1900) tells us that *sophia*, in its original sense, meant something like discerning taste.[2] So the original lovers of *sophia* were people who had cultivated a nuanced appreciation for the finer things, perhaps like the suave scoundrel Lando Calrissian, who – despite his

Bespin mining installation being infested by Imperial forces ready to abduct his friends – can't help but pause and admire Leia's beauty! During the time of Socrates and Plato, the word *sophia* had evolved to carry a grittier connotation, close to something like practical "know-how."[3] In this second sense, the canny and resourceful Han Solo, not Yoda, would be the wisest philosopher.

The philosophical rivals of Plato and Socrates, the Sophists, were teachers of rhetoric and masters of persuasion, adept at swaying the masses. Sophists rejected the idea that there were universal standards for things like Justice, Truth, and Beauty, arguing instead that these ideals vary greatly, depending on one's point of view. One of these Sophists, Thrasymachus, was an intimidating thinker who would've been admired by the Sith. His arguments with Socrates and Plato also give us a clear sense of why Plato would find Plagueis paradoxical. Where Plato believed that there's no way to understand justice apart from wisdom, Thrasymachus argued that there was no way to understand justice apart from *power*. Where Socrates and his philosophical friends struggle to find an all-encompassing definition of *justice*, Thrasymachus cuts through their debate by asserting forcefully that "the just is nothing else than the advantage of the stronger."[4]

This is *precisely* the worldview of the Sith, for whom talk of right without might is a childish fairytale and the wise man who thinks he can somehow transcend the vagaries of power is a fool. We see the Sith follow Thrasymachus's teaching during the siege of Naboo in *The Phantom Menace* when Darth Sidious orders Nute Gunray to commence the Trade Federation's invasion. Expressing more concern for his own wrinkled hide than any actual ethical principles, Gunray timidly asks Sidious, "Is that legal?" Sidious hisses a reply that would've made Thrasymachus smile: "I will *make* it legal." Sidious knows that the law is just a tool waiting to be used by anyone wise enough to see that there is no justice beyond power, and that enough power can make anything just. In *Revenge of the Sith*, when Palpatine is revealed to be Sidious and is confronted by Mace Windu, who tells him, "The Senate will decide your fate," Sidious exclaims, "I *am* the Senate!" Sidious learned this philosophy of life from his master, Darth Plagueis, who long before the invasion of Naboo taught him that the Sith will triumph over the Jedi because "[t]he Sith are not placid stars but singularities. Rather than burn with a muted purpose, we warp space and time to twist the galaxy to our own design."[5]

Plato opposed this cynical view that might makes right. He knew that Athens had transformed, from an admired city-state that had bravely turned back the massive invading forces of the Persian Empire at the battles of Salamis and Platea, into yet another despised empire that was shattered by the Spartans during the Peloponnesian War. This occurred because the Athenians were swayed to the "Dark Side" teachings of the Sophists, convincing themselves that the powerful doing as they will is not injustice, but rather "a necessary law of their nature [that] they rule wherever they can."[6] Plato argued that this idea ultimately destroys whomever follows it, whether an individual or an entire city-state. Instead of a notion of justice as "might makes right," Plato sought a definition of justice that doesn't rest merely on power, but ultimately on wisdom.

"Unlimited Power!"

Plato would have admired the Code of the Jedi that brought millennia of peace and prosperity to the Galactic Republic after the Battle of Ruusan:

> *There is no emotion; there is peace.*
> *There is no ignorance; there is knowledge.*
> *There is no passion; there is serenity.*
> *There is no death; there is the Force.*

Consider now the Sith Code as taught by Darth Bane:

> *Peace is a lie, there is only passion.*
> *Through passion, I gain strength.*
> *Through strength, I gain power.*
> *Through power, I gain victory.*
> *Through victory, my chains are broken.*
> *The Force shall free me.*

Where the Jedi seek peace through mindfulness and control of their feelings, the Sith hope to *use* passion, power, and strength for the ultimate goal of freedom. As Plagueis explains the difference, "Remember why the Sith are more powerful than the Jedi, Sidious: because we are not afraid to feel."[7] The Sith want to be free from convention, morality, government, law, and ultimately even the limits of the Force itself. This sort of freedom is what philosophers refer to as *negative freedom* because it is freedom *from* control, a freedom that says, "*Don't limit me!*"[8] But Plato teaches that no wise person should ever walk this path, as it is ultimately self-destructive. The truly wise see that this sort of freedom is not liberation: it is its own cage.

Plato asks us to imagine that our soul has three parts: the rational, the spirited, and the appetitive. When we are in balance, reason rules over the other two parts of the soul. Such a balanced person has the virtue of justice because they function the way they should: every part of the soul performs its proper function. Just as the eye is meant to see and the hand is meant to grasp, reason is meant to lead and everything else is meant to follow. A wise person is one whose reason rules their soul and is practiced at making good judgments. We should be suspicious of the freedom that the Sith long for, Plato argues, because "there exists in every one of us ... a terrible, fierce and lawless brood of desires, which it seems are revealed in our sleep."[9] Instead, the wise person must find a balance in which he satisfies his *necessary* desires – such as the desires for food, sleep, and sex. In short, the ethically good person *is* the wise person for Plato. Once he truly knows the good, he always at least *tries* to do good. This leads to a startling conclusion: for the wise person, *conscious acts of evil are impossible.*

Moving from the small canvas of the individual to the larger canvas of the state, Plato says that the just state is one guided by the truth that "each one man must perform one social service in the state for which his nature was best adapted."[10] In the case of a person's soul, the rational part of the soul enlists the help of the spirit, or willpower, in controlling and subduing the passions. This allows us to live good and ethical lives – genuinely free lives – where our reason guides us through "a life of significance, of conscience," the kind of life that Sidious knows Anakin seeks to live. Similarly, a just *state* is one in which the naturally wise rule while everyone else fulfills his or her individual function.

When we succumb to the notion that freedom means indulging our appetites or spirit as the Sith do, then our corrupted soul becomes our own inescapable prison. The freedom sought by the Sith *should* be its own worst punishment for Plato. The Sith, by hoping to use appetite and spirit as means to freedom, are in fact forging their own bonds of slavery. Their quest for unlimited power leads inevitably to their spirit and appetite having power over them. And yet, this does not happen to Plagueis.

Darth Plagueis the Wise

To be sure, Plato's theory *is* plausible, given many tales of the Sith and others seduced to the Dark Side. The Dark Jedi Maw, for example, was a Boltrunian Jedi who gave into his selfish inclinations and became a grotesque and deformed vessel of pure, seething hatred.[11] Most famously, Anakin Skywalker, despite his exceptional connection to the Force, was never able to fully control his fear – first for his dear mother Shmi, who was tortured and killed by Tusken Raiders, and later for his beloved Padmé after having a premonition of her death in childbirth. Darth Sidious deftly exploited Anakin's passionate attachment to Padmé, using it to lure him to the Dark Side. The result was that Anakin suffered the last two decades of his existence as a twisted monster: a single, living, burning wound of passion encased within a dark prison of wires and armor plates.

However, the wisest of all Sith avoided these fates. Plagueis is undeniably evil from the point of view of Plato and the Jedi. He sacrifices others in service of his ambition to visit vengeance on the Jedi and conquer the galaxy for the Sith. He does not hesitate to put his will, rather than his reason, in charge of his Muunian soul. He does not seek peace by subduing his spirit and appetite: he fans them like the flames of a forge in which he crafts his ambitions. However, none of the other qualities that Plato associates with evil apply to him. He is capable of great violence and brutality, but yet is fully able to restrain himself when the time is right. He is a calm and careful scientist – even if a morally repugnant one – who experiments on living creatures in order to learn as much as he can about the Force. His plot to take over the Munn financial empire of Damask Holdings unfolds over decades, just as his plan to murder his own master, Darth Tenebrous, took a human's lifetime to come to fruition. Indeed, his connection to the Force is so great that many believe it was his manipulation of the Force that created Anakin, the Chosen One. Instead of descending into the madness and corruption that Plato and the Jedi foresaw for anyone who deviates from their path, Plagueis held his own steady course for decades toward the most ambitious vision of all. He did not merely want to crush the Jedi and bring the galaxy to heel: as he told his droid One One-Four Dee, his goal was nothing less than "to extend my life indefinitely. To conquer death."[12] This wise Sith Lord was a Platonic paradox: a restrained, patient, and rational being who used violence, passion, and lies in his quest for power.

More disturbing to Plato than the mere existence of an evil yet wise being would be the fact that Darth Plagueis mostly *shares* Plato's vision. In the *Republic*, Plato describes a just city-state as an analogy for the ethical soul. In both cases, the rational element works with the spirited element, and together they

> will preside over the appetitive part which is the mass of the soul in each of us and the most insatiate by nature of wealth. They will keep watch upon it, lest, by being filled and infected with the so-called pleasures associated with the body and so waxing big and strong, it may not keep to its own work but may undertake to enslave and rule over the classes which it is not fitting that it should, and so overturn the entire life of all.[13]

Plato's concern that reason rule over spirit and appetite is *precisely* Plagueis's motivation for destroying the Jedi and conquering the universe on behalf of the Sith. He hopes to call forth

> a scouring storm that would lay waste to everything antiquated and corrupt, and pave the way for a new order in which the Sith would be returned to their rightful place as the stewards of the galaxy, and before whom all the diverse species would bow, not only in obeisance and fear, but in gratitude for having been drawn back from the brink.[14]

Plato and Plagueis agree that the average ignorant citizen is too foolish to accept his own inability to govern himself, and so wise rulers must rely on deception in order to protect the masses from themselves. Plato calls this opportune falsehood "the noble lie."[15] Similarly, the Sith use deception to trick the Republic into giving the Sith the power they need in order to finally protect the lesser beings from their own craven instincts, and bring peace and order to the galaxy. Finally, Plato argues that members of the proper city should practice selective breeding, matching wise with wise, strong with strong, in order to produce the best rulers and guardians for the city.[16] Likewise, Darth Plagueis the

Wise was the fruit of selective breeding: his master Darth Tenebrous paired Plagueis's Force-sensitive father Caar Damask with a Force-sensitive female Muun in order to maximize the chances that their offspring would be worthy of Sith training.[17] Plagueis himself carried on this eugenic legacy in using the Force to influence the midi-chlorians to create life.

So what are we to make of this? Perhaps Plagueis is not really *evil*: it might be that the sentients of the galaxy are so prone to disorder and self-destruction – just look at the dysfunctional Galactic Senate in *The Phantom Menace* – that only the Sith's dreadful medicine is strong enough to cure the malady of ignorance. If true, then the Jedi are merely prolonging a terminal illness by defending the Galactic Republic. On the other hand, perhaps Plagueis is not really *wise*: it might be that, no matter how patient, a creature driven by such self-centered ambition and so void of ethical principles is at best lucky and would never be suited to rule the galaxy fairly, as Plato envisions the rulers of his ideal republic doing. Perhaps Plagueis's own spirit and appetite would have devoured him in time if his apprentice hadn't consumed him first in a storm of Sith lightning while he slept. But perhaps Plato was simply wrong about wisdom, freedom, and justice, and we'd make better sense of Plagueis's contradictions and paradoxical nature by looking at him through the lens of a philosopher who, like Plagueis, scoffed at the Jedi-like ideals propounded by Plato. Friedrich Nietzsche can help us understand why Plagueis rejected the view of wisdom, justice, and freedom advocated by Plato without succumbing to the beast of his own spirit and appetite. Nietzsche looked on Plato with the same revulsion and contempt that the Sith demonstrated as they watched the Jedi slowly lose their connection to the Force and to life itself; the Sith scorned them for failing to understand the nature of freedom and the meaning of life.

The Wisdom of Seeking a Life of Great Significance

Consider now the Code of the Anti-Christ as taught by Nietzsche:

> What is good?
> All that heightens the feeling of power, the will to power, power itself, in man.
> What is evil?

Whatever springs from weakness.
What is happiness?
The feeling that power increases – that resistance is overcome.[18]

One of the strongest affinities between Nietzsche and the Sith is that he challenges a supposedly benevolent philosophy that has duped everyone into thinking that its notion of value is the *only* notion of value. Just as the Sith hoped to pierce the Jedi's pretentions to selflessness, benevolence, and justice, Nietzsche aimed to expose the rotten truth about Socrates, Plato, and even Jesus of Nazareth. Nietzsche feared that the philosophies of these men had weakened civilization and made it decadent. They were perspectives that did not encourage vitality or bravery, but servility and obedience. They were *slave moralities* that preached "the wretched alone are the good; the poor, impotent, lowly alone are the good … and you, the powerful and noble[,] are on the contrary evil."[19] Instead, Nietzsche called on the rare, brave few to recover *true* morality, the ancient *master morality* that rejoiced in life, power, and vitality. Where the slave calls "good" those values that are useful for him, the master calls "good" those things that are in and of him and even his enemies if they be noble! The goodness of the noble is marked by "indifference to and contempt for security, body, life, comfort, their hair-raising cheerfulness and profound joy in all destruction, in all the voluptuousness of victory and cruelty."[20]

Nietzsche hoped we might replace the decadent morality with the moralities of ancient warrior castes, and the Sith also sought to walk away from the Jedi path that placidly pleads for the assistance of the Force (humbly wishing, "May the Force be with you"). Instead, the Sith would boldly stride the galaxy-spanning hyperspace lanes of the Rakata who built the galaxy's first great empire – the fabled Infinite Empire – by bending the Force to their will and, with it, countless star systems.[21] Whereas the Jedi often live lives with all the variety and excitement of Tatooine's Great Dune Sea, the Sith often seem to really enjoy life! What possible better image of "hair-raising cheerfulness and profound joy in all destruction" could there be than Darth Sidious cackling as he hurls gigantic senatorial pods at Yoda during their climactic battle in *Revenge of the Sith*?

The Jedi, like Plato, sought peaceful lives by restraining their spirit and appetite and by resisting the temptation to use their power needlessly. Nietzsche laments this error, and even more he regrets that

Plato's seductive charm led so many to follow his errant creed. Instead, it sounds like he is speaking words of encouragement to the Sith when he asks,

> [D]o you want a *name* for this world? A solution for all its riddles? A light for you, too, you best concealed, strongest, most intrepid, most midnightly men? – This *world is the will to power – and nothing else besides*! And you yourselves are also this will to power – and nothing besides![22]

Plagueis makes exactly the same point as he instructs Sidious on the essential difference between the Jedi and the Sith. He explains that the Sith follow the paths blazed by the first Force-users, the Rakata, who

> didn't pronounce judgment on their works. They moved planets, organized star systems, conjured dark side devices like the Star Forge as they saw fit. If millions died in the process, so be it. The lives of most beings are of small consequence. The Jedi have failed to understand this. They are too busy saving lives and striving to keep the powers of the Force in balance that they have lost sight of the fact that sentient life is meant to evolve, not simply languish in contented stasis.[23]

Where the Jedi and Plato taught that peace is our highest purpose in life, Nietzsche and the Sith counter that the peace they seek is natural only in the grave, and that life does not seek peace, but *power*. The Sith crave power to be free of any and all limits, even the ultimate limit of death.

In his allegorical masterpiece, *Thus Spoke Zarathustra*, Nietzsche included a chapter entitled "On the Despisers of the Body," in which the hero Zarathustra takes to task the decrepit philosophy that places spirit above the body. We could easily imagine him chiding Yoda for teaching Luke to despise his own body by teaching that "luminous beings are we, not this crude matter." Rejecting the age-old ideas that the "crude" body corrupts the "luminous" soul and that the wise person, conversely, is the one whose soul conquers their body, Zarathustra teaches, "There is more reason in your body than in your best wisdom. And who knows why your body needs precisely your best wisdom?"[24] The living body is the source of true wisdom, and more than anything it seeks power to live! Nietzsche believes that the brave person doesn't need the fairy tale about the eternal soul: once they accept the truth about the will to power, they will live for the sake of life – *real* life – and not fear the pain required to live a life of great significance.

The Jedi observe the death of the body calmly – perhaps a little *too* calmly – just as Socrates shows an eerie calm at dying needlessly for a crime he did not commit.[25] Yoda tries to keep Anakin within his Jedi flock by teaching him, after his premonition of Padmé's death, "Death is a natural part of life. Rejoice for those around you who transform into the Force. Mourn them do not. Miss them do not." The Jedi, like Plato and his master Socrates, seem to almost welcome the eternal peace of being free of the body. The Sith, on the other hand, cherish the body and seek ways to preserve it, strengthen it, even enable it to transcend death altogether. While some, like the Jedi, would call this power "unnatural," the Sith, along with Nietzsche, would smile and ask in return, What could possibly be *more natural* than wanting to live? What is more natural, for young Anakin to serenely accept the death of his mother or to satisfy his visceral urge for vengeance? What is more natural, for Anakin to sit idly by as his love faces death alone or *do anything within his power to keep her alive*? The Sith and Nietzsche argue that the Jedi and Plato have it exactly backwards: the natural philosophy is the philosophy that cherishes life, and the unnatural one is the one that slips calmly into death. As Nietzsche puts it, "All naturalism in morality, that is all *healthy* morality, is dominated by an instinct of life."[26] Plagueis was then the most moral and natural of all, for he focused, without apology, on the instinct of life by seeking to unlock the secret of an eternal existence.

The Force beyond Light and Dark

Yoda would be Plato's philosopher-of-choice from the *Star Wars* universe, as Yoda completely agrees with his view that the soul is the true source of wisdom, and that loving wisdom leads one to look beyond bodily life. Nietzsche would undeniably pick Plagueis and cheer him on in his quest for life everlasting in the physical realm. Let him be called evil, Nietzsche might say, for great men are always called evil by those who envy them. When the Jedi condemn the Sith for being evil, it is like when lambs complain, "These birds of prey are evil; and whoever is least like a bird of prey ... would he not be good?"[27] The Sith, for their part, feel no need to call the Jedi names or bleat about their faults. Instead, like the birds of prey, they "might view it a little ironically and say: '*we* don't dislike them at all, these good little lambs; we even love them: there is nothing more tasty than a tender lamb.'"[28] Let the Sith be despised and reviled and misunderstood in the darkness, for "[h]e shall be the greatest who can be the loneliest, the most hidden, the most deviating, the human being beyond good and evil, the master of his virtues, he that is overrich in will. Precisely this should be called *greatness*."[29]

Nietzsche offers a liberating wisdom in a verse worthy of preservation within even the rarest of Sith holocrons:

> The overcoming of morality, in a certain sense even the self-overcoming of morality – let this be the name for that long secret work which has been saved up for the finest and most honest, also the most malicious, consciences of today, as living touchstones of the soul.[30]

Not long before his wise and long life would come to an end at the hands of his apprentice Sidious, Darth Plagueis personally visited his vengeance on Ars Veruna – the corrupt and shameful ex-king of Naboo – for daring to assault his hidden lair on Sojourn. Having recently commanded a control over the Force that no known being had ever achieved, Plagueis killed his one-time ally by simply instructing his midi-chlorians to "return to their source." Veruna gasped an insult at Plagueis, saying he was no better than the dreaded Anzati brain-eaters. Plagueis replies, not by defending his actions in terms of conventional morality, but by asking, "What does *better than* mean to those of us who have passed beyond notions of good and evil?"[31] Plato and the Jedi give us a formula for how to be wise, and therefore good. Nietzsche and the Sith do not see themselves as *opposing* the teachings of their moralizing counterparts: they *transcend them*. They do not stand for evil that foils their good: they represent the hope that the truly great soul might live *beyond good and evil*.

Notes

1. Plato, *Socrates' Defense (Apology)*, in *Plato: The Collected Dialogues*, trans. Edith Hamilton and Huntington Cairns (Princeton, NJ: Princeton University Press, 1961), 9 (23b).
2. Friedrich Nietzsche, *The Pre-Platonic Philosophers*, trans. Greg Whitlock (Urbana: University of Illinois Press, 2001), 8.

3. Pierre Hadot, *What Is Ancient Philosophy?*, trans. Michael Chase (Cambridge, MA: Harvard University Press, 2004), 21.
4. Plato, *Republic*, in *Collected Dialogues*, 588 (338c).
5. James Luceno, *Star Wars: Darth Plagueis* (New York: Del Rey, 2012), 159.
6. Thucydides, *The Landmark Thucydides*, ed. Robert Strassler (New York: Touchstone, 2008), 354.
7. Luceno, *Darth Plagueis*, 193.
8. For one of the best treatments on the difference between positive and negative liberty, see Isaiah Berlin, *Two Concepts of Liberty* (Oxford: Clarendon, 1958).
9. Plato, *Republic*, in *Collected Dialogues*, 799 (572b).
10. Ibid., 674 (433a).
11. Stephen Sansweet and Pablo Hidalgo, *The Complete Star Wars Encyclopedia*, vol. 2 (New York: Ballantine Press, 2008), 295.
12. Luceno, *Darth Plagueis*, 57.
13. Plato, *Republic*, in *Collected Dialogues*, 684 (442ab).
14. Luceno, *Darth Plagueis*, 59.
15. Plato, *Republic*, in *Collected Dialogues*, 659 (414bc).
16. Ibid., 658 (414b).
17. Luceno, *Darth Plagueis*, 81.
18. Friedrich Nietzsche, *The Anti-Christ*, trans. R. J. Hollingdale (New York: Penguin Books, 1968), 115.
19. Friedrich Nietzsche, *On the Genealogy of Morals*, trans. Walter Kaufmann and R. J. Hollingdale (New York: Vintage, 1989), 34.
20. Ibid., 42.
21. Ryder Windham, *Star Wars: Jedi vs. Sith* (New York: Ballantine Books, 2007), 161.
22. Friedrich Nietzsche, *The Will to Power*, trans. Walter Kaufmann and R. J. Hollingdale (New York: Random House, 1967), 50.
23. Luceno, *Darth Plagueis*, 159.
24. Friedrich Nietzsche, *Thus Spoke Zarathustra*, trans. Walter Kaufmann (New York: Viking Penguin, 1966), 35.
25. Plato, *Phaedo*, in *Collected Dialogues*, 97 (115a–18a).
26. Friedrich Nietzsche, *Twilight of the Idols*, trans. R. J. Hollingdale (New York: Penguin Books, 1968), 45.
27. Nietzsche, *On the Genealogy of Morals*, 45.
28. Ibid.
29. Friedrich Nietzsche, *Beyond Good and Evil*, trans. Walter Kaufmann (New York: Vintage, 1989), 139.
30. Ibid., 45.
31. Luceno, *Darth Plagueis*, 322.

2

"You Are Asking Me to Be Rational": Stoic Philosophy and the Jedi Order

Matt Hummel

How does a young boy go from slave on Tatooine to angst-ridden apprentice, to conflicted Jedi Knight, to Sith Lord? The prequel *Star Wars* trilogy tells the origin story of the iconic sci-fi villain Darth Vader. When *The Phantom Menace* hit theaters in 1999, audiences eagerly anticipated Anakin Skywalker's transformation into the black-clad intimidator who blasted his way on screen more than two decades earlier. And from the moment the dusty little boy in Watto's shop asked Padmé if she's an angel, people wondered what the big turning point would be. Over the course of the prequel trilogy, it became apparent. It was Anakin's failure to understand the philosophical perspective of the Jedi that ruined his chance of becoming one.

The Jedi are "keepers of the peace." Just as they protect the galaxy, Jedi are also called upon to keep the peace *within themselves* by aligning their wills to the Force. This requires self-restraint, abstinence from worldly pleasures, a virtue-driven mindset, incorruptible fearlessness, and total belief in following the will of the Force. As Jedi Master Qui-Gon Jinn warns a young, overeager Anakin, "Training to become a Jedi is not an easy challenge, and even if you succeed, it's a hard life."

As we'll see, the principles of the Jedi Order closely mirror the "hard life" maxims of a school of philosophy known as Stoicism, represented by the slave-turned-philosopher Epictetus (c. 55–135). The comparison begins a long time ago in a city far, far away. ...

The Ultimate Star Wars and Philosophy: You Must Unlearn What You Have Learned, First Edition. Edited by Jason T. Eberl and Kevin S. Decker.

Master of the Stoic Arts

Both Anakin and Epictetus were slaves eventually freed by their wealthy masters, both lived in the era of a power-crazy emperor,[1] and both went on to study a life-changing discipline. While Anakin entered a well-established disciplinary order of more than "a thousand generations," Epictetus studied and built upon a tradition of Stoicism based on principles more than three centuries old.[2] For both Jedi and Stoics, philosophy is a way of life, not just a subject for study. Epictetus advised people to seek virtue through wisdom, to become conscious of what is and is not in their control, and to avert themselves from pleasure and pain by being aware of the present and practicing indifference.

A central claim of Stoic ethics is that only virtues and virtuous activities are good, and only vices and vicious actions are evil.[3] Stoic virtue is the capacity to recognize and use the advantages of a situation wisely, like recognizing that "greed can be a powerful ally" in manipulating an avaricious junk-dealer. Vice involves using advantages but solely for personal gain. In *Revenge of the Sith*, Palpatine tries to convince Anakin that the Jedi are just as lustful for power as the Sith. Anakin responds that the Jedi selflessly "care only about others," while the Sith "think inwards, only of themselves." For Epictetus, being virtuous and progressing toward personal excellence mean understanding the true nature of one's being and keeping one's moral character in the right condition.[4] The same could be said of the Jedi, who seek to align themselves with the will of the Force rather than selfishly exploit its power.

What is *power*? The Force provides great power to those who know how to use it, even those who don't fully know they have it. Qui-Gon says as much about young Anakin: "He has special powers. ... He can see things before they happen." Power, however, is more than just special abilities. Epictetus asserts that true power lies in the capacity to adapt oneself to circumstances by making proper judgments of what's in a person's control:

> Some things are up to us and some things are not up to us. Our opinions are up to us, and our impulses, desires, aversions–in short, whatever is our own doing. Our bodies are not up to us, nor are our possessions, our reputations, or our public offices, or, that is, whatever is not our own doing.[5]

I have power over my own mind. The opinions I hold, the intentions I form, the interests I develop, what I value, and to what I'm averse are all wholly up to me. What disturbs people is not what happens to them but their judgments on those happenings.[6] Stoic *strength of mind* is quintessential to Jedi training – keeping them from slipping into uncontrollable feelings like hate and anguish. The need for a well-disciplined mind is why the Jedi Council usually refuses to train people past a certain age. "Younglings" haven't lived long enough to form desirous attachments, so they can be trained more easily to be mindful of their feelings and cultivate detachment. Remaining calm in the face of adversity and controlling one's emotions no matter the provocation are qualities often referred to as "stoic." They're developed in the full Stoic sense by making proper use of one's awareness – in Jedi terms, being "mindful of the living Force."

Awareness is the ability to "see each particular event in the context of the whole."[7] The wisest Jedi can perceive events within the context of the will of the Force. When Obi-Wan stops an impatient Anakin from rushing into a bar after the bounty hunter Zam Wesell, he admonishes his padawan, "Patience. Use the Force. Think. He went in there to hide, not to run." Though it seems Obi-Wan is simply instructing Anakin in the simplistic ways of criminals, he's actually teaching a greater lesson about awareness of the Force – that it's a grand design that can be understood rationally. The Jedi would refer to it as the unifying Force that "binds" the galaxy together, creating an ultimate destiny.[8] Mastering awareness involves understanding the unifying Force along with its complement in the living Force, which "flows" through each passing moment.[9] Qui-Gon identifies the difference to Obi-Wan before their "negotiations" with the Trade Federation, instructing his padawan to "keep [his] concentration here and now, where it belongs," rather than become overly anxious about his "bad feeling." For Anakin, making proper use of his awareness would require steady practice of what Epictetus calls "indifference."

Since Jedi must focus on the present to determine the will of the Force, they must remain *detached* from whatever might distract their concentration, especially relationships with other people. Epictetus calls these potential distractions *indifferent*.[10] Matters of indifference have no intrinsic value, but one can make use of them in service of living virtuously or in accord with the will of the Force. Typically preferred are things like health, wealth, and companionship, while "dispreferred" are things like sickness, poverty, and social exclusion. Obi-Wan prefers not to fly, which he thinks "is for droids," but when flying a starfighter into battle is required to protect the galaxy – a fact beyond Obi-Wan's control – he's indifferent toward it. He judges the value of flying within the greater context of the living Force and so does his duty as a peace keeper.

Thus, the Stoic principles of the Jedi Order are revealed:

- Strive for wisdom and live virtuously by following the will of the Force, not seeking personal gain.
- Remain mindful of what is in one's control and so use the Force as a means for good.
- Maintain awareness of events within the context of the living Force.
- Do not be concerned with matters of indifference – things out of one's control.

A Jedi's strength of mind has greater value than the ability to execute a Force push. Epictetus was able to discern and practice Stoicism in our galaxy as well as any Jedi Master. But the latently powerful Anakin fails to understand the true path of Stoic philosophy for the "hard life" of a Jedi. Even if we knew nothing about Anakin's future as a Force-choke master, it would be evident over the course of the prequel trilogy that he's not destined to be a successful Jedi.

Unlimited Power?

It's hard to see Anakin in *The Phantom Menace* as anything other than an adventurous kid, a typical boy, with some keen abilities and a disregard for authority. What then causes Obi-Wan to warn his master, "The boy is dangerous"? Precisely the fact that Anakin *is a typical boy*, complete with a forward-looking vision and lack of patience. Young Anakin is very interested in status and power. He defensively corrects Padmé when she calls him a "slave": "I'm a *person* and my name is Anakin." He eagerly tells Qui-Gon he's the only human who can race pods and that he's built the fastest one ever. And he ambitiously wants to be the first person to see all the planets in the galaxy.

More importantly, young Anakin has misconceptions about power. He doesn't think of power in terms of good judgment but instead as the ability to do amazing things: "No one can kill a Jedi"; "I had a dream I was a Jedi. I came back here and freed all the slaves." Certainly, this is typical thinking for a young boy, and Qui-Gon seems convinced it's only a matter of "time and training" before Anakin realizes the true complexity of the Force and the passive approach to power through wisdom espoused by the Jedi.[11] True to Stoic form, the basics of Jedi teaching involve searching our feelings and using our instincts in wading through a complicated situation. But Anakin doesn't recognize the complexity of his circumstances, nor does he practice the Jedi way of making proper judgments. This troubles Obi-Wan, but he still agrees to train Anakin.

Anakin's fascination with power grows as he learns Jedi skills, and it manifests as arrogance when he brags that he's "really ahead of" Obi-Wan, claiming that he's ready to take the trials to become a Jedi Knight. Worse, his dreams of freeing all the slaves and visiting every planet get replaced by premonitions of his suffering mother and "intoxicating" thoughts about Padmé. With a growing lust for power and zero concentration on the will of the Force, Anakin becomes overly confident in his ability to prevent tragedies in his life. After Anakin's mother's death, Padmé consoles Anakin by reminding him that he isn't all-powerful and so shouldn't feel guilty for failing to save her. Anakin loses his cool, promising to someday learn to stop people from dying. This emotional scene shows how utterly devoid of peace Anakin is and how likely he is to turn to the dark side.

When Anakin suffers a nightmarish premonition of Padmé's death, he promises her that he won't let this dream become real – yet another misconception about power. Anakin's problem is a lack of self-reflection about whether his premonition about Padmé's death is real or what his role in it is. When it comes to Padmé, Anakin seems fully confident that he can stop her death, yet he admits he's completely powerless over his feelings of love for her. He's unable to "wish [his] feelings away" precisely because he doesn't understand the kind of power that's in his capacity. "Wishing his feelings away" is just what *is* in his power according to Epictetus; controlling the fates of others is not. Failure to see the difference leads Anakin straight to Palpatine, who convinces him that secret powers over life and death are within the arsenal of the dark side. Anakin takes on the mantle of Darth Vader to save his wife, but in the end, it doesn't matter. Padmé dies from losing the will to live – an arguably preventable disease by

Stoic standards – and Anakin suffers another blow to his conception of power. Even after Padmé's death, Anakin refuses to face the truth of his own powerlessness. Rather, he forsakes reason and remains sworn to the dark side.

"Fear Is the Path to the Dark Side"

Jedi Masters present a calm, stoic face to adversity and danger. They aren't thrill-seekers: "adventure, excitement, a Jedi craves not these things." Few Jedi would readily plummet from a hover-speeder in the all-day rush hour of Coruscant. Rather, the Jedi replace fear by opening themselves to the will of the Force, akin to surrendering the will to reason. Epictetus claims that reason is "where nature itself has fixed [people's] end."[12] Our ultimate goal is to discern and live harmoniously with nature.[13] The ultimate goal for Jedi is to decipher the will of the Force and conduct themselves accordingly. Jedi have nothing to fear by living within the Force's graces, even if it leads to death – for this is also the will of the Force – whereas the Sith fear death. Darth Plagueis the Wise experimented night and day to learn how to influence the Force to create life and overpower death;[14] and his apprentice, Darth Sidious, used cloning technology to create new bodies to incorporate his malevolent spirit.[15] For his part, Anakin's fear of death is rooted in the threat of loss.

Anakin's fear is palpable as he starts the journey with Qui-Gon on Tatooine. Anakin immediately turns back to his mother, expressing his fear of never seeing her again. Shmi Skywalker shows Jedi-like wisdom when she instructs Ani to consult his heart whether they'll see each other again. Shmi is essentially telling Anakin to search his feelings, to seek virtue through yet-unrevealed wisdom. The young Anakin wholly misses her point, shrugging it off as encouraging mom-talk. But the fear of losing his mother stays with him through his initial review by the Jedi Council when Yoda tells Anakin, "Fear leads to anger. Anger leads to hate. Hate leads to suffering." To suffer is to believe and behave contrary to the will of the Force – or of *nature*, as the Stoics would say.

Anakin's fear later leads him to experience nightmares and premonitions of death. His Jedi skills give him a clairvoyant vision of the future, but he never seeks the virtue of *understanding* what his visions mean; nor does he heed Yoda's warning: "Careful you must be when sensing the future, Anakin. Fear of loss is a path to the dark side." Instead of guiding his actions with reason, his fear leads him away from his duty to guard Padmé in order to save his mother from torment. Upon finding her, he suffers the pain that comes from not contemplating the will of the Force and is left only with the fear and remorse that his mother suffered terribly before dying in his arms. He slaughters the Tusken Raiders and broods in hatred over what they did to Shmi. The way in which Jedi face dread is important. In *Revenge of the Sith*, Obi-Wan hopes against hope that the security recordings at the decimated Jedi Temple will not show his friend attacking their fellow Jedi. Upon realizing the truth, however, Obi-Wan doesn't sink into despair and anger. Instead, he tries to figure out what he missed, consulting the Force for guidance in a matter beyond his own wisdom. Obi-Wan's trust in the Force shields him from the fear of loss of both his friend and the entire Jedi Order.

Perhaps our sympathy with Anakin's fear of losing the women in his life points to a valid criticism of the Jedi and their Stoic principles: what count as matters of *indifference*? On the refugee ship, Anakin makes the argument that Jedi are encouraged to love and that creating and maintaining bonds of "unconditional love" – which is how Anakin interprets the Jedi call to *compassion* – "is central to a Jedi's life." More likely than not, he's being openly facetious here in order to flirt with Padmé, but perhaps Anakin really does believe Jedi *should be allowed* to have relationships. It seems cold and inhuman to say that strong love for other people as well as thoughts of the suffering and deaths of those individuals are mere matters of indifference. Yoda, though, highlights the error in Anakin's argument. He reminds Anakin that "death is a natural part of life" and is to be celebrated as people "transform into the Force." Yoda is exhorting Anakin to be aware of the greater context of life itself – that even in death, beings are an extension of the living Force. It's not that love is forbidden, but love for the Force should be greater. There's no suffering when one lives according to the will of the Force; so Yoda invites Anakin not to mourn or miss those who are gone and not to fear the loss of others: "Learn to let go of everything you fear to lose." Yoda's sentiment rings true in Epictetus's *Handbook*: "If you want your children, and your wife, and your friends to live for ever, you are stupid; since you are wanting things that are not up to you to be up to you. ... Exercise yourself, then, in what is within your power."[16] Anakin has the power to control his fear, seek virtue, and even find solace through wisdom. But his misunderstanding of power only compounds his fear of loss, driving him to the dark side.

As we've seen, lust for power and fear of loss dominate in the downfall of Anakin Skywalker. But underneath all this, Anakin seems most guilty of un-mindfulness on a grand scale: he doesn't get it, and never has. Qui-Gon tries to explain midi-chlorians to him before embarking for Naboo. He tells Ani that midi-chlorians live inside all living cells and allow the Jedi to discern the will of the Force. Anakin can't understand Qui-Gon's lesson that tiny things can communicate in big ways. Even after ten years of training, he still fails to understand smaller events within the context of bigger pictures, a crucial mindset for the Jedi. While in pursuit of Count Dooku, Padmé falls out of the ship and Anakin gets into a shouting match with Obi-Wan about the greater good of the galaxy. The selfishness of the dark side peeks through their transaction as Anakin demands the ship turn around to rescue Padmé. Only by couching his argument in reference to Padmé's desires does Obi-Wan convince Anakin that the potential to end the Clone Wars before they really start is worth leaving Padmé behind. Obi-Wan understands power in Stoic terms. True power is awareness of the "divine governance" of all things – the will of the Force – even in the most trivial of human affairs, and to be "moved by it."[17] The wisest Jedi subordinate their lives to the life of the entire universe and recognize themselves as one piece of a greater whole. Anakin's ultimate downfall can be found in his placing his fears and desires for misunderstood power above the power of the greater order of all.

"From My Point of View, the Jedi Are Evil!"

The real tragedy of Anakin's story is something never shown in the films. Somewhere between *Attack of the Clones* and *Revenge of the Sith*, Anakin develops a dangerously close relationship with Chancellor Palpatine. Why he elects to confide in Palpatine is left unsaid other than Anakin's statement that "he's watched over me ever since I arrived here." Befriending Palpatine gets Anakin to start questioning the Jedi Order. Despite the twisted deceit of the Sith Lord, there are things about the Jedi way that seem to contradict the Stoic philosophy and are worth questioning.

For starters, the infamous Jedi mind trick threatens the idea that a person has control of their own thoughts.[18] The Jedi may reply that the Force persuasion technique is simply that – *persuasion*, not mind control. Yet Qui-Gon tries to use the Force to persuade Watto to accept Republic credits in exchange for a new hyperdrive. If the trick had worked on the Toydarian, Qui-Gon would've effectively stolen a hyperdrive, since the credits were worthless on the desert planet. Watto is a greedy dealer, so maybe he deserves to be swindled, but a Stoic wouldn't agree. A true Stoic would be concerned about the potential immorality of Force persuasion.

On a wider scale, the Jedi's agreeing to participate in the Clone Wars doesn't come across as a Stoic decision: it amounts to trying to influence an outcome beyond one's power. Epictetus calls the realization that there are conflicting opinions the very beginning of philosophy.[19] But entering the Clone Wars isn't a Jedi attempt to sway opinion in their favor. Rather, they're acting as "guardians of the Republic." It's also difficult to judge clearly the worthiness of either side in the conflict as both are masterminded by Darth Sidious. Blindness to the Sith's dealings shows a flaw in the Jedi's reasoning ability, a flaw they're conscious of and try to keep hidden. Their investigation of the Chancellor operates in the same kind of moral gray area as Force persuasion. When Anakin is asked to spy on Palpatine, he's being asked to cooperate in a deception that serves the Council's interest but is perhaps betraying its own principles, as he points out to Obi-Wan: "You're asking me to do something against the Jedi Code, against the Republic, against a mentor and a friend."

Finally, the attempted assassination of Palpatine more clearly accentuates what is suspect about the Jedi's belief in their inability to control others. Mace Windu and a cohort of Jedi approach the Chancellor initially to arrest him. But when the revealed Darth Sidious attacks and kills all but Mace Windu, the powerful Jedi Master is forced to fight back and corner the Sith. Anakin arrives in time to see Windu with his lightsaber at the Chancellor's throat. Sidious is clearly subdued and, with Anakin there, the plan could reasonably revert back to arrest. Mace, however, exclaims, "He's too dangerous to be left alive!" Despite Anakin's pleas to put Palpatine on trial, Mace raises his lightsaber for a deadly strike. Anakin protects Sidious for his own benefit, but in a way he's also playing the more Stoic role. While the Jedi are sworn to destroy the Sith, a full assault on the defenseless

Sidious doesn't fit the defensive, passive position of action guided by reason. Master Windu isn't heeding Master Yoda's lesson, "A Jedi uses the Force for knowledge and defense, *never* for attack." The will of the Force always seems to come into play when a Jedi slays a living being, like when Mace Windu defends himself against Jango Fett on Geonosis. The bounty hunter attacks him, and he eliminates his attacker; likewise when Obi-Wan kills General Grievous. But even those killings stand out as odd for the Jedi, who usually seem more content with disarming (literally) their foes. The preference to *neutralize* threats seems more in line with seeking virtue through wisdom than *elimination* of one's foes, even if they're genuinely evil. Jedi are called to refrain from desiring what isn't theirs and to refrain from lamenting what isn't in their control.[20] The existence of vice in the form of the Sith isn't in their control, and neither is Anakin's choice to hold a different point of view. Perhaps the Jedi's extreme attitude toward the Sith is what's actually causing the "imbalance" in the Force that Anakin is destined to correct.

"You Underestimate My Power!"

There's no doubt that Anakin Skywalker was a powerful Jedi, and his power seems to run in the family, something we can look forward to perhaps when Episode VII hits theaters – at the time of this writing, the latest plot rumor involves Luke having sequestered himself from the rest of the galaxy for the past ten years because he fears his inability to control his own power in the Force.[21] For all his power, Anakin assures his transition to the dark side by failing to learn the key principles of Stoic philosophy according to the Jedi Order. Virtue through wisdom, mindfulness, and the practice of indifference escaped the aspiring Jedi from day one. But maybe he has more self-knowledge than we give him credit for, since he plainly admits his failure when he awkwardly professes his love for Padmé: "You are asking me to be rational. That is something I know I cannot do."

Notes

1. Christopher Gill, "Introduction," in Epictetus, *The Discourses, The Handbook, Fragments*, ed. Christopher Gill, trans. Robin Hard

(London: J. M. Dent, Orion Publishing Group, 1995), xiii. According to the chronology of this book, Epictetus endured the reign of the Roman tyrant Nero. *The Discourses* was actually written by his student Flavius Arrian. *The Handbook* features maxims selected by Arrian that were drawn from *Discourses*, and *Fragments* are extracts from other ancient works that seem to be influenced by Arrian.

2. Ibid., xix.
3. Epictetus, *The Discourses*, 94, 123.
4. Ibid., 13, 65.
5. Ibid., 287.
6. Ibid., 289.
7. Ibid., 16.
8. http://starwars.wikia.com/wiki/Unifying_Force (accessed February 23, 2015).
9. http://starwars.wikia.com/wiki/Living_Force (accessed February 23, 2015).
10. Epictetus, *The Discourses*, 8–10, 86–87.
11. Ibid., 8.
12. Ibid., 17.
13. Ibid.
14. See James Luceno, *Star Wars: Darth Plagueis* (New York: Del Rey, 2012). For discussion of whether Darth Plagueis merits the appellation "the Wise," see chapter 1 in this volume.
15. See Tom Veitch et al., *Star Wars: Dark Empire Trilogy* (Milwaukie, OR: Dark Horse, 2010).
16. Epictetus, *The Discourses*, 291.
17. Ibid., 37.
18. Ibid., 8–10.
19. Ibid., 99.
20. Ibid., 274.
21. http://makingstarwars.net/2014/11/star-wars-episode-vii-state-luke-skywalker/ (accessed November 8, 2014).

3

The Jedi Knights of Faith: Anakin, Luke, and Søren (Kierkegaard)

William A. Lindenmuth

Luke Skywalker must make a decision at the end of *Return of the Jedi*. Will he ignore the utilitarian principle that he must kill his father to save the galaxy, or will he violate the ethical principle against dishonoring and murdering his own father and risk being turned to the dark side by the Emperor? Both are unacceptable to Luke. So he'll have to do something no one had believed possible for thousands of years: turn a Sith to the light side of the Force. Such a maneuver requires a leap of faith, and for that we turn to a man who knew just how hard it was: the Danish philosopher Søren Kierkegaard (1813–1855).

"I Can't Kill My Own Father"

Jedi Masters Yoda and Obi-Wan Kenobi ask Luke Skywalker to kill his father. They're obsessed with a prophecy that foretold the appearance of a "Chosen One" who would "bring balance to the Force." The Jedi had believed this meant that Luke's father, Anakin, would "destroy the Sith, not join them." Anakin's turn to the dark side led to the annihilation of all but a few Jedi.

Luke has an alternative interpretation in the form of a radical idea: to bring balance to the Force *without* killing his father. But how can this be done? After Yoda's death, Obi-Wan appears to Luke, who feels angry and betrayed. Obi-Wan had told him not that Darth Vader was

The Ultimate Star Wars and Philosophy: You Must Unlearn What You Have Learned, First Edition. Edited by Jason T. Eberl and Kevin S. Decker.
© 2016 John Wiley & Sons, Ltd. Published 2016 by John Wiley & Sons, Ltd.

his father but that he had murdered Luke's father. When Luke first asks how his father died, Obi-Wan dissembles, "A young Jedi named Darth Vader – who was a pupil of mine, until he turned to evil – helped the Empire hunt down and destroy the Jedi Knights. He betrayed and murdered your father." It isn't until he first faces Vader that Luke learns the truth. On Cloud City, Vader wants Luke to join him and complete his training, telling him that it's his destiny to "destroy the Emperor" and that they can "rule the galaxy as father and son." Darth Vader describes this as the "only way." Luke's response is to fall off the platform to an uncertain fate.

When Luke sees Obi-Wan after confronting Vader, he's understandably distressed. He interrogates him, "Why didn't you tell me? You told me Vader betrayed and murdered my father." Obi-Wan explains that Anakin was seduced by the dark side of the Force and when he became Darth Vader, he ceased being Anakin: "the good man who was your father was destroyed." Luke counters that there is "still good in him," that Anakin isn't dead. Obi-Wan responds, "He's more machine now than man, twisted and evil." He claims it is Luke's destiny to face Vader and destroy him. When Luke demurs, Obi-Wan responds, "Then the Emperor has already won."

Both the Sith and the Jedi believe that "balance" is the eradication of the opposing side, even though Obi-Wan himself says, "Only a Sith deals in absolutes." Luke is determined to face Darth Vader and the Emperor, but somehow not turn to the dark side or murder his father. He faces quite a dilemma when he finally confronts them simultaneously.

"Mostly Because of My Father, I Guess"

Abraham, a central figure in the Book of Genesis, was in a similar situation when God asked him to kill his own son. Abraham, whose name means "the father is exalted," was a biblical patriarch who had a special relationship with God. God promised Abraham that a great nation would be made of him, and a covenant would be formed with him. This would be an exclusive agreement that God would watch over and assist Abraham and all his descendants as long as they obeyed God's laws. God made this arrangement, promising the hundred-year-old Abraham and his ninety-year-old wife Sarah a son to be named Isaac.

It was through this son that God was to make Abraham's descendants as numerous as the stars in the sky and uphold His covenant.

Sometime later, God suddenly calls Abraham and commands, "Take your son Isaac, your only one, whom you love, and go to the land of Moriah. There offer him up as a burnt offering on one of the heights that I will point out to you" (Genesis 22:2). How can this be? How can the Lord – in whom Abraham has put all his faith, who gave him a son after a hundred years and promised to make a great nation through him – ask Abraham to kill this beloved son?

Søren Kierkegaard asked these hard questions. Writing in the early nineteenth century, he was bothered by how "easy" philosophers were making faith and Christianity. He believed that the "leap to faith" was, as Gotthold Lessing put it, an "ugly great ditch." Kierkegaard considered this problem, imagining a number of variations on the events of Genesis 22 and what they mean for ethics and faith. Stressing the separation between reason and faith, Kierkegaard argued forcefully that faith is more important than anything else.[1]

Let's complete the biblical story. The next morning after God speaks to him, Abraham saddles his donkey and brings Isaac and some servants on the trip to Moriah, telling his wife nothing. After travelling for three days, he tells the servants to wait for them to go and worship. As they head up the mountain, Isaac asks his father where the sheep is for the sacrifice. Abraham replies, "Son, God Himself will provide the sheep for the holocaust." He then ties Isaac to the altar and raises his knife. At that moment, an angel tells him to stop. Abraham has demonstrated his devotion to God, and the covenant will be fulfilled; Abraham's descendants will be blessed abundantly and made as "countless as the stars of the sky and the sands of the seashore ... because you obeyed my command" (Genesis 22:18).

Kierkegaard is in awe of this. He says he *can't comprehend* this story! "Abraham I cannot understand; in a certain sense I can learn nothing from him except to be amazed."[2] How did Abraham know it was God who asked him to do this? How did he know it wasn't a demon or nightmare? How can God have asked him to do this? How does he know he got the message right? How can God keep His promise if Isaac must die? Has Abraham gone crazy? Kierkegaard writes, "Who strengthened Abraham's arm, who braced up his right arm so it did not sink down powerless! Anyone who looks at this scene is paralyzed."[3]

Likewise, both Anakin and Luke experience premonitions of the future that cause them, like the Greek tragic heroes, to hubristically try to prevent them. Han, Leia, and Chewbacca are tortured on Bespin to command Luke's attention and bring him into the Emperor's grasp. Perhaps Palpatine also caused the young Anakin to envision Padmé's death and therefore feel compelled to take her protection into his own hands and solidify his quest for power. The dark side was crouching just around the corner.

"Something Is Out of Place!"

Some people might pass over the Abraham story, thinking it just a foolish myth – just as belief in the Force tends to be disregarded as an "ancient religion" to which some still have a "sad devotion" after the virtual extinction of the Jedi. But Abraham is treated as a father by adherents to the major world religions of Judaism, Christianity, and Islam, and as a paragon of virtue regarding *faith*. Kierkegaard thinks the story of Abraham and Isaac, as paralyzing as it is, is fundamental to understanding the human condition, and so he approaches it with "fear and trembling." It's important to Kierkegaard to try to understand this story, and it will help us understand Luke's situation. Luke stands in the reverse position. He's being asked to destroy his father, and the fate of the galaxy rests on his success. But how can the Force ask this of him? How can it be a holy act to be willing to kill one's own father or son? Kierkegaard asks, "If faith cannot make it a holy act to be willing to murder his son, then let the same judgment be passed on Abraham as on everyone else."[4] If we can't explain Abraham's act through faith, then he's as much a monster as anyone who'd kill his own son, and the same is true of Luke killing his own father.

Kierkegaard imagines a number of ways that this story could've happened. In one version, Abraham pretends it is he, and not God, who wants Isaac killed. In this way he prevents his son from imagining God "a monster" for ordering this sacrifice. An alternate version imagines Abraham going through the task, but losing his faith in the process, never forgiving God for ordering this sacrifice. In yet another, he tells it from Isaac's perspective, where Isaac sees Abraham clenching the knife "in despair," and Isaac loses faith in God.

Kierkegaard's point is that these are all much more believable and likely stories than the biblical one, which is a marvel: Abraham must simultaneously believe that he'll have to sacrifice Isaac and that he won't. God had promised Abraham descendants through Isaac; God has demanded Isaac's sacrifice. This is a confounding paradox that Kierkegaard thinks can't be explained away. Abraham is both *resigned* to losing Isaac and full of faith that he'll get to keep him at the same time. It's what Kierkegaard describes as a "double-movement." The first is a movement of "infinite resignation," in which Abraham gives up everything: his son, his wife, and his life. It's an ultimate surrendering, in which he becomes a "knight" of infinite resignation, a hero willing to lose everything.

The Jedi are knights in this fashion as well. Yoda doesn't want Anakin trained, as he's formed too deep an attachment to his mother and is accordingly terrified of losing her. "I sense much fear in you," Yoda tells young Anakin. When he loses his mother, Anakin slaughters the Sand People in revenge, and concentrates all his love and feelings of attachment on Padmé. It's this attachment that Chancellor Palpatine takes advantage of by tying his survival to Padmé's in Anakin's mind. When Anakin begins having premonitions of Padmé's death that echo his mother's, he goes to see Yoda, who counsels him, "Train yourself to let go of everything you fear to lose." Anakin can't comply and thus becomes a prisoner to his fears.

"I Find Your Lack of Faith Disturbing"

The movement of faith is a positive belief that somehow, through losing everything, one will gain everything. It's a complete and utter trust in God. This could mean that God will bring Isaac back from the dead, or stop Abraham before he kills him, which is what happens. But Abraham can't go about his task believing this. He can't "pretend" to kill Isaac or hesitate with the knife, as happens in the alternate versions that Kierkegaard imagines. He must be fully and totally committed to his duty. But his duty is also to love and care for his son! While the first movement is resignation, the second is faith, where one gains what one has lost. Abraham now becomes a knight of faith by trusting in God and his promise. Through losing Isaac, he also gains him.

Returning to Luke, he still must defeat Vader. The only way anyone imagines this can happen is if Luke kills him. Why must Luke face Vader? The Rebel attack on Death Star II would destroy Vader and the Emperor, but he must confront them anyway. As Abraham must sacrifice Isaac "For God's sake and his own sake,"[5] Luke must confront Vader for his sake and the Force's sake. He can't merely refuse to fight him on the grounds that the Jedi are not aggressive. To do so would be to turn his back on justice, his friends, and the fate of the galaxy. Darth Vader and the Emperor must be stopped, and Luke is the only one who can do it. But, besides the general obligation that we each have not to kill, this injunction applies all the more as a special duty not to kill our family members.

When Luke faces his father on Endor, he confidently reminds Vader that he was "once Anakin Skywalker, my father." That is the name of Vader's true self, a self he has forgotten. "I know there is good in you," Luke says. "The Emperor hasn't driven it from you fully." Luke doesn't believe that Vader will bring him before the Emperor, but he is wrong. Still, when Vader sends Luke to the Emperor, we witness Vader's evident hesitation. At some deep level, Luke has affected him.

"I Take Orders from Just One Person: Me!"

There are a number of heroic characters in the *Star Wars* saga, but one of the most interesting is Han Solo. One of the compelling aspects of his character is that he starts off as a "scoundrel." He's a smuggler, a rough, uncouth man who's in it for himself. "What good's a reward if you ain't around to use it?" he asks Luke when the Rebels are about to attack the Death Star. He's what Kierkegaard describes as the "aesthetic" man. His motivations are self-preservation and pleasure. Luke tells him, "Take care of yourself, Han. I guess it's what you're best at."

Luke loses everything shortly after we meet him in *A New Hope*. He resigns himself to "learn the ways of the Force and become a Jedi like my father." He's thrown into the next stage, what Kierkegaard calls the "ethical." This is the realm of the *hero*, the person who follows a moral code and adheres to certain universal principles regardless of the consequences, including the risk of his own life. Han makes the transition from the aesthetic realm to the ethical when he shows up near Yavin out of nowhere, at great personal risk to himself, his partner Chewbacca, and his ship. He clears Luke to take the shot that destroys the Death Star, and they all return in triumph. Leia says about him, "I knew there was more to you than money." Han again risks himself to save Luke when he goes missing in the freezing terrain of the ice planet Hoth. Kierkegaard's ethical stage also explains the great pains taken to rescue Han from Jabba the Hutt. The risk doesn't matter to the hero, though, as Kierkegaard describes, "The tragic hero relinquishes himself in order to express the universal."[6] Heroes are willing to sacrifice in order to protect something greater than themselves.

Everyone demands of Luke that he use his powers to kill his father, who's been responsible for so much evil. But Luke, sensing the good in his father, has to come up with a radically new plan. He can't kill his father, but he can't allow Vader to live. Luke is already a Knight of Infinite Resignation. He must go beyond if he's to truly defeat the dark side in Vader and his Emperor.

"It's a Trap!"

When Luke rushes off to Bespin to save his friends, Obi-Wan and Yoda urge him not to go. Luke retorts, "But I can help them! I feel the Force." Obi-Wan reprimands him, telling Luke that he can't *control* the Force and will be vulnerable to the dark side. Yoda reminds him of his "failure at the cave." After a training session in which Yoda teaches Luke that the Force is never to be used for attack, Luke senses something is wrong. Yoda tells him there's a nearby cave that "is strong with the dark side of the Force" into which Luke must go. What's in the cave is "only what you take with you." Luke begins strapping his utility belt on, but Yoda tells him, "Your weapons – you will not need them." Luke gives him a sidelong glance and straps them on anyway. Within the cave, an apparition of Darth Vader suddenly approaches and Luke extends his lightsaber. Vader mirrors him. There's a brief clash, then Luke beheads Vader. As Vader's head comes to a rest on the ground, the mask explodes, revealing Luke's visage underneath.

What exactly is Luke's failure? Was it that he brought his weapons in after Yoda told him not to? Was it that he resorted to violence and struck first? Was it that he's simply too tempted by the dark side and needs more discipline and training? Was it that he brought the "idea" of Vader in with him that caused him to materialize? It's at least a subtle foreshadowing that Luke is related to Vader, and that's why he sees himself in the mask. Much of a hero's arc is devoted to destroying the elements that connect them to the villain. His Aunt Beru had told her husband that Luke "has too much of his father in him," to which Owen replies, "That's what I'm afraid of."

Luke believes that convincing his father to return to the light side would be easier. He isn't prepared to face Vader and the Emperor together, and he thinks that he can turn Vader before being brought before the Emperor. Yoda's message must be ringing in Luke's ears: "Only a fully-trained Jedi Knight with the Force as his ally will conquer Vader and his Emperor." Luke knows he has to defeat them both, but he can't join the dark side and doesn't want to kill his father. What he learns and doesn't expect is that the Emperor wins if Vader kills Luke, but also if Luke kills his father. The Emperor never refers to Darth Vader as Anakin in front of Luke, but always as his *father*. Darth Sidious relishes his perceived ownership of the Skywalkers: "You, like your father, are now *mine*." Luke killing and replacing Vader with himself would continue Darth Sidious's habit of recruiting ever stronger apprentices.

Luke also thinks the joint sneak attack on the shield generator and the Death Star will succeed, but the Emperor tells him that it was all a trap of his design. He mocks, tempts, and threatens Luke, cajoling and goading him to fight. One of the final straws is the revelation that the Death Star is a "fully armed and operational battle station," which begins to fire on the Alliance fleet. Luke breaks down and crosses swords with Vader. He continually tries to stop the physical fight and keep the battle on the light side of Anakin against the dark side of Darth Vader: "I feel the good in you, the conflict," Luke tells him. Luke doesn't believe his father will kill him: "You couldn't kill me before and I don't believe you'll destroy me now." Vader lures Luke with the chance to save his friends if he turns. Luke's feelings flare at this and "betray him," revealing to Vader that Luke has a twin sister. When Vader threatens her, Luke loses control and launches a full-force attack on Vader, savagely swinging at him until he floors him and chops off his hand.

"That's Impossible!"

As with Abraham, Luke's "temptation is the ethical itself, which would hold him back from doing God's will."[7] Luke wants to kill Vader and, in many ways, it's the "right" thing to do. We think our fear is that Luke will turn to the dark side or die at Vader's hand. But what we really fear is that he'll do what Yoda and Obi-Wan demand of him: kill his father. The Emperor wins either way: Vader kills Luke – problem solved – or Luke kills Vader and takes his place at the Emperor's side. The Emperor believes he's engineered events so that he'll remain victorious regardless of the outcome. This is what the Emperor means when he says, "Young fool. Only now, at the end, do you understand." Luke realizes the only way that he can win is by surrendering everything. He can't murder his father and he can't join the dark side. In the same act, Abraham raises his blade while Luke casts his aside, but the meaning is the same. Luke can destroy Vader and yet simultaneously save his father, while Abraham symbolically sacrifices Isaac and God keeps his word.

This is the negative movement, the abandoning of all things: his friends, his cause, his life, his hopes – everything. As Kierkegaard speaks of Abraham, "[O]nly in this moment when his act is in absolute contradiction to his feelings, only then does he sacrifice Isaac."[8] Likewise for Luke, killing Vader is exactly what he wants to do. Darth Vader represents everything that Luke hates about the galaxy, and when he threatens Leia, it's the last straw. There's no composure here: Luke explodes at Vader, slashing and wailing on him until he beats him into submission, chopping off his hand just as Vader had done to him. He's seething, the pent-up rage bursting out of him as he pounds away, flecks of spit glistening on his open, panting mouth. He *hates* Vader, as in the moment before, ethically, Abraham "hates Isaac."[9] Luke's hatred has made him powerful. But if he strikes down either Vader or the Emperor "with all his fury," his "journey toward the dark side will be complete!" Earlier, Yoda teaches Luke that "a Jedi uses the force for knowledge and defense – never for attack."

Luke looks at Vader's smoking stump and then at his own mechanical hand. His eyes widen as he makes the connection that he's following in his father's path. Luke inhales deeply to calm and steel himself for what he's about to do. Yoda teaches him that he will know "the good side from the bad" when he is "calm, at peace, passive." He doesn't repeat the past. Determined, in the most difficult moment of his life, when he has more right to anger and revenge than anyone, he chooses faith instead. He trusts in the Force, even in the darkest place. "*Never*. I'll never turn to the Dark Side. You failed, your Highness. I am a Jedi, like my father before me." He doesn't repeat his father's mistake. The Emperor said that Luke's "compassion will be his undoing." Instead, it's what saves him – and Anakin. As Kierkegaard describes, "The knight will then have the power to concentrate the whole substance of his life and the meaning of actuality into one single desire."[10] Luke's desire is to get his father back.

Bringing Balance to the Force

Luke overcomes Vader in the lightsaber duel *through* anger, fear, and aggression. These are the exact things Yoda tells Luke to avoid, as "the dark side are they. Once you start down the dark path, forever will it dominate your destiny." But Luke *isn't* dominated by them, nor do they determine his fate. Both the Sith and the Jedi try to kill all of the other side. They don't want the other to exist. When Obi-Wan interprets the prophecy of the "Chosen One," he says it is "to destroy the Sith" in order to "bring balance to the Force, not leave it in darkness."

But this isn't balance. Only Luke sees the good in his father, and he's also the only one who possesses the composure to control his feelings and retract his lightsaber after defeating Vader. Unlike the young Anakin, Luke is able to resist the Emperor's temptations of power, revenge, and justice. By contrast, consider how Sidious manipulates Anakin to kill the unarmed (and dismembered) Count Dooku.

Luke realizes that killing Vader will not bring balance to the Force. He can't do what is demanded of him: he must do something more. "The knight of faith relinquishes the universal in order to become the single individual."[11] Luke somehow has faith that there's still good in his father, all evidence aside, and that they'll save one another. Discarding the lightsaber, Luke expresses both *resignation* and *faith*. He abandons everything he's fought for, while at the same time embracing it. He becomes a Jedi Knight of faith in this amazing act. While the Emperor tortures him with Sith lightning, he also accomplishes something no one ever thought possible: he turns a Sith good.

Clearly Vader sees his son suffering when the Emperor is electrocuting him, but it was Luke's casting aside his saber that made it possible. It isn't through mere sympathy that Anakin saves his son. Rather, Luke's commitment to the Force brings Anakin back. Darth Vader is willing to kill Luke: but what's amazing is Luke's ability not to do the same. Luke defeats Vader in the duel, but saves him in not ending it the way everyone has been telling him to. As Kierkegaard says, "it is only by faith that one gets to Abraham, not by murder."[12] It's only by faith that Luke gets to Anakin, not through killing him. "I've got to save you!" Luke says to his dying father. "You already have, Luke," Anakin replies.

Luke is warned by Yoda not to underestimate the powers of the Emperor, "or suffer your father's fate you will." Ironically, it's the Emperor who underestimates the power of the light side of the Force, having misplaced his faith in the dark side, as Yoda had forewarned him back in their duel on Coruscant. In the end, balance has been restored.

Notes

1. Søren Kierkegaard, *Fear and Trembling; Repetition*, trans. Howard Hong (Princeton, NJ: Princeton University Press, 1983).
2. Ibid., 31.
3. Ibid., 22.
4. Ibid., 30.
5. Ibid., 59.
6. Ibid., 75.
7. Ibid., 60.
8. Ibid., 74.
9. Ibid. What Kierkegaard is referring to is the challenging line of Luke 14:26, in which Jesus states, "If anyone comes to me and does not hate his own father and mother and wife and children and brothers and sisters, yes, and even his own life, he cannot be my disciple." Kierkegaard admits this is a "hard saying," but that he can understand it "the way one can understand a paradox." He explains, "The absolute duty can lead one to do what ethics would forbid, but it can never lead the knight of faith to stop loving. Abraham demonstrates this. In the moment he is about to sacrifice Isaac, the ethical expression for what he is doing is this: he hates Isaac." Luke's situation is reversed, because he must resist murder while Abraham must force it. The central idea is that all worldly concerns are subordinate to the higher religious demands of God, even if they contradict our normal ethical duties.
10. Ibid., 43.
11. Ibid., 75.
12. Ibid., 31.

4

Anakin and Achilles: Scars of Nihilism

Don Adams

The central story of the *Star Wars* saga, from *The Phantom Menace* to *Return of the Jedi*, is the story of Anakin Skywalker. We first see him as a gifted child and slave who is granted his freedom, but at the cost of leaving his mother – his only family. We see him develop into a powerful young man, a warrior of great distinction feared by his enemies. However, his power makes him arrogant and he feels that he's unjustly being held back, that he's not being treated by Obi-Wan and the Jedi Council as he deserves. When he discovers that his mother has died violently at the hands of Tusken Raiders, his anger is transmuted into blind, hate-filled rage and he goes on a killing spree in revenge. Fear for his wife Padmé is the last straw; he allies with the Sith Lord Darth Sidious, becomes Darth Vader, and slaughters the Jedi, even the *younglings*. The last vestiges of his humanity appear all but obliterated when "a new hope" arises in the form of his children, Luke and Leia. The dark side was unable to completely extinguish the father's love, and it is this love that overpowers Darth Vader, allowing Anakin to reemerge at the end of the epic saga and finally feel the connection to family that he had lost so long before.

Achilles, the greatest hero of the ancient Greek epic poem *The Iliad*, has a similar story. Although he was never a slave, he was a gifted young man separated from his family by a great war between the Greeks and the Trojans. "Wrath"[1] is the very first word of the poem,

The Ultimate Star Wars and Philosophy: You Must Unlearn What You Have Learned,
First Edition. Edited by Jason T. Eberl and Kevin S. Decker.
© 2016 John Wiley & Sons, Ltd. Published 2016 by John Wiley & Sons, Ltd.

and we see Achilles consumed increasingly by its dark power as the poem develops. His prowess makes him arrogant, and he feels that the Greek commander-in-chief isn't treating him as he deserves. Like Anakin, his anger is turned into blind, hate-filled rage when the person he loves most, his closest friend Patroclus, is killed by Hector, prince of the Trojans. In revenge, Achilles goes on a savage killing spree, slaughtering dozens of enemy soldiers until he finally kills Hector. But blood can't save Achilles from what he has become; in anguish, he drags Hector's body behind his chariot around and around Troy in an apparently endless cycle of rage, revenge, and despair. As with Anakin, only one thing is powerful enough to break this cycle: a father's love for his son. King Priam, Hector's father, begs Achilles to let him give Hector's body an honorable funeral. Priam weeps for his son, and when Achilles looks into Priam's eyes, he can't help but think of his own father and how he would weep upon learning of Achilles's death. This love of father for son reawakens Achilles's humanity, and he allows Priam to take Hector's body. Like Anakin, Achilles barely managed to reemerge from the greatest danger – and the greatest temptation – he ever faced: *nihilism.*

"[Not So] Hard to See, the Dark Side Is"

Moral nihilism is the view that there are no moral facts. Friedrich Nietzsche (1844–1900) is famous for defending moral nihilism:

> You know my demand upon the philosopher: that he take his stand *beyond good and evil* and leave the illusion of moral judgment beneath himself. This demand follows from an insight that I was the first to formulate, that *there are no moral facts.* Moral judgment has in common with religious judgment that it believes in realities that are not real. Morality is merely an interpretation of certain phenomena – more precisely, a misinterpretation.[2]

To see what Nietzsche means, consider the invasion of the planet Naboo by the Trade Federation in *The Phantom Menace.* Federation Senator Lott Dodd asks the Galactic Senate to send a neutral commission to ascertain the truth of Queen Amidala's "outrageous" claim. Such a commission might be able to come to an impartial judgment based on solid evidence that the Trade Federation had indeed unlawfully invaded Naboo. But, according to Nietzsche's nihilistic view of morality, no commission could ever come to an impartial judgment of Senator Palpatine's counsel to Queen Amidala: "Our best choice would be to push for the election of a stronger Supreme Chancellor. One who will take control of the bureaucrats, enforce the laws, and give us *justice*." While the *existence* of the invasion is an objective fact that can be established by a commission, in Nietzsche's view, the *injustice* of the invasion is merely one possible *interpretation of the facts*. Is justice in the eyes of the beholder?

Anakin gets his first lesson in nihilism from Chancellor Palpatine at the Opera House in *Revenge of the Sith*.

ANAKIN: The Jedi use their power for good.
PALPATINE: Good is a point of view, Anakin. The Sith and the Jedi are similar in almost every way, including their quest for greater power.
ANAKIN: The Sith rely on their passion for their strength. They think inward, only about themselves.
PALPATINE: And the Jedi don't?
ANAKIN: The Jedi are selfless. They only care about others.

Is the difference between good and evil all just a matter of perspective, a matter of interpretation? While battling on Mustafar, Anakin and Obi-Wan confront each other with their rival moral viewpoints:

ANAKIN: I should've known the Jedi were plotting to take over.
OBI-WAN: Anakin, Chancellor Palpatine is *evil*.
ANAKIN: From my point of view the *Jedi* are evil.
OBI-WAN: Well then you *are lost*!

Anakin hasn't quite learned Palpatine's nihilist lesson yet, for he's still employing a moral concept – "evil" – in reference to the Jedi. If Anakin follows the Sith Lord's teachings, then, like Nietzsche's "philosopher," he would venture "*beyond good and evil*." He would no longer think in terms of right and wrong, good and evil, but rather see those quaint notions as a sad devotion to an ancient, hokey religion. Good and evil are interpretations; they aren't facts – at least according to nihilism and Palpatine. If you still see the world in these terms, then perhaps you're merely accepting what you were trained to believe rather than clearly seeing reality for what it actually is.

Nietzsche developed his view by studying ancient Greek litera-ture, especially Homer's *Iliad*. It's not hard to see why. The wrath of Achilles is first aroused by a dispute over the distribution of war booty. No one disputes that it is right for the better to rule the worse, or for the better to have the lion's share of the booty.[3] But just who is *better*? On the one hand, Homer portrays it as an undisputed, objective fact that Agamemnon was king over more warriors than any other Greek. But, on the other hand, he also portrays it as an equally undisputed, objective fact that Achilles is the single mightiest warrior.[4] Obviously, Agamemnon thinks that the one who brought the largest contingent of warriors is the "best of the Greeks," and Achilles thinks that the great-est fighter is the best.[5] But these are clear instances of self-serving bias; both are equally *subjective*. Better and worse, right and wrong, seem to be matters of interpretation, depending upon one's point of view.

What happens next doesn't seem to be determined by right or wrong, but by force and violence. Because he commands superior numbers, Agamemnon sends a delegation and simply takes Achilles's war prize. Because he's the superior warrior, Achilles plans to settle the dispute by running his sword through Agamemnon or by manipu-lating the situation until Agamemnon is forced to pay him back three-fold, regardless of how many Greeks die as a result.[6] Morality drops entirely out of the equation: what matters is not good or evil – these warriors are beyond all that. What matters is one thing and one thing only: *power*.

"The Dark Side Is a Pathway to Many Abilities Some Consider to Be *Unnatural*"

Nihilism can feel like an attractive view at first, but it soon reveals its flaws. When Hector faces Achilles to fight to the death, he proposes that they fight honorably and swear that whoever wins will not defile the body of the defeated. Achilles refuses, saying that "between lions and men there are no trustworthy oaths, nor are there hearts of con-cord between wolves and sheep."[7] He means it: after killing Hector, Achilles insults his corpse, calling him a dog and shouting, "I wish that my rage and fury would free me to carve into your flesh and eat you raw!" There is a sort of intoxicating liberation that comes with allowing rage to take over; it can release us from the constraints we normally feel. But is this freedom, or is it voluntarily sinking into a pit from which we may be unable to return?

Achilles tries to defile Hector's corpse, but the gods Apollo and Aphrodite protect it day and night. Achilles's willpower is not infinite; there are real powers in the cosmos that are not subject to his choice, and he ignores them at his own peril. Apollo points out to the rest of the gods that, in his grief over Patroclus, Achilles has become deranged to the point that he no longer feels either compassion or respect. Achilles has made a stone of his heart so that he has become "like a savage lion, who with his great force and arrogant heart takes the sheep of men for his feast."[8] Achilles has become like the Tusken Raiders who, according to Cliegg Lars, "walk like men, but they're vicious, mindless monsters."

Apollo's simile is important because it makes clear that he is not merely expressing his own feelings. He's identifying an objective fact: human beings are not lions. It's perfectly appropriate for a lion to devour the uncooked flesh of sheep, but it would be truly monstrous for Achilles to carve into Hector's flesh and literally eat him raw. Compassion and respect are appropriate for us because we are people; we are not savage beasts. Here we have an objective basis for morality, a basis that could be confirmed by a neutral and impartial committee on a fact-finding mission. This "moral realism" is the *rejection* of nihilism: there are moral facts because there are facts about what kinds of relationships are appropriate for us. Compassion and respect for others save us from the poverty of selfishness. When we love someone, we open ourselves to being hurt by them, or being plunged into sorrow if something bad happens to them; but we do not make our lives better by turning our hearts into stone in order to protect ourselves from the pain of loss. Without compassion and respect, life is a bitter struggle to kill or be killed, as Darth Sidious heartlessly murdered his master Darth Plagueis. While that sort of life is suitable for lions and gazelles, people simply aren't designed to thrive that way.

After Hector's death, his father risks everything to beg Achilles for Hector's body so that he can give it a proper burial. With tears in his eyes, he pleads, "Respect the gods, and have compassion on me."[9] Priam's tears make Achilles think of his own father, and his heart melts. He weeps with Priam and grants an extraordinary claim on him from a mortal enemy. The common bond of humanity, whether with friend or foe, still makes legitimate claims on us.

The same kind of moral realism in Homer's poetry is displayed in *Star Wars*. Compare the Jedi and the Sith visually. The Sith Lord sits alone in his office, occasionally giving orders to his apprentice, following Darth Bane's "Rule of Two" established after the defeat of the Sith Order at the Seventh Battle of Ruusan: "Two there should be; no more, no less. One to embody power, the other to crave it." Nietzsche is quite correct that many things are matters of interpretation, but with the Sith there's only one interpretation: that of the master. In stark contrast, the Jedi High Council consists of twelve Jedi Masters who sit in a semi-circle to examine issues from all sides. Each listens to the others respectfully and gives their opinions due consideration. They may have different opinions, perspectives, or interpretations – particularly on crucial issues such as how to understand the prophecy of the "Chosen One" – but no one tries to win, as if discussion were simply a battle with words instead of lightsabers. Rather, the group works together to discover the truth and discern the best way to proceed; they also tolerate the contrary views of sometimes defiant Jedi Masters, such as Qui-Gon Jinn. Even the venerable Grand Master Yoda yields to the Council's collective will when they decide to allow Obi-Wan to train Anakin against his better judgment. We could say that they never lose sight of their "humanity," but since they're not all members of the human species perhaps we should say that they respect each other's "personhood."

Although Sith are similarly capable of living their lives respecting each other's personhood, they choose instead to act like animals without the capacity for prudent council: they try to overpower each other. When Darth Sidious had learned all he could from Darth Plagueis, he simply killed him in his sleep, without respect or compassion, the way a snake might slither into a bird's nest and swallow an egg. Similarly, when Darth Tyranus/Count Dooku's usefulness has come to an end and he kneels defeated at Anakin's saber point, Sidious actually *smiles* and casually instructs Anakin, "Kill him. Kill him now."

Nihilism – *It's a Trap!*

What Nietzsche and Palpatine fail fully to grasp is that morality is no more or less a matter of interpretation than other forms of perception. We see what we expect to see, and it can appear fully real to us even if it's a total illusion. Padmé relies on this fact when she devises her plan to retake Naboo. She understands that if the Gungans attack the droid army in force, Nute Gunray will mistakenly interpret this as the final battle for Naboo he's been expecting: he will send out his forces, allowing her to sneak into Theed Palace and capture him. Padmé has seen through the superficial appearance of power to the central weakness of Gunray's position.

All perception may be a matter of interpretation, but some interpretations are better than others. This is, roughly, the lesson learned by Immanuel Kant (1724–1804):

> Coincidental observations made without any previously thought-out plan can never connect up to form a necessary law, which reason seeks and needs. If reason is to be instructed by nature, then it must approach nature with its principles in one hand (since it is only by agreeing with principles that appearances can count as laws) and with its experiments (thought-out in accordance with those principles) in the other hand. Reason must not behave like a student who simply repeats what his teacher says; it must rather approach nature like an appointed judge who requires the witness to answer the questions put to him.[10]

The famous "problem of induction" asks, how can we be sure that the future will resemble the past? Kant solves this problem by expecting that we act not on our own "coincidental observations," but on *principle*, that we ask the hard questions and see if we can figure out how our subjective interpretations of events can connect to form a universal law. For example, ask ten witnesses to Obi-Wan's disarming (literally!) of Zam Wessel in a Coruscant nightclub what they saw, and you may get ten different stories. It takes an intelligent investigator to sift through the coincidental observations to find the objective truth that lies beyond all these subjective truths. But Kant's crucial insight is more than this. He titled his magnum opus the *Critique of Pure Reason* because he discovered that it isn't enough for reason to critique or judge the evidence of our senses. Reason must also be *self*-critical: we must question even our own point of view.

How are we to do that? Scientists answer this question (in part) with the concept of "reproducibility." Scientists present their findings to the scientific community so that others can try to reproduce their results. If the results you report turn out to be irreproducible, then those results will be dismissed as purely subjective and probably a result of some mistake (or deliberate attempt at deception) on your part. We've already seen this sort of approach in *The Phantom Menace*. The Jedi High Council includes twelve wise Masters who discuss and respectfully debate each other's viewpoints. Similarly, Padmé reveals her plan to capture Gunray to Captain Panaka, Boss Nass, and Qui-Gon in order to confirm that it is a good plan. Critical and self-critical inquiry is successful when we transcend our own limited perspective by treating one another with compassion and respect. In short, we have a greater chance of discovering the deeper principles of nature if we treat alternative points of view with the sort of respectful consideration they deserve.

By contrast, the Sith approach seems almost childish. Yes, they understand that in morality and other matters, subjectivity and interpretation shape our perceptions, but they lack the patience and humility – in short, the maturity – to engage in critical and self-critical inquiry. When a Sith faces obstacles or doesn't get what he wants, he throws a temper tantrum and uses the Force to get his way, or he sneaks behind everyone's back and manipulates the situation so that he gets what he wants. Sith behave just like Agamemnon and Achilles in Book 1 of Homer's *Iliad*: each one wants his way, and tries to overpower or manipulate others to do so.

The difference between Kant and Nietzsche on the subject of better and worse interpretations– between the patience and maturity of critical and self-critical inquiry on the one hand, and the impatience and immaturity of passionate subjectivity on the other hand – is evident in *Attack of the Clones*, just as the love between Anakin and Padmé is blossoming:

ANAKIN: I don't think the system works.
PADMÉ: How would you have it work?
ANAKIN: We need a system where the politicians sit down and discuss the problems, agree what's in the best interests of all the people, and then do it.
PADMÉ: That is exactly what we do. The trouble is that people don't always agree.
ANAKIN: Then they should be made to.
PADMÉ: By whom? Who's going to make them?
ANAKIN: I don't know. Someone.
PADMÉ: You?
ANAKIN: Of course not me.

PADMÉ: But someone.
ANAKIN: Someone wise.
PADMÉ: That sounds an awful lot like a dictatorship to me.
ANAKIN: Well, if it works. . . .

Anakin is effectively recommending the rejection of compassion and respect; instead, the most powerful among politicians could force the rest to agree with his own limited point of view. This is the real danger with the Senate granting Chancellor Palpatine "emergency powers" to defend the Republic against the growing Separatist movement – all due to Palpatine's behind-the-scenes maneuvering and the gullibility of Gungan Representative Jar Jar Binks – leading ultimately to Palpatine's self-declaration as "Emperor" and eventually the complete dissolution of the Senate so that only Palpatine's point of view will determine the course of galactic events. How would you like to be forced to agree with someone else's point of view when your own experience tells you that there is more going on?

In *The Empire Strikes Back*, Yoda agrees with Kant regarding looking for the deeper principles of nature binding on all of us in order to transcend our limited subjectivity:

> My ally is the Force, and a powerful ally it is. Life creates it, makes it grow. Its energy surrounds us and binds us. Luminous beings are we, not this crude matter. You must feel the Force around you; here, between you, me, the tree, the rock, everywhere.

The Force is universal, like the force of gravity; it touches all of us (not just the lucky few born with a high midi-chlorian count). But this quest for universal principles that transcend the subjectivity of the individual raises one final question: if the worlds of *The Iliad* and *Star Wars* reject nihilism in favor of moral realism, and they both do so by making the intersubjectivity of compassion and respect fundamentally important in the discovery of cosmic principles, what *moral universals* are at work in these worlds?

Homer's Greek heroes obey what we might call the "Pagan Golden Rule": *help your friends and harm your enemies*. This sounds harsh at first, but remember that an honorable warrior never loses compassion or respect for his enemies, "I have just learned that my enemy is to be hated only so much, since he may soon be my friend; and the friend

I help, I will help only so much since he may not always remain my friend."[11] Friends can become enemies if you take them for granted – as Count Dooku and the other Separatist leaders learn the hard way from Darth Sidious – but if you treat your friends with respect and compassion, they will probably remain loyal to you. The same is true for your enemies. As Abraham Lincoln once asked, "Do I not destroy my enemies when I make them my friends?"

This is ultimately what *Star Wars* and *The Iliad* reveal to be the root of the nihilistic trap. There are real moral facts because there are universal moral principles that bind all people together, and which we ignore at our own peril. It isn't always easy to be a true friend to someone, since you need to be understanding and patient with them, and from time to time you have to make yourself vulnerable to them. The same is true with our enemies. Hostility isn't always a simple matter of winning and losing; often we need to take the time to understand our enemies, to see things through their eyes to find common ground. Immature people are impatient and unwilling to approach others with both compassion and respect; instead, like Anakin in the face of bureaucratic wrangling, they try to force the solution they want on others. After succumbing to the temptations of the dark side in *Revenge of the Sith*, Anakin attempts to persuade Padmé to his point of view, sounding even less mature now than the little boy Padmé first knew on Tatooine: "I have become more powerful than the Chancellor. I can overthrow him. And together you and I can rule the galaxy, make things the way we want them to be!"

"Help Me Take This Mask Off"

Anakin and Achilles found that going down the dark path of nihilism can cost you dearly. Achilles was rescued from the monster he had become by seeing his own father in the tearful eyes of Priam. Anakin was saved by the devotion of his own son. Dying, he asks Luke to remove his helmet so that he can see his son with his own eyes rather than the eyes of Darth Vader, who could see only what his helmet allowed him to see. He had to make that direct connection with his son one last time. There wasn't much left of Anakin – he was "more machine now than man" – but it was enough. As Yoda *almost* said, "Fear leads to anger, anger leads to hate, hate leads to … nihilism."

Like Achilles, Anakin barely makes it back from his journey into nihilism.

Notes

1. All translations from Greek and German are my own.
2. Friedrich Nietzsche, *Götzen-Dämmerung, oder, Wie man mit dem Hammer philosophiert* (*Twilight of the Idols*), in *Werke in drei Bänden*, Band 2, ed. Karl Schlechta (Munich: C. Hanser, 1954), 979.
3. Homer, *The Iliad*, 2 vols. (Cambridge, MA: Loeb Classical Library, 1988), 2.198–206, 285–91; 1.121–9, 163–71.
4. Ibid., 2.576; 2.769.
5. Ibid., 1.91; 1.244.
6. Ibid., 1.194; 1.213; 9.653.
7. Ibid., 22.262–3.
8. Ibid., 24.41–3.
9. Ibid., 24.503.
10. Immanuel Kant, *Kritik der reinen Vernunft* (*Critique of Pure Reason*), in *Werke in zwölf Bänden*, Band 3 (Frankfurt am Main: Suhrkamp, 1977), 22.
11. Sophocles, *Ajax* in *Fabulae*, ed. Sir Hugh Lloyd-Jones and N.G. Wilson (Oxford: Oxford University Press, 1990), 678–82.

5

Dark Times: The End of the Republic and the Beginning of Chinese Philosophy

Kevin S. Decker

It is said that straw dogs were treated with the greatest deference before they were used as an offering, only to be discarded and trampled upon as soon as they had served their purpose.

– D.C. Lau[1]

The currents of philosophy have always been influenced by the culture in which thinkers live and work. In ancient China, the profound turmoil that eventually tore apart the Zhou dynasty (1122–221 BCE) led to social and intellectual unrest, out of which was born a new class of writers and thinkers who created the foundations for Chinese philosophy. These included Kongfuzi, better known as Confucius (551–479 BCE), the originator of Confucianism, and Laozi (sixth century BCE), the originator of Daoism.

There are historical and philosophical parallels with this Chinese time of uprooting in the "Dark Times" of the *Star Wars* universe: the period between the establishment of the Empire by Palpatine in the year 19 BBY (Before the Battle of Yavin) and the death of the Emperor and Darth Vader twenty-three years later. Few Jedi survive through the Dark Times, but they're the closest thing to philosophers we can find during the *Star Wars* saga's most intense period of oppression and wickedness. In particular, we can look to Dark Horse's *Dark Times* series for examples of three Jedi Masters who survived Palpatine's purge. Dass Jennir (a human), Kai Hudorra (a Bothan), and

The Ultimate Star Wars and Philosophy: You Must Unlearn What You Have Learned, First Edition. Edited by Jason T. Eberl and Kevin S. Decker.
© 2016 John Wiley & Sons, Ltd. Published 2016 by John Wiley & Sons, Ltd.

K'kruhk (a Whiphid) groped for ways of understanding morality, transcendence, honorable practice, and survivor's guilt. Looking at these Jedi through the lens of the Chinese philosophies of Confucianism and Daoism, we'll see what kind of evil – and what good – people are moved to do during Dark Times, whether in ancient China or the nascent Galactic Empire.[2]

Heaven's Mandate Is Not Constant

"In order to ensure the security and continuing stability, the Republic will be reorganized into the *first Galactic Empire*! For a safe and secure society ... ." With these words, Chancellor Palpatine declares himself Emperor and initiates the crucial political transformation around which the *Star Wars* saga revolves. Together with Order 66's scourge of the Jedi and the rise of Darth Vader as Palpatine's right hand, a new and harsh regime begins its rule over more than a thousand star systems. While core worlds loyal to the Imperial New Order enjoy relative security and stability as promised by Palpatine – at the very least, the Clone Wars that Palpatine engineered are over – the rest of the galaxy is plunged into political chaos as dissident civilizations are squeezed by the Empire's military gauntlet. There's also political fragmentation within local systems due to the elevation of fringe sector players, such as the greedy and vainglorious Hutts, the criminal organization Black Sun, and the corrupt Corporate Sector Authority.[3]

These kinds of events must've been in the mind of the Chinese originator of the ancient twofold blessing/curse, "May you live in interesting times." Near the end of the Old Republic, the political stresses of large-scale corporate violence and bureaucratic corruption motivate Queen Amidala to announce to the Galactic Senate, "I was not elected to watch my people suffer and die while you discuss this invasion in a committee. If this body is not capable of action, I suggest new leadership is needed." "Interesting times" also echo from a long time ago in our own corner of the galaxy, in the long, slow death of the Zhou Empire of China, a feudal government that fell apart from its center, living on in name only during the intellectually fertile Spring and Autumn (*Chunqiu*) period (722–476 BCE) and the Warring States (*Zhanguo*) period (475–221 BCE). These five hundred years were pivotal for early China because quickly shifting political boundaries and their attendant, bloody battles disrupted families and whole societies.

For example, "[I]n *Lu*, Confucius's native state, three sons of an earlier ruler, Huan Gong, had established branch lineages that had in the next two centuries become independent powers each with its own military citadel, and the nominal lord had become virtually helpless."[4] Among the aristocrats (Confucius's line included), a new class of the lowest-ranking "knights" (*shi*) served, like Japanese *samurai*, as highly mobile soldiers. By the end of the Spring and Autumn period, however, they had developed into a social and cultural literary elite.

Evidence of the deep scarring of the late Zhou political and social catastrophe can be found in the emphasis that many *shi* placed on having *de*, variously translated as "virtue," "potency," or "moral force."[5] In its humble beginnings, *de* simply represented a feeling of gratitude, but it can also represent the distinctive virtue of great rulers:

> a good king acquires and enhances [*de*] by offerings to the spirits, and by gifts of goods, authority and confidence to subordinates, as well as by opening his ears to advice. Conversely, he would squander all this power by self-indulgence, lack of restraint, arrogance or cruelty.[6]

Whether a ruler has *de* or not represents a moral constraint on power: Heaven (*tien*) grants *de*, but it may take it away based on the moral failures of bad kings. Good kings remain on their thrones because they have the "Mandate of Heaven." Bad rulers, however, lose the Mandate anywhere the people no longer tacitly accept the ruler's authority, usually because of a lack of prosperity and order, which is spiritually and emotionally connected with the ruler's influence.

But *why* do rulers lose the Mandate of Heaven? One answer is they've simply lost favor with Heaven, the ways of which are mysterious – the earliest reference to the Mandate we have gravely intones that it "is not to be presumed upon."[7] But certain *shi* saw this as cold comfort for living through the Warring States and Spring and Autumn periods. Instead, they spoke of the essential unity of people and Heaven.[8] Their alternate approach distinguished early Chinese philosophies from the mysticism and divinatory practices that preceded them.

K'Kruhk's Story

When Plato of Athens (429–347 BCE) thought about social order and disorder, he identified the soul (*psyche*) of the individual as a microcosm of the larger community. His philosophy of "as within, so without" explained the degree of justice in a citizenry as a whole by referring to the degree of order or disorder in each citizen's *psyche*. Similarly, the ancient Chinese thought that political and social chaos were quite unnatural because "'Heaven, Earth and the Human' has a profoundly mysterious mutual interconnection or correspondence." In fact, the ground for this "interrelated holistic entity" that was the Chinese cosmos bears more than a little resemblance to the Force. The Daoist Laozi says of it:

> There was something undifferentiated and yet complete,
> Which existed before heaven and earth.
> Soundless and formless, it depends on nothing and does not change.
> It operates everywhere and is free from danger.
> It may be considered the mother of the universe.
> I do not know its name; I call it *Dao*
> If forced to give it a name, I shall call it Great (*Da*).[9]

In the *Dark Times* series, Jedi Master K'Kruhk struggles to keep his mind and spirit ordered, but is hampered by the burden of his charge – caring for and protecting his adoptive padawan, Chase Piru, and the younglings of Soaring Hawkbat Clan. In a chillingly drawn scene, his quest begins with clone troopers mixing with the admiring younglings, a scene that ends with the squad receiving Order 66 and opening fire. K'Kruhk launches into action to protect them, losing his temper and furiously shouting, "Why?!" Fleeing the Hawkbats' home, they settle on an unnamed moon with Chase as their new instructor and K'Kruhk as their protector. After two months there, they've formed their own sort of family:

> So much has changed in the past two months. Then he had a war to fight, and responsibilities to an entire galaxy – and the Jedi Order. Now this group of younglings is his only worry. K'Kruhk is not sure which burden has weighed more heavily on him. When they first arrived – crash-landed – on this world, the wounds of betrayal and of the personal loss he had suffered were still raw. At that time K'Kruhk desired only solitude ... or, though he hates to admit it to himself, to lash back at the Sith and their minions.[10]

An attack on the group by space pirates leads K'Kruhk to once again forget his discipline as he uses his lightsaber and other weapons to decimate the opposition. After the violence, K'Kruhk seeks redemption through Piru, telling her, "My emotions were not very Jedi-like, were they? I was in the war for so long, I guess some of the war got into me …. In trying to save something I cared about, I may have lost it … forever."[11]

Laozi might suggest that K'Kruhk has lost authentic connection with the *Dao*, the Chinese parallel of the Force. Because of his stressors, K'Kruhk is clashing with the world rather than finding his natural place in it. A Daoist like Laozi would say that K'Kruhk needs to practice *wu-wei*, which literally means "no action" but actually means something like aligning oneself with the Force rather than fighting against it. Laozi explains, "If a tree is stiff, it will break. The strong and the great are inferior, while the tender and the weak are superior."[12] This Daoist advice will be difficult for most Westerners to sympathize with, but K'Kruhk finds an able interpreter in Master Zao, a blind Veknoid Jedi modeled on the famous sightless swordsman Zatoichi of Japanese films.[13] After they meet in a refugee camp on the planet Arkinnea, Zao instructs him, "The Force is a great ally, and it can lead you where you need to go. But you must always be open to follow. If you decide you already know where it is leading, you may take the wrong path. Be aware, observe, but do not assume."[14] Zao thus follows a path not typical of the Jedi, skirting the borders of the Clone Wars, "follow[ing] the Force and never [taking] sides."[15]

Zao and K'Kruhk, however, are tested by the corruption of the refugee camp administrators, who are killing their former separatist charges rather than helping them. Despite Zao's attitude of *wu-wei* toward violent resistance, he admits that, confronted by the massacres perpetrated by the Arkinneans against Separatist refugees, "Perhaps it is a mercy that there are no survivors here to perpetuate the next cycle of revenge … though the Force cries out for justice for these victims."[16] Zao thus explores the tension between K'Kruhk's deep-seated need for revenge, the conventional demands of justice, and the need for spontaneous, positive action – another meaning of *wu-wei*. Yet, by protecting the younglings – even as one shows a tendency toward turning to the dark side – Zao and K'Kruhk learn the meaning of the seemingly paradoxical Daoist slogan, "Even the sage regards things as difficult, and therefore he encounters no difficulty."[17] Zao does this by reflecting on the fact that the murder of the refugees shouldn't represent an

insuperable obstacle to positive action, while K'Kruhk's timely intervention with Sidirri forestalls her attraction to the dark side.

Dass Jennir's Story

According to Confucius, the commitments of *wu-wei* and the simple
complexity of the *Dao* obscure the need for people in dark times to create virtuous communities by focusing on what it means to be human
(*ren*) and acting steadfastly in service of that idea. We read an ancient
moral tract like Confucius's *Analects* "in order to understand the com-
plexities associated with the process of moral reasoning as the early
Confucians understood it," and so learn "from experiences of enlight-
ened people in the past, that is, understanding of how others may have
acted admirably or fallen short of particular requirements."[18]

Dass Jennir, a human Jedi and the central protagonist of the *Dark
Times* series, worries about falling short of Jedi requirements in
the absence of a standing Jedi Order.[19] Jennir's encounter with Kai
Hudorra, another Jedi attempting to keep to the shadows on Coruscant, reveals their fundamental differences in the face of tragedy.
When Hudorra inquires as to whether Jennir intends to attack the
clone troopers at the temple, he replies, "I would not throw my life
away so hastily – or so vainly … but neither am I done fighting for the
principles on which the Republic was based."[20] But what are those
principles, given the facts that Darth Sidious had been subverting the
Senate for years and that leading politicians at the end of the Old
Republic, including Mon Mothma, stood uncertain of where the Jedi's
commitments lie?

Confucius would've seen this muddle as calling for the "rectification
of names" (*zhengming*), a realignment of ways of speaking and thinking with hard reality. Likewise, there is a fascination in the world of
Star Wars, particularly among the Sith, with concealed identities and
the significance of names – "Darth" being a title bestowed upon newly
sworn Sith Lords, for example. Because of the pictographic nature of
Chinese, the close fit between words and reality has always been of
importance to Chinese thinkers. "Each Chinese character (or name:
ming) has a particular meaning, and how the characters are combined,
for instance, to form a compound name or a proposition, is an important matter."[21] Confucius himself taught:

If names are not rectified, then language will not be in accord with truth. If language is not in accord with truth, then things cannot be accomplished. If things cannot be accomplished, then ceremonies and music will not flourish. If ceremonies and music do not flourish, then punishment will not be just. If punishments are not just, then the people will not know how to move hand or foot. Therefore the superior man will give only names that can be described in speech and say only what can be carried out in practice.[22]

For his part, Dass Jennir returns to what it means to be "Jedi" in helping the Nosaurian separatists on New Plympto against the clone army. Jennir is recruited by the Nosaurian Commander Rootrock, who tells him, "I can sympathize with a former foe who has discovered that he was doing the wrong thing for what he thought were the right reasons – but all who have died in the war believed they fought for what was right."[23] This recalls the preamble to the record of the Clone Wars' conclusion in the Journal of the Whills, in which it is stated, "There are heroes on both sides."[24] Yet Jennir is in for a series of moral tests that threaten to dislodge his principles. Developing a close attachment with one Nosaurian, Bomo Greenbark, Jennir pitches in to find Bomo's family when they're taken by slavers. But Bomo's wife is already dead, and when Jennir finds and interrogates the Chagrian slaver who has sold Bomo's daughter, he ends up killing the slaver to keep him quiet. In fact, as his enraged expression shows when he pulls the trigger, he does so with extreme prejudice.

This is a choice, Jennir admits, that "mean[s] departing from the Jedi path. Possibly forever."[25] He not only departs from the Jedi path but also, when Bomo's daughter is consumed by a "cultivated" cannibal who buys slaves for his gruesome menus, Jennir kills the culprit and thereby deprives Bomo of his vengeance. Greenbark repudiates Jennir, leaving him alone to follow a path of his own, a path he's afraid will "lead to nowhere."

Driven by his guilt over not saving Bomo's family, Jennir interferes in a feud between T'surr spice runners and Chagrian slavers. Posturing like a cross between Clint Eastwood and Japanese cinema's Toshiro Mifune, Jennir's transformation into a vigilante "Jedi with no name" is complete – he even sports a futuristic version of the classic wide-brim Ronin hat.[26] "As a Jedi, Jennir was a peacekeeper – protecting the innocent – supporting the laws of the Republic ... but without law – with the Republic – he will become a peace*maker*."[27]

Given Confucius's emphasis on ritual propriety (*li*) and social order, it might seem like the role of peacemaker is the best that Dass Jennir can hope for while living in the fragmented galactic fringe. As with the breakdown of the Zhou dynasty in China, decency and discipline seem to have no place in a post-Jedi world. Yet, in the Confucian stress on acting in a way to encourage the essential humanity (*ren*) of oneself and others to flourish, there's still a higher-order path for Jennir: "A superior man in dealing with the world is not for anything or against anything. He follows righteousness as the standard."[28] *Ren* implies that each person still has duties to oneself and others despite social breakdowns, and that many of those duties, rather than simply iron-clad rules bereft of thinking or feeling, must be dictated by one's *virtue*. We're not born with virtue, but must cultivate it, which is the central motivating force of Confucius's philosophy. Virtue isn't so much a way of *being* – as the ancient Greek virtues of Plato and Aristotle are often understood – but a way of *relating*:

> One who can practice five things wherever he may be is a man of humanity [*ren*] …. If one is earnest, one will not be treated with disrespect. If one is liberal, one will win the hearts of all. If one is truthful, one will be trusted. If one is diligent, one will be successful. And if one is generous, one will be able to enjoy the service of others.[29]

Critics of notions of "virtue" complain that we're told what the virtues are, but we're not told their definitions and how to employ them. Confucius's *Analects*, like many ancient Chinese texts, is an effort not simply to provide answers to such questions but also to encourage *reflection* by individuals who want their virtue to flourish. This suggests that dark times are less a threat to moral thinking and acting than are unchanging, static codes of rules that merely *simulate* virtue instead of encouraging its genuine growth, even if *conflict* is necessary for this to occur.

Conflict certainly dogs Dass Jennir. With duplicitous Ember Chankali, a woman who plays Jennir off against two gangs on the planet Telerath, tagging along, Jennir crashes his ship and ends up having to save Ember from bandits. They grow closer as a result, and the correctness of how this relationship *feels* to Jennir allows him to turn his life around. His love and devotion toward Ember redeem him as a Jedi – Confucius well understood the positive power of such feelings – rather than any act of justice or vengeance he carries out as a "peacemaker."

Kai Hudorra's Story

While K'Kruhk, aided by Master Zao, might be working toward becoming a Daoist sage, and Dass Jennir's search for a meaningful role in dark times illuminates Confucian truths, we haven't yet said anything of Master Hudorra. With his padawan Noirah Na, Hudorra, a Bothan, escaped Order 66 thanks to the sacrifice of another Jedi, Na's master. Like Jennir, Hudorra is sorely tested; but unlike Jennir, he soon loses his faith and his way. Hudorra finds that Palpatine's plan to not only destroy but also *discredit* the Jedi has worked. "The Jedi tried to overthrow the Republic!" a denizen of a local bar proclaims. Hudorra challenges, "But the Jedi led the war to *preserve* the Republic, not to control it!" To his chagrin, another barfly responds, "Either way, who needs them? The war is over."[30] On Coruscant, he and Na witness the killing of a rebellious Jedi on the steps of the Jedi Temple, and Hudorra drops both of their lightsabers in a waste disposal unit and gives Na this extraordinary advice: "Forget about the temple. Forget the Jedi Order. Forget everything you've learned about the Force. I am no longer your master ... and you are no longer a Jedi."[31] He then sends Na – a fifteen-year-old girl taken from her home by the Jedi before ever knowing her family – into the crowds of Coruscant, a converse image of young Anakin fatefully leaving his mother, Shmi, to become a Jedi, while Na will never be one again.

Hudorra's complete rejection of the idealism he sees in Jedi like Jennir is similar to the critics of Confucianism led by Mozi (470–391 BCE), called Mohists. Often identified as spiritual minimalists concerned more with earthly costs and benefits than spiritual transcendence, Mohists nonetheless were ethically critical of serious, concrete problems in Chinese culture like the exploitation of the peasantry by large landowners and the dissolution of traditional families. Their criticisms stemmed from the principle that "correct ethical assessment must take into account the sum total of good and evil for all concerned."[32] They thus also condemned war and violence: "Now does it mean that to annex a state and destroy an army, injure and oppress the people, and throw the heritages of sages into confusion will benefit Heaven?"[33] Mozi would've agreed with Hudorra that fighting the power in dark times is a losing game.

And a life of withdrawal suits Hudorra. The next time we encounter him, he's the prosperous owner of The Lucky Twi'lek, a fortress-like casino on Kestavel. There, the Dark Jedi Master Beygor Sahdett betrays Dass Jennir and Hudorra to Darth Vader. After an Imperial assault on the casino, Hudorra dies at Vader's hands in order to give Jennir and his allies time to escape. He leaves Jennir a holo-recording in which he says with confidence that the Jedi Order survives in Jennir: "At first I resented you for bringing this battle to my doorstep, but after hearing of your exploits – and your sacrifices .... I knew that I could not allow you to throw your life away on a fight we had so little chance of winning."[34] Hudorra's conscience must've been troubled indeed for him to so quickly give up his comfortable life to a suicide mission. Ironically, given Mohism's seemingly narrow, utilitarian focus, it is Jennir's virtuous example that moves Hudorra to fight to the end. Despite Hudorra's sacrifice, Jennir is heartened by the slain master's last words: "I can go to my fate secure in the knowledge that in the galaxy a vital spark of the Jedi remains. May the Force be with you all."[35] The convergences and departures in the struggles of K'Kruhk, Jennir, and Hudorra stand as a poignant reminder: just as the contours of philosophy are always shaped by society and culture, it's equally true that everyday pragmatism, the engine of society and culture, has little inspiration to create a better world without the force of philosophical ideals, even in dark times.

Notes

1. Lao Tzu, *Tao Te Ching*, trans. Dim-cheuk Lau (Harmondsworth, UK: Penguin Books, 1963), 61.
2. An excellent accompaniment to this chapter is Walter [Ritoku] Robinson, "The Far East of *Star Wars*," in *Star Wars and Philosophy*, ed. Kevin S. Decker and Jason T. Eberl (Chicago: Open Court, 2005), 29–38. While Robinson focuses on the influence that Zen Buddhism and Daoism have had on the martial arts philosophy that informs the Jedi, I discuss the response of early Chinese philosophers to "dark times" in its moral and political respects.

3. See Brian Daley, *The Han Solo Adventures* (New York: Del Rey, 1992); and Steve Perry, *Shadows of the Empire* (New York: Bantam Spectra, 1996).

4. David Shepherd Nivison, "The Classical Philosophical Writings," in *The Cambridge History of Ancient China*, ed. Michael Loewe and Edward L. Shaughnessy (New York: Cambridge University Press 1999), 748.

5. Ibid., 749.

6. Ibid., 750. Max Weber calls this "charismatic authority," which provided the legitimacy for many "Oriental" states and which "rest[ed] on devotion to the exceptional sanctity, heroism or exemplary character of an individual person, and of the normative patterns or order revealed or ordained by him"; Weber, *Economy and Society: An Outline of Interpretive Sociology* (New York: Bedminster Press, 1968), 214.

7. Edward L. Shaughnessy, "Western Zhou History," in *The Cambridge History of Ancient China*, 314.

8. Wing-Tsit Chan, ed., *A Source Book in Chinese Philosophy* (Princeton, NJ: Princeton University Press, 1963), 3.

9. "The Natural Way of Laozi," in *A Source Book in Chinese Philosophy*, 152.

10. Randy Stradley et al., *Star Wars: Dark Times*, vol. 1 (Milwaukie, OR: Dark Horse, 2014), 203–4.

11. Ibid., 276.

12. Chan, *A Source Book in Chinese Philosophy*, 174.

13. Thanks to Terry MacMullan for the connection made here. As played by Shintaro Katsu, Zatoichi was the central character of twenty-five immensely popular films in Japan set in the mid-nineteenth century and released in cinemas between 1962 and 1973. Zatoichi's charm is that he doesn't present himself as a warrior; he's a masseur by profession; while in *Dark Times*, Zao is an accomplished chef.

14. Randy Stradley et al., *Star Wars: Dark Times*, vol. 2 (Milwaukie, OR: Dark Horse, 2014), 254.

15. Ibid., 251.

16. Ibid., 279.

17. Chan, *A Source Book in Chinese Philosophy*, 169.

18. Karyn L. Lai, *An Introduction to Chinese Philosophy* (New York: Cambridge University Press, 2008), 21.

19. With his full white beard and his hair cut short, he's evocative of Ralph MacQuarrie's concept art for "General Luke Skywalker," a character brought to life in Dark Horse's miniseries *The Star Wars*.

20. Stradley et al., *Dark Times*, 1:49.

21. Lai, *Introduction to Chinese Philosophy*, 111.

22. Chan, *A Sourcebook in Chinese Philosophy*, 40.

23. Ibid., 33.

24. The Journal of the Whills is how the history of that galaxy far, far away has become known to us: http://starwars.wikia.com/wiki/Journal_of_the_Whills (accessed November 8, 2014). In its cinematic form, the preamble quoted is the opening crawl of *Episode III: Revenge of the Sith*.

25. Stradley et al., *Dark Times*, 1:132.

26. Classic Ronin films starring Mifune include Akira Kurosawa's *Yojimbo* (1961) and *Sanjuro* (1962); the influence of Kurosawa's films on George Lucas's approach to *Star Wars* has been well documented. Eastwood's Western versions of the "man with no name" include Sergio Leone's *A Fistful of Dollars* (1964), *For a Few Dollars More* (1965), and *The Good, the Bad and the Ugly* (1966).

27. Stradley et al., *Dark Times*, 2:47. A similar character arc is undertaken by Obi-Wan Kenobi during his self-imposed exile on Tatooine, although he stays more true to the Jedi path; see John Jackson Miller, *Star Wars: Kenobi* (New York: Del Rey, 2013).

28. Chan, *A Sourcebook in Chinese Philosophy*, 26.

29. Ibid., 46–7.

30. Stradley et al., *Dark Times*, 1:26.

31. Ibid., 47.

32. Lai, *Introduction to Chinese Philosophy*, 59.

33. "Mozi's Doctrines," in *A Source Book in Chinese Philosophy*, 227.

34. Stradley et al., *Dark Times*, 2:454.

35. Ibid.

Episode II
ATTACK OF THE MORALS

6

Chasing Kevin Smith: Was It Immoral for the Rebel Alliance to Destroy Death Star II?

Charles C. Camosy

Those of us who are fans of both Kevin Smith and *Star Wars* have been treated to several delicious references to a galaxy far, far away in his movies. From giving one of his films a *Star Wars*–esque title (*Jay and Silent Bob Strike Back*), to creating bar scenes explicitly inspired by *the* famous Mos Eisley cantina (*Dogma*), to writing Hooper X's devastating and hilarious response to the proposal that Lando Calrissian is a "strong black role model" (*Chasing Amy*), Smith's movies out their creator as a fellow *Star Wars* geek.[1]

But one particular Star Wars reference stands above the rest. In *Clerks*, Randal and Dante discuss whether it was immoral for the Rebel Alliance to attack and destroy Death Star II in *Return of the Jedi*. Noting that the unfinished space station likely had "independent contractors working on that thing," Randal argues that they were "casualties of a war they had nothing to do with." After all, these workers are likely "just trying to scrape out a living" and were "innocent victims" of "left wing militants." A local roofer overhears Randal's argument and claims that contractors have to consider their personal ethics and politics when taking a job. He once refused to take a job from well-known gangster, and, wouldn't you know it, the contractor who took the job was killed during a hit from a rival gang. Moral of the story: let your most deeply held values and instinct for self-preservation guide the decision to take a contracting job, not your wallet.

The Ultimate Star Wars and Philosophy: You Must Unlearn What You Have Learned, First Edition. Edited by Jason T. Eberl and Kevin S. Decker.
© 2016 John Wiley & Sons, Ltd. Published 2016 by John Wiley & Sons, Ltd.

This brilliant and rich scene presents several important philosophical questions.[2] At bottom, Smith's concern is a question for moral philosophy: "Was the Rebel attack on Death Star II immoral?" Since the attack appears to have killed so many innocent people, maybe it's even fair to call it an *act of terrorism*. Several related questions also present themselves. What does it mean to be innocent? Was helping to build the Death Star morally blameworthy? Even if the Rebel attack wasn't terrorism, it could still be seriously immoral. Was the damage caused by the Death Star's destruction *proportionate* with the good that was gained?

Scum and Villainy: The Anatomy of a Terrorist Act

Especially for *Star Wars* fans who identify deeply with the Rebels, the idea that the destruction of Death Star II might be terrorism could be jolting. In responding to Smith's challenge, the first thing we need is a definition of terrorism. In public discussions, *terrorism* is often used simply as a rhetorical device to paint one's enemies, making them seem like barbarians lacking basic decency or humanity. As philosophers, though, we need to be more precise with our definition, and then apply it consistently in each and every case we encounter, regardless of our politics or other interests.

Terrorism means something only within a specific way of thinking about right and wrong, or, more generally, an ethical theory or framework. One very popular and powerful ethical framework is utilitarianism, which views the moral life as about producing the greatest good for the greatest number, maximizing pleasure over pain or happiness over unhappiness.[3] For a utilitarian, moral rules exist as merely "rules of thumb" that generally work to produce the best consequences. Because utilitarians generally do not recognize exceptionless rules, they would simply ask us to consider whether killing the innocent – in the long run and overall – is likely to produce good consequences. So although he didn't kill Han and Leia, Lando Calrissian seemed to be thinking in utilitarian terms when he made a deal to betray the Rebels to the Empire in return for freedom and security for the inhabitants of Cloud City.[4]

But most thinkers espousing "just war theory" reject the utilitarian view.[5] Using rule-based ethical frameworks, they argue that certain actions are so horrific, so thoroughly at odds with what's right, that they can never be done under any circumstances. Acts like torture, forcing prisoners to fight against their own side, using weapons of mass destruction, and gang rape would be considered "intrinsically evil acts." Just war theorists think that utilitarians are mistaken in holding that the only important moral consideration is whether an act ultimately produces good consequences. Instead, we should follow exceptionless moral rules against doing such evil things – even when doing so might give us a substantial advantage. Vader's torture of Han in Cloud City, or the building of a Death Star (which, of its very nature, is a weapon of mass destruction), may have produced significant benefits – such as bringing order to an unruly galaxy – but most just war theorists would reject both as intrinsically evil.

Just war theory also prohibits the killing of innocent noncombatants: any intentional targeting of innocents is to be considered a terrorist act. Indeed, it is only from within this kind of rule-based theory that terrorism makes any sense as a concept. Terrorism violates the exceptionless moral rule forbidding the intentional targeting of innocent people, as becomes clear if we examine the destruction of Death Star II within a just war ethical framework.

But hold on a minute. Let's take some time to discuss this in committee. Aren't innocents killed in every major conflict? If we called it *terrorism* every time an innocent person is killed in war, wouldn't virtually every player in virtually every conflict around the world be considered a terrorist group? This important question can be answered by thinking more carefully and precisely about what *targeting* means in our original definition of terrorism.

Innocent Voices Crying Out in Terror: From Madrid to the Death Star

In 2004, an al Qaeda–inspired group, apparently in an attempt to influence Spanish national elections three days hence, set off ten bombs in four trains during the peak of rush hour in Madrid. They killed almost 200 innocent people and wounded almost 2000. By almost everyone's account, this was a brutal and horrific act that deserved to be called *terrorism*.

But suppose someone defends the bombers by using the ethical framework from the last section. Simply because noncombatants are killed in war doesn't mean that such an act is terrorism. Suppose they argue that the government of Spain, as a supporter of the war on al Qaeda in Iraq, was a legitimate military target. The ultimate end or goal of the attack was to get this government out of office, and the civilian deaths, while regrettable, were just collateral damage – just as in a situation of all-out war.

But terrorists almost never have the death of civilians as their *ultimate* goal. What makes terrorists deserve near-universal condemnation is that they intentionally use the death of the innocent as a *means* to accomplish what they are really after. Consider Grand Moff Tarkin's decision to obliterate millions of innocent people by destroying Alderaan. While his ultimate goal was to deter other systems from rebelling against the Empire ("No star system will dare oppose the Emperor now"), the means by which he accomplished this goal meant the death of millions of innocent people. This clearly makes it a terrorist act.

As I wrote these pages, I was regularly confronted by the terrible news reports of the death of innocent Palestinian civilians in Israel's latest conflict with Hamas. Some reports describe Israeli attacks as terrorism. While their military response to Hamas' attack may be *disproportionate* (as we'll discuss further in this chapter), and therefore seriously wrong, it's a mistake to think of Israel's response as *terrorism*. But why isn't this just the bias of a pro-Israel view? It is true that the Madrid bombers, Tarkin, and the Israeli military all engaged in acts that led to the death of civilians. But while they all produced the same outcome, there's more to consider than just *which* consequences were produced. If we accept terrorism as a moral category of action, we also need to think about *how* the consequences were produced. Israel used TV and radio broadcasts, telephone calls, text messages, and even leaflets to warn innocent civilians to leave the areas that would be attacked.[6] Their stated goal was to destroy Hamas' offensive capability, and the death of civilians was not intended at all. Far from targeting them, Israel tried to get innocent civilians to leave the areas they were planning to attack.

Not so with the Madrid bombers. They used the death of the innocent civilians as the *means* of achieving their objectives. They targeted innocent people for death, and that makes them terrorists. In helping my students figure out whether innocents were targeted in any given situation, I've given them a tool that they playfully call the *Camosy pissed test*. I ask them to do a thought experiment in which innocents were *not* killed in the attack and then imagine whether the person or group acting would be "pleased or pissed" that no innocent people were killed. If the Madrid bombings had killed no one, it is clear the bombers would have felt that their purpose wasn't accomplished. This is because the death of civilians was the means by which the bombers were attempting to resist the Spanish government's support of the Iraq war.

The same is true of Tarkin's use of the Death Star to destroy Alderaan. At first, it seems like he's simply threatening the planet's destruction to force Princess Leia to reveal the location of the hidden Rebel base. Once Leia appears to "break" and reveals the location as Dantooine, Tarkin should've ceased operations and either sent his scout ships to Dantooine or found a different way to persuade Leia. Instead, he orders his men to "continue with the operation" and "fire when ready." When Leia protests, he responds with glee, "You're far too trusting. Dantooine is too remote to make an effective demonstration. But don't worry, we'll deal with your Rebel friends soon enough." The truth is that Tarkin has two goals: leveraging the princess and instilling terror in the minds of any planets that may oppose the Empire. Having apparently succeeded in the first goal with the mere threat of destroying Alderaan, only its actual destruction would accomplish the second goal. This makes Tarkin a terrorist.

What about Israel? Suppose their bombings killed no Palestinian civilians. They would have felt as though their information campaign to clear the area was successful. Not only did killing the innocent have nothing to do with achieving their ultimate goal of destroying Hamas' offensive capability, but each time such killing happens, it actually damages their goal by turning the opinion of their allies (and indeed most of the world) against them.

But suppose our imagined defender of the Madrid bombers protested this view by noting that plenty of attacks by Western militaries target civilians as well but don't get slapped with the *terrorism* label. One classic example might be the United States' bombings of Hiroshima and Nagasaki – which killed tens of thousands of innocent people, including thousands of infants and very young children. The United States clearly targeted civilians in an attempt to break the will of the Japanese leadership with the ultimate goal of producing their unconditional surrender. If we apply our definition consistently, we are forced to admit that this is another (particularly atrocious) act of terrorism.

But many defend the US decision – and the defense often goes something like this: "Okay, killing innocent people is generally a very bad thing, but how many millions of Japanese and American soldiers would have had to die in order to conquer Japan through a traditional ground invasion? Isn't that worse? Isn't the death of thousands preferable to the death of many millions?" But notice that this is utilitarian reasoning. By saying that something is terrorism, we are saying that *nothing* justifies it, no matter how good. Intentionally targeting the innocent is *never* justified, no matter the consequences.

We are now ready to return to the destruction of Death Star II: was it a terrorist act? The station itself is clearly a legitimate military target. Indeed, if the Empire's use of the previous station against Alderaan is any guide, the new one would also have been used to kill many billions of innocent civilians. But remember that the space station, though operational, was still under construction at the time it was destroyed. Kevin Smith's brilliant *Clerks* scene asks us to consider the innocent workers who were killed in the attack. Was the Rebel attack another example of terrorism?

Absolutely not, and the reason should now be clear. While the Rebels foresaw the death of the innocent contractors, they did not intentionally *target* them. Their deaths were not the means by which the Alliance accomplished its goals of destroying the station, killing the Emperor, and ultimately ending the war. Indeed, when we apply the Camosy pissed test, we see that the Rebels would've been quite happy if, on the day of the Battle of Endor, all the innocent people on board took the day off to go hiking somewhere on the forest moon. The Rebel attack, through it resulted in the death of innocent people, did not intentionally target them. It was not a terrorist act.

Doubling Their Efforts: Were the Death Star Workers Innocent?

Okay, it wasn't terrorism – but so what? All this means is that the Rebel attack didn't violate an exceptionless moral rule. The horrific evil of killing the innocent – though not intended – could still be morally wrong because this evil is disproportionate to the good that might come out of it. If true, this would still make the act very seriously wrong. I suspect this concern is what many have in mind when they criticize Israel's killing of innocent Palestinians in their bombing of Hamas targets. At a certain point, doesn't the evil of so many civilian deaths become disproportionate to the good to be gained by more attacks? Israel's attacks on Hamas have killed many, many innocent civilians, and the destruction of Death Star II caused the death of many, many innocent workers.

But *were* they innocent? The workers building Death Star II are different from the innocents of Gaza, Hiroshima, Alderaan, and Madrid in that these workers were actively contributing to the evil intention and military goals of the enemy. Returning to the roofer's point in *Clerks*, shouldn't we say that the Death Star's workers were blameworthy for deciding to work for such an evil organization? Doesn't this make them something less than innocent?

In order to respond to these important questions, we need to know who was actually doing the work of building the new space station. The first Death Star was built while in orbit around the prison planet Despayre. Prisoners from this planet (many of whom, given the Empire's history, were likely innocent) – along with a "veritable army" of Wookiees – were used as slave labor in building the first space station.[7] But it turned out that these slaves weren't efficient workers, not least because they would revolt from time to time. We have less evidence of who built Death Star II, but given that it was much larger and built much more quickly, it is likely that the Empire rejected slave labor in favor of different and faster techniques. This suggests that much of the work was being done by droids – but recall Moff Jerjerrod's response to Darth Vader when confronted about construction being behind schedule. He says, tellingly, "I need more men." Especially because it included quarters for humanoid "shell construction crews,"[8] it seems likely that both people and droids built the second Death Star.

But *which* people? Xizor Transport Systems appears to have been involved,[9] but these were just the crews ferrying materials to the job site. What kind of humanoids made up the actual construction crews? Given that the Emperor put construction plans on such a strict schedule (necessary for the battle station to be "fully armed and operational" in time for the Rebel attack), he probably wouldn't have trusted outside contractors with such an important task. What options are left? There seem to be two: (1) graduates of the volunteer Imperial Academy and (2) clones. It is likely there were some of each on the station, but given the special military training that academy graduates received, it makes sense that the Empire would prefer to make use of them in actual military situations. Perhaps a few graduates of the Imperial Academy's engineering or project management programs were on board when Death Star II was destroyed, but the vast majority of "men" to which Jerjerrod refers were probably clones.

Were these workers innocent? Graduates of the Imperial Academy volunteer their service and would therefore have not been innocent. But they probably made up a very small percentage of the total number of workers. There were probably some people working for Xizor Transport Systems in the blast area as well. Did these workers make a free choice to work for the Empire? It's difficult to say. Probably some workers did have a choice, while the ruthless Prince Xizor coerced others.[10] In any event, these deaths also would have been a small percentage of the total number of workers. The overwhelming majority would have been clones and droids.

Do clones count as "innocent people" as we are using the term? Does it make sense even to call them "people" in the first place? I would argue that they most certainly count. Essentially, each of them is an identical twin of Jango Fett, and much like other identical twins, each clone has his own personality and other distinctive characteristics, as evidenced by key troopers such as Captain Rex and Commander Cody in *The Clone Wars* and *Revenge of the Sith*.[11]

What about droids? Could a *machine* really be a person? This is a deep philosophical question that we can't take on here.[12] We can note, though, that the *Star Wars* galaxy is one of the best places to encounter beings who, despite being very different from us, are nevertheless persons. Jabba the Hutt, Boss Nass, Chewbacca, Watto, and many other strange aliens all have something recognizably "personal" about them.

But what exactly makes them all persons? This is a hotly contested question in moral philosophy. One common answer is something like *self-awareness*. Each of these alien beings has an intelligent mind, capable of recognizing the fact that it exists. This gives them the capacity to value their own lives, which in turn gives them moral status.

Indeed, if we were to kill them, they would be deprived of a life they value and would prefer to continue living.

Could droids have self-awareness? There seems to be no reason in principle why they couldn't. The aliens just mentioned are also machines, that is, *organic* machines. Is there any reason why non-organic machines couldn't also be persons? In the *Star Wars* galaxy, most droids appear to have self-aware intelligence, and upon reflection, maybe it isn't an outlandish view to consider them persons. Most people who watch R2-D2 and C-3PO know intuitively that they share something in common with, say, Luke and Chewie, that makes all four of them persons.[13]

Assuming that they are persons, we can ask whether clones and droids working on Death Star II were *innocent* persons. What was their level of moral responsibility? It seems obvious that droid workers – having been built and programmed to behave in certain ways, along with being limited by restraining bolts – were forced labor and not morally responsible for their actions. Indeed, though there was a Droid Abolitionist Movement led by those who argued that droids had rights and should be free to determine their own destiny,[14] most of the galaxy simply thinks of droids as slaves to be used as mere tools or objects. The droids working on the Death Star II during the Battle of Endor had no freedom and were therefore were not morally responsible for helping to construct a terrorist weapon of mass destruction.

But what about the clones? They had a bit of freedom under the command of the Jedi during the Old Republic, but under the command of the Emperor they had virtually none. Conceived, born, and raised simply to serve the Empire – essentially "programmed" to obey orders such as Order 66 to kill their Jedi generals with no reason given – they were essentially conscripted soldiers with no choice in the matter. Like the construction droids who were also destroyed that day, they died as slaves who had no choice to be anywhere else.

"They're Gonna Bust Up Vader's Hood" ... for a Proportionate Reason?

The Rebel attack did not aim at the death of innocent people, so it wasn't terrorism. But in determining whether the attack was morally justified, we still need to ask whether the Alliance had a serious enough reason for engaging in an attack that they foresaw would kill many, many innocent persons if successful. Just how many? Boasting a diameter of over a hundred miles, and a total population of two million humanoids, the completed Death Star II would have been simply enormous. Can we use these facts to make a broad estimate as to how many innocent clones and droids would have been onboard working on the station when it blew? Especially, given the fact that most of the droids were likely significantly smaller than hominoids (with no quarters for sleep and other off-duty activities), and how quickly the station was being built, I think we can safely say "millions."

What kind of good must be achieved to justify a military attack that, even if unintentionally, kills millions of innocent persons? If the Alliance had killed this many innocents in attacking, say, a single Star Destroyer, we would without hesitation conclude that the attack was immoral. Eliminating a Star Destroyer may be a legitimate military objective, but the relatively minor good achieved is out of proportion with the monstrous consequences produced.

The destruction of Death Star II is a very different situation. This station was built to avoid the vulnerabilities of the first Death Star and, once complete, would have wrought untold havoc. In addition to destroying many planets and intentionally killing many billions of innocent people, it would have easily defeated the Rebellion and assured the Empire of an indefinite stranglehold on the galaxy. But its destruction, along with the death of the Emperor himself, saved many billions of lives. The defeat of the Empire brought with it a new era of peace and justice, defended by a New Republic and the return of the Jedi order – at least until the Yuuzhan Vong showed up. Given these kinds of circumstances, the good achieved seems proportional to the evil produced; thus, we should conclude that the Rebel attack on Death Star II was not morally wrong.

The Good Guys Lens

Despite having a deep love for *Star Wars*, and having watched *Jedi* many, many times, I include myself among the fans who failed to ask the central question of this chapter. From the opening scenes of *A New Hope*, the "culture" of *Star Wars* conditions us to root for the Rebels. Looking at the movies through this lens can blind us to the questionable decisions of those we are told are the "good guys." The ability to challenge the dominant cultural lens through which most of us look at the world and ask critical questions of our own "side" is as rare today as it is important. Kevin Smith repeatedly challenges versions of the stories we're culturally conditioned to accept.[15] This is especially important if we care about protecting many innocent and vulnerable people who are ignored and even killed in the name of peace and justice, even it's to "restore freedom to the galaxy."

Notes

1. Smith's Instagram account revealed that he was one of the special few invited to check out the set of Star Wars VII. I would have teared up as well! http://instagram.com/p/p4W_kDRy8D/?modal=true (accessed July 21, 2014).

2. I see the signs of Smith's theological background as well. Raised in the Roman Catholic intellectual tradition – which insists on careful critical thinking – Smith's questions are always willing to challenge the dominant narrative (i.e., the Rebels are always the "good guys"). Furthermore, Catholic just war theory (which largely serves as the historical basis of just war theory in the secular West) never permits the intentional killing of the innocent, even for what some would say is a "good reason." That moral commitment lies at the foundation of this challenge in this scene.

3. For the two most famous originators of the position, see John Troyer, ed., *The Classical Utilitarians: Bentham and Mill* (Indianapolis, IN: Hackett Publishing, 2003). For perhaps the best-known utilitarian work being done today, see Peter Singer's *Practical Ethics* (New York: Cambridge University Press, 2012).

4. For an ethical analysis of Lando's decision, see Richard H. Dees, "Moral Ambiguity in a Black-and-White Universe," in *Star Wars and Philosophy*, ed. Kevin S. Decker and Jason T. Eberl (Chicago: Open Court, 2005), 39–54.

5. Though there are some who would go with Cicero instead, I would argue that contemporary just war theory has its roots with St. Augustine, and in particular his *City of God*. St. Thomas Aquinas built on Augustine's work, particularly in his *Summa Theologiae*, questions 40 and 64. Much of what Augustine and Aquinas had to say on these matters was wildly influential, and even found its way into the 1949 Geneva Conventions. For an alternative view of just war theory, see Jeff McMahan's *Killing in War* (New York: Oxford University Press, 2009).

6. http://www.nytimes.com/2014/07/09/world/middleeast/by-phone-and-leaflet-israeli-attackers-warn-gazans.html?ref=middleeast&_r=1 (accessed September 4, 2014).

7. Stephen J. Sansweet, Pablo Hidalgo, Bob Vitas, and Daniel Wallace, *The Star Wars Encyclopedia* (New York: LucasBooks, 2008), 176.

8. Kristin Lund, Simon Beecroft, Kerrie Dougherty, and James Luceno, *Star Wars: The Complete Locations* (New York: LucasBooks, 2005), 167.

9. Though not official EU sources, this is the view of http://starwars.wikia.com/wiki/Death_Star_II and http://starwars.wikia.com/wiki/Xizor_Transport_Systems (both accessed August 23, 2014). The company's existence, at least, is confirmed in *The Star Wars Encyclopedia*, 342–3.

10. For more on the background of Prince Xizor and his criminal syndicate Black Sun, see Steve Perry, *Shadows of the Empire* (New York: Bantam Spectra, 1997).

11. For more on the personhood of clones, see Richard Hanley, "Send in the Clones: The Ethics of Future Wars," in *Star Wars and Philosophy*, 93–104.

12. For a detailed discussion of droid "personhood," see Robert Arp, "'If Droids Could Think . . . ': Droid as Slaves," in *Star Wars and Philosophy* (2005), 120–31. See also the chapters by Dan Burkett (chapter 20) and Jim Okapal (chapter 16) in this volume.

13. Some may reject this definition of *personhood*. Especially if one is a Christian, personhood may go beyond self-awareness and have something to do with the capacity to love. But, even here, I think we can see that relationships between droids and humanoids (Artoo and Luke, Chewie and Threepio, etc.) and even between droids (Artoo and Threepio) can be characterized by sacrificial care and love – recall Threepio's offer to donate any of his circuits or gears to help repair Artoo after the Battle of Yavin.

14. Sansweet et al., *The Star Wars Encyclopedia*, 209.

15. Although not everything that Kevin Smith challenges in his movies, in my view, is worth challenging. For instance, some of the racist remarks that his characters attempt to "reclaim" simply have no place in moral discourse.

7

The Ballad of Boba Fett: Mercenary Agency and Amoralism in War

David LaRocca

"As you wish." It's the quintessential response of a servant to his master, and in the case of the Dark Lord of the Galactic Empire, Darth Vader, it's the best thing to say when he gives an order. But what if the command is morally dubious? The virtues of service – loyalty, honor, discipline, ability – may give way quite readily in the face of a charge of moral turpitude. When the boss says *kill*, is obedience the only fitting reply? Perhaps it is for a soldier ranked in a chain of command, but what about an independent, freelance mercenary who is paid to follow orders? In what is principally an economic relationship, does the mercenary have more (or less) discretion when accepting assignments – especially if they're morally suspect? Might the mercenary be more susceptible to bribery, and thus potentially more likely to take up with the highest bidder – not necessarily the "right side"? In order to survive financially, must the mercenary necessarily be *amoral* – focused on payment for work completed, instead of the ethics of his tasks or the merits of the moral claims made by his clients (or their enemies)? In considering these questions, we turn to the fiercest bounty hunter in the *Star Wars* galaxy.

The Ultimate Star Wars and Philosophy: You Must Unlearn What You Have Learned,
First Edition. Edited by Jason T. Eberl and Kevin S. Decker.
© 2016 John Wiley & Sons, Ltd. Published 2016 by John Wiley & Sons, Ltd.

Darker Than the Dark Side

Boba Fett's cultural significance – and his robust and enduring fan base – stands in striking contrast with his minimal screen time, and even more so with his infrequent and tersely spoken lines. With Boba Fett, a small head tilt, as well as how he cradles his gun – signaling contemplation and competency – become important signs. George Lucas's addition of a clip showing Fett flirting in the "special edition" of *Return of the Jedi* stirred scandal since the gesture seemed so out of character; the actor who originally portrayed Boba Fett (Jeremy Bulloch) was dismayed by the intervention.[1] With so little of Fett to judge, the inclusion of a few new seconds' worth of behavior can upend or give rise to whole new theories of character, motivation, and conduct.

It's true that the Expanded Universe fleshes out Fett's life and exploits, yet commentary on them is inspired by a remarkable dearth of scenes featuring Fett on film. As with many gnomic figures, it's plausible that Fett's allure and significance are partly explained by his infrequency on screen coupled with his reticence when he's there. Fett's quiescence is highlighted to comedic effect in the recent Shakespearean adaptation *The Empire Striketh Back*, in which his "As you wish" is followed by a lengthy Shakespearean-style soliloquy that reveals his inmost reflections.[2]

Still, he is a pivotal figure – Darth Vader's most trusted and effective bounty hunter – and significant plot points shift around Fett. As a bounty hunter – occupying an intermediate position between the perennial antagonisms of the Empire and the Rebel Alliance; Vader and Luke; Jabba and Han – Boba Fett also becomes a fitting icon of moral ambiguity. Though Fett is clearly loyal to Darth Vader – or at least the rewards that Vader offers – he isn't motivated by Vader's beliefs or ambitions. We must wonder, then, what drives Fett to act, especially on matters of morality? Is there any evidence that suggests Fett acts for any reason other than profit?

If the answer to this last question is "no," then we might believe that he's an amoralist: that is, *neither* a moral relativist who believes there are many potentially valid positions on value, *nor* an ethical egoist who believes his own values to be the proper (and sufficient) source of judgment about what's good. Boba Fett's status as an intermediary – say, between Vader and the Rebels – might make him seem a moral relativist. Or perhaps his isolation and independence might recommend his credentials as an egoist. Yet, as we look closer at the very few occasions he's on screen, the more prominent, but darker, implication is that Fett has altogether removed himself from the project or practice of moral judgment. He may be a self-employed, freelance contractor, but he's not going to sort out the nuances of your moral dilemmas. So, what Fett – the epitome of a gun for hire – can help with is a consideration of the virtues and vagaries of the role of mercenaries as such.

Daddy Issues, Decapitation, and the Family Business

As is often the case with characters in *Star Wars*, Boba Fett has father issues. He's the son of Jango Fett, a renowned bounty hunter, who in turn is the "father" – or, more precisely, "clone template" – to the entire Grand Army of the Republic. Each of the clone soldiers is genetically modified for unquestioning obedience, but, as a stipulation of Jango's contract with the Kaminoans, he was provided an "unaltered clone" to raise as his son, Boba. This makes Boba "genetically identical to Jango Fett" and thus "a cross between a son and a very late identical twin."[3] During the Battle of Geonosis, which sets off the Clone Wars, Boba witnesses his father's beheading by Jedi Master Mace Windu.

While Luke didn't discover who his father was until adulthood – receiving a parental (and imperial!) command to join him on the dark side – Boba was still a child when he faced the decision of whether or not to follow his father's path. The orphaned Fett thus undertakes vocational discernment prematurely, lacking, by contrast, the steadying and orienting moral influence of Uncle Owen on the young Luke. Moreover, Luke encounters a surrogate father in the form of Ben Kenobi, a Jedi whose ethical clarity is pivotal for Luke's capacity to turn away from the dark side but later compassionately turn toward his dying father. Boba, on the other hand, not long after the Battle of Geonosis, begins running in the company of bounty hunters like Aurra Sing.[4]

Bounty hunting in Boba's work occupies a gray zone between the white of his clone trooper brethren and the black of Vader. Lucas, in fact, describes Fett's origins as a "split" from his earliest vision of Vader.[5] Even Boba's outfit is a mercurial gray/green, cobbled together from various parts and places, including his father's Mandalorian armor.[6]

Boba may be a "good son" who takes up his father's business, unlike Luke who actively resists Vader's offer, but the business itself is a troublesome affair. Bounty hunting is the trade of an independent contractor, the industry of a gun for hire, the labor of a mercenary. The bounty hunter accepts a commission from a client – not commands from a superior, which Boba's cloned brethren are conditioned to obey – and this implicates the mercenary agent in a position of making choices. As his decisions are made voluntarily (i.e., knowingly), he is morally culpable for his actions based on such decisions. In maturity, however, Fett doesn't seem to weigh the relative merits of his clients' claims versus their enemies' (as a moral relativist would), or take moral comfort from his own self-centered needs and desires (as an ethical egoist would). Instead, Fett has made the choice to withdraw from the moral order as a whole. When Solo's life is threatened by the carbonite-embalming process, Fett isn't concerned with Solo's life as a person, but *strictly* whether he'll be alive so that Fett can be paid by Jabba. Like a good delivery man who signs the insurance papers before the fact, Fett elicits Vader's reassurance that Fett will be paid his bounty even if Solo dies. Relieved of his preoccupation with monetary compensation, Fett remains faithful to the contract.

Moral Manager or Moral Mangler?

In light of Boba's genetic uniformity with the clone troopers of the Republic (and later Imperial) army, despite his significant personality differences, let's consider the ethics of bounty hunting, especially in relation to military ethics in the conduct of war. While fans may admire Fett's reserve, reliability, efficacy, independence, and even apparent code of Mandalorian honor, his mercenary role introduces certain ethical quandaries. This is because Fett's daily work involves kidnapping, killing, and otherwise operating beyond the strictures of a military chain of command.

If Boba Fett, in his gray zone between Rebellion and the Empire, is the embodiment of amoralism, what can we say about the use of mercenaries and independent contractors in our own world – such as Blackwater (now called Academi) and Halliburton in the U.S. wars in Iraq and Afghanistan – not to mention the expanding use of U.S Special Forces? The U.S. government and such companies have undertaken "a sophisticated rebranding campaign aimed at shaking the mercenary image and solidifying the 'legitimate' role of private soldiers in the fabric of U.S. foreign and domestic policy, as well as that of international bodies such as the UN and NATO."[7] As part of this "campaign," "Mercenary firms are now called 'private military companies' or 'private security companies,'" and the hired agents are referred to as *private soldiers* or *civilian contractors*.[8] These euphemisms give rise to the suspicion that something of moral significance is being hidden.

What are the criteria for being a mercenary? The most common definition states that a mercenary is "motivated to take part in the hostilities [of armed conflict] essentially by the desire for private gain, and, in fact, is promised ... material compensation substantially in excess of that promised or paid to combatants ... ; is neither a national of a Party to the conflict nor a resident of a territory controlled by a Party to the conflict; ... [and] has not been sent by a State which is not a Party to the conflict on official duty as a member of its armed forces."[9] Given this definition, Boba Fett qualifies as a bona fide mercenary. He's motivated by money, unmotivated by the causes or reasons for warfare, and unaffiliated with a particular state and its military apparatus – including the enlisted soldiers, despite his genetic relationship to them. Mercenaries stand apart, above, over, and in between the conflicts of others. They are interlopers hired to exercise their specialized skills – not moral philosophers called up to adjudicate the nuances of value. When Obi-Wan Kenobi and Anakin Skywalker "disarm" the bounty hunter Zam Wesell after her attempt on Padmé Amidala's life, their interrogation uncovers her utter disinterest in the ethical dimension of her foiled assassination:

OBI-WAN: Do you know who it was you were trying to kill?
ZAM: It was a Senator from Naboo.
OBI-WAN: And who hired you?
ZAM: It was just a job.

Unlike his clone counterparts, Fett, together with fellow bounty hunters Zam Wesell, Aurra Sing, Dengar, Zuckuss, IG-88, Bossk, and 4-LOM, are capable of independent decision making. They are not "programmed" to follow orders. Yet, even though Fett very much grows into his father's son, he and other "soldiers of fortune" are still caught between the needs and goals of the Rebellion and those of its adversary, the Empire. Indeed, the existence of that tension is the *condition* for the mercenary's business. Likewise, in contemporary warfare, when governments hire independent contractors, moral accountability and responsibility become sullied and strained. Conflict between dominant parties is good for the mercenary trade and the bounty-hunting business. It does not, however, clarify the moral justifiability of activities carried out in the name of the employer.

Mercenary Motivation and Ethical Action

Must mercenary work invite amoralism? Or can the motivations that give rise to mercenary behavior sometimes be understood as moral? Our inquiry has to move beyond fan-boy adulation of Fett's "cool" qualities and the allure of his lifestyle as a freelancer. Instead, Boba Fett's status as a mercenary forces us to ask whether there is an identifiable and important moral difference between the military acts of states and those of mercenaries. Does a government's use of mercenaries in a war mean that such a conflict can't be a *just war*? After all, mercenaries' acts of violence are motivated, not by patriotic loyalty and values held dear, but by their wish for private financial gain.[10] Does the introduction of a "free market" in the conduct of war transform moral questions into merely *economic* ones? The name *bounty hunter* indicates the issues at hand. Is the hunt only for rewards (bounty or booty)? And what kind of *hunting* is happening – a secretive but nonviolent search, or a guns-drawn, take-no-prisoners, bloody approach? Either way, the mercenary or bounty hunter, like the enlisted soldier, may kill defensively or offensively.

What if there were a mercenary who decided "to fight only in wars where legitimate nation-states are under threat of invasion"?[11] Could there be such a "good mercenary"? Compare a nongovernmental employee or a freelance journalist who strikes out for a newly war-torn region to lend aid or to cover the event through word and image. The "good mercenary" would be similarly motivated to help, but would also be better paid than a soldier. The mercenary would be authorized like a soldier to use both offensive and defensive tactics, but independently of the state's military chain of command. Think, for example, of soldiers who fight for the United Nations in the role of "peacekeepers," and "who do not fight for their country of origin, [but] who [do] fight for monetary and professional reasons."[12]

The contemporary philosopher Michael Walzer lends additional credence to the notion of the "good mercenary." Walzer describes the mercenary as a fighter who may exercise a "certain sort of freedom in choosing war," unlike the conscripted private (or engineered clone trooper).[13] For the enlisted soldier, ordered into combat, writes Walzer, "We assume that his commitment is to the safety of his country, that he fights only when it is threatened, and that then he has to fight (he has been 'put to it'): it is his duty and not a free choice."[14] But in making an analogy with a medical professional, Walzer warns us that we may dismiss too readily the notion of a mercenary who feels a duty to seek service in a conflict: "[The mercenary] is like a doctor who risks his life during an epidemic, using professional skills he chose to acquire but whose acquisition is not a sign that he hopes for epidemics."[15]

Repeated screenings of *The Empire Strikes Back* and *Return of the Jedi* may have convinced many viewers that Boba Fett's iconic status as an "antihero" was grounded in the appearance of amoralism being at the heart of mercenary work. Yet it may be the case that the "arguments which purport to demonstrate some morally salient differences between mercenary violence and violence perpetrated by regular national soldiers" are found wanting.[16] The common attributes cited to ethically distinguish mercenaries from soldiers – money, motives, and the meaning of war – all fail "to provide a clear case for the moral inferiority of mercenarism *per se*."[17]

If the world of *Star Wars* is mapped onto our own, the Galactic Empire can be seen as a legitimate state – Palpatine having been duly granted "emergency powers" by the Galactic Senate during the Clone Wars, and then elevated from Supreme Chancellor to Emperor in a chorus of "thunderous applause." This would make the Rebels *terrorists* – as director Kevin Smith has implied.[18] On the other hand, the typical fan's "point of view" is that the Empire is *tyrannical*, and the insurgency against it is justifiably carried out by a band of anti-Imperial "freedom fighters" – not unlike the eighteenth-century "patriots" who liberated the fledgling colonies in America from the imposing tyrannical regime of King George III of England.

Boba Fett's role and his decisions again prompt the question of whether a mercenary's motives may be corrupted by the morally unjustifiable aims of his employer in hiring him. If it is possible that Fett is a "good mercenary," is he morally compromised by working for the wrong boss? Would Fett-as-mercenary be morally better if he switched sides and worked for the Rebellion? This question helps us ask what we *really* find objectionable about the mercenary. Is it that he's getting paid? Or that he may aid a "side" we judge morally loathsome? Or perhaps – and here is amoralism again – that he doesn't *choose* a side at all? In the opening crawl for *Revenge of the Sith*, we learn that "there are heroes on both sides" of the Republic versus Separatist dispute. We can understand, and potentially justify, the moral motivations of an "enemy" even if we don't agree with them, but it's more difficult to understand or justify the *amoral* stance of a mercenary. If there are legitimate reasons for the state to expand the use of mercenaries in the current age of terrorism – along with its varied forms of imposed force, from conventional ordnance to biochemical weapons to cyberattacks – do we need to rethink our moral assessment of the state, the mercenary, or both?

Gray Areas: Fett and Amoralism

In *Star Wars*, there's an obvious moral "grammar" in many celebrated aspects of the films, from choice of words ("dark side," "Death Star") to costuming (black cloaks, red robes, fear-inducing masks) to mechanics (flawless Imperial ships versus the clunky *Millennium Falcon*). These qualities are usually framed as binary opposites, perhaps precisely so that the extremes can be complicated by the areas in between, just as Vader and Luke debate whether there is still "good" in the person who seems (and is costumed) to embody the epitome of evil.

In this realm where dichotomies and binary relationships are made to be dissolved or contested,[19] we find the irony that Boba Fett's moral ambiguity – his literal and figurative grayness – may actually bring some measure of light, however faint, to the Empire's penetrating darkness. Meanwhile, the virtues of the bounty hunter, while often appearing at direct odds with our Rebel heroes, become pragmatically beneficial when Princess Leia, disguised as the Ubese bounty hunter, Boushh, cunningly barters with Jabba for the price of the "captured" Chewbacca. Jabba concedes, "This bounty hunter is my kind of scum, fearless and inventive." Is that praise for the wiles of the bounty hunter or for the Rebel princess *beneath* the mask? Even Boba Fett offers her a subtle nod of respect after she nearly kills him and everyone else in Jabba's throne room with a thermal detonator. It seems, then, that the mercenary's grayness can also have a potent effect when mixed with the moral purity of the Rebel Alliance's cause.

Just as Han Solo, Luke Skywalker, and Darth Vader have entered popular culture as emblems of certain characteristics and behaviors – the scoundrel, the questing hero, the terrifying overlord – so has Boba Fett become a figure of mythic significance. Perhaps it's precisely the uncanny imbalance between his paltry screen time and his resonance in thinking about moral ambiguity that compels us to inquire "*Why?*" Nostalgia among those who grew up watching him is certainly part of the explanation – particularly for those who acquired a first-release Boba Fett action figure with an actual firing jetpack rocket before there was a safety recall. But as we've seen, such sentiments may get in the way of clear critical thinking about Fett's true role in the saga. Yet, while mercenaries have been a part of human culture since the first leader paid someone else to do his dirty work, Fett's particular features – the father issues, the mantle of inherited vocation, the individuality and independence of the job, the satisfactions and rewards of work effectively and efficiently done – all coalesce to make him a character with broad appeal and increasingly wide intellectual and philosophical significance. We can, in short, learn much about our own individual moral conduct, the government's responsibilities, and the ethics of war by considering Vader's favored go-to bounty hunter. In particular, we may see that there may not be much *moral* difference between the enlisted soldier and the hired mercenary – both proclaiming "As you wish" in response to their superiors' orders, as Fett to Vader and Vader to the Emperor – and that amoralism is – perhaps surprisingly, for most who feel compelled by deep moral considerations – a central part of human political and military life.

Though Boba Fett met what seemed to be an inauspicious end in *Return of the Jedi*, perhaps the scene of his death can be instructive. It's a kind of apathetic comment on the denial to Fett of a "good death" so familiar from the traditions of the warrior, knight, samurai, cowboy, and soldier. Fett ignominiously falls into a giant mouth, and the last sounds we hear are a scream and a generous belch. That's it. There is no grand standoff, no chance to give meaning to one's end, no death with dignity and pride. This is the death of the most notorious and effective bounty hunter in the galaxy – at least until he escapes the Sarlaac in the Expanded Universe and embarks on more adventures tormenting his favorite quarry, Han Solo. Later he admits that he only ever had a *personal* vendetta against the Jedi who killed his father: "Just wanted to remind you, Solo, that my personal fight was always with the Jedi. You were nothing more than cargo."[20] Eventually, Fett evolves from a mercenary to become the Mandalore, leader of his father's people, although he never gives up his bounty hunter ways.[21] Later, just as her mother employed the bounty hunter persona for pragmatic effect in Jabba's palace and earned Fett's momentary respect, Jedi Knight Jaina Solo sought out Fett to train her in a specifically non-Jedi fashion so that she could defeat her fallen brother, Darth Caedus.[22]

In his life, and even in his apparent death, Boba Fett remains a mercenary for our times. We're not done thinking about him yet. It's fitting, then, that a stand-alone Boba Fett feature film is in development to resurrect him again for our entertainment and contemplation.

Notes

1. "Confessions of a Bounty Hunter: An Interview with Jeremy Bulloch," Starstore.com (September 10, 1998).
2. Ian Doescher, *The Empire Striketh Back: Star Wars, Part the Fifth* (Philadelphia: Quirk Books, 2014), 92–3.
3. Richard Hanley, "Send in the Clones: The Ethics of Future Wars," in *Star Wars and Philosophy*, ed. Kevin S. Decker and Jason T. Eberl (Chicago: Open Court, 2005), 95.
4. *Star Wars – The Clone Wars*, "Death Trap."
5. See, for example, Pete Vilmur, "Proto-Fett: The Birth of Boba," October 16, 2012, http://archive.today/ew8HZ (accessed February 23, 2015).
6. Ibid.
7. Jeremy Scahill, *Blackwater: The Rise of the World's Most Powerful Mercenary Army* (New York: Nation Books, 2007), 425.
8. Ibid.
9. See *Protocol Additional to the Geneva Conventions of 12 August 1949* (APGC77) from 1977. This protocol is not endorsed by the United States.
10. For further discussion of the "just war theory," see Charles Camosy's chapter in this volume (chapter 6).

11. Tony Lynch and A. J. Walsh, "The Good Mercenary," *Journal of Political Philosophy* 8, no. 2 (2000): 141.
12. Ibid., 141n22.
13. Michael Walzer, *Just and Unjust Wars: A Moral Argument with Historical Illustrations* (New York: Basic Books, 2000), 27.
14. Ibid.
15. Ibid.
16. Lynch and Walsh, "The Good Mercenary," 153.
17. Ibid., 142. In *Return of the Jedi*, the Emperor arrives on the Death Star and informs Vader of his scheme to turn Luke to the dark side. Vader's reply? "As you wish." Vader isn't a mercenary, but the Emperor's second-in-command, so this mode of relation to his superior stands out as an overt and intriguing parallel with Fett's conduct as a mercenary: executing orders without much, if any, regard for their moral import. The phrase "As you wish" – common to both Vader and Fett – reinforces the thesis that there may not be much difference between the enlisted soldier – no matter his or her rank – and the paid mercenary.
18. For a detailed analysis of Kevin Smith's characterization of the Rebels as potential "terrorists" in his film *Clerks*, see Charles Camosy's chapter in this volume (chapter 6).
19. For an alternative discussion of ethical ambiguity in the *Star Wars* saga, see Richard Dees, "Moral Ambiguity in a Black-and-White Universe," in *Star Wars and Philosophy* (2005), 39–54.
20. James Luceno, *Star Wars – The New Jedi Order: The Unifying Force* (New York: Del Rey, 2003).
21. Karen Traviss, *Star Wars – Legacy of the Force: Revelation* (New York: Del Rey, 2008).
22. Ibid.

8

How Guilty Is Jar Jar Binks?

Nicolas Michaud

> Senators! Dellow felegates! In response to this direct threat to the Republic, mesa propose that the Senate give immediately emergency powers to the Supreme Chancellor!
> – Gungan Representative Jar Jar Binks of Naboo

Jar Jar Binks might be the most hated individual in the *Star Wars* universe. I've often wondered, while wallowing, Gamorrean-like, in my loathing for the floppy-faced idiot, why no one has ever seen fit to blame Jar Jar for anything more than being annoying. It is fun to Binks-bash; gather a group of *Star Wars* fans, and sooner or later you'll hear about various ways they'd like to see Jar Jar eliminated from the galaxy – if George Lucas can digitally insert characters seamlessly, why couldn't he delete one? Occasionally, a younger fan might come to Jar Jar's defense, arguing that he's charming, funny, and good for the children in the audience. What you don't hear often are questions like "How about the fact that Jar Jar is responsible for the rise of the Empire?" Of all the things that we hate about Jar Jar, why don't we talk about *that* one?

True, Binks was manipulated into this action. He couldn't have known that Chancellor Palpatine was a Sith Lord. And, after all, he was doing his best to do what he believed Senator Amidala would've done. But can we really ignore the fact that his action cost billions

The Ultimate Star Wars and Philosophy: You Must Unlearn What You Have Learned, First Edition. Edited by Jason T. Eberl and Kevin S. Decker.
© 2016 John Wiley & Sons, Ltd. Published 2016 by John Wiley & Sons, Ltd.

of lives? The Clone Wars, the Rebellion, and even the destruction of Alderaan all have their start with Jar Jar's singular choice to grant an already powerful man even more power, in effect making the Galactic Senate powerless in comparison – as Palpatine proclaims when confronted by Mace Windu, "I *am* the Senate!" As a result, untold millions of intelligent entities became slaves to the Empire, the Jedi Order was all but completely destroyed, and a thousand years of peace and prosperity came to an end. Maybe Jar Jar should have to answer for his choice – whether it was intended or not. Too much was lost to simply absolve him because he didn't know any better. Because we're dealing with issues of praise and blame, we need to look deeply into the case of Jar Jar, so that we can come to the most reasonable verdict possible. If our verdict is that Jar Jar is *guilty*, it may even be arguable that he deserves *execution* for his crime of galactic proportion – something more than a few *Star Wars* fans would pay good money to watch in 3D IMAX with THX surround-sound.

"Mesa Cause One, Two-y Little Bitty Axadentes"

Again, Jar Jar didn't *mean* to cause the collapse of the Empire, and it's not like he did it all by himself. There were a lot of other people who helped Palpatine rise to power: Count Dooku, Anakin Skywalker, even the Jedi generals who fought Palpatine's trumped-up war for him. According to contemporary philosopher Thomas Nagel, there's more to morality than consequences or intentions; there's also *moral luck*.[1] Of particular interest to our discussion is *resultant moral luck*. Jar Jar did not have total control over the consequences of his actions, so, at least to some degree, those consequences are a matter of luck. The problem is, though, that while Jar Jar didn't mean to do harm, his actions, in part because of bad luck, did in fact cause great harm.

We like to think that someone can be innocent because he simply *didn't mean* to do something bad, which would include Jar Jar. On the other hand, we sometimes blame people for the consequences of their actions despite their best intentions, especially when those actions are thoughtless or due to negligence. In *that* case, Jar Jar would be guilty. To Nagel, this means that luck *does* play a role in our moral judgments. In fact, he argues that if we try to remove luck from the equation and only judge people for what they have control over, we might not be able to make any moral judgments because there are no events over which we have complete control!

Imagine two universes that have identical Luke Skywalkers in them. In both, Luke is driving a landspeeder through Mos Eisley at top speed. In the first universe, Luke looks down at his comlink and, as a result, accidentally runs down a child crossing the street and kills her. Imagine that, in the second universe, everything is exactly the same, except when Luke looks down at his comlink there's no child crossing the street and so he doesn't incur any negative consequences for his poor driving decisions. It seems obvious that only the first Luke is morally blameworthy for killing the child. But *both* Lukes are guilty of reckless driving. Since we're assuming that everything else in the two universes is the same, had the child been crossing the street in the other universe, the second Luke would have killed her too. So does it make sense to blame one Luke, but not the other, when the consequence was only a matter of luck?

This is a difficult question: should we praise Darth Vader for motivating Leia's confession of love to Han Solo by carbon-freezing him? Should we blame Obi-Wan Kenobi for training someone who turned into a mass-murdering, child-killing maniac? (Obi-Wan did feel some guilt over what happened, telling Anakin in the midst of their duel on Mustafar, "I have failed you, Anakin! I have failed you!") Neither event was intentioned, yet they both led to morally significant consequences. What about a Bothan spy who tries to assassinate Vader but misses and accidentally kills an innocent bystander? Should he be found guilty of murder? Or what if the bounty hunter Dengar aims his blaster in a can't-miss kill-shot at Admiral Ackbar's head, but a split-second before he fires, his competitor IG-88 fires his blaster rifle and kills the Admiral first? While IG-88 should get the bounty, it's not clear that Dengar isn't also morally culpable for Ackbar's death since his laser bolt would've killed Ackbar if IG-88's hadn't gotten there a millisecond earlier.

Moral blame and praise are not easily assessed by consequence alone. We can blame Luke for reckless driving in *both* cases, regardless of whether he kills a little girl or not. As Nagel would point out, whether he's culpable for killing the girl, accidentally or not, is a matter of *luck*. The same goes for someone who's *not* trying to do something good but accidentally does something fantastic, like Vader bringing Leia and Han together. Should we thank Vader for using Han as a test subject for a risky process due to the accidental good that resulted, in the same way that we would condemn Luke and Jar Jar?

Oopsies Daisies, Meesa Killed Billions. Whoopsie!

On one hand, if we're inclined to simply forgive Jar Jar for bringing about the tyrannical Empire with an "Oopsies daisies!" and a shrug, we're not taking seriously the fact that consequences do matter, even in matters of moral luck. But if we take consequence into consideration, we must consider giving Vader praise for helping Leia and Han find love, though that may be a tough pill to swallow. On the other hand, if we decide that someone should be held responsible only for their *intentions*, then the reckless landspeeder driver who kills the child crossing the street because he was playing with his comlink isn't guilty of murder because he wasn't *trying* to kill the child.

Contemporary philosopher Susan Wolf suggests that Nagel has placed us in a false dilemma: we need not consider morality as either a purely intention-based *or* consequentialist affair. The two positions aren't necessarily the only choices for moral decision making. There's also the consideration of what a *virtuous* person should do. This third option considers what *kind of people* we should be. We can ask ourselves, "How would a virtuous person address these problems?" A virtuous person would *feel bad* about killing a child, even if it wasn't his intention. So, despite the fact that moral luck seems to lead to some odd results, it isn't unreasonable for us to hold the Luke who kills the child by his recklessness more guilty than the one who doesn't because *he should in fact feel worse*. Wolf writes, "The position for which I have argued states ... that blameworthiness is solely a function of faultiness. In other words, equal fault deserves equal blame. At the same time, my position holds ... that different effects call for different responses – including different emotional responses in the agents whose behaviors bring about these effects."[2] If I have not killed a child, then it's reasonable for me not to feel guilty. One would hope, though, that a virtuous Luke who does not kill the child would nevertheless feel tremendous guilt for his recklessness if he found out that someone else who took his same actions killed a child.

Similarly, Jar Jar should feel a great deal of guilt over his actions in the Senate, though well meaning, because they caused so much strife. And, as such, it isn't unreasonable for the rest of us to hold him accountable for that event. What about Vader's freezing of Han? If Vader's aim was to be a virtuous person by bringing two people together in love, then perhaps he *should* be praised; however, it's clear that Vader does not embody the virtues of a romantic matchmaker. We can consider how Vader would reflect on his own actions: it's unlikely (because he's not virtuous) that he feels particularly good about inadvertently provoking Leia's confession of love.

The way a person feels (or *should* feel) about a particular action they perform – whether or not they regret it, for example – plays a role in whether we should blame them or not. Jar Jar should feel guilty for killing millions, and that fact gives us reason to say that he is, to some degree, blameworthy. Another way of putting this is that we have good reasons for holding people responsible for their actions, if those actions have consequences about which they should feel bad. Binks's actions weren't *just* accidental. Though he didn't intend them, they came from a decision that was hasty and not well thought-out. He's clearly not as guilty as a person who *intended* to bring about these events – like Palpatine or his Chagrian Vice Chancellor Mas Amedda, who muses provocatively in the presence of Jar Jar and the other Loyalist senators, "If only Senator Amidala were here" – but he is blameworthy nonetheless, because he should reflect on what he did with shame and remorse. If he's a virtuous person, though, we can also credit him for his remorse and recognize that he's still a good, if annoying, person.

Kant Decide

There's at least one eminent philosopher who would strongly object to all this: Immanuel Kant (1724–1804). After all, it sounds like I'm blaming Jar Jar because of his bad luck, despite the fact that he was trying to do the right thing. Kant's ethics are focused on intentions, the reasons *why* people choose to act as they do. He argued that we can only hold people blameworthy or praiseworthy for what they *intend* to do because the consequences of our actions are beyond our control. Simply put, blaming people for things they can't control isn't morally fair.[3]

Kant famously claimed that *ought* implies *can*, stating, "For if the moral law commands that we *ought* to be better human beings now, it inescapably follows that we must be *capable of being better human beings.*[4] To blame Jar Jar may be unreasonable, not just because he didn't have bad intentions, but also because he may have had little ability to choose otherwise – after all, he doesn't seem to have a lot of political acumen. This doesn't mean that Jar Jar's choice in the Senate wasn't free. It means only that, if we look at his case, we can see that he's constrained in his actions because of the information he has before him and the meager statesgunganship abilities with which he has to work.

There are causal forces at play in granting Palpatine emergency powers that may have been inescapable for Jar Jar. He knew war was imminent; he knew the Senate was frozen in inaction; he knew the planet he represented was in immediate peril. And so we might say that Jar Jar, given the situation he found himself in, couldn't have behaved otherwise. Kant argued that we can only be blamed for those actions that we could've avoided doing. We're asking whether, given the situation, Jar Jar simply couldn't have made another decision that would likely have led to better consequences. If so, he wasn't genuinely free and thus can't be held accountable.

It's important to note that Jar Jar doesn't get off *that* easily from a Kantian perspective. Kant argued that we must do what's right out of the intention of having a good will – *because what we intend is a moral law.* This requires some explanations because we need to know how to figure out what the moral law is. Kant argued that logic and consistency are the best way to determine morality. We have a tendency to be very biased, and often make exceptions for people we love or people we hate. We are more inclined, in other words, to save the people we love and kill the people we hate. Kant, though, thought that making these kinds of exceptions made little sense when dealing with morality because *everyone can't make them!* If we all made these exceptions, everything would fall apart. Moreover, we don't want people killing us just because they hate us.

So Kant developed the *Categorical Imperative.* This "universal rule" tells us that we should only do things that can rationally be made a law for everyone else too. If I want to kill someone, for example, then I can't just make an exception for myself because I really, really hate them. I have to consider what it would mean if the idea "Each of us should kill people we hate" was a universal moral law. I see that this would be a bad rule, not just because it would produce a rather unpleasant galaxy to live in but also because the rule couldn't be followed. That kind of rule contradicts itself, both because we don't want it done to us and because of the inevitable consequence that we would all die and therefore couldn't follow the rule. So, given that, we need to recognize that there are moral laws that are beyond our own personal wishes and biases, and it is that law that should motivate us to act. *And* it is our *duty* to follow that law. We know it's our duty because when we really think about it, logic tells us that the rule makes sense and that the only reason to break the law is because we want an exception. When we act out of our own personal bias, we can't really call ourselves "moral." After all, we didn't act because of the moral law, but because we *wanted* the consequence. We should only be praised, therefore, according to Kant, when we act from the "good will" – out of respect for the moral law!

We can only say that Jar Jar is praiseworthy, according to Kant, if Jar Jar's action is motivated solely because it's the right thing to do. If he's acting for any selfish reason, even out of love for his fellow Gungans, then he isn't doing the morally correct thing; he's doing it for some reason other than "reverence for the *law*." In such a case, Jar Jar wouldn't be much different from Anakin Skywalker, who betrays the Jedi and plunges the galaxy into tyranny, not because he truly believes it's the morally right thing for him to do – although Palpatine does a good job of twisting his mind in this way – but more so out of his self-centered love for Padmé and desire to save her from premature death.

What if we give Jar Jar the benefit of the doubt? Let's say that he did act in service of, and out of respect for, the moral law? Using logic and reason, and leaving his own feelings out of it, Jar Jar decided that the moral law required granting emergency powers to Palpatine. The fact that Palpatine decided to do great evil with those powers isn't Jar Jar's fault. Jar Jar can't be blamed for the evil that others do, only for the evil that *he* intends to do.

So we're left with two major concerns: should we still be worried about moral luck if, following Kant, we just concern ourselves with intentions? And is Jar Jar's decision even free, and thus open to blame? Despite Kant's excellent points, we still have to worry about moral luck. The consequences of our actions are important, at the very least because they inform others about our likely intentions. Other people don't have access to our thoughts, or vice versa; no one can know for sure what another person actually *meant* to do. So we take into account both the consequences of a person's actions and her reaction to those consequences in order to help us judge her actions *and* her intentions. If someone repeatedly commits a harmful action and shows no remorse, we can infer that her intentions aren't good.

If we were to put Jar Jar on trial, the case couldn't be based solely on his intentions. Maybe, in the court of Jar Jar's own mind, he's a Kantian and absolves himself. Without access to his thoughts, we might still find Jar Jar guilty on the grounds that Nagel laid out: it's not because he intended for anyone to be killed, but because of his *negligence*, that Jar Jar is indirectly responsible for granting power to someone who would turn out to be a tyrannical mass murderer. But was Jar Jar *free* to make a different decision? Given his lack of political insight and the information Jar Jar had at hand, maybe he seems negligent only in hindsight: maybe he really *couldn't* have done otherwise.

(In)Sidious Motives

If Kant is right, we can only be held responsible if we're truly free to do other than what we did in fact choose. But it turns out this may not be the case. Contemporary philosopher Harry Frankfurt has responded to Kant's argument in a way that turned the philosophical world upside down.

Let's say that Palpatine, using a Sith mind-trick, has invaded Jar Jar's mind. He's able to tamper with Jar Jar's intentions to move him to grant Palpatine emergency powers. Palpatine wants to keep his actions hidden from the Jedi, so he triggers the mind-trick only if Jar Jar decides *not* to propose granting him emergency powers. On the other hand, if Jar Jar, of his own free will, decides in favor of the emergency powers, the mind-trick will not be triggered and Palpatine's use of the Force goes completely undetected. Given these options, Jar Jar *cannot do other than* make the motion to give Palpatine emergency powers. If Jar Jar doesn't choose to make the motion, he'll be forced to do so; and, if he chooses to do so on his own, then no mind-trick is necessary. Either way, Jar Jar can't do otherwise. In such a case, where we've completely eliminated Jar Jar's freedom to choose otherwise, could he still be blameworthy?

Even if Palpatine had planned to use such a mind-trick, we have no evidence that he actually did. So it's fair to say that Jar Jar didn't make the choice to grant Palpatine emergency powers *because he couldn't do otherwise*. Rather, he made the choice because he *wanted* to. Can't we be blamed for making choices that we want to, even if those choices are constrained by factors outside our control? It seems that Frankfurt does a lot of damage to Kant's notion of "ought implies can," but this doesn't really make Jar Jar any more or less guilty. Frankfurt's example works because it shows that a person's choice is their own so long as it stems from their own character and desires, regardless of whether their freedom is being impeded by factors outside their control or knowledge. In this case Jar Jar, at least so it seems, was *trying* to do good. Even worse, Palpatine was so in control of the situation, and had everyone so deceived, that Frankfurt's example seems to work against Jar Jar's moral culpability. It might well be that *no matter what Jar Jar did*, Palpatine still would have found a way to obtain emergency powers. In other words, if Jar Jar knew what Palpatine was up to, he would've done otherwise, but because he didn't know, he made a grievous error.

Jar Jar was, like most of the Senate, a *victim* of Palpatine's deceptions. So, even though the consequences were grave, and Jar Jar's decision hasty, he can be absolved for what he did. We have no evidence he acted negligently, like Luke recklessly driving his landspeeder. Given all of the information he had at hand and considering the imminent danger to the Republic, his decision was likely a good one. In fact, he was trying to bring about good, as his many other actions – clumsy as they may be – suggest. His case wasn't just a matter of luck or accident. He lacked true control over his actions due to Palpatine's deception, and so it seems Jar Jar Binks is not guilty of killing millions. *However*, I maintain he remains guilty of being painfully obnoxious ... surely that's sufficient reason for an execution (or at least a digital deletion)!

Notes

1. Thomas Nagel, *Mortal Questions* (New York: Cambridge University Press, 1991), 28.

2. Susan Wolf, "The Moral of Moral Luck," *Philosophical Exchange* 31 (2001): 1.

3. See Immanuel Kant, *Groundwork of the Metaphysics of* Morals, 2nd ed. (New York: Cambridge University Press, 2012).

4. Immanuel Kant, *Religion within the Boundaries of Mere Reason and Other Writings* (New York: Cambridge University Press, 1998), 70.

9

"Know the Dark Side": A Theodicy of the Force

Jason T. Eberl

DARK HELMET:	No, we can't go in there. Yogurt has the Schwartz. It's far too powerful.
SANDURZ:	But sir, what about your ring? Don't you have the Schwartz, too?
DARK HELMET:	Naw, he got the upside, I got the downside. See, there's two sides to every Schwartz.

–Spaceballs (1987)

Ever since Obi-Wan Kenobi first introduced the concept of "the Force" to Luke Skywalker in *A New Hope*, fans have pondered and debated its nature: what exactly *is* the Force? Why does it have *two* sides? How are the "light" and "dark" sides related to each other? As is well known, George Lucas invented the Force as a fictional stand-in for the diversity of spiritual metaphysics found in Western and Eastern philosophical and religious worldviews – for instance, the energy of *qi* in Chinese philosophy or the person of God in monotheistic religions like Judaism, Christianity, and Islam. The depersonalized Chinese concept fits the side of the Force described by Obi-Wan as "an energy field" that Jedi, Sith, and other Force-sensitive beings are able to channel through their minds and bodies to accomplish extraordinary mental and physical feats – such as telekinesis and manipulating the weak-minded.[1] The Force, however, is also like a personal God

The Ultimate Star Wars and Philosophy: You Must Unlearn What You Have Learned, First Edition. Edited by Jason T. Eberl and Kevin S. Decker.
© 2016 John Wiley & Sons, Ltd. Published 2016 by John Wiley & Sons, Ltd.

in that it purportedly has a *will*. Jedi Knights and Masters expend a great deal of time in meditative contemplation attempting to discern the will of the Force for how their individual lives, as well as galactic-scale events, should unfold. As in Earth's major monotheistic religions, there are even *prophecies* about future events and persons of significance – such as the prophecy referring to Anakin Skywalker as the "Chosen One" who "will bring balance to the Force."

As we know, though, that particular prophecy wasn't fulfilled in the way the Jedi had hoped it would be, as Obi-Wan expresses in anguish after defeating Anakin on Mustafar: "You were the Chosen One! It was said that you would destroy the Sith, not join them! Bring balance to the Force, not leave it in darkness!" Nevertheless, Anakin does eventually fulfill the prophecy, destroying both the Sith Lord Darth Sidious and himself in a final act of personal redemption. In another essay written not so long ago, not so far away, I argued that Anakin could've *freely chosen* both to turn to the dark side and to bring himself back to the light, despite his prophetic destiny.[2] The existence of a God's-eye perspective on the future still leaves Anakin – and later Luke – free to make choices for which they're each morally responsible.

When it comes to freely willed actions for which individuals can be held morally accountable, it isn't only humans like Anakin, Luke, you, or me who may be subject to moral evaluation. If there's a God – or a Force – responsible for willing the universe's unfolding physically and historically, we can also question the sort of moral code such a being is bound by, and whether there are justified reasons for allowing – or, perhaps what may be even worse, *willing* – horrendous evils that afflict millions of innocent sufferers, from the Holocaust on Earth to the destruction of Alderaan. This concern – known as the *problem of evil* – raises two kinds of serious doubts about an all-powerful, all-knowing divine being. If evil exists, could such a being exist? And if such a being does exist, should we praise it as essentially *good*? Various responses to this problem – known as *theodicies* – have been put forth throughout the history of Western philosophy. We'll examine the theodicy offered by the Christian philosopher and theologian, St. Augustine of Hippo (354–430 CE). While our examination of Augustine's theodicy won't answer all questions regarding the problem of evil,[3] it can help us explain the nature of the dark side of the Force to which Anakin succumbed.

"Now I Shall Show You the True Nature of the Force"[4]

Before we can effectively examine the problem of evil and Augustine's response to it, we first need to understand what his view of *evil* is and how it relates to good. Augustine understands the difference between "good" and "evil" to refer to a real, objective distinction in moral value, but these words don't refer to distinct types of *things in the world*.[5] Rather, Augustine claims that there's only *one* reality, and that reality is intrinsically good. Evil doesn't exist in itself, but only as a *lack* of being, of goodness – just as blindness is nothing other than a lack of the power of sight:

> For what is that which we call evil but the absence of good? In the bodies of animals, disease and wounds mean nothing but the absence of health; for when a cure is effected, that does not mean that the evils which were present – namely, the diseases and wounds – go away from the body and dwell elsewhere: they altogether cease to exist. … Just in the same way, what are called vices in the soul are nothing but privations of natural good. And when they are cured, they are not transferred elsewhere: when they cease to exist in the healthy soul, they cannot exist anywhere else.[6]

There are two broad categories of evil in Augustine's view. One is the inevitable by-product of God creating other beings: since no other being can be *perfect* as God is, every created being must lack some measure of being and goodness. The other type of evil arises out of the bad intentions of conscious, rational beings. This is the basis on which *moral responsibility* can be assigned to them. Luke says much the same in conversation with his nephew, Jacen Solo:

> It's true that the Force is unified; it is one energy, one power. But … the dark side is real, because evil actions are real. *Sentience* gave rise to the dark side. Does it exist in nature? No. Left to itself, nature maintains the balance. But we've changed that. We are a new order of consciousness that has an impact on all life. The Force now contains light and dark because of what thinking beings have brought to it. That's why balance has become something that must be *maintained* – because our actions have the power to tip the scales.[7]

Like Luke, Augustine argues that *moral* evil – that is, evil done *intentionally* by a person – is solely the fault of that person. For Augustine, the fault is found in the misuse of a person's God-given free will. We'll examine this theodicy through the lens of two heroic Jedi who fall from grace: Anakin Skywalker and his grandson, Jacen. We'll also see how Augustine's view of the nature and relationship between good and evil opens up the possibility of Anakin's eventual redemption.

"I Will Be the Most Powerful Jedi Ever!"

Anakin Skywalker awakes from a nightmare; however, as Anakin had told his wife, Padmé, "Jedi don't have nightmares." Rather, Jedi receive premonitions through the Force. In this case, Anakin foresees Padmé's death in childbirth. Having failed to save his mother after similar premonitions, Anakin vows to Padmé that he won't let his vision become real. To that end, Anakin seeks advice from Master Yoda. But instead of offering him a way to save Padmé, Yoda gives him some unexpected and, for Anakin, unsatisfying counsel: "Train yourself to let go of everything you fear to lose." Anakin's reaction makes it clear that he's not going to follow this advice. Later, he's offered a different perspective by another mentor, Chancellor Palpatine:

PALPATINE: Let me help you to know the subtleties of the Force.
ANAKIN: How do you know the ways of the Force?
PALPATINE: My mentor taught me everything about the Force, even the nature of the dark side.
ANAKIN: You know the dark side?
PALPATINE: Anakin, if one is to understand the great mystery, one must study all its aspects, not just the dogmatic narrow view of the Jedi. If you wish to become a complete and wise leader, you must embrace a larger view of the Force. Be careful of the Jedi, Anakin. Only through me can you achieve a power greater than any Jedi. Learn to know the dark side of the Force and you will be able to save your wife from certain death.

Why is Yoda right and Palpatine wrong? How could it be evil for Anakin to want to save his beloved wife? The first point Augustine would make about Anakin's turn to the dark side is that, while he's certainly been subject to manipulation by Palpatine throughout his mentorship, it's ultimately Anakin's own *will* that is the source of his moral downfall:

> A perverse will is the cause of all evils ... what could be the cause of the will before the will itself? Either it is the will itself, in which case the root of all evil is still the will, or else it is not the will, in which case there is no sin. So either the will is the first cause of sin, or no sin is the first cause of sin. And you cannot assign responsibility for a sin to anyone but the sinner; therefore, you cannot rightly assign responsibility except to someone who wills it.[8]

Consider Augustine's words using this example: when Obi-Wan Kenobi uses a Jedi mind-trick to convince Elan Sleazebaggano that he doesn't want to sell death sticks and should go home and rethink his life, we can't morally praise Elan for following Obi-Wan's advice, because his will was being directly manipulated. Similarly, if Anakin turned to the dark side because Palpatine used a Sith mind-trick on him, we shouldn't hold Anakin morally accountable for all the evil he does as Darth Vader. Anakin, though, isn't weak-minded like Elan, and his will remains free of such direct influence. While Palpatine subtly seduces Anakin, he's only able to have an effect because Anakin's will is *open* to Palpatine's influence.

Within Augustine's Christian worldview, Palpatine would be analogous to the serpent in the Garden of Eden (Genesis 3:1–15). While the serpent in that story plays a role in humanity's fall from moral innocence, the ultimate blame lies with Adam and Eve. In this role, Palpatine first offers Anakin recognition of his talents in place of the Jedi Council's continual humbling: "It is upsetting to me to see that the Council doesn't seem to fully appreciate your talents. Don't you wonder why they won't make you a Jedi Master?" Like the serpent, Palpatine plays upon the pride and envy of those tempted to pursue knowledge of good and evil in defiance of God's command. Palpatine's seduction culminates in his offer to help Anakin develop the power to save Padmé: "The dark side of the Force is a pathway to many abilities some consider to be unnatural." Clearly, the Jedi consider such "unnatural abilities" to be immoral, so Anakin must turn to Sith teaching in order to learn them.

Is there anything wrong with Anakin wanting to save Padmé? A man's devotion to his wife and his desire to save her life are in themselves good. But what's wrong here isn't the goal Anakin is attempting to achieve, but the *means* he employs. Padmé challenges Anakin on this very point after learning from Obi-Wan that he's turned to the dark side and led the slaughter of the Jedi Temple, including younglings:

PADMÉ: Anakin, all I want is your love.
ANAKIN: Love won't save you Padmé, only my new powers can do that.
PADMÉ: At what cost? You're a good person don't do this ... Anakin, you're breaking my heart! You're going down a path I can't follow!

Augustine identifies the source of moral evil as "inordinate desire" for "temporal goods":

> So we are now in a position to ask whether evildoing is anything other than neglecting eternal things, which the mind perceives and enjoys by means of itself and which it cannot lose if it loves them; and instead pursuing temporal things ... as if they were great and marvelous things. It seems to me that all evil deeds – that is, all sins – fall into this one category.[9]

We may at first think that the evil depicted in *Episode III* is essentially the *actions* Anakin does once he pledges himself to Palpatine. Augustine contends, rather, that what's essentially evil is the *inordinate desire* – in this case, to save Padmé at any cost – that animates such actions. Although Padmé's life is certainly good, it's nevertheless a good bounded by time's limits: she was born and one day, no matter what Anakin does, she will die.

Conversely, God and love for God are *eternally* good and the source of a human being's perfect (i.e., complete and abiding) *happiness*. If a person possesses love for God, he can't lose that love or the happiness that comes along with it, unless he wills to do so. Loving God means willing in accord with God's will. Unfortunately, according to Augustine, the "original sin" of humanity as told in the story of the Garden of Eden was to give in to the serpent's temptation and turn away from God in defiance of God's will for humanity. Similarly, Yoda and the other great Jedi Masters strive to discern the will of the Force and to find peace and joy by acting in communion with the Force. Anakin, however, pridefully seeks his own vision of happiness in defiance of the will of the Force and the lesson Yoda attempts to teach him about ordering his desires.

Anakin wants the power to save Padmé. He's clinging to a good that'll always be subject to potential loss. This leads, according to Augustine and Yoda, not only to committing evil deeds out of fear of losing those goods, but also to an anguished life:

> All wicked people, just like good people, desire to live without fear. The difference is that the good, in desiring this, turn their love away from things that cannot be possessed without the fear of losing them. The wicked, on the other hand, try to get rid of anything that prevents them from enjoying such things securely. Thus the wicked lead a criminal life, which would be better called death.[10]

Augustine's recommendation to turn our love away from transitory goods also includes our beloved friends and family. Scripturally, Augustine finds a basis for his view in Christ's exhortation, "Whoever comes to me and does not hate father and mother, wife and children, brothers and sisters, yes, and even life itself, cannot be my disciple" (Luke 14:26). Although the word "hate" seems rather harsh, Augustine understands Christ's teaching to refer to one's love for friends and family, and even his own life, as *subordinate* to love for God – *the* eternal good. Augustine came to this realization through his own self-reflection concerning the paralyzing grief he felt after the death of a dear friend.[11] Grief, for him, is a torment for the "wicked"; those who've focused their love on God, on the other hand, won't suffer at the death of a loved one. Yoda gives the same advice to Anakin: "Death is a natural part of life. Rejoice for those around you who transform into the Force. Mourn them do not. Miss them do not."

Now, when Augustine says that "the wicked lead a criminal life, which would be better called death," he isn't condemning such people from a moral "high ground." Instead, his view is based on his psychological analysis of how a person whose moral character is inclined toward inordinate desire – a vice that Augustine terms *cupidity* (*cupiditas*) – suffers from an embattled soul:

> In the meantime cupidity carries out a reign of terror, buffeting the whole human soul and life with storms coming from every direction. Fear attacks from one side and desire from the other; from one side, anxiety; from the other, an empty and deceptive happiness; from one side, the agony of losing what one loved; from the other, the passion

to acquire what one did not have; from one side, the pain of an injury received; from the other, the burning desire to avenge it.[12]

Anakin's anguished cry upon learning of Padmé's death, as well as his hatred for Obi-Wan as he lay dismembered on the burning sands of Mustafar, evidence the wisdom expressed by Yoda when he first meets Anakin and discerns his fear of losing his mother: "Fear is a path to the dark side. Fear leads to anger; anger leads to hate; hate leads to suffering." Not only does Anakin, as Vader, cause tremendous suffering to others, but also he himself suffers the tragic results of his own inordinate desires.

"You Were My Brother, Anakin! I Loved You!"

Anakin's grandson, Jacen Solo, isn't driven to the dark side by the fear of losing someone he loves. Jacen realizes this when he time-drifts through the Force to Anakin's purging of the Jedi Temple and senses his grandfather's roiling emotions.[13] On the contrary, faced with an ancient Sith prophecy seemingly about himself, Jacen is willing to "immortalize his love" by killing her for the sake of peace and justice in the galaxy. He believes his selflessness in pursuing what seems to him to be his moral duty will protect him from becoming evil – even as he becomes the Sith Lord Darth Caedus.[14] In the end, Jacen does kill someone he loves – Mara Jade Skywalker – and also suffers the loss of respect and admiration from his apprentice, Ben, Mara and Luke's son. The prophecy is finally fulfilled, though, when he irrevocably loses the love of his own daughter, Allana. While Anakin's love for his children is what ultimately redeems him, Jacen's willingness to sacrifice this primordial love places him *beyond* redemption.[15]

Augustine believes that *love*, when directed toward God, is an eternal good. Unlike the inordinate love of temporal goods characterizing the vice of cupidity, Augustine ranks the virtue of love directed toward God – which he terms *charity* (*caritas*) – as the highest of all virtues, even more so than faith in God or hope for eternal life:

> For when we ask whether someone is a good man, we are not asking what he believes, or hopes, but what he loves. Now, beyond all doubt, he who loves aright believes and hopes rightly. Likewise, he who does

not love believes in vain, even if what he believes is true; he hopes in vain, even if what he hopes for is generally agreed to pertain to true happiness, unless he believes and hopes for this: that he may through prayer obtain the gift of love.[16]

While love for God is paramount in Augustine's view, it also extends to other persons, since God loves them as well. There's thus nothing wrong with Anakin loving Padmé, or Jacen loving Tenel Ka and Allana, so long as that love is *rightly ordered*.

So a sign of a depraved moral character would be found in a person who lacks an appropriate love for others. In his quest to bring peace and justice to the galaxy – a noble goal in itself but, as the history of both the *Star Wars* galaxy and our own shows, one that's fleetingly transient[17] – Jacen tragically sacrifices "an ordinary man's precious connection to other beings – love, trust, and intimacy. He could never recover any of it."[18] At the moment of surrender to his dark fate, Jacen's "heart – irrelevant, fragile, expendable – broke."[19] Anakin inordinately desires his beloved's life, and this leads him to a life of tremendous evil. In the end, though, he hasn't lost the capacity to love in a proper fashion, and thus, as Padmé, and later Luke, both sense, "There is still good in him."

The moral corruption that was the consequence of Anakin's inordinate desire to save Padmé doesn't end with her death. Encased forever in life-sustaining armor, Anakin has evidently surrendered to the dark side, despairing of any possible redemption for himself. As his apprentice, Shira Brie/Lumiya, describes him, "Vader wasn't a galaxy-conquering psychopath. He was a sad man whose one love in life had died, and whose one anchor to the world of the living was, yes, a galaxy-conquering madman."[20] Vader himself confesses to Luke on Endor, "It is too late for me, son."

Augustine considers a human being's will to be *free* when it's oriented toward the objective source of *happiness* – what's eternally good, God. Conversely, when a person desires temporal goods inordinately, he willingly *enslaves* himself to those inferior goods and his desire for them: "Nothing can make the mind a slave to inordinate desire except its own will."[21] Freedom to do evil, according to Augustine, isn't *true* freedom, and our desire for temporal goods should always be subordinated to our desire for the eternal good.

But Anakin also seems to *enjoy* the power the dark side provides him as he mercilessly Force-chokes incompetent Imperial officers or those whose lack of faith in the Force he finds "disturbing."[22] Augustine sees that those who cling to temporal goods also tend to fail to moderate their desires in accord with eternal justice. In other words, the more a person is able to gain the power to fulfill his desires, the less inclined he is to restrain himself out of regard for the needs or interests of anyone else.[23] Anakin, gaining power alongside Chancellor Palpatine, no longer moderates his desire for power and control; he even goes so far as to tempt Padmé, and later Luke, to help him overthrow Palpatine: "I am more powerful than the Chancellor. I can overthrow him. And together, you and I can rule the galaxy, make things the way we want them to be!" In short, moral corruption begets ever more moral corruption – or, as Yoda puts it to Luke, "If once you start down the dark path, forever will it dominate your destiny. Consume you it will, as it did Obi-Wan's apprentice."

"If the Force Is Life, How Can There Be Life without the Force?"[24]

Even if we grant all of Augustine's claims, the problem of evil still remains: why did God give moral agents freedom of will if God knows that most of us will misuse it at some point and, in doing so in some cases, bring horrendous suffering to others?[25]

Augustine's answer is that free will is something *good* insofar as it allows us to be oriented toward a loving relationship with God and, by extension, other persons. Like other goods, however, it can be misused. Augustine draws an analogy to the use of one's body:

> Consider what a great good a body is missing if it has no hands. And yet people use their hands wrongly in committing violent or shameful acts … many people use their eyes to do many evil things and press them into the service of inordinate desire; and yet you realize what a great good is missing in a face that has no eyes. … So just as you approve of these good things in the body and praise the one who gave them [i.e., God], disregarding those who use them wrongly, you should admit that free will, without which no one can live rightly, is a good and divine gift. You should condemn those who misuse this good rather than saying that he who gave it should not have given it.[26]

The prosthetics of Vader's life-supporting armor provide Anakin's electronic "eyes" and mechanical "hands," which he may use to wield a lightsaber either in defense of innocent aliens or to slay Jedi who escaped Order 66. Anakin's body isn't what's evil, but rather his *misuse* of it. Analogously, each individual human being is morally responsible for the use of his own free will, which Augustine insists must be aimed at the eternal good – God – and not misused in pursuit of earthly objects of desire we might mistakenly believe will lead us to happiness: "Everyone wills to be happy but not everyone can be; for not everyone has the will to live rightly, which must accompany the will to live happily."[27]

Jacen shows this kind of understanding of the Force when expressing concern about how his brother, Anakin Solo, seems to be misusing the Force to satisfy his "personal hunger for glory. ... The Force is a method of serenity and truth, not an outward-projecting tool to be used to further any single person's perception of good."[28] Anakin later comes to realize that there may be something to reality more fundamental than the Force, "something of which the Force was a manifestation, an emanation – a tool. ... The Force was the servant of that truth."[29]

For Augustine, this more fundamental truth is God, whose gift of free will – which is a great good in itself – is essential to leading us toward loving union with God. Augustine defines evil, not as a thing in itself, but as the misuse of one's free will. Similarly, the dark side of the Force doesn't refer to any part or aspect of the Force – which is itself entirely good – but instead to its willful misuse. Free will and the Force thus have the potential to be used for good or evil – as former Jedi, Vergere, warns the Yuuzhan Vong priestess, Elan: "The Force is a sword with two edges, mistress. Cut one way and vanquish. But be careless on the backswing, or allow your mind to wander, and you risk undoing all you've accomplished. ... Such power should be reserved for those with the strength to heft the sword and the wisdom to know when to wield it."[30]

Notes

1.   For more on the Chinese philosophical conception of the Force, see Walter [Ritoku] Robinson, "The Far East of *Star Wars*," in *Star Wars and Philosophy*, ed. Kevin S. Decker and Jason T. Eberl (Chicago: Open Court, 2005), 29–38. Further discussion of the capacities the Force endows upon its users can be found in Jan-Erik Jones's essay, "'Size

Matters Not': The Force as the Causal Power of the Jedi," in the same volume, 132–43.

2. See Jason T. Eberl, "'You Cannot Escape Your Destiny' (Or Can You?): Freedom and Predestination in the Skywalker Family," in *Star Wars and Philosophy* (2005), 3–15.

3. A complete response to the problem of evil has to address not only the evil that results from choices of moral agents (e.g., wars, slavery, the making of the *Star Wars Holiday Special*), but also the evil that results from the natural conditions of the created universe (e.g., natural disasters, diseases, Gungans). Augustine's theodicy, as discussed here, focuses only on the former, although Augustine also has a response to the latter kind of evil. At one point, Luke reflects on the existence of natural evil and concludes, "It was the way of the Force that some should survive and others perish. Death without malicious intent, for nature didn't have a dark side" (James Luceno, *Star Wars – The New Jedi Order: Jedi Eclipse* (New York: Del Rey, 2000), 64). This may be a satisfactory account of natural evil in the *Star Wars* universe insofar as the Force, despite having an apparent "will," isn't understood to be an intelligent, creative entity responsible for the existence of the universe with the physical causal laws that determine its nature. It remains an open issue, however, for God as understood by traditional monotheistic religions.

4. Emperor Palpatine to Luke, as recalled by the latter in James Luceno, *Star Wars – The New Jedi Order: The Unifying Force* (New York: Del Rey, 2003), 266.

5. For alternative views of evil and the nature of the dark side, see George Dunn's chapter in this volume (chapter 17).

6. Augustine, *Enchiridion on Faith, Hope, and Love*, trans. J. B. Shaw (Washington, D.C.: Regnery, 1961), ch. III, §11; ch. IV, §14.

7. *The Unifying Force*, 267–8. By "sentience," Luke is referring to a level of consciousness that includes the capacity for rational thought and intentional action. This term, however, most properly refers to any level of conscious awareness; thus, not only human beings, Wookiees, and Muuns, but *all* animal life, is sentient. Luke is also drawing a false dichotomy here between sentience and "nature," since sentience is an emergent property from the natural evolutionary process.

8. Augustine, *On Free Choice of the Will*, trans. Thomas Williams (Indianapolis: Hackett, 1993), bk. III, §17.

9. Ibid., bk. I, §16.

10. Ibid., bk. I, §4.

11. See Augustine, *Confessions*, trans. F. J. Sheed, 2nd ed. (Indianapolis: Hackett, 2006), bk. IV, chs. 4–9.

12. *On Free Choice of the Will*, bk. I, §11.
13. See Karen Traviss, *Star Wars – Legacy of the Force: Bloodlines* (New York: Del Rey, 2006), 79–82.
14. See ibid., 372–7. The full prophecy can be found in Karen Traviss, *Star Wars – Legacy of the Force: Sacrifice* (New York: Del Rey, 2007), 3.
15. For further discussion of the redemptive power of Anakin's love for his children, see Charles Taliaferro and Annika Beck's chapter in this volume (chapter 10). Luke is also drawn back from the dark side through the love of his sister, Leia, in Tom Veitch et al., *Star Wars: Dark Empire Trilogy* (Milwaukie, OR: Dark Horse, 2010).
16. *Enchiridion*, ch. XXXI, §117.
17. For a comparison of the relative historical progression and recession in *Star Wars* and in human societies on Earth, see Nancy R. Reagin and Janice Liedl, eds., *Star Wars and History* (Hoboken, NJ: John Wiley & Sons, 2013).
18. Karen Traviss, *Star Wars – Legacy of the Force: Revelation* (New York: Del Rey, 2008), 71. At one point, Jacen – now Darth Caedus – muses that "he had not sacrificed the ability to love – only the ability to be loved in return"; Troy Denning, *Star Wars – Legacy of the Force: Inferno* (New York: Del Rey, 2007), 104. I believe, however, that Jacen is deluding himself; for one can only have the ability – the virtue – to love if he's able to *actualize* that love, which isn't compatible with Jacen's consistent betrayal of his friends and family.
19. *Bloodlines*, 377.
20. Aaron Allston, *Star Wars – Legacy of the Force: Betrayal* (New York: Del Rey, 2006), 362.
21. *On Free Choice of the Will*, bk. III, §1.
22. Although Anakin's grandson, Ben Skywalker, learns from the grandson of a junior Imperial officer that Vader was capable of compassionate loyalty to those who found favor with him: "My granddad thought the world of him. When he got badly burned on a mission and had to be discharged from the Imperial Army, Lord Vader made sure he was taken care of for the rest of his life. Whatever some people say about Vader, monsters don't look out for lieutenants" (*Sacrifice*, 154).
23. See *On Free Choice of the Will*, bk. I, §15.
24. Matthew Stover, *Star Wars – The New Jedi Order: Traitor* (New York: Del Rey, 2002), 67.
25. As I discussed in my previous essay, Augustine conceives of God as having *perfect* knowledge by virtue of possessing an *eternal* perspective over the entire temporal continuum all at once.
26. *On Free Choice of the Will*, bk. II, §18.
27. Ibid., bk. I, §14.

28. R. A. Salvatore, *Star Wars – The New Jedi Order: Vector Prime* (New York: Del Rey, 1999), 82.

29. Greg Keyes, *Star Wars – The New Jedi Order: Conquest* (New York: Del Rey, 2001), 238.

30. James Luceno, *Star Wars – The New Jedi Order: Hero's Trial* (New York: Del Rey, 2000), 165. I'm very grateful to George Dunn, Kevin Decker, and Bill Irwin for helpful comments and edits on earlier drafts of this chapter.

Episode III

REVENGE OF THE ALLIANCE

"Like My Father before Me": Loss and Redemption of Fatherhood in *Star Wars*

Charles Taliaferro and Annika Beck

When Darth Vader makes his revelation to Luke Skywalker, "*I am your father,*" in *The Empire Strikes Back*, the shocking, unbelievable substance of his claim to fatherhood isn't put into perspective until Vader's backstory is completed in 2005's *Revenge of the Sith*. But in 1980, it wasn't certain that Vader was telling the truth; even James Earl Jones, Darth Vader's voice, didn't trust his own character's statement when he read it in the script: "I thought," he stated in an interview, "He's lying. I have to see how they carry this lie out."[1] At the time, we could only wonder if perhaps Vader was seeking to manipulate Luke into accepting an alliance to rule the galaxy in a paternal lineage as co-Emperors or for them both to serve under Vader's master. *The Empire Strikes Back* leaves us in suspense: we're given a hint that Vader is telling the truth – why else would Luke react with the kind of horror he does if his own feelings didn't confirm he was the offspring of a moral monstrosity? We've observed a completely unexpected overture by an arch-villain to our hero, seemingly to provide him with safety and power, and yet, at the end of *Episode V*, we're left in the (perhaps tantalizing) dark. Eventually, we learn the truth that Luke is indeed the son of the great Anakin Skywalker, once a Jedi Knight who served the Galactic Republic well, but through murder and betrayal became Darth Vader.

The Ultimate Star Wars and Philosophy: You Must Unlearn What You Have Learned,
First Edition. Edited by Jason T. Eberl and Kevin S. Decker.
© 2016 John Wiley & Sons, Ltd. Published 2016 by John Wiley & Sons, Ltd.

The six episodes of *Star Wars* reveal that Anakin's love for his mother, Shmi, and later his wife, Padmé, turns into a disastrous obsession with saving their lives. Desiring the continued life of those we love, and actively taking steps to preserve their lives, are both natural and often praiseworthy, *but not at all costs*. This is especially apparent when the cost involves killing innocent persons and aligning oneself with great powers that violently suppress dissent, and also annihilate populated planets. With the benefit of hindsight, observing the peculiar, dramatic moment when Vader declares his paternity, there's a painful portrait of how fatherhood can go wrong. Fatherly love should be evident in caring for the health and good of one's children, seeking to safeguard them from harm and to encourage their integrity. However, Vader promises his son's survival only on the condition that Luke will serve his own monstrous, tyrannical master. Utilizing a *philosophy of love and goodness* to show how the parent–child relationship may be lost or regained, we'll examine the transition in Anakin's life from a natural love of others to a distorted, toxic caricature of love.

Early Attachment

Anakin's struggle with finding a way to balance love and detachment emerges in his infancy and childhood. Supposedly conceived by midichlorians, Anakin has no father. One advantage to this is that he has his mother's undivided love and devotion, which he'd otherwise have to share with a human father. But it may be precisely because of this that Anakin develops his compulsive tendencies. That is, he doesn't have to share his mother's love, and so he doesn't learn how to feel anger or grief in the course of emulating a good father in a healthy family. When Anakin is given the opportunity to realize his dreams, he makes a promise: "I will come back and free you, Mom." This is a promise he will keep, but not in the way he intends. He believes he'll use his exceptional powers to save his mother. The Jedi, however, train highly efficient, wise guardians, not super-powerful free agents who can exercise their powers to do whatever they want. Master Yoda senses that Anakin's desire for power is linked to an unhealthy attachment to his mother. Yoda questions him, "Afraid to lose her I think, hmm?" Anakin protests, "What has that got to do with anything?" To which Yoda counsels, "Everything! Fear is the path to the dark side. Fear leads to anger. Anger leads to hate. Hate leads to suffering. I sense much fear in you."

Yoda's warning echoes the teaching of the Stoics. Today, the advice to "be stoic" is a recommendation not to show your emotions: that you should "keep your chin up" and stop crying. But the Stoics in Ancient Greece took a position that was slightly different and more in line with the Jedi: they emphasized the need to understand what we love and care about. If you love someone or something that is not immortal or indestructible, its loss will be a source of great sorrow if you have treated it as if it might exist forever. The Stoic philosopher Epictetus (c. 50–120 CE) is especially clear when he admonishes his followers to realize that the people they love are human beings who will die, and to see that inevitability as a part of their relationships. So, the Stoic philosophers did want us to avoid some emotions, especially the painful suffering we feel when someone or thing we love dies. However, they wanted us to avoid these emotions not through repressing or disguising our feelings, but through avoiding what they saw as unwise or compulsive attachments.

Anakin's all-consuming love and devotion to his mother gradually lead to his dreadful disorientation in which he becomes blind to the importance of caring for others. When faced with personal adversity, he relies heavily on his own feelings rather than living in light of the wisdom of his elders or striving for harmony with the feelings of others. This is evident in how he copes with personal distress, not in the Stoic way of addressing the cause of suffering (excessive attachment), but through hiding his feelings, first denying to Padmé that Jedi have nightmares when he's experiencing visions of his mother's suffering, and then later in terms of his reluctance to tell Padmé his premonition of her own death in childbirth or confess his jealousy at how close Obi-Wan is becoming to her. At this juncture, we can see how Anakin is led to vices slowly by way of his pursuit of apparent goods. His loving devotion to his mother is admirable, right? It seems so, until it leads him to deceive those he loves and, ultimately, to have such a distorted view of the value of others that he has recourse to murder.

When Anakin leaves his closest confidante, his mother, on Tatooine, he is drawn to his savior Qui-Gon, the only man who has ever believed in him. But this attachment is cut short by Darth Maul's malice, and Anakin loses his first father figure almost as soon as he has found him. This fleeting relationship foreshadows the temporary nature of

Anakin's future paternal relationships (loving Obi-Wan as a father, then turning to Palpatine, then considering overthrowing him for absolute power). Obi-Wan Kenobi fills his master's shoes, and Anakin eventually sees him as "the closest thing I have to a father." Still, the lack of a *stable* father figure drives Anakin to thrill seeking rather than soul searching, as he fails to exercise the detachment that Yoda counsels (in accord with the Stoics). Additionally, as we've noted, he's distracted by thoughts produced by his already-cemented attachment with his mother.

Failed Detachment

Anakin's obsession with his mother's welfare doesn't comply with the Jedi ideal to abandon "attachment" with anything or anyone who might jeopardize their mandate to guard the peace and security of the Republic. When Anakin finds his mother dying in captivity among Tatooine's Tusken Raiders, he is racked by guilt at not having found her sooner. In finding her and allowing her to die in a loving embrace, Anakin partly vindicates his mother's praise years before: "You have given hope to those who have none." But not enough hope, in Anakin's mind: "Why couldn't I save her? I know I could have," he laments. The virtue of humility –in this case, Anakin admitting his own natural limitations and focusing on being grateful that he was able to offer his mother some sense of peace before she died – is not present. Humility would require Anakin to understand the things that are out of his control, as the Stoic Zeno of Citium (334–262 BCE) might have put it. We see here how an inflated belief in his own powers and his refusal to find consolation in his mother's last words fuel his excessive self-blame. It also inflates his unquestioned confidence that he, Anakin, knows *what should or should not* happen to those he loves.

Anakin's lack of humility allows his originally admirable love for his mother to become the driving force that leads him into an increasingly damaged, vain sense of himself and his duty, exemplified in his exchange with Padmé upon his return: "I will be the most powerful Jedi ever. I promise you. I will even learn to stop people from dying." Anakin would do anything to resurrect his mother – a natural desire for an unnatural power. From a Jedi perspective, this disordered passion is not the only sin Anakin is to commit, since what's far worse than an inordinate attachment to those who have died is the act of killing innocents. When Shmi exhaled her last breath, Anakin took his rage – but also perhaps his resentment of his own perceived inadequacy – out on her captors, including women and children. He knows, as a Jedi, that he should be "better than this." He should be able to see that he could have done no more for his mother, that her situation was outside of his control, and let it go, but Anakin's originally healthy feelings of love have devolved into destructive hate.

Choosing a Father

Kneeling at his mother's grave, he swears, "I won't fail again," and transfers his affection to Padmé, about whom he's dreamt since their first meeting.[2] When Padmé reveals she is pregnant, Anakin finds himself again beset with nightmares about a woman he loves: this time it's Padmé dying in childbirth. He promises he "won't let this dream come true" and reaches out to Master Yoda for advice. Yoda admonishes, "Fear of loss is a path to the dark side.... Death is a natural part of life. Rejoice for those around you who transform into the Force. Mourn them do not, miss them do not. Attachment leads to jealousy. A shadow of greed that is." Anakin must "let go" of everyone to whom he's become attached; for as much as he loves her, Padmé is not an object he can own, but another "luminous being" connected to the Force.

At the same time, Anakin begins to see Obi-Wan as more of a jealous brother while Palpatine takes on more of a fatherly role in their relationship. When Palpatine tells him the legend of Darth Plagueis, who could manipulate the midi-chlorians to "create life," keeping his loved ones from dying (and could possibly be responsible for Anakin's conception),[3] Anakin's interest is piqued. Palpatine tempts Anakin with a path that will give him great power: "The dark side of the Force is the path to many abilities some believe to be unnatural." At last, Palpatine's true identity is revealed, and at first Anakin reacts with disgust; but Darth Sidious promises that, if he pledges his allegiance, Anakin can "save [his] wife from certain death." His disgust dissolved by his desire for this power, Anakin's solemn pledge of allegiance seals his fate.

Ironically, the lengths to which Anakin is willing to go for Padmé will destroy the democracy she risked her life countless times to protect. After his rampage at the Jedi temple and on Mustafar, Anakin sheds a tear; perhaps this is a moment of bitter guilt, suppressed by his obsession with saving Padmé at all costs, as he couldn't save his mother. The conflict within Anakin is really a conflict between the measured stoicism he has been taught by the Jedi and his desire to master things outside his realm of control. Even when Padmé tries to persuade her love to return home and end the bloodshed, he is adamant that he must gain power: "Love won't save you, Padmé. Only my new powers can do that." He assures her that he can "overthrow" his dark mentor and that he and Padmé can "rule the galaxy" together. But Anakin's change destroys her "will to live," leaving Anakin devoid of her life and love, a slave to the Emperor.

It's important to note that it isn't just the Stoic tradition that warns against such attachment.[4] Both Eastern and Western philosophical traditions assert that wisdom and proper love require a certain measure of detachment or resistance to passions, especially when such passions are not guided or restrained by reason. Ancient Greek philosophers like Plato and Aristotle; traditional Jewish, Christian, and Islamic philosophers; in addition to the Buddha, Confucius, and Laozi all teach us that passionate desire and even deep love for others require the use of practical wisdom. The kind of unrestrained, passionate desire to control circumstances that we see in Anakin at this stage in his life is just what many thinkers have warned against in their philosophies.

Vader's Deformed Fatherhood

When Obi-Wan begins Luke's training as a Jedi, the boy perhaps sees Obi-Wan as a vestige of what he believes his father was, connecting to him on a deeper level than that of teacher and student. But Obi-Wan doesn't have much time to teach Luke, for he must face his father. Obi-Wan is as confident as ever, for he, unlike Vader, has accepted his own mortality and convergence with the Force. Obi-Wan's death bears a similar significance to Luke as Qui-Gon's death had to Anakin, but, as we shall see, Obi-Wan's self-sacrifice offers us a hint about how Anakin's perverse parenting of his children may be resolved. Before looking to that end, let's survey the problems Vader creates as a parent.

In *The Empire Strikes Back*, Vader's moral compass begins to right itself. He certainly desires to please his master and gain power for the

Galactic Empire, but he's also feeling more. Perhaps his heart raced when he learned that his wife had indeed lived to give birth and that he had not destroyed her entirely but that part of her, their son, lived on. He also could have been racked with guilt yet again about orphaning his own son. "He's just a boy," he asserts when the Emperor refers to him as "a new enemy," perhaps hoping that the Emperor will not harm his son yet. But the Emperor is unmoved and insists on the boy's destruction until Vader introduces the idea of making Luke "a powerful ally." With this proposition, Vader satisfies his own cognitive dissonance; by bringing Luke over to the dark side, he will save the boy (as he couldn't save Padmé) and also increase his own power.

Meanwhile, Luke is making discoveries of his own under Yoda's tutelage. In the Dagobah cave, Luke literally faces his own similarities with his father. When he severs the head of the apparition of Darth Vader, he finds his own face behind the mask. Luke is uniquely vulnerable to the dark side – quick to risk all for his loved ones – and could become the very evil he seeks to destroy. In Cloud City, Luke is offered that opportunity. Beaten back and clutching his severed forearm, Luke is forced to listen to Vader solicit him. Just as Sidious offered his teaching to his young apprentice whom he affectionately called his son, Vader now offers his service to his true son: "With our combined strength, we can end this destructive conflict and bring order to the galaxy." He asserts that the Emperor is vulnerable and could be defeated and that "together we can rule the galaxy as father and son." But like his mother, Luke would rather risk death than help stamp out freedom's last hope in the galaxy. While he walked into Vader's trap at Cloud City because he acted on his attachment to his friends, he doesn't allow this attachment to control his moral compass. He does not take Vader's offer of power in hopes that he can right the wrongs of the galaxy through their partnership: that was Anakin's mistake. Instead, Luke focuses on what he can do alone in the situation, and he decides he would rather brave a nasty fall.

Savior by Sacrifice

The revelation, disturbing as it is, cultivates in Luke a deep compassion for the father he never had. In *Return of the Jedi*, Luke seeks to persuade his father to desert the dark side in a bizarre case of role reversal. Luke seems to be acting more like the father than Vader, as Luke tries to turn him back to "the good side," as if the villain is a lost child. Luke echoes his mother's words when he tries to persuade Leia that his mission isn't foolhardy: "There is good in him. I've felt it. I can save him. I can turn him back to the good side. I have to try." Luke is willing to brave danger and death if it means he can convince his father to return to a healthy life, but he will not do so at the cost of the Rebellion; it is his fight, and his fight alone.

Luke did indeed put too much faith in his father's humanity. Vader is so twisted by the dark side that he's willing to bring his son before his master, knowing that if he refuses to succumb to him, his son will be killed and he may have to do the killing. It does indeed lead to their final confrontation, where Luke (younger, stronger, and eventually fired by rage when Vader threatens to turn Leia to the dark side) gets the better of him. He amputates Vader's mechanical arm, and the Emperor delightfully bids him, "Take your father's place at my side." But the frayed wires protruding from Vader's sleeve remind Luke of his own mechanical hand. Once again, Luke sees how easily he could become like his father, and that perhaps he has already begun the journey. Suddenly, Luke resists. He straightens and tosses his weapon aside. "I'll never turn to the dark side," he insists. And, as if to offer proof, he proclaims, "I am a Jedi, like my father before me," and nods toward Vader's crumpled form.

When the Emperor pummels him with Sith lightning, Luke turns to his father in agony: "Father please, help me!" Perhaps Vader recalls that same suffering he experienced at the hands of Dooku's Sith lightning, but the last time he was in this situation was the moment he decided to defend Sidious from Mace Windu. After an agonizing period of nonintervention, he lunges forward, picks up the Emperor, and drops him into the core of the new Death Star, absorbing much of the lightning himself. Certainly dying, he begs Luke to help him remove his mask. He looks upon his son admiringly, and when Luke insists, "I've got to save you," he responds, "You already have, Luke." Luke's compassion gave Anakin the opportunity to sacrifice himself for his son, his daughter, and a return to the democracy his wife so loved. This is Vader's redemption and an act of true fatherhood. In fact, Anakin's dying wish is for his daughter to know that Luke "was right" about the good left in his soul. Perhaps it's a promise that, had he lived, he would have tried to make up for torturing her on the Death

Star and for using her as leverage to turn Luke. Maybe he could have loved her like he did her mother.

Vader's self-sacrifice is powerful because it fulfills what Vader should have done much earlier: sacrifice his own inflated sense of self, sacrifice his pursuit of power in the name of what seemed to him to be love, and sacrifice his scheme to save his son by leading Luke deeper into the heart of darkness. But his inability to "let go" prevented him from acting in the principled way his son does. Vader cannot go back in time to make such sacrifices and become the loving father that he ought to have been, but he can sacrifice his life now, dying in Luke's place, as Obi-Wan did in *A New Hope*. While Obi-Wan didn't give his life to bring about atonement for his own past wrongdoings, his sacrifice perhaps foreshadows how Vader, much later, can also save Luke through self-sacrifice.

A Lesson on Love

The drama and trauma displayed in *Star Wars* allow us to recognize how an admirable love can lose its value, and in fact can become what motivates people to outrageously wicked acts. The good of the love in such relationships needs to be tempered by humility and wisdom, otherwise the apparent good of such love is merely an appearance that can be used to try to justify increasingly base and cruel acts. Ultimately, *Star Wars* shows us how such poisoned familial relations may be in some way redeemed or salvaged (in part) by revealing truths about those relations (truths about parentage, past wrongs, and so on) and through heroic, costly self-sacrifice.

The lessons learned from a story about events that took place "a long time ago in a galaxy far, far away" may not have obvious parallels for humans in this galaxy. But the films can still stimulate us to consider practical proposals for a philosophy of love, especially familial love: the importance of accepting our limitations as mortals and realizing that loving another person means loving someone who is vulnerable to harm and death; and that healing and repair in family relations may be enhanced by self-sacrifice. In the real world, if your relationship with your father or mother has been unhealthy, then it's not likely that your parent will have to rescue you from a blast of Sith lighting, or that your mother or father must destroy an evil Emperor by throwing him into the reactor shaft of a Death Star. Happily, though, there are other routes to display love through heroic self-sacrifice in our world that are less dramatic, yet just as expressive.

Notes

1. As quoted in an interview for the DVD Documentary *Empire of Dreams: The Story of the Star Wars Trilogy*, dir. Kevin Burns (2004).
2. Their relationship has been a topic of much discussion – see especially Jason T. Eberl, "'You Cannot Escape Your Destiny' (Or Can You?): Freedom and Predestination in the Skywalker Family," in *Star Wars and Philosophy*, ed. Kevin S. Decker and Jason T. Eberl (Chicago: Open Court, 2005), as well as Eberl's chapter in this volume (chapter 9). Therefore, an in-depth analysis will not be included here except to show that Anakin's desire for the power to save Padmé is one of the chief reasons – if not *the* chief reason – why Anakin turns to the dark side. This change is achieved as Anakin's relationship to Obi-Wan changes and his association with Palpatine becomes stronger.
3. This theme is explored in more depth in James Luceno, *Star Wars: Darth Plagueis* (New York: Del Rey, 2012).
4. For more detail on the connections between *Star Wars* and Stoicism, see Matt Hummel's chapter in this book (chapter 2).

11

The Friends of a Jedi: Friendship, Family, and Civic Duty in a Galaxy at War

Greg Littmann

Give yourself to the dark side. It is the only way you can save your friends. Yes, your thoughts betray you. Your feelings for them are strong.

– Darth Vader, *Return of the Jedi*

The heroes and villains of the *Star Wars* saga are probably the most widely recognized fictional characters in the Western world. How many people couldn't identify Darth Vader, or C-3PO, or Luke Skywalker standing with his lightsaber blazing? Almost forty years after George Lucas first unveiled an entirely new mythology to a dazzled public, the saga remains part of our culture, with *Star Wars* merchandise stacked on toy aisle shelves and the upcoming seventh film in the series poised to be a blockbuster through sheer brand loyalty. Why does the series have such lasting appeal? One reason is that so many of the central themes are universal and timeless. In particular, the saga is a celebration of friendship and family bonds. Though it's a story of conflict and warfare, grand political concerns about the fate of the galaxy are kept in the background, as the story focuses more on action and the relationships among the main characters. In fact, for Luke, Leia, and Han, ties to friends and family are stronger motivations than duty to society, as they prioritize helping their loved ones over saving the galaxy from the Empire.

The Ultimate Star Wars and Philosophy: You Must Unlearn What You Have Learned, First Edition. Edited by Jason T. Eberl and Kevin S. Decker.
© 2016 John Wiley & Sons, Ltd. Published 2016 by John Wiley & Sons, Ltd.

Pals over Politics: Motivations of a Hero

When we first meet Luke, he wants to leave Tatooine to join the Rebellion, but he puts the interests of his Uncle Owen and Aunt Beru first, staying to help them on their moisture farm. He complains about staying and claims that he hates the Empire, but doesn't run away to join the fight. Ben Kenobi seems to understand that Luke is more easily motivated by personal attachments than civic loyalties. When he tries to convince Luke to leave the farm and join him in his quest, he tells him, "*She* [Leia] needs your help," not "*The galaxy* needs your help."

In *The Empire Strikes Back*, Vader uses Luke's loyalty to his friends to set a trap for him. He subjects Han and Leia to torture in Cloud City, knowing that Luke will sense their pain and be unable to resist coming to help them. Luke puts his Jedi training with Yoda on hold, leaving Dagobah to undertake a rescue mission, despite Yoda's warning, "If you end your training now – if you choose the quick and easy path as Vader did – you will become an agent of evil." Yoda is aware that this is a trap set by the Emperor in order to convert Luke to the dark side. If the Emperor were to succeed, the Rebellion would be lost. Yet even Yoda frames Luke's choice in terms of how Luke can best serve his friends, not his society. Yoda counsels, "Decide you must how to serve them best. If you leave now, help them you could; but you would destroy all for which they have fought, and suffered."

Similarly, in *Return of the Jedi*, Luke risks his life to rescue Han by confronting Jabba the Hutt on Tatooine. Given how vital Luke is to the Rebel cause, he's taking an enormous risk with the freedom of the galaxy in order to look after his buddy. Strikingly, when the Emperor finally succeeds in making Luke lose his temper in an effort to turn him to the dark side, he does it not by taunting him about the fate of the galaxy, but by taunting him about the impending deaths of his friends.

Luke is no less willing to risk the freedom of his society for the sake of his father. Darth Vader is the Emperor's right hand; but Luke, who has killed many Imperial officers and soldiers, refuses to slay his dad. "I can't kill my own father," he insists to Obi-Wan. He isn't even moved when Obi-Wan responds, "Then the Emperor has already won. You were our only hope." Luke just can't bring himself to execute his old man, even if the price is victory for the Empire. Of course, Obi-Wan is wrong that the Emperor will automatically win because Luke won't kill Vader. Luke understands that there's some good left in Vader and that it's possible for him to turn against the Emperor instead. All the same, Luke takes a huge gamble by relying on Vader to turn, and in so doing, puts the interests of his father before the needs of the oppressed galaxy.

Leia is already devoted to her civic duty when we first encounter her in *A New Hope*, risking her life to smuggle the Death Star plans to Alderaan for the Rebellion. But even Leia's devotion to the common good counts less than her devotion to her friends. In *Return of the Jedi*, she joins Luke in risking her life to rescue Han from Jabba the Hutt. Given her exalted leadership position in the Rebel Alliance, she's not simply taking a personal risk to help her friend but also risking the future of the galaxy.

Han is slower to develop a public spirit than are Leia or Luke. When Luke first meets him, he's interested only in making a profit through smuggling, not fighting the Empire. Even when Han helps to rescue Leia from the Death Star, he tells her, "Look, I ain't in this for your revolution and I'm not in it for you, Princess. I expect to be well paid. I'm in it for the money." Han at first refuses to join the Rebel attack on the Death Star, complaining, "What good's a reward if you ain't around to use it?" When the *Millennium Falcon* swoops in to save the day at the last moment, it's to save Luke's life by firing on Vader's TIE fighter. Han can turn his back on the Rebellion, but can't let his buddy face death alone.

Things change by the time of *The Empire Strikes Back*. Han is helping the Rebels on Hoth without any mention of reward. Still, he's getting ready to leave in order to pay off Jabba, despite Leia's insistence that the Rebellion needs him. Once again, where public spirit fails to move Han, personal loyalty wins out. When he hears that Luke hasn't returned from patrolling the frozen wastelands, he delays leaving to search for him, despite the dangerous falling temperature. Likewise, when the time comes for Hoth to be evacuated, his first concern is for his friends, refusing to leave until he assures that Leia has escaped safely.

Luke Skywalker and Other Mythic Heroes

The overwhelming loyalty that the heroes of *Star Wars* feel for friends and family is a traditional feature of heroes, from ancient history to today. For the heroes of the Ancient Greek epics *Iliad* and *Odyssey*, loyalty to friends and family is a paramount virtue, while the good of outsiders is barely considered. Whereas the Rebellion is fought to bring "freedom to the galaxy," the Trojan War depicted in the *Iliad* is fought because King Agamemnon has to avenge the honor of his brother, whose wife has been seduced and taken away. For this, Agamemnon allows the deaths of countless Greek and Trojan soldiers, and eventually destroys the entire city of Troy. At one point, the mightiest Greek hero, Achilles, goes AWOL from the battle because of a slight to his honor, sulking in his tent while the other Greeks die on the field. But when Achilles' best buddy Patroclus is killed by the Trojan hero, Hector, Achilles returns to the fight in order to have his revenge. In *Star Wars*, heroes rescue their friends rather than avenge their deaths, but in rushing off to save one another from Cloud City or Jabba the Hutt, they maintain the tradition of being primarily motivated by friendship rather than the ongoing war.

Likewise, in the *Odyssey*, Prince Telemachus quests to rescue his father, King Odysseus, who's been lost at sea for twenty years, much as Luke quests to rescue his father, Lord Vader, who's been lost to the dark side of the Force for twenty years. Where Vader saves Luke in turn by killing the Emperor, the returned Odysseus saves Telemachus from rivals who've used the king's absence to muscle in on his turf. Together, father and son wreak bloody vengeance, securing the young man's inheritance of the kingdom of Ithaca – just as Vader, before his redemptive conversion, tries to convince Luke to join him in overthrowing the Emperor so they can "rule the galaxy as father and son."

To these ancient heroes, it would seem obvious that Luke, Leia, and Han do the right thing when they place loyalty to their friends and family over their civic duty to fight the Empire. However, more than six hundred years after the Trojan War, philosophers in Athens questioned traditional beliefs regarding how people should live. The most influential of them believed that people have a duty to their society that goes far beyond what most people thought.

Leaving Han Solo in the Freezer

Socrates (469–399 BCE) believed that the only important thing to achieve in life is being good. He was such a zealot for doing his civic duty that when he was unjustly condemned to death, and his friends tried to rescue him from prison, he refused to go, claiming that he owed it to Athens not to break the law. In allowing the state to execute him, he was placing his duties to the people of Athens over the interests of his friends. His friends, who all wanted him to escape, regarded him as a great teacher of wisdom – he was a veritable Yoda to them. But Socrates saw his friends' benefit, and his own life, as less important than the need to do right by his society. He thought that to leave without the city's permission would be "mistreating the people whom we should least mistreat."[1]

If Socrates were advising Luke, Leia, and Han, he'd surely urge them to do their duty to their society before looking after the good of their friends, which might mean obeying the Empire's laws, even at the cost of their lives. Perhaps Socrates would've advised Leia to follow his example and refuse to go with Luke and Han when they attempt to rescue her from the Death Star, on the grounds that, as a citizen of the Empire who turned Rebel, she has a duty to submit to the death penalty. If so, Socrates would certainly have condemned the Rebellion as a whole, telling Luke to go farm moisture and Han to find an honest job.

I doubt that Socrates would go so far, though, because he thought there are limits to our duties to obey the law. When he was ordered by the Athenian government to help in the arrest of an innocent man as part of a bloody political purge, he refused. Since Socrates thought that the most important thing in life is being good, it's hard to see him failing to support the fight against a system that's not merely corrupt but devoted to evil as a matter of principle. Also, when Socrates submitted to Athenian judgment and accepted his execution, he based his acceptance on the grounds that he had implicitly made a *just agreement* with the city to abide by its laws, by virtue of having lived his whole life in Athens and raising his own children there. After all, he could've left at any time if he didn't like the city's laws. Luke, Leia, and Han, however, cannot simply choose to leave the galaxy if they don't approve of the Empire's laws. Even on a remote Outer Rim planet like Tatooine, Imperial stormtroopers will freely harass citizens and casually kill peaceful moisture farmers if it serves the Empire's interests. Perhaps this means that there's no binding, implicit agreement between the Empire and its citizens that would morally compel them to obey its laws.

If Socrates would support the Rebellion, he'd chide Han for being so slow to do his duty as a citizen, urging him to join up at once, rather than concerning himself with his personal profit. Socrates himself served with distinction as a soldier defending his city from the invading Persian army. He would clearly side with Yoda in urging Luke to continue his Jedi training on Dagobah instead of flying to Cloud City to rescue Leia and Han. He'd also tell Luke and Leia to leave Han to the mercies of Jabba the Hutt until the civil war is over. As the last of the Jedi and an influential leader, they are too valuable for the Rebellion to risk losing for Han's sake.

Socrates's student, Plato (427–347 BCE), accused the people of his day of placing too much emphasis on their private loyalties rather than on their public duties. In his *Republic*, Plato describes the perfect independent city, in which everyone must work for the good of the state. The citizens are trained and assigned their jobs in whatever way will serve the public interest best. Plato thought that the damage done by the way that people prioritize the interests of their family over the interests of their community is so awful that he wanted to abolish the family in the ruling and military classes. He recommended that children be taken away at birth to be raised by the state "so that no parent will know his own offspring or any child his parent."[2] Children raised this way would see the whole populace as their family and dedicate all their loyalty to the city. Even marriage is abolished in this class, except for temporary marriages that last only as long as it takes for two people selected by the state to breed. For Plato, the way that Vader offers his son a position of political power so that they can rule together would be a prime example of political corruption driven by family loyalties.

For the everyday citizenry, however, Plato believed in some strict familial duties. He recommended that the state ban the mythological story in which the chief Greek god, Zeus, kills and overthrows his own father, Kronos. The crime of killing one's father is so awful that the story could corrupt society: "Nor should a young person hear it said that in committing the worst crimes he's doing nothing out of the ordinary, or that if he inflicts every kind of punishment on an unjust father, he's only doing the same as the first and greatest of the gods."[3] Plato judges Zeus's actions in the story as contemptible, even though Kronos is so wicked that he's been eating his own children for fear of one day being overthrown by them. Plato would thus approve of Luke's reluctance to kill Vader despite how it might benefit the galaxy.

With the exception of forbidding patricide, Plato would advise our heroes to place civic duty ahead of the good of their friends or family. It's even possible that Plato would assert that civic duty includes *not rebelling*. The Rebels fight to "restore freedom to the galaxy," but Plato put little stock in freedom. He had a passion for law and order, and he believed that, ideally, ordinary citizens would do as they are told by the government without question and make no political decisions at all. The Emperor and Vader, however, despite their claims to be bringing "peace, freedom, justice, and security" in reorganizing the Old Republic into the First Galactic Empire, govern in ways that fit an erroneous (according to Plato) concept of justice as "the advantage of the stronger."[4] So, even a strict authoritarian like Plato would likely advise Luke, Leia, and Han to make fighting the Emperor and Vader (short of killing their father) their first priority.

Whereas Plato wants to restructure society to keep people's attention focused on their duties to the state, his student Aristotle (384–322 BCE) emphasizes the importance of giving preference to our friends and family. He writes in his *Nicomachean Ethics*, "It is a more terrible thing to defraud a comrade than a fellow-citizen, more terrible not to help a brother than a stranger, and more terrible to wound a father than anyone else,"[5] while "to confer benefits is characteristic of the good man and of virtue, and it is nobler to do well by friends than by strangers."[6] But Aristotle also thinks it can be more important to serve our entire community than those close to us: "though it is worthwhile to attain the end merely for one man, it is finer and more godlike to attain it for a nation or for city-states."[7] In fact, our duty to serve the state is so great that we should regard individual citizens as *state property*, since people can survive only as members of a group: "Neither must we suppose that any one of the citizens belongs to himself, for they all belong to the state, and are each of them a part of the state, and the care of each part is inseparable from the care of the whole."[8] For example, Aristotle believed that the state should provide universal compulsory schooling in accordance with a state-approved curriculum, to ensure that the citizens grow up to be useful members of society.

Despite the extent to which he values friendship, Aristotle would probably also advise our heroes to put their duty to the Rebellion first. He would emphasize that they should rescue their friends if they can, but not if it requires seriously risking the war effort. But what about Luke killing Vader? On the one hand, Aristotle claims that our duties to our fathers are so strong that it is "more terrible to wound a father than anyone else." On the other hand, the sheer number of other people who Luke would be hurting by not confronting his father might be so great that it outweighs his duty as a son. Aristotle does raise the question of whether it is *ever* all right to even disobey one's father; but he never answers it, except to note that there are limits to what even a father is owed.

Your Friends or Your Galaxy?

You will have to make up your own mind, but I think that the philosophers of Athens get closer to the truth than the heroes of the Trojan War, in that they think we should sometimes place our civic duty over the interests of those closest to us. This doesn't mean that we should never treat our friends and family better than people with whom we have no connection. But it does mean that even apparently heroic acts of loyalty between friends and even family can really be acts of moral failure. If we want to do right, it isn't enough to do well by the people we care about most. We must ask how our actions affect *everyone*. Han should've joined the Rebellion immediately after he abandoned the Imperial Academy, Luke should've stayed on Dagobah to complete his Jedi training, and Luke and Leia should've left Han in Jabba's clutches. Perhaps most importantly, Luke should've killed his father rather than taking the risk of trying to redeem him.

Stories about friendship and familial loyalty move us in a way that stories about the performance of civic duty don't. But weighing the actions of fictional characters like Luke and his pals can help us reflect on how we should act in the real world. Is it all right if we live our lives like the heroes of *Star Wars*, placing our loyalty to the people close to us far ahead of our sense of duty to strangers?

In some ways, the moral views of these early philosophers move us too far toward civic duty and away from the traditional values of loyalty to friends and family. Plato and Aristotle are wrong to turn the citizens into something akin to state property. People are happiest when they are allowed to be in charge of their own lives, which is why the Rebels are right to fight for freedom for the galaxy. Plato is especially wrong that we should encourage loyalty to the state by abolishing the family as children's guardians in favor of raising them in state institutions. The love of a family is good for children's development. While Luke and Leia may have benefited by being removed from their father's care, it's fortunate that the Larses and Organas were ready and willing to take them in – Bail Organa assures Yoda and Obi-Wan when he volunteers to raise Leia, "She will be loved with us." On the other hand, in some ways the philosophers don't take us far enough from traditional values in their notions of how to balance family and civic loyalties. Both Plato and Aristotle explicitly make the harming of one's father one of the worst of crimes; and, in Plato's dialogue *Euthyphro*, Socrates questions the wisdom of a young Athenian lawyer who is bringing charges of murder against his own father in court. Such loyalties raise the possibility of letting family interests get in the way of important civic duties, whether by refusing to kill one's evil father or by family corruption on a less dramatic scale. The bottom line is that good moral reasoning requires doing some math. It isn't enough to ask simply. "Who do I care about?" without also asking, "How many people will my actions affect, and how much?"

Notes

1. Plato, *Crito*, in *Plato: Complete Works*, ed. John M. Cooper (Indianapolis, IN: Hackett, 1997), 50a.
2. Plato, *Republic*, in *Plato: Complete Works*, Book V, 457d1–2.
3. Ibid., Book II, 378b7–c2.
4. Ibid., Book I, 339a.
5. Aristotle, *Nicomachean Ethics*, in *The Complete Works of Aristotle*, ed. Jonathan Barnes (Princeton, NJ: Princeton University Press, 1984), Book VIII, 1160a4–6.
6. Ibid., Book IX, 1169b11–13.
7. Ibid., Book I, 1094b9–11.
8. Aristotle, *Politics*, in *The Complete Works of Aristotle*, Book VIII, 1337a27–9.

12

Light Side, Dark Side, and Switching Sides: Loyalty and Betrayal in *Star Wars*

Daniel Malloy

Loyalty is like the Force: it has a light side and a dark side, and it surrounds and binds us all. Each of us, whether Jedi or Sith, Rebel or Imperial, is ensnared in a complex web of loyalties: to family, friends, and coworkers, as well as to institutions, governments, and countries. Each of these loyalties makes claims on us and places us under obligations.

On the light side, our loyalties bind us, turning mere groups of people into something more – families, communities, causes, and so on. Our loyalties tell us who we are and give us our place in the world. A human being without any loyalties is like Aristotle's man without a city – either a beast or a god, but not a man.[1] Furthermore, our loyalties can inspire us to great acts. They can motivate us to do the right thing when we may be inclined otherwise. They can even motivate acts that go above and beyond anything that could be reasonably expected of us.

On the dark side, those same loyalties can trap us and restrict us. They can inspire us to awful acts in the names of those to whom we're loyal. They can incline us to do wrong when we wish to do right. Those who are completely loyal may be convinced to do *anything*.

It's thus hardly surprising that philosophers have never come to any sort of consensus about loyalty. Attitudes range from Josiah Royce's (1855–1916) belief that loyalty to "loyalty itself" is a sufficient basis

The Ultimate Star Wars and Philosophy: You Must Unlearn What You Have Learned,
First Edition. Edited by Jason T. Eberl and Kevin S. Decker.

for a system of ethics[2] to Philip Pettit's contention that whatever value we place on loyalty is based on its ability to motivate people to immoral acts that favor *us*, nothing more.[3] Philosophers can't even agree on what loyalty is, much less whether it's a good thing. I will argue that the value of loyalty itself is exaggerated, and that its true value is derived from other valuable personality traits.

Betrayed by a Droid

The first question we confront is what exactly loyalty is. Is loyalty a *moral* concept, or simply a way of describing an *emotional connection* between individuals or groups? If it's a moral concept, is there a *duty* to be loyal? Or is loyalty a *virtue* of good character? In everyday speech, we treat it equally as both. We say that Lando should've been loyal to his friends instead of selling them out to the Empire, or that Luke was right to remain loyal to his friends rather than join the Emperor, implying that loyalty is a duty. But we also praise Chewbacca for his loyalty to Han over many years, implying that loyalty is a virtuous character trait.

One thing that's clear about loyalty is that it's *relational*: loyalty is always the loyalty of one thing to another. But what kinds of things can be loyal? And what kinds of things can they be loyal to? As to the first, a basic level of cognition and feeling seems necessary for something to be loyal. Han is loyal to the *Millennium Falcon*, but the *Falcon* is incapable of reciprocating. What basic level of cognition and feeling is required is subject to some debate, though. Whether, for example, a droid could be loyal would depend on answers to a variety of questions – starting with whether droids are sentient at all.[4] Within the *Star Wars* universe, however, most of the on-screen characters, human and nonhuman, are the kinds of beings that can be loyal or disloyal. Certainly, no one would question Chewbacca's loyalty – not twice, anyway.

On the low end of the scale of cognition and feeling required for loyalty, we might consider pets. Although pets, particularly dogs, are often considered paragons of loyalty, they're actually too low on the scale of cognitive ability to be actually loyal. Consider Talon Karrde's pair of canine vornskrs, Sturm and Drang, from Timothy Zahn's *Thrawn* trilogy. When Sturm or Drang disobeys Karrde, is it being disloyal? Hardly; it's just being a vornskr. And since no action on its part would be considered disloyal, it shouldn't be considered loyal either. It should be considered a vornskr, and kept well fed.

This test could likewise be applied to whether droids can be loyal. If a droid could act in a way we'd call disloyal, then a droid can also be loyal. But this test implies something controversial about loyalty: that acts of loyalty are *voluntary*. Josiah Royce claims that all loyalty is voluntary. Likewise, what George Fletcher calls our "historical self" – the past ties that forge our identities – has some influence over what we may be loyal to, but the choice is ultimately ours.[5] On the other hand, Fletcher argues that at least some loyalties tied to our "historical selves" aren't voluntary but still impose obligations. I agree with Royce: the historical self provides the basic materials of our loyalties – it determines what we can be loyal to. But it doesn't determine what we will be or what we are loyal to. That determination is our choice, which may be more or less difficult depending on the context. What we align ourselves with is up to us, at least to an extent. Luke, for example, isn't a disloyal person because he feels no special attachment or loyalty to his home planet of Tatooine – telling Obi-Wan, "I'm never coming back to *this* planet again." Despite being his home planet, Tatooine has no claim to Luke's loyalty.

But it's plain that the choice of what we're loyal to isn't completely unrestricted. When Grand Moff Tarkin threatens to destroy Leia's home planet of Alderaan unless she tells him the location of the Rebel base, she's caught between conflicting loyalties to Alderaan and the Rebel Alliance. What does it mean to be loyal to either of these? Alderaan is (was – sorry!) a planet, but also a people, a culture, a government, a history, a collection of traditions and customs, an ecosystem, and many other things besides. The Rebel Alliance is a cause, but it's also an organization, a collection of assets, and a group of people. In each case, it's legitimate to ask what the object of Leia's loyalty is.

Royce argues that loyalty is always loyalty to a *cause*. If Royce is right, then Leia's conflict is between her loyalty to the cause of Alderaan (the interests of her people and government) and the cause of the Rebel Alliance (the overthrow of the Empire). In her mind, it seems safe to say, the two were linked, until, as a prisoner of the Empire, she's confronted with the reality of the Death Star orbiting Alderaan. The idea that loyalty is always to a cause seems to limit it to being political in some fashion. Royce, though, defines "causes" broadly enough that essentially anything can be a cause: even lovers aren't really loyal to one another, but to the "cause" of their love.

Royce's analysis has been criticized for being too abstract.[6] Perhaps, on the contrary, all loyalty is really loyalty to *persons*, whether individuals or groups. Andrew Oldenquist claims that Royce's notion of a cause fails to distinguish between a loyalty and an *ideal*. If Leia is committed to the ideal of freedom, then she's committed to it in all times and places. On the other hand, if she's committed to her home planet of Alderaan, that commitment is particular to her. She's loyal to it because it's *her* home planet. Luke, not even loyal to his home planet of Tatooine, can neither be loyal to Corellia, Alderaan, or Coruscant, because he has no connection to them.

This is how our historical selves limit the options for our loyalty. Loyalty is based not just on any sort of relationship but also on a *connection* the loyal person feels to the object of her loyalty. The things and people to which we can be loyal must be *ours* in order for our actions toward them to be based on loyalty, rather than just affection or general goodwill toward them.

Simon Keller has proposed a "thin" theory of loyalty, in which loyalty should be primarily understood in terms of *motive*. An action is motivated by loyalty if three conditions are met: it's at least partially emotional; it involves a response to the object of loyalty; and it's defined by reference to a particular relationship that the subject believes to exist between herself and the object.[7]

Consider Luke's decision to leave Dagobah and go to Bespin to try to rescue Han and Leia. It was a partially emotional, and not wholly rational, decision. The rational course of action would've been to complete his training so that he could defeat the Emperor and, as Yoda said, "honor what they fight for." Instead, Luke left because he was pulled by his feelings for Han and Leia. The fact that it was *Han* and *Leia* who were in danger is important. Luke, being a good person, wouldn't want to see anyone hurt unnecessarily. But while he was training on Dagobah, many people were being hurt all over the galaxy. It was only the peril faced by his friends that could motivate him to action. He responded to their suffering, not because it was greater than others' or because they were more important, but because they're *Han* and *Leia*. They shared a particular connection with Luke: they were *his* friends.

What makes Keller's view unique is that it strips loyalty of moral content. Loyalty is an *emotional connection*, but not one that obliges us in any way. If Keller is correct, then the place of loyalty in morality can be limited solely to a tool for understanding the motivations behind certain actions. Let's look at the complex role that loyalty plays in motivating the actions of a particular group of *Star Wars* characters: the Sith.

The Loyalty of the Sith

The Sith represent an interesting paradox: in order for a Sith Lord to be loyal, she must betray. A Sith Lord – following Darth Bane's Rule of Two – who refuses to betray her master isn't a loyal Sith. But there are any number of reasons why an apprentice might not betray her master, and not all of them represent a betrayal of the Sith code. A Sith apprentice who defends her master's life, when she could just as easily kill him and assume the mantle of "master" herself, might do so for perfectly good Sith reasons. Similarly, not every Sith apprentice who betrays her master remains a loyal Sith. Vader's final betrayal of his master was also a betrayal of the Sith.

Perhaps discussing loyalty among the Sith puts too much strain on the concept of loyalty itself. Can a relationship founded on the idea that one party must eventually betray the other be a relationship of loyalty? Consider Anakin Skywalker and Darth Sidious. From the very day that Sidious took Anakin as his apprentice, the newly christened Darth Vader was plotting his master's downfall. After revealing his relationship to Luke, Vader's first thought is that they should unite and overthrow Sidious. Betrayal is built into Vader's relationship with his master, as it is in every Sith bond. The apprentice may be obedient to the master, but it would be a stretch to say that she is loyal. The apprentice's interest in the master is mostly in her *own* interest in the master's ability to teach her dark side skills. Once the master has fulfilled that purpose, the apprentice no longer has any use for him.

The betrayal of a Sith master by his apprentice, then, isn't a violation of loyalty, since you can't violate what doesn't exist. In fact, it remains an act of loyalty, provided the betrayal is based on proper Sith motivations, such as the desire for power. As Darth Bane's Rule of Two states, the role of the master is to have power, the role of the apprentice to crave it. The apprentice who kills her master to acquire power, as Darth Sidious did when he killed Darth Plagueis, or as Darth Vader proposed both to Padmé and to Luke, remains a loyal Sith: not to her master, but to the Sith itself. Betrayal of one's master involves loyalty to the master, not as a person, but as a member of the Sith Order.

And then there's the final betrayal by Darth Vader. In the end, Vader did what he'd been scheming since his Sith apprenticeship began: he turned on his master. But he also turned on the ideals of the Sith. His betrayal was motivated by un-Sithlike loyalty. That's the odd thing about the Sith – in order to be a loyal Sith, one can't be motivated by loyalty. Even betraying one's master out of loyalty to the Sith is to betray the Sith. The betrayal must be motivated by a craving for power, not by loyalty or principle.

Loyal Soldiers of the Empire

It may seem that loyalty is a good thing. After all, Vader's betrayal of the Sith was motivated by loyalty to Luke and Leia, and it was the right thing to do. But remember that Vader also joined the Sith out of loyalty. Anakin Skywalker agreed to become Darth Sidious's apprentice out of loyalty to Padmé, in hopes of saving her life. We generally hold loyalty to be a good thing, but what if loyalty is misplaced? What if we are loyal to something we shouldn't be? Stormtroopers, for example, are supposed to be fanatically loyal; but does that make them good?

To begin with the most severe criticism, Philip Pettit argues that loyalty is either redundant or immoral. If I'm loyal to a person or cause insofar as it fits my morality, then loyalty is redundant – it simply tells me to do what my conscience has already told me. On the other hand, if my loyalty goes beyond my morality, then it makes me an accomplice to actions or causes I should consider immoral. Pettit's argument gets to the core of moral philosophers' discomfort with loyalty. Other critics of loyalty focus on its *partiality*.[8] A central tenet of most moral theories is that we should judge and act impartially, without prejudice or bias. When Obi-Wan tells Yoda that he can't kill Anakin, who's like a brother to him, even after witnessing Anakin's betrayal of the

Jedi, he's revealing his partiality toward Anakin despite the fate of the galaxy hanging in the balance.

Furthermore, similar cases should be treated similarly, without regard to one's personal connections or relations. But loyalty is a bias – a loyal person favors the thing to which she's loyal because of her particular relation to it. Imagine a scenario where Chewbacca has to choose between saving Han and saving a droid carrying a key piece of information for the Rebel Alliance. He can't save both. If he saves Han, he'll have lived up to the terms of his life-debt while possibly handing ultimate victory to the Empire. If he saves the droid, the Empire will surely fall. If it were anyone but Han, Chewie would certainly save the droid. But it's *Han*. So Chewie's loyalty to Han may prevent him from doing the right thing.

Loyalty can conflict with morality, and thus loyalty isn't always a good thing. However, there are reasons to think that we need loyalty. As Royce and Fletcher argue, being loyal is at the core of our identities, especially loyalties linked to our "historical selves." In fact, loyalty may be a *necessary condition* for a moral life. Oldenquist contends that loyalty isn't so much a virtue or a duty, but is the condition for even being virtuous or having duties, insofar as they require us to first have a connection with a certain community. Only within a community can we be virtuous or owe duties – outside of it, there's no right or wrong.

We see acknowledgement of this viewpoint in the Sith tradition of taking on a new name with the title "Darth." It's a common rite of passage for potential Sith apprentices to rid themselves of all connections to their past lives – to shed the loyalties of their former identities. Palpatine had to kill his family to become Darth Sidious. Anakin only became Vader after brutally severing his ties to the Jedi. But those connections are only *part* of loyalty. Boba Fett was connected to the Mandalorians, but only became loyal to them late in life when he took on the role of Mandalore.[9] There's an *act of will* that turns a connection into a loyalty – and thereby obliges us to the object of that loyalty. It's thus easy to see why betrayal of any sort invites our unease. Even if a person were to betray a corrupt institution like the Empire, the act of betrayal itself would make her a constant object of suspicion. No one trusts a traitor, even if the traitor betrayed our enemies. The traitor has done something almost impossible to imagine ourselves doing: she's given up a part of who she is.

The Solo House Divided against Itself

While conflicts between loyalty and morality are real and difficult, they're rare in comparison to conflicts between loyalties. These two kinds of conflicts aren't mutually exclusive, since a single decision can involve a conflict between distinct loyalties, or between loyalty and morality. Since we've already seen that morality isn't always our best guide when it comes to issues of loyalty, let's focus here on conflicting loyalties. They are, after all, plentiful in both *Star Wars* and everyday life.

Unfortunately, while philosophers acknowledge this problem, they have very little to offer by way of practical advice or guidance to resolve it. Royce argues that, when confronted with conflicting loyalties, we should be loyal to "loyalty itself." What Royce means by this rather cryptic statement is that, in choosing between loyalties, we should opt for the one that strengthens the ability of others to be loyal to their respective causes. Since loyalty, according to Royce, is a central value in human life, we ought to act to preserve and enhance it wherever possible. If a Force-adept must choose between the light side and the dark side, the Jedi and the Sith, and feels equal loyalty to both, she has good reason to choose the light side because it encourages order and discipline without unduly interfering with the freedom to choose one's loyalties. The dark side, on the other hand, sows chaos and conflict and is, at least in Bane's line of the order, founded on betrayal. But in this case, loyalty needn't even enter into the decision. Simple morality can dictate the choice, without any reference to loyalty at all.

What should we do when the causes vying for our loyalty have equal claims? Consider the events that led to the Second Galactic Civil War in the *Legacy of the Force* series. At its start, there are competing sides in Corellia and the Galactic Alliance, each with what appear to be valid political claims. Corellia wishes to maintain a military for defense purposes, while the Galactic Alliance has called for disarmament. To complicate matters further, the Solo family is caught in the middle. Leia and the twins are loyal to the Alliance, while Han can't help but support his native Corellia. None of them can simply avoid the conflict. So we have a situation in which each member of the family has to choose between loyalty to family or to cause.

Unfortunately, Royce's loyalty to loyalty offers no guidance here. There seems to be no right decision for anyone involved. But since choosing between loyalties inevitably involves being disloyal to (if not outright betraying) the other, a better approach in thinking about conflicting loyalties might be to look at the morality of disloyalty and betrayal. It's a strange fact about discussions of loyalty that even those, like Keller, who think that it's not a moral concept still accept that disloyalty and betrayal are moral concerns.

Betrayal at Bespin; or, Why Lando Was Right

Given evident conflicts between competing loyalties, or between loyalty and morality, it seems that betrayal and disloyalty of various sorts are not only inevitable but also commonplace. Our reactions to betrayal, however, are anything but commonplace. To be disloyal is generally treated as the worst of crimes. But why should that be? Some betrayals are certainly disastrous for the party betrayed – just think of Bane's betrayal of the Sith or Anakin's betrayal of the Jedi. In both cases, betrayal led to the near annihilation of the betrayed party.

But that's not always the case. Some betrayals inflict little to no damage on the betrayed and may even prove beneficial. Think of Darth Bane's later attempt to betray his apprentice, Darth Zannah,[10] or Darth Teneberous's similar attempt to betray Darth Plagueis.[11] In both cases, the betrayed party came out better for the confrontation, with Darth Zannah assuming the mantle of Sith master and Darth Plagueis acquiring Darth Venamis as a subject for his experiments. These are nevertheless viewed by the betrayed in the same way as more egregious betrayals. So, the wrongness of betrayal isn't simply found in the harm it does to the betrayed, because the betrayed isn't always harmed by disloyalty. But something is harmed: the relationship between the two parties. When a loyalty has been betrayed, it can never be returned to its original state. An act of betrayal may not destroy a relationship, but it will alter it inevitably and irrevocably.

These thoughts can guide us when confronted with conflicting loyalties. In a situation where I must betray one loyalty or another, I have to weigh the loyalties against each other. Several factors can be taken into account. First, are the loyalties equally obligating? Loyalty to family generally takes easy precedence, for instance, over loyalty to a sports team. Second, what would be the relative severity of each of the respective betrayals? If betraying A will lead to A's death, while betraying B will lead to B losing some money, then I should betray B. Third, assuming the loyalties are *equally* obligating and the harms caused by the betrayal are *equally* severe to the betrayed, are the loyalties of equal importance to me, or is preserving one worth sacrificing the other? Finally, connected to this last concern, I should consider the relative strength of the respective relationships involved in the conflicting loyalties. Some relationships are strong enough to withstand betrayals, while others aren't.

Judged by this measure, Lando's decision on Bespin to betray Han was the right one.[12] If he hadn't done so, the Empire would've taken over Cloud City, subjecting all of its residents to the tender mercies of an Imperial military governor – and that's the best-case scenario! It's also conceivable that Lord Vader's annoyance would've taken the more direct form of simply blowing up Cloud City. Furthermore, Lando and Han's relationship was strong enough to cope with the betrayal – they're both scoundrels, and they both know it. They've double-crossed each other before and remained friends. On the way to Bespin, Han even admits that he doesn't entirely trust his old friend. He's just the best bet in a bad situation.

"So Be It ... Jedi!"

Loyalty, it seems, isn't very valuable. It can't resolve moral dilemmas for us, and in fact it creates more than a few of its own. Its usefulness in determining the correct course of action is negligible, in no small part because loyalty is just as likely to be felt toward bad causes and bad people as toward the good.

Still, there's an argument to be made that loyalty is valuable for the effect it has on its subjects. Loyal people seem to be better people all around than nonloyal people. Loyal people commit themselves to causes and to other people. They value the good of something other than themselves. Luke is disappointed when Han is "turning his back on" the Rebellion just before the Battle of Yavin, preferring to take his reward to pay off some old debts. When Han returns to save the day, Leia exclaims, "I knew there was more to you than money!" When Han's decision catches up with him and he falls victim to his unpaid debt to Jabba the Hutt, his friends risk everything to save him out of loyalty. Alternatively, the entire philosophy of the Sith is inimical to loyalty, and thus betrayal is the definitive act of a Sith.

Loyalty itself may not be all that good, but it represents a combination of other factors that generally are good. Commitment, dedication, and selflessness are all valuable traits for a person to have. This is why, where the Sith are incapable of loyalty, the Jedi are defined by it. Realizing that his friends were in danger, Luke could no more remain on Dagobah than Threepio could quit whining. To do so would've been to give up Luke's very essence, and that of the Jedi. When Yoda and Obi-Wan urge him to abandon his friends, it's out of their own sense of loyalty – not to Han and Leia, of course, but to the Jedi Order and all the friends they've already lost in the fight against the Emperor. Luke doesn't have those loyalties – there is no Jedi Order anymore for him to be loyal to. But *his* friends and *his* Rebel Alliance demand his loyalty.

Notes

1. Aristotle, *Politics*, trans. Carnes Lord (Chicago: University of Chicago Press, 2013), 41.
2. Josiah Royce, *The Philosophy of Loyalty* (New York: MacMillan, 1918).
3. Philip Pettit, "The Paradox of Loyalty," *American Philosophical Quarterly* 25 (1988): 163–71.
4. For discussion of whether droids are sentient or have moral status, see Dan Burkett's and James Okapal's chapters in this volume (chapters 20 and 16 respectively).
5. George Fletcher, *Loyalty* (New York: Oxford University Press, 1993).
6. Andrew Oldenquist, "Loyalties," *Journal of Philosophy* 79 (1982): 173–93; and John Ladd, "Loyalty," in *The Encyclopedia of Philosophy*, vol. 3, ed. Paul Edwards (New York: MacMillan & The Free Press, 1967), 97–8.
7. Simon Keller, *The Limits of Loyalty* (New York: Cambridge University Press, 2007).
8. See William Godwin, *An Enquiry Concerning Political Justice* (New York: Oxford University Press, 2013), 52: "What magic is there in the pronoun 'my' that should justify us in overturning the decisions of impartial truth?"

9.   Karen Traviss, *Star Wars – Legacy of the Force: Revelation* (New York: Del Rey, 2008).

10. Drew Karpyshyn, *Star Wars – Darth Bane: Dynasty of Evil* (New York: Del Rey, 2009).

11. James Luceno, *Star Wars: Darth Plagueis* (New York: Del Rey, 2011).

12. For another argument supporting Lando's decision, see Richard H. Dees, "Moral Ambiguity in a Black-and-White Universe," in *Star Wars and Philosophy*, ed. Kevin S. Decker and Jason T. Eberl (Chicago: Open Court, 2005), 39–54.

13

Guardians and Tyrants in the Republics of *Star Wars* and Plato

Adam Barkman and Kyle Alkema

Early in *The Phantom Menace*, the Jedi Knights are described as "the guardians of peace and justice of the galaxy." This is echoed early in *A New Hope*, when Obi-Wan Kenobi tells Luke Skywalker, "For over a thousand generations the Jedi Knights were the guardians of peace and justice in the Old Republic, before the dark times, before the Empire." So whichever of the two trilogies you start with, the initial image of the Jedi is identical. The Jedi – upholders of peace and justice – align themselves with the light side of the Force, while the Sith align themselves with the dark side. Although the Jedi are guardians of the galaxy, they refrain from ruling directly, acting as willing servants of the Old Republic. The Sith, however, are only too happy to rule and mete out their own brand of justice.

In his *Republic*, Plato (429–347 BCE) has his mentor, Socrates, search for a definition of justice through conversation with various characters. Let's take Socrates and Plato, his star padawan, as our guides in illuminating the nature of justice in relation to both the latter's hypothetical Republic as well as the Old Republic of the *Star Wars* galaxy.

The Ultimate Star Wars and Philosophy: You Must Unlearn What You Have Learned, First Edition. Edited by Jason T. Eberl and Kevin S. Decker.

Dysfunctional Democracy

In the *Republic*, Socrates's search for justice follows many paths, one of which explores the different types of political states. Socrates argues that there are five, arranged in a hierarchy from best to least.

Democracy, that modern champion of liberty, comes in surprisingly low on Socrates's list: second from the bottom. While democracy is *fair* in theory because of its commitment to equality, Socrates argues that it fails in practice whenever there's an abuse of power.[1] Imposed equality leads to anarchy. The ruled become like the rulers, and the rulers like the ruled; fathers become like children, and children like fathers; then the same follows with teachers and pupils, young and elders, and finally slaves and freemen.[2] Too much freedom leads to too much slavery, opening up the door for a tyrant to reach in and snatch power.

The Old Republic, as a representative democracy, aims at pure democracy but will always fall short since it's impossible for each rational being on thousands of planets to have a say in *everything*. In *The Phantom Menace*, the Galactic Senate degenerates into endless bickering and debating that fail to lead to positive action, while Senator Palpatine blames the weakness of democracy on a lack of care for the common good. The bureaucrats, says Palpatine, rule the Senate, and they're not concerned with acting for the good of the people. Queen Padmé Amidala of Naboo can only reply to Palpatine, "It is clear to me that the Republic no longer functions." This allows Palpatine to weave his web and gain more power for himself.

In *Attack of the Clones*, Anakin Skywalker and Senator Amidala demonstrate the trajectory of Plato's thinking when they engage in a semi-serious debate about the politics of the Republic. Anakin, in contrast to Padmé, has lost faith in the power of the Senate to make constructive decisions. According to Padmé, it's not the system that's the problem, but rather the reality that people can't always come to agreement. Anakin's quick retort is that someone should make them agree – "someone wise." She can only say in response, "Sounds an awful lot like a dictatorship to me." This conversation foreshadows Palpatine seizing power from the virtually powerless Senate, exactly as Plato might predict in this situation.

Tyranus Rex

Democracy leads to *tyranny*, says Plato, when an evil man seizes power.[3] Too much liberty, ironically, leads to enslavement. The tyrant begins as a champion of the people, raised up as their hero. In a time of need, the tyrant springs up as a protector, a guardian.[4] He always seems pleasant and respectful at the outset, and everyone is fooled.[5] The smiles are fake, though, and hide the true nature of a monster – for Plato, a "werewolf-like creature" – lurking underneath.[6]

This is precisely how Darth Sidious becomes the Galactic Emperor. In the guise of the wise and benevolent Chancellor Palpatine, he seems only to care for the good of the Republic. Secretly, however, he pulls the strings that begin with the conflict between the Trade Federation and Naboo, prompting Queen Amidala to introduce a vote of "no confidence" against Chancellor Valorum, paving the way for Palpatine to become the new Chancellor. He then stays in power long after his term should've ended by maintaining conflict in the galaxy, ensuring that he remains the people's hero. He instigates the Separatist movement through his apprentice, disaffected Jedi Master Count Dooku; influences Gungan Representative Jar Jar Binks to initiate a motion granting him emergency powers; establishes the Grand Army of the Republic; and fuels war throughout the galaxy.[7] *In*sidious, to say the least.

In contrast to Socrates, Thrasymachus, one of the antagonists of Plato's *Republic*, believes that the only proper rulers are those who hold and wield power for their own happiness.[8] For Thrasymachus, *injustice* is stronger than justice, and the power deriving from injustice can be used to rule over people. An unjust ruler's subjects are forced to attend to their ruler's interests and make him happy – this kind of ruler is a tyrant, a malevolent dictator.[9] It's thus fitting not only that Separatist leader Count Dooku takes on the Sith name of "Darth Tyranus," but also that the Separatists' terrifying battleship at the beginning of the Clone Wars is called *Malevolence*. Thrasymachus doesn't see the tyrant as bad, though. If someone is able to hold power over people, then by all means it's in his interest to do so and thus he *should* be a tyrant.

The Sith are selfish tyrants who use their power to pursue their own interests. As Anakin observes shortly before his fall to the dark side,

"They think inwards, only about themselves." Long before the rise of Darth Sidious, the Sith Brotherhood of Darkness tried to prevent fratricidal war among the Sith by giving all Sith the same status, but this was undone by a Sith Lord who instituted the "Rule of Two." A master would train an apprentice in the ways of the dark side of the Force until the apprentice became more powerful, killed the master, and chose a new apprentice. Plato describes tyrants as treacherous, telling us that they would never know true freedom or friendship. How true this is for the utterly unjust Sith![10] Even though they may think they are free, the Sith can't know true freedom because they're bound by their tyranny and their fear of losing their power. The only path to freedom for tyrants is to give up their power, something the Sith would never do.

Ironically, Anakin's progress to the dark side is largely driven by the tyrant Darth Sidious himself, behind his mask as Chancellor Palpatine. Socrates's words in the *Republic* sound prophetic here: "They will, therefore, lie at his feet begging and honoring him, taking possession of and flattering beforehand the power that is going to be his."[11] Palpatine recognizes Anakin's potential and can't resist turning him to the dark side. He stokes Anakin's ego by claiming that he'll become "even more powerful than Master Yoda." He plays on Anakin's frustration with the Jedi Council, whom he believes is holding him back from his full potential. And ultimately he promises Darth Vader the freedom to become a tyrant like his new master.

Plato argues that a tyrant must purge his state of enemies to consolidate his power.[12] The Emperor begins his purgation through Order 66, instilled in the ever-obedient clone army, by declaring the Jedi traitors to the Republic. Later, he declares himself sole head of the Galactic Empire when he dissolves the Senate in *A New Hope*. The newly completed Death Star has given him enough power to use fear to keep everyone in line.

Socrates's and Thrasymachus's different perspectives about justice allow Plato to examine the injustice of tyrants. Sidious and Vader follow the trajectory he lays out: both are initially proclaimed heroes of democracy yet end up being democracy's downfall. The Sith, as tyrants, occupy the other end of the spectrum from the Jedi, the guardians of justice. Perhaps, though, there are more similarities than appear at first glance.

Guardians of Their Galaxy

Whereas the Sith crave to be rulers, the Jedi are content to be guardians of their galaxy. According to Plato, this is why the Sith are unjust tyrants and why the Jedi would make the best rulers. Plato's vision of what the best rulers should be like includes envisioning them as both the best philosophers and the bravest warriors – *guardians*.[13] True rulers care only for their subjects; they're servants who sacrifice themselves for the sake of the city. In order to serve, they must be able to defend against the enemies of the state, both inside and outside.

A guardian must be swift, strong, brave, and full of spirit (*thumos*).[14] He must be dangerous to his enemies yet gentle to his friends.[15] Guardians must be the greatest and most courageous heroes on the battlefield. All of these qualities are required of the Jedi, who can both serve as wise mediators and also fight bravely when needed: "aggressive negotiations" – that is, negotiations with a lightsaber, as Anakin tells Padmé in *Attack of the Clones* – are often required when attempting to restore peace and justice.

Though the guardians must be adept at warfare, they must also be able to blend their courage with *temperance*.[16] Courage is bold action in the face of danger, and temperance is proper self-control. Guardians should not be quick to laugh, which may seem strange at first, but their task is a serious and solemn one.[17] The Jedi, though they may have a sense of humor, are usually business-first types of heroes. Guardians must be able to obey superiors and be in control of their desires and emotions.[18] They must deny themselves possessions, says Socrates, so that they aren't perverted by greed – just as the Jedi give up attachments, even family, in order to serve the Order and the Republic.[19]

Guardians must also be reluctant to rule, ruling not out of a desire to wield power but out of a sense of duty to serve.[20] Mace Windu is reluctant to have the Jedi Council take control of the Republic if Chancellor Palpatine refuses to give up his emergency powers after General Grievous is defeated. The Jedi see it as necessary, but not ideal. The Sith, on the other hand, see this as a power grab: the Jedi must want power, because in their minds everyone wants power. As Palpatine lectures Anakin, "All who gain power are afraid to lose it, even the Jedi."

Plato stresses the importance of guardians as *true philosophers* dedicated to the freedom of the state.[21] Hence, knowledge trumps mere martial ability. True philosophers are truthful, temperate, selfless, gentle, just, with a keen memory, quick to learn, noble, gracious, and virtuous.[22] Quite the list: just how rare would these guardians be?

Socrates distinguishes between those who will be the rare blend of philosophy and spirit and those who are defined more by their strength of spirit than by their talent for philosophy. Those select few who excel in philosophy would be elevated to rulers, and the rest would be their subordinates and be in charge of protecting the state: *auxiliaries*.[23] The rulers would also exemplify *true love*, which is attached to the highest good, love of beauty and harmony.[24] Anakin explains to Padmé that the Jedi are not forbidden to love, but rather, "compassion, which I would define as unconditional love, is central to a Jedi's life." Attachment and possessions are forbidden for the Jedi, however. Although it's Darth Sidious who tempts Anakin to the dark side through the power it can have over death, it's Anakin's attachment to Padmé that makes the temptation possible. Plato, too, denies his guardians strong exclusive relationships, yet he did allow male and female guardians to enter into partnerships of a sort.

After looking at Plato's views on failed democracy, unjust tyrants, and just guardians, we've come to Socrates's definition of justice. We have justice in the state when each individual is put to the use for which nature intended him, or when one attends to one's own duties.[25] When all citizens are content with their station in life, performing their own tasks well and not interfering with the tasks of the other classes, there will be harmony and unity, justice will reign, and the state will be happy. This is in sharp contrast to Sidious's tyrannical declaration, "Once more the Sith will rule the galaxy, and we shall have peace."

But Socrates is less interested in justice in the state than in the *soul*. Indeed, all talk about politics in the state has been in order to find it in the soul.[26] Everything written about the state must be taken metaphorically. Hence, justice in the state mirrors justice in the soul, where each part of the soul acts in its proper, natural way. Plato divides the soul into three levels: the rational aspect is above the spirited part, which is above the appetitive part – just as the guardians are above the auxiliaries, who are above the rest of the citizens.[27] Plato's point is that the happiest person will be the one whose soul is in harmonious order: when reason rules the spirit and the appetite, the soul is just, and this person will act justly. True happiness is a type of flourishing that does not require material wealth. Rather, true happiness is tied to justice, which is wrapped up with wisdom, goodness, and beauty.[28]

Plato's ideal state is clearly unattainable in this world, as Socrates almost admits in the end. Nor does it seem desirable from our perspective since it goes against most things entailed by the ideals of human rights, equality, and freedom.[29] Why do the rulers have the authority to decide who does what? What if the rulers were to tell me that it's in my nature to be a merchant or a producer, for example, but I hate selling or producing things and I desperately want to be a philosopher? The rulers are fallible, too, which Plato admits. People want to choose for themselves, and this seems to be a good thing. If they don't have the potential to achieve their goal, they'll find out soon enough, but they should be welcome to try. Furthermore, despite what Plato might say, greed, envy, and pride will probably always be in conflict with imposed order.

Plato says some things that are a product of his time but cause discomfort today. Though Socrates claims that marriage will be held sacred, he proposes that the rulers will play matchmakers to put the best specimens together and encourage them to have children.[30] Socrates and his companions developed a method for encouraging the guardians to breed with each other, thus preventing the "lesser stock" from having children. Under "a throng of lies and deceptions," the rulers should make it look like chance was responsible, and not themselves.[31] The children would then be grouped together and raised by nurses (those who by nature are best suited to take care of the young).[32] Similarly, the Jedi identify young children who are strong in the Force at an early age (so early that, by age nine, Anakin is already too old), take them from their families, and raise them with other younglings in the Jedi Temple.

Jedi and Present-Day Guardians

As we have seen, the Jedi are on the side of justice, so long as we understand justice to mean "to treat each as it ought to be treated." Treating each as it ought to be treated means doing the right thing, and in order to do the right thing you first need to know what the right thing to do is. Yoda teaches Luke Skywalker that he'll be able to know the good from the bad when he is "calm, at peace, passive. A Jedi uses the Force for knowledge and defense, never for attack." When Palpatine and Anakin discuss the difference between the Jedi and the Sith, Anakin defends the Jedi by saying that "the Jedi use their power for good." Before his training is completed on Dagobah, Luke wants to leave to help his friends. Yoda and Obi-Wan don't want Luke to leave even though his friends are in trouble – not because they don't care about his friends, but because his training is more important. Luke needs more knowledge of the light side of the Force to protect him from the temptations to tyrannical power proffered by Darth Vader and the Emperor: "If you end your training now," Yoda warns, "If you choose the quick and easy path, as Vader did, you will become an agent of evil."

If the good is something we can have some understanding of, then Anakin, Yoda, and Plato are most likely right. The Jedi are selfless servants who sacrifice their lives for the safety and well-being of others, and that seems to be a pretty good thing. Platonic guardians and Jedi alike, therefore, should be the most virtuous of all people – they must exemplify the four cardinal virtues of courage, temperance, wisdom, and justice. Their rational nature should control their feelings and desires: reason looks up at the sun (Plato's metaphor for the highest good), while feelings such as anger, fear, and aggression blind them to the truth and lead to the dark side.[33] The best rulers will be the best Jedi who pursue goodness, justice, and wisdom while also being courageous and noble fighters. The Jedi Council are very close to the picture painted by Plato of the ideal guardian-philosophers – the only thing lacking is their power to rule. They are servants of the Republic, which Plato would see as absolutely essential for any guardians, but they also take orders from weak and corruptible Republic politicians.

Lightsaber-Wielding Philosophers

Plato's views in the *Republic* mirror the different types of rule in the *Star Wars* galaxy surprisingly well: democracy is vulnerable, tyrants only care about their own interests, and guardians of peace and justice are the state's best chance for flourishing. While democracy fails, allowing the Emperor to become a malevolent tyrant, the Jedi Council is cut off in its service to the Republic. Perhaps if the Jedi Council had

had more power in ruling while still serving the people, then the Sith would've had a harder time establishing themselves.

The conclusion that Socrates reached is that the public tyrant is the most miserable person imaginable, but the guardian – the philosopher who rules by serving – will be the happiest.[34] The happiness of the individual and the happiness of state and society are linked. If Plato was right that a society denying goodness and truth runs the risk of losing sight of the most important things, then happiness is at stake for all of us.

If Plato *was* right, does this mean that democracy is doomed to failure? That seems unlikely, but the warning is relevant. Democracy triumphs over tyranny at the end of *Return of the Jedi*. We'll have to wait and see what the consequences of this are in Episodes VII through IX. Will Luke Skywalker erect a new Jedi Order with a Jedi Council that pursues true philosophy and holds more power? One thing is almost certain: the Jedi of the New Republic will still be the guardians of peace and justice. As long as justice is pursued and the importance of truth is maintained, there is a new hope for the future. Truth is a beacon, an ally of the light side, but it can also be endangered. The dark side can cloak the truth in shadows, clouding it from sight.

Notes

1. Plato, *The Republic of Plato*, trans. Allen Bloom, 2nd ed. (New York: Basic Books, 1991), 565d, 244.
2. Ibid., 562d–563b, 241.
3. Ibid., 575d, 256.
4. Ibid., 565c, 244.
5. Ibid., 566d, 245.
6. Ibid., 565e–566a, 244–5.
7. For an analysis of Jar Jar Binks's moral culpability for his part in the Republic's downfall, see Nicolas Michaud's chapter in this volume (chapter 8).
8. Plato, *Republic*, 343d, 21.
9. Ibid.
10. Ibid., 576a, 256.
11. Ibid., 494c, 174.
12. Ibid., 567c, 246.
13. Ibid., 543a, 221.

14. Ibid., 375a, 52.
15. Ibid., 375c, 52.
16. Ibid., 389d, 67.
17. Ibid., 388e, 66.
18. Ibid., 388e, 67.
19. Ibid., 390d, 68.
20. Ibid., 342e, 20–21.
21. Ibid., 376b–c, 53; 395b–c, 73–4.
22. Ibid., 485c–487a, 164–7.
23. Ibid., 414b, 93.
24. Ibid., 403a, 82.
25. Ibid., 423d, 101; 433a, 111.
26. Ibid., 368e–369a, 45.
27. Ibid., 441c–e, 121; 443c–e, 123.
28. Ibid., 443e, 123; 473d, 153; 508d–509b, 189.
29. Ibid., 592b, 275.
30. Ibid., 458e, 137; 459e–460a, 139.
31. Ibid., 459c, 138; 460a, 139.
32. Ibid., 460c, 139.
33. Ibid., 508d–509b, 189.
34. Ibid., 576e, 257; 578b, 259.

Episode IV
A NEW HERMENEUTIC

14

Pregnant Padmé and Slave Leia: *Star Wars'* Female Role Models

Cole Bowman

The *Star Wars* universe is dynamic, thrilling, and inspired. It is space opera in its truest sense, combining an intricate web of political maneuvering, space battles, romantic subtext, and the occasional duel to the death with lightsabers. But there's an imbalance in the Force, and it's not the one that concerns the Jedi. There's an imbalance of gender roles in everyone's favorite space saga, with the vast majority of characters played by males while the female parts are minimized at nearly every turn. But the underlying problem of womanhood in *Star Wars* might be even more insidious than Darth Sidious himself. It can be tough to be a woman in any universe, but perhaps it's especially so in a galaxy far, far away, where the only obvious female role models are a princess and a queen both intimately related to the dark lord trying to rule them all.

So, why is it difficult to embrace a strong female identity anywhere, let alone in the midst of intergalactic war? Women are expected to fulfill many disparate roles during their lives, so it's little surprise that there's a conflict raging within many women about who they're supposed to be in the absence of strong role models to emulate. Do any of the women in *Star Wars* have what it takes to bring *feminism* to the Force?

The Ultimate Star Wars and Philosophy: You Must Unlearn What You Have Learned, First Edition. Edited by Jason T. Eberl and Kevin S. Decker.

"I Am Not a Committee!"

While Princess Leia and Queen Amidala are instantly recognizable figures in popular culture, the questions persist: do they represent women positively? Are they strong feminists or damsels in disguise? Can they inspire people in the same way that the men of the films can?

What does it mean to be a strong female role model? Depending on whom you ask, the criteria can be very different, all predicated on distinct views of what it actually means to *be* a woman. It's thus extremely difficult to articulate what it means to be a "strong woman" in nearly any *human* context, let alone in a galaxy with such diversity of species and races that droids and Wookiees can have a celebration alongside humans and Ewoks. Because of this, female role models presented in the media are often left critically unexamined. They're simply accepted as "good enough" if they are at all different than the stereotypical depiction of women within our own culture. For the most part, though, such "good enough" images of femininity really aren't representative of true strength for feminists.

What does it mean to be a *strong* woman? It's much the same as being a strong man, but with different body parts. The vast majority of feminist philosophers would agree with this standpoint, to varying degrees. It's important, then, to understand what *feminism* means. Feminism is *not* an institution that aims to denigrate men and assert a dominant female paradigm. Instead, feminism is an institution that insists upon an equal footing for both sexes, whether in Toronto or on Tatooine: "Feminism is the radical idea that women are people."[1]

There are many voices striving for equality of the sexes, which have codified into branches with their own specific approach. *Radical feminists* argue that a "strong woman" eschews all of the stereotypes that have been placed upon women by a long history of patriarchy. *Ecofeminists* take this idea further by pointing to the intersection between oppression of women and the environment as a means of empowerment. *Liberal feminists* call for an absolute equality between the genders on all levels, whereas *cultural feminists* find strength in the differences between the genders. Each of these perspectives is valid, but there's no *überfrau*, no "superwoman," they could all agree on to embody their *ideal* strong woman.

Therein lies one problem of trying to depict any sort of honest female role model: no single woman can represent all of what it means to be a woman, no matter how strong she is. You can't, by definition, be both a strong example of motherhood and a strong example of a woman who chooses not to have children. This is the first place where *Star Wars* falls short. While Leia is awesome, she can't represent every aspect of a woman's experience. She's just one laser-shooting rebel space princess. How can we expect her to be the whole package of feminist strengths?

"The Force Is Strong with This One"

What we want from female characters is the same as what we want from male characters: to be dynamic and interesting, as well as to display growth in response to challenges. In the six *Star Wars* movies, there are only a limited number of women who even have a *chance* at meeting these ideals. Can we consider them strong women?

In the original trilogy, there's only one major female character: Princess Leia Organa, a member of the Alderaanian royal family and a leader in the Rebel Alliance. She is without a doubt a powerful role model for young women. Unfortunately, besides Leia, Aunt Beru has the largest female role in the original trilogy, and she's killed about a quarter way through *Episode IV*. Thankfully, though, Leia is as dynamic as you can get, challenging the men she encounters at every turn by outshooting, outmaneuvering, and outquipping them – telling Grand Moff Tarkin to his face, "I recognized your foul stench when I was brought on board." The entire original trilogy hinges on her, since she incites much of the action in the first place. Leia's ambition is literally spelled out in the opening crawl: "Pursued by the Empire's sinister agents, Princess Leia races home aboard her starship, custodian of the stolen plans that can save her people and restore freedom to the galaxy." Everything else that happens starts with Leia's bravery and is carried through by her tenacity. *Leia is a strong woman.*

In the prequel trilogy, there are more women in the foreground, including Shmi Skywalker and several female Jedi. This generation of films, however, fails in much the same way the original trilogy does in representing women. Queen Padmé Amidala of Naboo is the only truly significant female role. In fact, she's the *only woman* with a speaking role at all in *Episode III* – unless you count the deleted scenes featuring Mon Mothma.

Like Leia, Padmé is a key figure in the action of the prequel trilogy. From the very beginning, she's shown to be quick-witted and resilient. In order to save her people, she fights bravely against the Trade Federation. During the Clone Wars, it's *her* political and military savvy that gives the good guys the edge they desperately needed. Along with Mon Mothma, she challenges the growing power of Chancellor Palpatine with the Delegation of 2000, which leads to the formation of the Rebel Alliance. It's easy to see where her daughter, Leia, might have gotten some of her own strength.

While Leia and Padmé are typically recognized as the feminist icons of *Star Wars*, they're not all the films have to offer. Queen Amidala's young handmaidens – Sabé, Cordé, and Dormé – provide us with fine examples of strong women. Chosen for their close resemblance to Padmé, they act as handmaidens and decoys for the queen from a young age. They trained with Padmé extensively in order to imitate her correctly in the event they should be needed to stand in for the queen. They were also trained as warriors able to defend the queen if necessary. They are fluent in several languages, and despite the stress that undoubtedly comes from their position impersonating the queen, they act effectively in Amidala's stead even during tense encounters.

While these women are undoubtedly influential in the story, it's important to note the criticism they've received as representatives of women in *Star Wars*. Each has been supposedly typecast in a different way, opening up the criticism that they act in ways that stereotype women as a whole. Each has been placed into a position that shows the specific mechanisms of oppression against women that feminists have fought to dismantle. What turns heroines to stereotypes so quickly?

"Aren't You a Little Short for a Stormtrooper?"

If there were a Jedi Order of feminism, Simone de Beauvoir (1908–1986) would undoubtedly be on the Council. As a cornerstone of feminist philosophy, Beauvoir's influential book, *The Second Sex*, predicted many of the issues that fueled what's called *Second Wave feminism*.[2] These issues include a frank look at sexual and reproductive rights for women, women's relationship to religion, their access to education, and many others. Beauvoir focuses on how women have been relegated into specifically oppressive roles throughout history, such as motherhood and sexual objectification. These roles have been rarified into stereotypical "places" for women to occupy as a result of patriarchy. What might Beauvoir have to say about the way Padmé and Leia relate to these roles?

While Padmé is a powerful political leader and a dynamic woman, the acme of her role in the prequel trilogy comes with the birth of her twin children. The plot is even framed around a climactic buildup for that very moment, and so her importance in the film can be seen as being reduced to the births. While it's important for the entire story arc that the two were born in that way, it's easy to be left wondering what happened to the brilliant Padmé introduced in *The Phantom Menace*. Does Padmé's pregnancy relegate her to being a stereotype?

Not by a long shot. Motherhood is not an impediment to feminism. It's true that motherhood has been seen in this way by a number of feminist thinkers, such as radical feminist Andrea Dworkin, who contends that "[women being] trained to be mothers from infancy on means that we are all trained to devote our lives to men."[3] That is, by becoming a mother, Padmé has automatically cast herself into a role of oppression, according to this view.

While this criticism has some teeth in the feminist dialogue, its use against Padmé involves an unfounded failure in judgment. The stereotypical, oppressive role that a woman must fulfill in becoming a mother, as described by Dworkin, has no basis when it comes to the former queen of Naboo. The criticism of motherhood as Padmé's primary role is based on a distorted vision of what she's accomplished up to that point.

The fact that Padmé Amidala is Luke and Leia's mother doesn't make her a stereotypical caricature of femininity. At the conclusion of *The Second Sex*, Beauvoir ruminates on an ideal future in which "motherhood would be freely chosen," as it is in Padmé's case. Just like anything else that she's accomplished, being a mother is a *part* of her story, not the whole of it. She's still the woman who fought against the Trade Federation and called for a vote of "no confidence" in Chancellor Valorum in the Galactic Senate.

The most important feminist issue raised by Leia's presence in the original trilogy is *sexuality*. While a social perspective on sex and sexual identity is integral to feminist dialogue, its real power is what it wields over an individual. An individual's place within the sexual spectrum, and therefore their place in relation to everyone else, other sexual identities, and social institutions, becomes a characteristic part of what makes them *who they are*. Sexuality, however, has been used as an oppressive tool for centuries. When Leia is held captive in Jabba the Hutt's court, wearing the infamous gold bikini, she becomes a representative of the power of female sexuality. Because her outfit also involves a neck-chain attached to a crime boss, her situation is blatantly oppressive. Does this render Leia merely a token of sexual objectification?

Certainly not! Even when chained to Jabba, Leia exerts *command* over her sexuality. While both Han and Jabba – in quite different ways – attempt to gain control over Leia's sexuality, she accepts neither of them. She *intentionally* got herself into Jabba's company to help Han. Once captured, she uses her sexuality to exploit the situation, placing herself in a position to kill Jabba with her own chain at the opportune moment. In *The Empire Strikes Back*, Leia asserts her sexuality when she kisses Luke in front of Han as a means of subverting Han's claim over her:

HAN: [with a smug smile] You didn't see us alone in the south passage. She expressed her true feelings for me.

LEIA: [just before kissing Luke] Well I guess you don't know everything about women yet.

By keeping command of this aspect of her life – though it's only one part of her experience – Leia retains strength despite the challenges she faces. Of course, Leia eventually gives into Han's charms, but she does so on *her* terms.

This brings up another stereotype that seems to plague Leia: the lovelorn damsel as shown through her devotion to Han. While the spice-running scoundrel might not be everyone's idea of a suitable mate, he is the Princess's – and that's all that really matters. Similarly, one of the major complaints about Padmé is the nature of her relationship with Anakin. While it's necessary for them to be together sexually to produce the twins, their relationship isn't the highest exemplar of a functioning marriage. Both of them even recognize at the outset of their courtship that a secret marriage "would destroy us." But should the fact that Padmé is married be a defining criticism of her character? Can Leia be in love and still be a strong woman?

For an answer, we can turn back to Beauvoir, an unabashed proponent of female sexuality, who yet provides an interesting insight on love:

> On the day when it will be possible for woman to love not in her weakness but in her strength, not to escape herself but to find herself, not to abase herself but to assert herself – on that day love will become for her, as for man, a source of life and not of mortal danger.[4]

Anakin's dependence on Padmé isn't a source of abuse for him on the dark side of the force, so why should the inverse be true? When Han brazenly attempts to rescue Leia, his place as a masculine hero is never brought into question. Just the same, the love these women have is a source of strength for them, not weakness. The fact that Leia goes out of her way to rescue Han from Jabba is one of Leia's defining feminist functions: in a dramatic turn of events, the princess saves the rogue! She thus singlehandedly turns the "damsel in distress" dynamic on its head. Her mother shows similar strength when facing execution in the Geonosian arena. Chained with Padmé and Obi-Wan to huge posts as vicious beasts slowly approach, Anakin displays his misplaced chivalrous chauvinism:

OBI-WAN: Just relax, concentrate.
ANAKIN: What about Padmé?
OBI-WAN: She seems to be on top of things.

Not needing two Jedi warriors to rescue her, Padmé had freed herself from her chains and climbed to the top of the post, ready to battle the razor-clawed nexu coming for her.

"You Have Your Moments – Not Many of Them – but You Do Have Them"

Betty Friedan, a cornerstone of Second Wave feminism, famously states in her book, *The Feminine Mystique*: "You can have it all, just not all at the same time."[5] Friedan intends this exhortation for individual women, assuring them that there are various stages to their lives' fulfillment. This idea also summarizes the real problem with women in *Star Wars*. When any figure is presented as strong, they can be easily torn open by some sort of ill-placed criticism: Leia is too sexualized, Padmé is just a vessel of motherhood, and Shmi Skywalker doesn't fight Watto to go with Anakin. The problem is that, as Friedan suggests, we can't "have it all" with any of these women. Yet, we keep trying to find that *perfect* feminist role model in the media.

Since Leia is the only major female character within the original trilogy, her decisions can be seen as representative depictions of women overall. Moreover, anything she does unwisely or poorly – like blowing up Jabba's sail barge with innocent slaves still inside – *sends a message about all women*. If there were greater representation of women, however, there wouldn't be a problem with evaluating Leia as an individual character versus Leia as a representative of women overall. Even Mon Mothma's wisdom isn't enough to take the focus away from Leia in the original trilogy because her part is relatively miniscule.[6]

Let's consider a reversal of this situation for some context. Imagine that all the characters in everyone's favorite space opera are female except one: Han Solo. Luke Skywalker becomes Lucy Skywalker, Lando Calrissian becomes Lindsay Calrissian, and Darth Vader is Dorothy Vader. Everything about the plot and interactions between the characters remains the same, except for how Han is able to relate to the universe around him. Rather than being one example of many men, he now typifies a kind of "male essence" in the story. Anything he does is the sole exemplar of male behavior. So, when Han shoots Greedo (now Gretta), it makes all men look impulsive and violent. When Han tells Leia she could "use a good kiss," *all* men look oppressively chauvinistic.

Every one of the women in *Star Wars* has her own flaws, but that's part of what makes them such good feminists. If any of them were "perfect," they would appear both above the need for relationships with the other characters and impractical as objects of the audience's interest. If any of them were the "whole package" of feminist ideals, they'd be unrealistic and unrepresentative of any sort of real experience of womanhood. So while it's reasonable that women should be able to "have it all," this won't be attainable by any single person at any single time. Ultimately, *Star Wars* gives us a handful of excellent leaders who are strong women. But they are relegated to the fringes of their own society, and they are simply too few in number to represent accurately women as a whole.

Furthermore, the women of *Star Wars* are actually extremely marginalized. It just happens that the women who do get our attention occupy the kind of margin we can look at and say, "Well that's not so bad, is it? She gets to be a queen!" But the fact that Padmé and Leia are important political figures appears to be the only reason that they are even *able* to have a say in anything that happens. Other than royalty, how many speaking roles do women have in the six movies? In the original trilogy, there are only six women who speak. Period. Leia, a princess, constitutes *one-sixth* of the speaking roles for women in these movies. In the prequels, there are fourteen other than Padmé Amidala. While that number still isn't great, it's certainly better.

But the important issue is that Leia and Padmé are allowed to speak more than anyone else because of their *position*. Both of them are verbally clever and are frequently quoted by fans. I'd bet that when Leia or Padmé are mentioned, your mind recalls such classics as "Aren't you a little short for a stormtrooper?" and "So this is how liberty dies, with thunderous applause." Now call to mind one of Shmi's lines. How about Aunt Beru's? There's a good chance you can't, which is fair, because you're not really meant to. You're really only supposed to pay attention to these "important" women in the male protagonists' lives. In this way, Padmé and Leia have become yet another stereotype – *the affluent few*. They are both royalty and are, therefore, inherently important regardless of their gender. They're separated from the rest of women because of their position, causing another schism in the sisterhood of the Force.

As a result, Padmé and Leia are put in the position of being mouthpieces for womankind, despite there being several degrees of separation between their social situation and the rest of the women populating the *Star Wars* galaxy. Leia and Padmé can't accurately voice the needs of different species and classes, considering the alienation from everyday life they experience as high-ranking members of the social echelon – even when traveling with Anakin in disguise "as refugees," Padmé wears fine clothing with an elaborate headdress while Anakin lugs around two large suitcases that presumably aren't filled with dozens of his Jedi robes. But these individual women shouldn't have to bear the burden of representing all women.

Most of the other women in the *Star Wars* saga, despite their potential to be strong women themselves, are never given a chance to express their strength. Aunt Beru raises Luke to become a hero. Shmi deftly maneuvered her life as not only a single mother but also a *slave* on remote Tatooine. Mon Mothma not only was a senator, but also openly defied Emperor Palpatine and eventually became the first Chief of State of the New Republic and a mentor to Leia. Were any of these women allowed more than a few lines, undoubtedly we'd truly see their strength. Were they given a voice, they would be feminist role models.

But, as always, there is hope. Let's not forget about our courageous handmaidens, Sabé, Cordé, and Dormé. Unlike Padmé and Leia, they present dynamic figures without relying on the trappings of royalty and influence. Yes, they sometimes dress as the queen and act in her stead, but they have no actual authority. Yet, they're still featured as women worth looking up to. They're resilient and clever. They fearlessly stand in for the Queen of Naboo, and Cordé even gives her life in the other woman's stead. These handmaidens stand as silent but ready sentinels while Padmé holds court on Naboo, reaching out of the margins and bridging the gap between the royal women of *Star Wars* and others who might someday speak.

The problem for any strong woman, no matter who she is or when she lives, is the social situation in which she makes her life. Caitlin Moran writes of this struggle:

> For throughout history, you can read the stories of women who – against all the odds – got being a woman right, but ended up being compromised, unhappy, hobbled or ruined, because all around them, society was still wrong. Show a girl a pioneering hero – Sylvia Plath, Dorothy Parker, Frida Kahlo, Cleopatra, Boudicca, Joan of Arc – and you also, more often than not, show a girl a woman who was eventually crushed.[7]

Context matters. No matter how wonderful a feminist figure is, her effectiveness and legacy can be sustained only if the society around her allows this to happen. Leia can only be a true heroine of our story if audiences accept her as one. Padmé can only lead us to the light

PREGNANT PADMÉ AND SLAVE LEIA 171

side if we follow her. Sabé, Cordé, and Dormé can give voice to the marginalized women of the galaxy only if we listen.

The women of *Star Wars* are tough-as-nails and aren't afraid to show it, if they're given a chance. Taken individually, they offer just as much as any of the individual male characters. They're strong, witty, and certainly a "Force" to be reckoned with. But their numbers are few, and they dwell on the margins of society. Perhaps the next great battle in that galaxy so far, far away will be that of the women, fighting their way to equality behind a tactician queen, a warrior princess, and a resourceful handmaiden.

Notes

1. Marie Shear, "Review of *A Feminist Dictionary*," *New Directions for Women* (May–June 1986): 6.
2. Modern feminism is typically divided into three distinct "waves," which each pertained to certain issues of women's liberation. First Wave feminism took place between the late nineteenth and early twentieth centuries and was concerned mostly with a woman's right to vote. Second Wave feminism came later, predominantly during the 1960s. This was succeeded by Third Wave feminism, which began in the 1990s; its major focuses included discussions of feminist intersectionality, queer theory, sex positivity, and reproductive rights.
3. Andrea Dworkin, *Our Blood* (New York: Perigee, 1981), 58.
4. Simone de Beauvoir, *The Second Sex* (New York: Vintage Books, 1989), 708.
5. Betty Friedan, *The Feminine Mystique* (New York: Norton, 1963), 36.
6. While *Return of the Jedi* is 134 minutes long, Mon Mothma's speech lasts for only 39 seconds.
7. Caitlin Moran, *How to Be a Woman* (New York: Harper Perennial, 2011), 10.

15

Docile Bodies and a Viscous Force: Fear of the Flesh in *Return of the Jedi*

Jennifer L. McMahon

Through its characters and the epic challenges they face, the *Star Wars* saga contributes to a variety of serious and long-standing philosophical discussions. It offers insights on personal identity, the tension between free will and determinism, and the nature of good and evil. Though other chapters in this book deal with these grand topics, this chapter addresses a very specific one: how a single scene in the saga serves to reflect a popular and problematic contemporary view about people. The scene in question occurs in *Return of the Jedi* when Jabba the Hutt holds Princess Leia captive in his court on Tatooine. Using the philosophy of Susan Bordo, Jean-Paul Sartre, and Michel Foucault, we'll see that Leia's captivity scene reflects modern society's hatred of fat and its preoccupation with the control of bodies, particularly the female body.

"Me Chaade su Goodie"

Throughout human history, stories have not only entertained audiences but also reflected and reinforced societal values, often unconsciously. Stories present us with ideal characters who we might seek to emulate, and these characters help establish standards regarding what should be valued, including standards involving gender. This is no less true for George Lucas's *Star Wars* saga than it was for Homer's

The Ultimate Star Wars and Philosophy: You Must Unlearn What You Have Learned, First Edition. Edited by Jason T. Eberl and Kevin S. Decker.
© 2016 John Wiley & Sons, Ltd. Published 2016 by John Wiley & Sons, Ltd.

Odyssey. When one thinks about *Star Wars*, iconic male characters immediately spring to mind: Luke Skywalker, Obi-Wan Kenobi, Han Solo, and Darth Vader. But when it comes to characters that epitomize femininity, there's but one in the original trilogy: Princess Leia Organa.[1]

To be sure, Leia is present in many memorable scenes in the original trilogy. There's the scene in *A New Hope* where Luke, like a space-traveling Tarzan, swings her to safety from a legion of stormtroopers. Likewise, in a moving scene in *The Empire Strikes Back*, she declares her love to Han Solo before he's encased in carbonite. However, for most viewers, no sequence is more memorable than Leia's captivity in *Return of the Jedi*. Here, the despot Jabba the Hutt holds a scantily clad Leia prisoner. Though the scene is short, its effect is significant, due primarily to the visual structure of the scene. The sequence opens shortly after Leia has infiltrated Jabba's palace in an effort to free Han. After her attempt fails, he's thrown into a cell while Leia is cast into a different form of captivity. Transfigured from liberator to captive, Leia is shown nearly naked, wearing nothing but a gold bikini and stout metal collar. Jabba holds Leia by this collar with a thick chain, forcing her to recline in front of him, at times pulling her tightly against his belly while he strokes her, a luscious prize subject to the rapacious appetite of her captor.

When compared with Leia's other scenes, the difference is striking. Though many scenes in the saga highlight Leia's beauty, none foreground her body so explicitly. Leia is typically dressed in pants or long skirts, or adopts male dress for purposes of battle or disguise. Even scenes that obviously highlight Leia's physical femininity focus on specific features, such as her carefully styled hair, instead of wholesale emphasis on her figure. By contrast, Leia's captivity scene puts her body on display. The focal point is her *form*, not her *function*, which creates a disturbing subtext. Captivity scenes, a staple in the Western literary tradition, are consciously or unconsciously "structured ... in specific ways to give shape and meaning to the captivity."[2] Though the scene serves a story purpose, its images speak volumes about our contemporary fear of fat and cultural preoccupation with being thin.

Two characters dominate this scene: Jabba and Leia. Jabba is a personification of fat and modern Western culture's negative perception of fat. Because he isn't easily recognizable as a certain type of being (e.g., a dog or human), he doesn't appear as something or some*one* that is fat, but as an embodiment of fat *in itself*. He's an amorphous colossus of flesh who suffers a sort of inertia by virtue of his titanic mass. He has only two vestigial arms that pale in size to his voluminous core – their apparent purpose is simply to procure more for him to eat, and he's almost always eating. Hapless creatures are regularly stuffed, still squirming, into his cavernous mouth. Indeed, Jabba's wide mouth is an apt symbol of his voracious appetite; it dominates his face and is made more threatening by the slimy tongue that slithers regularly from it. When Leia is first captured, Jabba has her brought close to him while he snakes his tongue out toward her; the novelization of *Return of the Jedi* offers this grotesque description: "Foul beast that he was, Jabba poked his fat, dripping tongue out to the princess, and slopped a beastly kiss squarely on her mouth."[3] Jabba's colossal figure, gravelly voice, frequent belching, and the ever-present spittle coating his lips, combine to offer a damning portrait of *appetite*, inviting revulsion on the part of the audience. Gross in both literal and figurative senses, Jabba is a formidable threat in the saga's narrative. As a personification of fat, he also represents what many people, particularly women, dread, struggle against, and are bound to by fear.

Leia is the visual contrary to Jabba. Though captivity scenes traditionally focus on torture and bodily denigration, this scene instead celebrates the body, or at least a certain type of body. As the camera pans across Leia's reclining figure, she is reminiscent of a classical depiction of Venus and other representations of ideal femininity, such as nudes by artist Peter Paul Rubens, save for the volume of flesh present.[4] In contrast to Jabba, Leia is supremely lithe. Whereas his flesh appears clotted and gelatinous, her skin is tight and her muscles are clearly defined and smooth. Leia is thin and toned, without a trace of cellulite or excess fold of skin. Whereas Jabba personifies fat, Leia epitomizes the contemporary ideal of the thin body. She is beauty; he is beast.

Other elements in the scene reinforce the visual vilification, or disparagement, of fat and the idolization of being thin. Like Jabba himself, two other beasts connected to Leia's captivity are gross personifications of what's generally assumed to be the cause of fat: uncontrolled desire. The rancor that Luke battles is a ravenous, huge-mouthed, many-toothed monster. The rancor's defeat by Luke's Jedi ingenuity depicts a triumph of mind over matter. Then we meet the Sarlaac, a creature that also personifies insatiable hunger. Depicted as a cavernous mouth gaping open in the desert – with or without its digitally added beak – the Sarlaac is a subterranean worm that digests its victims for over a thousand years and punctuates each feeding with a decisive belch. Once again, Luke uses his Jedi wits to escape consumption. Like Jabba, these creatures are visual contraries to Leia and negative symbols of appetite.

In contrast with Jabba and his uncontrolled appetite, Leia operates as a model of control – more specifically, as a model of the disciplined body. Leia illustrates what follows from "chaining the body," particularly food intake through the throat. Reading the image of her thin body as a kind of text in code, her ideal form is shown to be the consequence of constraining desire. Initially mastered by appetite, in a Hegelian reversal, she turns the tables on Jabba, choking him with the chain linked to her collar. She becomes flesh's master rather than its slave. She finds her freedom by fighting (and killing) fat.

"Oh, I Can't Bear to Watch!"

Susan Bordo has analyzed the contemporary vilification of fat and the recent cultural fascination with an exaggerated ideal of thinness. Identifying herself as a "philosopher of the body," Bordo attributes criticism of fat to our culture's "heritage of disdain for the body," a disdain that stems from our historical tendency to elevate the mind over the body. Bordo cites Plato's mind–body dualism, reinforced by René Descartes (1596–1650), as the root of our "pathological" fascination with the thin body. Furthermore, she argues our "desperate fixation on our bodies" is disproportionately oriented toward the *female* body by virtue of our cultural tendency to associate femininity more closely with embodiment. This emphasis on controlling and subjugating the body, particularly the female body, has produced an unrealistic and unhealthy ideal of feminine beauty, one that gets "thinner and thinner," "tyrannizes" women, invites the emergence of eating disorders, and "limits female possibilities" by encouraging women to be focused on the achievement of an "elusive" and unsustainable body type.[5]

The "anorexic aesthetic" that Bordo describes persists today.[6] The radical ideal of thinness she critiques is clearly one that Princess Leia epitomizes and reinforces. The visual celebration of thinness evident in Leia's captivity scene creates and bolsters normative standards for feminine beauty because "the rules for femininity have come to be culturally transmitted more and more through the deployment of standardized visual images," and the more popular and pervasive the image, the more force it exerts. Whether male or female, we're indoctrinated to *social norms*, and increasingly those norms are conveyed through images in the media, which "tell us what clothes, body shape, facial expression, movements, and environment [are] required" for us to be socially acceptable.[7] The unrealistic ideal of feminine beauty that dominates our visual culture not only threatens women's health and self-esteem, but also affects attitudes toward and opportunities for women, and shapes expectations for peoples' bodies generally. Bordo laments that "emaciated" figures are in vogue, and as a result many now "dread becoming fat" more than anything else.[8] "It is a dreadful irony," Bordo states, "that at a time when women are occupying more social space than ever before, [they] should be relentlessly, obsessively striving to contract the amount of physical space [they] take up."[9]

Bordo's work is anchored in French philosopher Michel Foucault's (1926–1984) account of "docile bodies."[10] Docile bodies are modified from their natural condition and assumed to be improved through discipline and "constraint." Docile bodies are desirable because they're more compliant and "manipulable." While it's fair to say that controlling the body is of interest to individuals, Foucault's focus isn't an individual's *personal control* of her body, but the degree to which our bodies are controlled by *impersonal forces* that seek various sociopolitical ends. The production of docile bodies stabilizes and promotes *hegemony* – that is, existing power structures, whether political or ideological. Furthermore, docile bodies, rendered susceptible to outside manipulation, become so habituated to their regime of control that they *regulate themselves* after initial indoctrination. They're bodies that, once mastered, master themselves.

As many feminist theorists like Bordo have noted, controlling the female body helps sustain patriarchal privilege. But the reason for controlling bodies generally, or for pursuing an ideal of thinness, requires further explanation than Foucault provides. Here we have to turn to

Foucault's predecessor, French existentialist Jean-Paul Sartre (1905–1980), whose work helps explain the preoccupation with controlling the body and the vilification of fat in Leia's captivity scene.

A "Slimy Piece of Worm-Ridden Filth"

According to Sartre, existence has two fundamental aspects: "being-in-itself" (matter) and "being-for-itself" (consciousness). He emphasizes that while these aspects of existence can be distinguished from one another for analysis, they're ultimately bound to one another. In particular, humans are a combination of being-in-itself and being-for-itself. We are *conscious bodies*, composites of matter and mind. Whereas Descartes conceived of mind as a fundamentally different substance than body – immaterial and able to exist on its own – Sartre emphasizes that consciousness occurs in, and is wholly dependent on, the body. Though Sartre asserts that consciousness *feels* itself separate from the body and the world, it can never be liberated from either one: "the body is presented as being the condition of existence for consciousness."[11] Sartre states that the body is that "first ... original, [and] concrete relation" without which I "would not be at all." Most importantly, the body "is the in-itself made manifest."[12] This is certainly a different attitude from Yoda's dualistic exhortation that "luminous beings are we, not this crude matter" as he pinches Luke's shoulder.

Sartre explains that, though dependent upon material conditions, consciousness itself isn't material. Instead, it represents the potential for *reflective awareness* of material existence that emerges within certain types of material beings – most notably, humans. A human being's reflective consciousness makes *self-determination* possible by virtue of the ability to apprehend one's bodily experience from a critical distance, affording the opportunity to choose how to engage in a situation rather than having one's behavior determined by instinct or emotion.

For all its benefits, though, consciousness is *alienated* from its body and situation; in coming to understand material existence from a critical distance, consciousness doesn't always like what it finds. As Sartre's character Roquentin discovers in the novel *Nausea*, being-in-itself appears as anything but innocuous. At the root of a chestnut tree, Roquentin sees material existence in its raw *formlessness*. Examining the otherwise innocuous root, Roquentin experiences a frightening epiphany:

> Existence has suddenly revealed itself. It had lost the harmless look of an abstract category: it was the very paste of things ... the diversity of things, their individuality, were only an appearance, a veneer. This veneer had melted, leaving soft, monstrous, masses ... all in disorder, a frightful obscene nakedness.[13]

Roquentin's fear extends to his perception of his own body because it too is material in nature. In a mirror, he recognizes "nothing of [his] face," seeing rather something without any definitive features, akin to a "jellyfish."[14] As these passages indicate, consciousness compels us to recognize that the order and qualities we think we find in reality are not intrinsic to it, but fabricated by consciousness. Beneath all the determinations we place on existence, determinations that give life order and meaning, being-in-itself lurks in its gross undifferentiated form, a form the colossus Jabba personifies.

One bodily quality Sartre focuses upon is "the slimy" (or viscous), which repels consciousness because it bears the primal stamp of being-in-itself. The slimy is symbolic of being-in-itself in its raw "nude" form and "in flaunting abundance."[15] When consciousness apprehends being in its primal state, it is *terrified*, because the slimy reminds consciousness of its fundamental fragility and finitude. Sliminess reminds consciousness that disorder lurks beneath everything, and that, at death, it will be "swallowed up by the In-itself."[16] Roquentin faces life stripped of the appearance of intrinsic order and value, and proclaims, "Existence is what I'm afraid of ... I hated this ignoble mess. Mounting up ... high as the sky, spilling over, filling everything with its gelatinous slither ... I choked with rage at this gross, absurd being."[17] Huge, gross, and gelatinous? It sounds almost like Jabba.

Consciousness's concern over the slimy readily transfers into a fear of the flesh in general and a desire to regulate the body. Sartre maintains that consciousness has a deeply ambivalent relation to the flesh upon which it depends. Simply put, consciousness fears *engulfment* by the flesh. The *Star Wars* saga capitalizes on this fear for dramatic effect – when Leia appears to be engulfed by Jabba's belly as he pulls her against his massive frame, when Luke is momentarily engulfed by the rancor's giant claw as he's pulled toward its yawning mouth, and when Boba Fett is literally engulfed by the cavernous Sarlaac. Flesh takes on an essentially "insipid" and "nauseous character."[18] As an analogue of being-in-itself, the physical body becomes a predictable target of disgust and thereby an object of conscious regulation. We seek to regulate the body because it's the source of some of our deepest anxieties: we're acutely aware that consciousness loses itself to the body in sleep, it slips away in cases of extreme pain or cold, and it's forever lost upon physical death.

Consciousness gives us the power to apprehend being-in-itself, but not the power to escape our *dependency* on it. The fundamental dependency and immaterial nature of consciousness lead Sartre to characterize it as "thin." By contrast, he describes being-in-itself as effectively *fat* by virtue of its ubiquity and fullness. Consciousness's "basic fear of engulfing Being"[19] predisposes it to be averse to that which is abundant and without obvious use or form, as these things call to mind being in its primal state. Here we have a potential explanation for the perennial cultural anxiety over the body and efforts to control it, as well as the tendency to vilify fat and celebrate the thin body. Whereas excess flesh or fat is suggestive of the slow and surreptitious conquest of consciousness by being, the thin body is indicative of consciousness's victory over the body. Leia captivates audiences partly because she epitomizes this victory.

"Soon You Will Learn to Appreciate Me"

Sartre helps us appreciate why consciousness fears engulfment by the flesh. Like Sartre, Bordo suggests that the evident "dread" of fat and "relentless pursuit of slenderness" are less about gender bias than about "general anxieties about the body ... and physical vulnerabilities."[20] Regardless of gender, people are inevitably concerned about the fragility of their existence, as well as their unavoidable susceptibility to illness, decay, and death – all based upon our physical embodiment. Deep inside our consciousness lies the desire to be "something other than flesh."[21] But beyond this, the "specter of 'fat' ... codes [this] generation's anxieties about the body."[22] "Fat ... is the enemy" because it represents everything that is difficult to get a handle on, resists control, and threatens to overwhelm the individual.

In some circumstances, this fear of existence is directed toward the body, sometimes the female body, but there's no need to focus exclusively on the feminine. The problem isn't the female body, but material existence generally.

Bordo focuses on our contemporary obsession with being thin because she wants to encourage resistance to it. Though regulating the body does help us "feel autonomous and free," when that regulation harnesses the individual to "an obsessive body practice" then it "limits … possibilities."[23] Bordo promotes resistance to the prevailing standard of thinness by drawing attention to the damaging influence of widely disseminated images like that of Leia in her infamous "gold bikini."[24] Sadly, Leia's bondage represents the plight of many contemporary women, particularly subjugation to fear of the flesh, while Leia herself represents an unrealistic ideal of feminine beauty.

Fear of the flesh and a desire to control bodies, however, are not restricted to women. They're expressive of a deeper anxiety regarding embodiment that has been culturally conferred upon women more than men due to our cultural association of women with the body. While Leia's captivity scene focuses mostly on the despot Jabba, in reality the scene empowers a more oppressive master in the form of *Leia*. Leia helps chain women to an insidious and tyrannical ideal of feminine beauty, demanding that they be unrealistically and unsustainably thin. This is just as problematic and pernicious as our cultural vilification of fat. Showcasing Leia's supremely slender form reinforces our prevailing, yet deeply problematic, ideal of feminine beauty, as well as our tendency to vilify fat. As Sartre explains, however, physical being isn't bad; we depend on our bodies. Hence, we need to suspend our fear of the flesh and instead take responsibility for our fears and the unrealizable wishes they produce. We need to embrace *life* in all its forms – as the Force does – rather than yoking ourselves to ideals that impoverish our experience.

Notes

1. For more details on what Leia's singular female influence means for the role of women in *Star Wars*, see Cole Bowman's chapter in this volume (chapter 14).

2. Gary Ebersole, *Captured by Texts: Puritan and Postmodern Images of Indian Captivity* (Charlottesville: University of Virginia Press, 1995), 9.

3. James Kahn, *Star Wars: Return of the Jedi* (New York: Del Rey, 1983), 26.

4. If the term *Rubenesque* refers to one who is sumptuous and fleshy, then the only Rubenesque figure in the frame is Leia's dark double: Jabba.

5. See Susan Bordo, "Docile Bodies, Rebellious Bodies: Foucauldian Perspectives on Female Psychopathology," in *Writing the Politics of Difference*, ed. Hugh Silverman (Albany: State University of New York Press, 1991), 204–13.

6. Susan Bordo, *Twilight Zones: The Hidden Life of Cultural Images from Plato to O. J.* (Berkeley: University of California Press, 1997), 58.

7. Bordo, "Docile Bodies, Rebellious Bodies," 207.

8. Susan Bordo, "Anorexia Nervosa: Psychopathology as the Crystallization of Culture," *The Philosophical Forum* 17, no. 2 (1985–6): 79.

9. Bordo, "Docile Bodies, Rebellious Bodies," 203.

10. Michel Foucault, *Discipline and Punish: The Birth of the Prison*, trans. Alan Sheridan (New York: Vintage International, 1995), 135.

11. Christine Daigle, "Where Influence Fails: Embodiment in Beauvoir and Sartre," in *Beauvoir and Sartre: The Riddle of Influence*, ed. Christine Daigle and Jacob Golomb (Bloomington: Indiana University Press, 2009), 35.

12. Jean-Paul Sartre, *Being and Nothingness*, trans. Hazel Barnes (New York: Washington Square Press, 1956), 405, 407.

13. Jean-Paul Sartre, *Nausea*, trans. Lloyd Alexander (New York: New Directions, 1964), 127.

14. Ibid., 16–17.

15. Ibid., 134, 128. Whereas consciousness is fragile and "nothing substantial" (17), being-in-itself is "dense" (773), "full" (29), and "*massif*" (28). Being-in-itself is undifferentiated totality that lacks necessity and is therefore fundamentally "superfluous (*de trop*)" (29).

16. Ibid., 777.

17. Sartre, *Nausea*, 134.

18. Sartre, *Being and Nothingness*, 444, 509.

19. Naomi Greene, "Sartre, Sexuality, and the Second Sex," *Philosophy and Literature* 4:2 (1980): 200.

20. Bordo, "Anorexia Nervosa," 111.

21. Bordo, *Twilight Zones*, 107.

22. Susan Bordo, "Reading the Slender Body," in *Body/Politics: Women and the Discourses of Science*, ed. Mary Jacobus, Evelyn Fox Keller, and Sally Shuttleworth (New York: Routledge, 1990), 89, 83.

23. Bordo, "Docile Bodies, Rebellious Bodies," 213.

24. For a satirical commentary on the pervasiveness of this image of the feminine among sci-fi/fantasy fans, which also makes the argument of this chapter for other genre franchises, check out this cosplay PSA: http://youtu.be/t4m6CrBUvWw (accessed November 2, 2014).

16

Of Battle Droids and Zillo Beasts: Moral Status in the *Star Wars* Galaxy

James M. Okapal

During the Clone Wars, an uncounted number of planets were invaded, ecosystems ravaged, and humans, nonhumans, and droids killed, destroyed, or deactivated. Some may think that the decisions leading to these results weren't necessarily *moral* decisions, but merely tactical or strategic decisions, following from an assumption that some of these things aren't worthy of moral consideration. Are entire ecosystems morally considerable? If not, then there'd be nothing morally wrong with Grand Moff Tarkin using an uninhabited planet to demonstrate the Death Star's effectiveness instead of Alderaan. But what about nonhuman creatures that may live on that "uninhabited" planet? Would it be okay for Tarkin to destroy a planet full of banthas and dewbacks? This question can arise because, throughout the *Star Wars* saga, we see nonhuman species with different levels of status: some have representation in the Galactic Senate, such as Wookiees and Mon Calamari; others aren't active in galactic politics, but nevertheless are accorded a degree of respect, such as Jawas, Tusken Raiders, and Ewoks; and still others are seen as property, pets, or pests, such as droids, aiwha, banthas, and mynocks. We must wonder: how are these distinctions made? And why are they important in determining which actions are morally acceptable?

These distinctions, in part, concern whether the creatures involved have *moral status*. As ethicist Rosalind Hursthouse notes, the *concept*

The Ultimate Star Wars and Philosophy: You Must Unlearn What You Have Learned,
First Edition. Edited by Jason T. Eberl and Kevin S. Decker.
© 2016 John Wiley & Sons, Ltd. Published 2016 by John Wiley & Sons, Ltd.

of moral status "is supposed to divide everything into two classes: things that have moral status and are within 'the circle of moral concern' and things that do not, which are outside the circle."[1] *Theories* about moral status can help us answer a variety of questions about events that occur throughout the *Star Wars* saga, like the following: is it morally acceptable for Han Solo to casually kill a mynock chewing on the *Millennium Falcon*'s power cables? Does it make a *moral* difference whether Han shot first in his final encounter with Greedo the Rodian? Is it morally acceptable for Anakin Skywalker to permanently deactivate battle droids? And what about the Zillo Beast? Is it more like a mynock whose death is barely noticed or more like Greedo whose death is a source of controversy?

"Where Are You Taking This … *Thing*?"

So how do we know what counts as merely a "thing" in the *Star Wars* galaxy? The philosopher Benjamin Hale provides a useful starting point when he distinguishes the terms "moral considerability," "moral relevance," and "moral significance."[2] If something is *morally considerable*, then we should include it in our moral deliberations, since it isn't a mere thing. If something isn't morally considerable, then we shouldn't include it in our moral deliberations. Suppose that what determines moral considerability is having a humanoid appearance and being biological and bipedal. Given this, humans such as Han Solo are morally considerable, as well as Wookiees like Chewbacca. A species can be morally considerable even when its physical features include additions such as headtails. So Twi'leks, or Togrutas like Ahsoka Tano, would be morally considerable. On this definition of moral considerability, however, neither mynocks nor Hutts would be morally considerable since they're not bipedal, nor would destroyer droids, since they aren't even biological organisms. Although humanoid robots like battle droids and C-3PO and cyborgs such as General Grievous or Darth Vader present difficult cases, once those cases are resolved, we should be able to determine whether the creature in question is morally considerable or not, full stop.

Unlike moral considerability, the concept of *moral significance* comes in degrees and becomes relevant when measuring the amount of importance assigned to an entity's moral rights or preferences if these competing moral claims can't all be fully satisfied. Assume that the Zillo Beast is morally considerable. In the relevant *Clone Wars* episodes, the main issue is whether to kill it, contain it, or relocate it. If the Zillo Beast is morally considerable, there's a presumption against killing it because one of the two most basic rights of any morally considerable being is not to be killed and not to be enslaved. But these rights are only *presumptions*. "The Zillo Beast Strikes Back," a *Clone Wars* episode that aired in 2010, takes place on the densely populated Coruscant, where the population consists of morally considerable individuals who had no say in the transfer and experimentation being done on the beast. Killing the Zillo Beast is justified by this calculation: the combined lives of the bystanders have more moral significance than the life of a single, rampaging Zillo Beast.

Finally, *moral relevance* identifies the properties a creature must have in order to be morally considerable; it also determines the creature's degree of moral significance. Consider our previous example of humanoids: the properties that are essential to being "humanoid" suggest whether a creature is morally considerable or not. Suppose we define being "humanoid" as being a biological organism *with appendages radiating from a torso*. This means that R2-D2 and other droids not shaped like a human can't be morally considerable. Jabba the Hutt, though, *will* count as morally considerable – his two tiny arms may not do much other than pick up squirming and squealing reptiles to eat, but they do radiate from his torso. Furthermore, the number, length, or degree of function of the appendages could be used to identify an entity's level of moral significance. Jabba, with only two short, almost useless, appendages, might be less morally significant than Han Solo, who has two legs and two arms, all of which are longer and more useful than Jabba's arms. Focusing on these properties will also change the moral significance of Chewbacca. Due to the arboreal nature of Wookiees and their incredible strength, which allows Chewbacca to rip a droid's arm from its socket, Chewbacca has longer, stronger, and more useful arms than Han and so would have comparatively greater moral significance. But it seems strange to say that a creature's moral significance depends on whether he can reach the blasters on the top shelf of the armory or not. So, what creature features might be better indictors of moral relevance?

"We Cannot Allow the Destruction of an Innocent Life Form"

Theories of moral relevance, understood in terms of the properties a creature must have to be morally valuable, fall into two important categories: those that focus on *physical* properties and those that focus on *psychological* properties.[3]

Two popular views on moral relevance that focus on the physical are the *biological* and the *genetic* views. The biological view says that what's *alive* is what deserves moral considerability and significance. One version of a biological view is Albert Schweitzer's idea that we should have a "reverence for life." According to Schweitzer, "[A]ll life is valuable and we [humanity] are united to all of this life."[4] Based on the interconnectedness of life, he defines *good* acts as consisting in "maintaining, assisting and enhancing life," while *evil* acts tend to "destroy, to harm or to hinder life."[5] For Schweitzer, if something is alive, then it's morally considerable.

The Jedi would appear to share this view. Obi-Wan Kenobi describes the Force as "an energy field created by all living things. It surrounds us, and penetrates us; it binds the galaxy together." Mace Windu, in the *Clone Wars* episode "The Zillo Beast," notes that it goes against Jedi principles to kill innocent life forms. Schweitzer's "reverence for life" view would also explain why Jedi don't think too much about droids. Droids are not biological entities, so they're not alive and not morally considerable. When all the battle droids are permanently deactivated at the end of the Clone Wars, this action is not similar to genocide or to wiping out an ecosystem. It is neither moral nor immoral.

A problem here is that the focus on life doesn't include a theory of moral significance, which leads to some odd conclusions. If all life is *equally* valuable, then any act that would harm or destroy an organism would be forbidden to the Jedi. As an organism, though, a Jedi must eat other living things, even if it's only plants. But if all living things are equally valuable, then eating pan-fried zucchini is no better or worse than eating Han-fried Greedo. So, while life might be a basis for moral considerability, it can't be the only property in a theory of moral relevance because it's not clear how it could be a basis for moral significance.

The genetic view of moral relevance focuses on a creature's *genome*. Suppose that all humans, Wookiees, and other mammalian, humanoid species in the *Star Wars* galaxy have a similar genetic makeup. Similarity to the human genome could possibly be the physical property that determines moral considerability and significance – although maybe it's the Wookiee genome that's the foundation of moral status. Suppose mammalian species like Twi'leks or Togrutas have only minor differences in their genomes – thus their headtails and skin color. These species would be *almost* as significant as humans – perhaps to the degree that, for all practical and political purposes, they are treated equally. Rodians, on the other hand, are reptilian in nature, suggesting that their genome differs significantly from that of humans. This would make them less morally significant, and so there'd be no moral qualms about Han shooting first. Zillo Beasts would be even less significant, and battle droids, lacking genetic material altogether, would have no moral significance or considerability.

Of course, genetic views of moral status can lead to a morally suspect xenophobia – (the unreasonable hatred or fear of the strange or foreign) or human chauvinism (the unjustified and zealous favoring of humans over other species). Emperor Palpatine – the representation of pure evil in the *Star Wars* saga – believed humans were superior to all other species; it was thus a remarkable challenge for the Chiss Mitth'raw'nuruodo to rise through the Imperial ranks to become Grand Admiral Thrawn.[6] A related problem is that each species would tend to use its own genome as the baseline for a theory of moral relevance, whether Hutts, Rodians, or humans. In order to avoid relativism, a genetic view needs to show why any one particular species should be favored, while also showing it doesn't just rely on idiosyncratic physical properties of that species. This would show, however, that physical properties aren't really the basis of moral relevance and that we ought to look to *psychological* properties.

"Besides Being the Last of Its Kind, This Creature May Be Intelligent"

Two psychological theories are based on *sentience* or *agency*. A focus on sentience says that the capacity to experience pleasure and pain, and enjoyment and suffering, is the key to moral relevance. If an entity has the capacity for these feelings, then it's morally considerable: as philosopher of animal rights Peter Singer says, "If a being suffers, there can be no moral justification for not taking that suffering into consideration."[7] But it's a mistake to think that all beings that can experience pleasure or pain are equally morally significant. As John Stuart Mill (1773–1836) pointed out, there are different types of pleasure and enjoyment as well as pain and suffering related to levels of complexity and to the ability to perceive that complexity.[8] Humans and their mammalian pets can experience the pleasure of eating popcorn drenched in a hydrogenous solution masquerading as "butter" in a movie theater, but humans can also experience "higher" pleasures. They're able, for example, to enjoy John Williams's epic musical score when an Imperial Star Destroyer first appears overhead on the big screen in the opening of A New Hope – all while enjoying the "butter"-drenched popcorn. Different capacities for enjoyment and suffering can be the basis for different levels of moral significance: if Luke Skywalker is capable of more kinds of complex enjoyments and sufferings than a rancor, then, when conflicts arise between the interests of Luke and those of a rancor, Luke's interests would outweigh the rancor's. To resolve the conflict, it would be okay morally for Luke to drop the door on the rancor's head in Jabba's Palace, although maybe the tears of the rancor's keeper should be taken into account as well.[9]

Sentience views run into problems, however. One problem is that it seems to cast the net of moral considerability too wide. While the set of morally considerable things is far smaller than a "reverence for life" view would have it, a sentience-based view would question the permissibility of eating meat, experimenting on animals, and using animals for clothing or transportation. If the Republic had really granted moral considerability and significance to all sentient beings, the Star Wars galaxy would have been very different. So, it appears that battle droids suffer. After all, they express desires to avoid jobs that will lead to their destruction. C-3PO whiningly makes statements like "We seem to be made to suffer. It's our lot in life." And R2-D2 lets out an electronic "scream" when spit out by the creature in the Dagobah swamp, and also when shot by a stormtrooper while trying to open the Imperial bunker on Endor. If droids really can suffer, then it seems that arbitrarily shutting them down, selling them to

Tatooine moisture farmers, or otherwise using them as tools should cease.

There would be similar implications for many other creatures in the *Star Wars* galaxy. Given the availability of technological means of transport, a sentience-based view would say that it'd be morally unacceptable to use banthas, dewbacks, or aiwha for transportation. Furthermore, to experiment on the Zillo Beast to learn the secrets of its impenetrable armor would be wrong. In "The Zillo Beast Strikes Back," Dr. Sionver Boll raises moral concerns about Chancellor Palpatine's command to conduct deadly experiments on the Zillo Beast because it appears to be intelligent. Palpatine isn't moved by this reasoning, insisting that the Zillo Beast is just an animal, a savage beast, and thereby not morally considerable.

In overriding Dr. Boll's challenge, Palpatine might be adopting an *agency*-based view of moral considerability and significance.[10] There are two types of agency: *mere* agency and *moral* agency.[11] Mere agency is the capacity to act on purposes, to be able to make plans and act on them. In other words, it's the ability to have and successfully achieve goals. In order to have agency, a creature needs to have *interests*, to be able to conceive of a future in which those interests might be fulfilled or frustrated, and so think of the *means* to bring about fulfillment. Despite Palpatine's doubts, the Zillo Beast may qualify for moral considerability on the mere agency view. It seems, for example, to understand that Palpatine is a threat to its existence. Once the Zillo Beast escapes, it appears to seek out Palpatine to kill him. First, it attacks a video screen broadcasting a message from Palpatine. Then it goes to the Galactic Senate to find Palpatine, attacking his escape transport in the process. This suggests that the Zillo Beast possesses mere agency: it has goals and makes choices in an attempt to achieve those goals, which would make it morally considerable.

Droids, however, don't seem to have this kind of agency. In Barbara Hambly's novel *Children of the Jedi*, Nichos Mar is a Jedi initiate who died of a disease and whose lover had his memories and personality downloaded into a droid. Throughout the story, the limitations of now being a droid are explored, and it's concluded that Nichos the droid isn't identical to Nichos the human. As Nichos the droid puts it, "A droid cannot go against his basic programming, or restraints placed on his programming if they do not conflict with the deepest level of motivational limiters."[12] Nichos the droid realizes that he lacks the *autonomy* of Nichos the human. While his former lover was being tortured, tried, and set for execution, Nichos the droid "would have done anything to help her. Except that, since I was programmed not to interfere with them, it was literally something I could not do."[13] In other words, droids, even droids with a transplanted human consciousness, are not even mere agents, let alone moral agents.[14]

Palpatine himself appears to be a mere agent when he lies, cheats, kills, and even creates and manages both sides of a galactic civil war in order to achieve his interests. But we often expect more out of political leaders. It isn't enough that they be mere agents and pursue their goals by any means available; they should also be *moral* agents. The best-known view of moral agency is based on Immanuel Kant's (1724–1804) idea of *autonomy* (derived from the Greek words *auto*, "self," and *nomos*, or "law"). Being autonomous means being able to control your behavior in accordance with laws or rules. The way Kant sees it, we use our moral autonomy when we discover universally applicable rules and then modify our behavior accordingly. If Palpatine were a moral agent, we would expect him to have some qualms about the immoral choices he makes to bring about his rise to power. As it is, however, he seems not to care one way or another about the death and destruction he causes in becoming emperor. This lack of concern could be seen as his failure to grant moral considerability to anyone in the galaxy. This attitude – that nothing in the galaxy should get moral considerability – suggests a lack of moral agency: if Palpatine sees everything and everyone as a mere tool, then he is a sociopathic agent for whom moral questions never arise. An alternative interpretation would be that Palpatine is just a *bad* moral agent – he recognizes that other creatures are morally considerable, but chooses not to follow any rules about how to treat them. Which interpretation we choose will affect whether we agree with Mace Windu that "he's too dangerous to be left alive."

Unlike sentience-based views that may include *too many* things in our moral deliberations, agency-based views seem to include *too few*. So, for example, cognitively impaired humans and animals would not be morally considerable on this view because they often lack even mere agency.[15] While it would be wrong for Jabba the Hutt to kill, enslave, or torture a normal adult Twi'lek, a moral agency view suggests that it's perfectly okay to do any of these things to Twi'leks who suffer from severe mental disorders: there's no difference between feeding a mentally disabled Twi'lek to a Sarlacc and dropping a bunch of cabbages into the Pit of Carkoon.

"I Applaud Your Moral Stance, Doctor. Principle Is in Short Supply"

We've only begun examining the numerous moral status issues that emerge in the *Star Wars* galaxy, as they do in our own. In particular, the story of the Zillo Beast confronts us with questions about moral considerability, significance, and relevance. There are many more related questions, however, that we don't have the space and time to consider here and now. What about the moral status of clones? Are they somehow less morally significant than nonclones? After all, they were apparently unable to refuse to obey the orders of the leaders of the Grand Army of the Republic, especially Order 66. Do defective clones like Clone 99 have less moral significance because of their deficiencies? What about Darth Vader, General Grievous, or the resurrected Darth Maul? As "more machine now than man," are they still morally considerable given that droids appear to be outside the circle of moral concern? All of these questions are interesting, but you, Padawan, will have to explore them yourself.[16]

Notes

1. Rosalind Hursthouse, "Virtue Ethics and the Treatment of Animals," in *The Oxford Handbook of Animal Ethics*, ed. Tom L. Beauchamp and R. G. Frey (New York: Oxford University Press, 2011), 120.
2. Benjamin Hale, "Moral Considerability: Deontological, Not Metaphysical," *Ethics & the Environment* 16, no. 2 (2011): 37–61.
3. For a different, and more in-depth, discussion of the topic of moral status, see Mary Anne Warren, *Moral Status: Obligations to Persons and Other Living Things* (New York: Oxford University Press, 2000). Views she discusses that are not included in this chapter because of space are ecological relation views and caring views of moral relevance.
4. Charles R. Joy, *Albert Schweitzer: An Anthology* (Boston: Beacon Press, 1967), 248.
5. Ibid., 259–60.

6. Timothy Zahn, *Star Wars: Heir to the Empire* (New York: Bantam Books, 1992).

7. Peter Singer, "All Animals Are Equal," in *Animal Rights and Human Obligations*, ed. Tom Regan and Peter Singer (Englewood Cliffs, NJ: Prentice Hall, 1989), 78–9. See also his *Animal Liberation*, rev. ed. (New York: Harper Collins, 2002).

8. John Stuart Mill, *Utilitarianism, on Liberty, Essay on Bentham*, ed. Mary Warnock (New York: Penguin Books, 1962), 260–2.

9. David Schmidtz, in his "Are All Species Equal?" *Journal of Applied Philosophy* 15, no. 1 (1998): 57–67, uses the term *vulnerability* to refer to this difference in complexity and how it justifies giving preference to humans over other species.

10. For one agency-based view of moral considerability, see Tom Regan, *The Case for Animal Rights* (Los Angeles: University of California Press, 1983).

11. For an in-depth discussion on the different types of agency, as well as the category of moral patiency, see Evelyn Pluhar, "Moral Agents and Moral Patients," *Between the Species* 4 (1988): 32–45.

12. Barbara Hambly, *Star Wars: Children of the Jedi* (New York: Bantam Books, 1995), 272.

13. Ibid., 271.

14. For further discussion of the moral status of droids, see Dan Burkett's chapter in this volume (chapter 20); Robert Arp, "'If Droids Could Think ... ': Droid as Slaves," in *Star Wars and Philosophy*, ed. Kevin S. Decker and Jason T. Eberl (Chicago: Open Court, 2005), 120–31; and David J. Gunkel, *The Machine Question: Critical Perspectives on AI, Robots, and Ethics* (Cambridge, MA: MIT Press, 2012).

15. For a discussion of someone who believes animals have not just mere agency but also moral agency, see Mark Rowlands, "Animals That Act for Moral Reasons," in *The Oxford Handbook of Animal Ethics*, 519–46.

16. I'm grateful to Jason Eberl, Kevin Decker, and William Irwin for the copious comments and corrections made to earlier drafts of this chapter. I would also like to thank Trish Donaher, Heather Urbanski, Leah Foster, and Tim Madigan for their help and encouragement in writing this chapter and in exploring philosophy through popular culture.

Episode V

METAPHYSICS STRIKES BACK

17

Why the Force Must Have a Dark Side

George A. Dunn

"May the Force be with you" is a standard blessing and parting phrase exchanged by members of the Jedi Order and others in the *Star Wars* universe, much like the traditional *dominus vobiscum*, "The Lord be with you," of ancient and medieval Christendom. Yet if there really is, as a skeptical Hans Solo puts it, "one all-powerful Force controlling everything," then you're going to have it with you, like it or not. "Its energy surrounds us and binds us," says Yoda, describing the Force as an active and creative power. As a power that "binds," the Force is what organizes the energy that produces living creatures, permitting us to exist as distinct but interrelated individuals. It is, according to Obi-Wan Kenobi, the immanent creative power that "binds the galaxy together." Yet Yoda also describes the Force as that into which we "transform" when we die, implying that the energy of the Force is also the very "stuff" of which the universe is made. The ubiquitous Force is at once the creator of every finite entity *and* the medium in which it creates. What the poet Epimenides said of Zeus, the supreme being of the ancient Greek world, also seems to apply to the Force: it is the element in which "we live and move and have our being."[1] Just try having the Force *not* be with you!

There's a word for this metaphysical worldview. It's called *panentheism*, formed from the Greek words for "all" (πᾶν/pân), "in" (ἐν/en), and "god" (θεός/theós) – "everything is in God."[2] Everything

The Ultimate Star Wars and Philosophy: You Must Unlearn What You Have Learned, First Edition. Edited by Jason T. Eberl and Kevin S. Decker.
© 2016 John Wiley & Sons, Ltd. Published 2016 by John Wiley & Sons, Ltd.

is encompassed within one overarching, divine reality, which has been variously named in religious traditions – Brahman (in India), 道 (Dào) (in China), God (in the West), and the Force (in a galaxy far, far way). The *Star Wars* saga is often interpreted as a modern update of the ancient panentheistic worldview, translated into a crowd-pleasing pop culture vernacular. It's an appealing worldview that emphasizes the essential connectedness of all things, but in thinking through its implications we encounter a difficulty. The Force is said to have a "will" that communicates itself to the Jedi in various ways, including through the midi-chlorians that Qui-Gon Jinn says "constantly speak to us, telling us the will of the Force." The Jedi feel confident that they can't go wrong trusting in the "will of the Force." But wait a minute. If the Force contains everything, must it not also contain evil? How can we make sense of the *dark side* of the Force?

Evil Sure Seems Pretty Damn Real Here on Alderaan

The *Star Wars* saga is an epic tale of good versus evil, light versus dark, freedom versus tyranny, Jedi versus Sith, with the mysterious "will of the Force" rallying the armies of light in their war against the armies of darkness. The evil opposing the "will of the Force" is something real, and – if the power-hungry Emperor Palpatine and the cruel Darth Vader are any measure – it's a formidable force in its own right. The idea of combining a ubiquitous Force, allied with the good, with belief in a great cosmic battle between good and evil is the germ from which the *Star Wars* saga grew, according to George Lucas:

> The Force evolved out of various developments of character and plot. I wanted a concept of religion based on the premise that there is a God and there is good and evil … I believe in God and I believe in right and wrong.[3]

There's nothing unusual about wanting to combine belief in God with belief in the reality of evil. Indeed, for many religious believers, they fit together like an evil right hand snugly ensconced in the glove of Darth Vader.[4] Yet, it's no mean task to reconcile a robust conception of evil – evil as a genuine power in the world – with the panentheistic conception of a good God or Force that encompasses and infuses everything.

If the Force is the vital energy that animates everything, if everything ultimately emerges out of the Force, then everything that happens, whether for good or evil, would seem to be attributable to the Force. But if the same Force is present in both weal and woe, goodwill and malice, then our judgments of good and evil seem to be the product of a one-sided perspective that reflects nothing more than our all-too-human preferences. "Good is a point of view," Chancellor Palpatine tells Anakin, and perhaps he's right. To the Force, it's all the same. In short, a serious commitment to panentheism seems to dissolve the distinction between good and evil as thoroughly and relentlessly as the Mustafar's lava melts flesh. According to Indian philosopher Swami Prabhavananda (1893–1976), "If we say, 'I am good,' or 'I am bad,' we are only talking the language of maya [the world of illusion]."[5] We need to transcend the illusory standpoint that takes the opposition of good and evil as real – though one suspects the Swami might whistle a different tune were a Death Star suddenly to appear in orbit above his home planet.

"Here Goes Nothing"

An alternative to dismissing the distinction between good and evil as illusory is to treat only *one* of them as unreal. Evil, on this view, isn't something that actually exists in its own right. It's simply the absence of good, a lack rather than a tangible presence. When that Death Star blasts Alderaan into oblivion, the evil consists in the sudden loss of a lot of goodness: the cultural treasures of the people of Alderaan – except for the invaluable moss painting *Killik Twilight*[6] – the natural beauty of the planet; and the lives of countless sentient beings. When Obi-Wan reports feeling "a great disturbance in the Force, as if millions of voices suddenly cried out in terror and were suddenly silenced," he isn't reacting to some evil the Force is doing. Rather, he's sensing something the Force is suffering: an eruption of absence, similar to the pain and trauma you'd experience if your hand were suddenly severed by the swift stroke of a lightsaber. The evil isn't something that *is*, but rather the nothingness where a hand or a planet should be. Understanding evil as an *absence* allows us to reconcile our "one all-powerful Force" encompassing everything with the opposition between good and evil, reinterpreted as the opposition between the all-embracing Force and the gaping holes of nothingness that puncture the Force and tear open its fabric like the horrible maw of a Sarlaac erupting from the Great Pit of Carkoon.[7] When something evil comes our way, our response should be the same as Lando Calrissian's commentary on the Battle of Endor: "Here goes nothing."

Known as the *privation* theory of evil, this view is closely associated with the Christian philosopher Augustine of Hippo (354–430). It's a matter of controversy whether Augustine should be called a panentheist, but he did equate God with Being-in-Itself, the most complete and fulsome expression of existence, as well as with the Good-in-Itself, the epitome of every form of perfection. On this view, *being* and *goodness* are correlates of each other, so that everything else that exists has a share of goodness simply by existing. In fact, the more "being" you have, the better you are. But how can one thing have more being than another? And what does more being have to do with being better? Augustine believes that a thing's being and its goodness both have a common root in the presence of "measure, order, and form." Consider one particular form of goodness, the phenomenon of *beauty*, and one particular instance of beauty, the lovely Padmé Amidala. Her loveliness results from the stunning effect produced by her *form* and by the *ordering* of her body's parts in a *measured* or properly proportioned way (her nose not too big, her neck not too short, and so on). Were her figure and features to become drastically deformed – so that she came to resemble Jabba the Hutt – her beauty would be greatly diminished. And if she were to lose *all* measure, order, and form, she'd simply cease to *exist* as a human being.

Or consider the *Millennium Falcon* – not as aesthetically pleasing as the lovely Padmé, but extraordinarily good in its own way. It may initially look like "a piece of junk," but if it were literally just a heap of haphazardly arranged and oddly shaped machine parts, it'd never get off the ground. Not only wouldn't it be a very good space freighter – it wouldn't be a space freighter at all! "She may not look like much, but she's got it where it counts," says Han, adding, "I've made a lot of special modifications myself." Needless to say, those modifications have to do with measure, order, and form, improving the arrangement of parts to maximize their functionality.

Finally, consider the moral virtue of Yoda. Like the *Millennium Falcon*, he may not be pretty, but to the extent that he's virtuous he possesses an inner beauty, which many classical philosophers would argue consists in the order he's imposed on his passions. By contrast, the savage immoderation of Anakin's passions – their lack of measure – turns him into a villain.[8] As Augustine puts it:

> Where these three things [measure, order, and form] are present in a high degree there are great goods. Where they are present in a low degree there are small goods. And where they are absent there is no good. Moreover, where these things are present in a high degree there are things great by nature. Where they are present in a low degree there are things small by nature. Where they are absent, there is no natural thing at all.[9]

Diminish a thing's measure, order, and form, and you diminish its goodness. Subtract *all* measure, order, and form, and you're left with *nothing*.

"I've Got a Very Bad Feeling about This"

The privation theory of evil offers a way to reconcile the goodness of the all-encompassing Force with the reality of evil. The Force, binding both galaxies and living beings together, is the source of the measure, order, and form that make things good. Of course, not everything is equally good, and some things are just plain bad – like Darth Maul's rage and Jar Jar Binks's voice – but that's not because the Force itself is evil. Rather, it's because the Force is not as powerfully present at all times and places. This theory comes with solid credentials and boasts an impressive pedigree in Western philosophy,[10] but it may not be entirely adequate to explain evil in the *Star Wars* universe. To begin, it's not clear how nothingness or absence can find a foothold within the cosmology espoused by Yoda, which resembles a certain outlook associated with the Chinese philosophy of Daoism.

The story is told of how the Chinese philosopher Zhuangzi (c. 369–286 BCE) was visited by his friend Huizi after the philosopher's wife died. Huizi was shocked to find his friend, who he expected to be grieving over his wife, occupied with drumming and singing. Zhuangzi, like Yoda, was known to exhibit an impish, playful streak, but his scandalized friend complained that to indulge in this sort of merriment on a day of mourning was going too far. Zhuangzi, however, offered an explanation for his unconventional behavior:

> I peered back into her beginnings; there was a time before there was a life. Not only was there no life, there was at time before there was a form. Not only was there no form, there was a time before there was 氣 (*qi*). Mingled together in the amorphous, something altered, and there was the 氣; by the alteration in the 氣 there was form, by alteration of the form there was the life. Now once more altered she has gone over to death.[11]

Zhuangzi regards his late wife as simply a fleeting form assumed by 氣, the Force-like energy Daoists believe pervades the cosmos. To borrow Augustine's language, Zhuangzi's wife came to be when 氣 assumed a certain "measure, order, and form" and passed away when that "measure, order, and form" was dissolved back into the 氣 from which it came. Zhuangzi doesn't grieve because he doesn't regard his wife's death as her annihilation, but rather her transformation, her reversion to 氣, which will now take on other forms. Yoda regards death in a similar light, encouraging Anakin to accept it as something natural and necessary: "Rejoice for those around you who transform into the Force. Mourn them do not. Miss them do not." Whether you call it the Force or 氣, living beings are just one of the many transient forms it assumes, and it's folly to get too attached to any of them. But if the dissolution of "measure, order, and form" is a natural part of life, if there's no pit of nothingness and no real loss, but only a ceaseless process of transformation, where is the *evil*?

Yet, like Obi-Wan sensing the destruction of Alderaan, Yoda's Daoist equanimity is shattered when the violent dissolution of individual lives into the Force is especially abrupt, large-scale, and brutal. Witness his palpable anguish as Order 66 is executed and virtually the entire Jedi Order is exterminated in one fell swoop. We'd be very surprised were we to learn that Yoda went home later that day and marked the occasion by merrily drumming and singing like Zhuangzi. How could he not mourn the transformation of so many noble Jedi into lifeless corpses? How could he rejoice? Can we experience such wholesale slaughter as anything other than a grievous evil? Even Zhuangzi confides to Huizi that his initial reaction to his wife's death was a sense of loss – a response to the passing of a loved one that is as natural as death itself. Admittedly, the sorrow and distress that Yoda and Zhuangzi experience come upon them unbidden, but that doesn't mean that such a "bad feeling" isn't the way that morally sensitive beings register the presence of real misfortune and evil. Just as a Jedi may have an intuitive sense of the Force, all sentient beings might have a visceral awareness of evil that registers through our emotions. In any case, even though both Yoda and Zhuangzi hold there's no real loss in the universe, only an endless succession of transformations, at least some of those transformations conform to our ordinary understanding of evil.

Empirical Reality Strikes Back

Another, perhaps more compelling, reason why the privation theory of evil doesn't fit well with the metaphysics of *Star Wars* is the simple fact that the Force, far from being absent whenever evil is afoot, is abundantly present. Consider the villainous Darth Vader. While the headstrong and impetuous Anakin Skywalker may have lacked proper "measure, order, and form" due to the "inordinate" strength of his undisciplined fear, anger, and other passions, the mature Darth Vader possesses tremendous self-discipline, allowing him, in good Sith fashion, to make effective use of those passions rather than simply letting them run riot in his soul. As Obi-Wan describes Anakin to Luke, "When I first knew him, your father was already a great pilot. But I was amazed how strongly the Force was with him." Anakin's seduction by the dark side wasn't a matter of the Force in him being diminished; nor did his soul shed all measure, order, and form when he became a black-caped, armor-encased despot in training. In fact, once his turn to the dark side was complete, he emerged considerably more "forceful" and more orderly in his passions, but also more evil than ever before. We find some of the most dazzling displays of excellence – in the form of skill, intelligence, acumen, self-control, fortitude, endurance, and daring – in those who are most wicked. Meanwhile, the good are often pretty mediocre. Who do you find more impressive: Darth Vader or starship pilot Ric Olié? "Who's Ric Olié?" you ask? Exactly my point!

As the philosopher Friedrich Schelling (1775–1854) pointed out, the privation theory reduces evil "to something merely passive, to limitation, lack, deprivation, concepts that are in complete conflict with the actual nature of evil. For the simple reflection that only man, the most complete of all visible creatures, is capable of evil, shows already that the ground of evil could not in any way lie in lack or deprivation."[12] Lucas seems to agree, which is why evil in *Star Wars* is *not* a privation but an aspect of the Force. As an artist, Lucas takes his bearings from human experience rather than abstract reason. Evil isn't typically experienced as a mere lack or absence, but as an aggressive, terrifying presence. We encounter evil as active malice and hatred, as an assault on people and things we love, as violent passions that cripple the will and set us on a path of self-destruction, and as the piercing experience of pain.

That's why in almost all popular mythologies – from primitive religions to *Star Wars* – evil has been depicted as a menacing and fearsome power actively opposing the good. Both have reality, and one isn't simply the privation of the other. This view often goes by the name *Manichaean dualism*, referencing the views of the Persian prophet Mani (c. 216–274), who believed that the cosmos was an interminable battle pitting the forces of Light and Goodness against the opposing forces of Darkness and Evil. Both were roughly equal in power, so there was slim hope that the good would eventually get the upper hand and completely vanquish evil.

The perennial popularity of Manichaean dualism is a testament to how well it captures something essential in our experience of evil. Most philosophers, however, have favored some form of privation theory – unless, like Swami Prabhavananda, they've simply dismissed the opposition between good and evil altogether. Some have had religious commitments that gave them a stake in denying the reality of evil in a universe purportedly governed by an all-powerful and perfectly good deity; but there may be a more fundamental motive, pertaining to the very nature of philosophical reason. Philosophers have always aspired to uncover an underlying unity behind the cluttered mess of our experience. Reason craves coherence like Luke Skywalker craves adventure. The philosophical mind – like the scientific mind – wants to connect the dots, reveal the big picture, and unite as many diverse phenomena as possible under a single explanatory principle. What could be a greater affront to the rational mind than the prospect that reality might ultimately consist of two irreducible, incommensurable, and eternally opposed principles? In ordinary life, we experience evil as an assault on the integrity of our bodies, our communities, and perhaps even our souls. To the philosopher, it's what frustrates our aspiration to integrate everything in our experience into a single, coherent, intelligible whole.

Schelling, who rejected privation theory as untrue to our experience, felt the attraction of Manichaean dualism, yet as a philosopher he couldn't abandon his desire for unity:

> Driven by this argument [against privation theory], one can be tempted to throw oneself into the arms of dualism. This system, however, if it is really thought as the doctrine of two absolutely different and mutually independent principles, is only a system of the self-destruction and despair of reason.[13]

With its cosmic powers of darkness and light locked in a titanic struggle, the *Star Wars* universe may seem to be thoroughly Manichaean.[14] Yet it's apparent that Lucas shares Schelling's philosophical aspiration to find unity behind the diversity of our experience, despite the reality of evil. Ultimately, the Force is one. Ultimately, the Force is good. Yet the Force has a dark side. How is that possible?

Bringing Balance to the Force

Like most philosophers before him, Schelling sought to understand the cosmos as a single, unified whole. But he thought the attempts of most of his philosophical predecessors fell flat because they insisted on treating the world as though it consisted of mere *things*, bloodless and inert chunks of matter pieced together to form a whole in the same way that hunks of metal are fitted together to form a TIE fighter. For Schelling, however, the world was *alive*: "In the final and highest judgment, there is no other Being than will."[15] In agreement with Jedi teaching, Schelling insisted that at its deepest core the world we inhabit is pulsing with living energy, animated by a vital and dynamic Force that surges through each and every thing, including each of us. This animating Force, which he called "God," has a will that "is the purest love: there can never be a will to evil in love."[16] Love, for Schelling, is a creative power seeking to build up and to unify, forging harmony and cooperation to the fullest extent possible. Free of attachment and possessiveness, it's the very same "unconditional love" that Anakin tells Padmé "is central to a Jedi's life."

What about evil? Schelling's primal will is also like the Force in that it has a dark side. In fact, he argued that the will absolutely *must* have a dark side in order to exist, though that dark side isn't always or necessarily evil. It becomes evil only when it constitutes itself as a "Separatist" force resisting the will of love. Schelling called the primal will's dark side its "ground." Everything, he claimed, must have a ground, something distinct from itself that makes its existence possible, and this applies to the divine will as much as anything else. Yet the divine will differs in having its ground within itself – in the form of a dark, obscure urge to bring itself into existence, "the yearning the eternal One feels to give birth to itself" that's the precondition for its emergence into the light as the will of love.[17] This dark ground is analogous to our passionate nature, those drives through which we assert our existence in an often-hostile world and which are most intense in the violent emotions of fear and anger. The Sith draw upon those drives to connect with the dark side of the Force. From Schelling's perspective, the dark ground from which the Sith take their power is distinct from the Force itself, since it is the will of the Force (or of God) that the dark ground should submit to the light of love like a good padawan to his master.

Only in the divine will is the passionate ground of existence pressed entirely into the service of creating and sustaining a rational order. In mortal creatures like us, however, the dark ground of our being can develop a will of its own and become as unruly as the mosh pit at a Max Rebo gig:

> [E]verything in the world is, as we see it now, rule, order and form; but anarchy still lies in the ground, as if it could break through once again, and nowhere does it appear as if order and form were what is original but rather as if initial anarchy had been brought to order. This is the incomprehensible base of reality in things, the indivisible remainder, that which with the greatest exertion cannot be resolved in understanding but rather remains eternally in the ground.[18]

Schelling's language of "rule, order, and form" is reminiscent of Augustine's association of being and goodness with "measure, order, and form," just as his talk of an "incomprehensible base of reality in things" reminds us of Zhuangzi's primal, amorphous 气 (*qi*). For Schelling, all order is the ordering of some earlier chaos. In the natural world, this original chaos threatens to return in the form of disease and natural calamities. In the human psyche, the dark ground is the egocentric will and its cravings. These aren't bad in themselves, since they're what fuel our will to exist, spurring our drive to build city-planets, make babies, and defend our loved ones from Tusken Raiders. Without that dark ground, we couldn't exist, let alone flourish.

But if that dark ground must always be present, it's benign only as long as it stands in the right relationship to our higher nature, heeding the will of the Force to participate in a richly creative way with others in sustaining a livable world. When the dark side asserts itself in defiance of the will of love, when the healthy self-will that ought to serve self-preservation transforms into the desire to dominate and exploit everything around it, then it becomes a dark power for evil and destruction. "Anger, fear, aggression – the dark side are they," warns Yoda, indicating what happens when the drives that ground our lives refuse to serve any ends higher than themselves. Those drives are rooted in the Force, but the Force doesn't will anything evil, even though the ground of evil, the dark side, must be present for the Force to exist. Whether that dark ground becomes a force for human flourishing or for death and destruction depends on how it comes to be ordered in relation to the higher "will to love" that should govern our lives. Ordering it rightly is perhaps what it means to "bring balance to the Force."[19]

Notes

1. Epimenides, *Cretica*, quoted approvingly and applied to the Christian god by the apostle Paul in Acts 17:28.
2. Panentheism is similar to pantheism, the belief that God is simply identical to the totality of things that exist. They differ in that although panentheism regards God as the power that animates the universe, it regards God as in some way more than the world, which is contained in God. Obi-Wan Kenobi seems to endorse this panentheistic

interpretation of the Force as something greater than the visible world when he says, "It's an energy field and something more. ... An aura that at once controls and obeys. It is a nothingness that can accomplish miracles" (George Lucas, Donald F. Glut, and James Kahn, *The Star Wars Trilogy* [New York: Del Rey, 2004], 143).

3. Quoted in Ryder Windham, *Star Wars Episode 1: The Phantom Menace Scrapbook* (New York: Random House, 1999), 11.

4. See Paul Davids and Hollace Davids, *The Glove of Darth Vader* (New York: Bantam Spectra, 1992).

5. Swami Prabhavananda, *The Spiritual Heritage of India: A Clear Summary of Indian Philosophy and Religion* (Hollywood, CA: Vedanta Press, 1979), 203.

6. See Troy Denning, *Tatooine Ghost* (New York: Del Rey, 2003).

7. This view accords with one theory about the Yuuzhan Vong, who appear not to exist within the Force, that they had been "*stripped* of the Force" due to the "whole people turning entirely to the dark side" (James Luceno, *Star Wars – The New Jedi Order: The Unifying Force* (New York: Del Rey, 2003), 171–2; and Greg Keyes, *Star Wars – The New Jedi Order: Conquest* (New York: Del Rey, 2001), 239.

8. See Jason T. Eberl's chapter in this volume (chapter 9).

9. Augustine, "On the Nature of the Good," in *Augustine: Earlier Writings*, ed. J. H. S. Burleigh (Louisville, KY: Westminster John Knox Press, 1953), 327.

10. In addition to Augustine, this theory is associated with the ancient school of Neo-Platonism, as well as with the dominant strain within Christian theology.

11. *Chuang Tzu: The Inner Chapters*, trans. A. C. Graham (Indianapolis: Hackett, 1981), 123–4. Chuang Tzu is how the philosopher 庄子's name was spelled under the old Giles–Wade system of transliteration. Under the currently standard system of pinyin, it is spelled Zhuangzi. I have altered Graham's translation slightly. The word 形 (*xíng*), which he translates as "shape," I render as "form." Graham translates 气 as "energy." I leave 气 untranslated.

12. F. W. J. Schelling, *Philosophical Investigations into the Essence of Human Freedom*, trans. Jeff Love and Johannes Schmidt (Albany: State University of New York Press, 2006), 36.

13. *Philosophical Investigations into the Essence of Human Freedom*, 24.

14. See Mark Rowland's discussion of *Star Wars* in his book, *The Philosopher at the End of the Universe: Philosophy Explained through Science Fiction Films* (New York: St. Martin's Press, 2004), 209–32.

15. Ibid.

16. Ibid., 42.
17. Ibid., 28.
18. Ibid., 29.
19. I am very grateful to Jason T. Eberl, who commented on an earlier draft of this chapter and made numerous suggestions that were of tremendous help in making it better.

What Is It Like to Be a Jedi?
A Life in the Force

Marek McGann

What is it like to be a Jedi? As an order of monastic knights, spiritual and ascetic, you might imagine their experience of the galaxy around them to be mystical, ethereal, almost abstract. It's clear that their world is very different from our own, that their awareness of the universe is more encompassing, richer. The Jedi call that other, mystical aspect of reality they perceive *the Force*.

Jedi *feel* the Force, as if it were tangible. It's not some vaporous, ghostly thing – it surrounds, penetrates, and binds us. Jedi speak about the Force akin to how a fish might talk about the ocean. Everything a Jedi does is immersed in the flow of the Force's eddies and currents. Its power is viscerally felt. When Alderaan is destroyed, Obi-Wan Kenobi puts his hand to his chest and stumbles, feeling faint and barely able to remain standing. From light-years distant, the sense of millions of voices crying out in terror and being suddenly silenced is something that literally takes the veteran Jedi's breath away. Just *trying* to lift his X-wing out of the swamp exhausts Luke Skywalker, leaving him panting for air, while even Yoda heaves a sigh of effort once he's done the job. For a group of spiritual beings, the Jedi are a very physical bunch.

This doesn't come as much of a surprise, however, if you consider the ideas of Maurice Merleau-Ponty (1908–1961).[1] Merleau-Ponty was interested in *consciousness*, what the raw form of our experience

The Ultimate Star Wars and Philosophy: You Must Unlearn What You Have Learned, First Edition. Edited by Jason T. Eberl and Kevin S. Decker.
© 2016 John Wiley & Sons, Ltd. Published 2016 by John Wiley & Sons, Ltd.

tells us about ourselves and about reality. *Phenomenology* involves paying attention to what we're aware of in a way that avoids forcing it into conceptual boxes or making prior assumptions about it. In his phenomenological philosophy, Merleau-Ponty made a few key observations, and primary amongst them is that, as living beings, we always perceive the world around us through our bodies, from an "embodied" perspective.

"Life Creates It, Makes It Grow"

There's just no getting away from the fact that we're made of meat, blood, and bone. If you're alive, you have a body that plays a crucial role in all your perceptions and everything you do. Some see the inherently bodily form of our experience as a challenge to understanding the mind, worrying about how we might reconcile the ideas of mind and body.[2] For Merleau-Ponty, it's a mistake to separate the two in the first place.

The Jedi don't make that mistake. When introducing someone to new ways of experiencing the universe around them, making them more aware of and sensitive to the Force, they don't try to avoid dealing with the body, or stop the person from being aware of the brute realities of being alive. In fact, Jedi training tends to reinforce a student's awareness of their own body and that they're a living being. Jedi younglings and padawans must put their body to new uses, perform new tasks, and learn new skills in physical activities that have profound effects on the way they see the world around them.

Obi-Wan gives Luke his first lesson in interacting with the Force through a challenging physical problem – using a lightsaber to block energy bolts from a hovering seeker remote. The challenge involves wielding a new tool, being acutely aware of where his body is and its relationship to the remote, and reacting both quickly and accurately to a strike. The motivation to do the task properly is as down-to-earth and physical as it gets – avoid being shot. If Luke is to succeed, he must develop a new kind of awareness, not through a mystical abstraction, but through the experience of his own body and its place in what's happening, in the flow of events in the world.

Later, Yoda takes Luke through a grueling series of activities: running an obstacle course, along with acrobatic challenges such as handstands, leaps, and somersaults. These aren't the kind of things you'd imagine would help a person become more aware of an ethereal Force. Such physical efforts push the young trainee to his limits, but they're much more than just exercise. They force Luke to become more conscious of his body, his own living being, and how he copes with the demands of what he's doing, thus unlocking new ways of experiencing and engaging with the world around him.

"You Must Unlearn What You Have Learned"

The Jedi figured all of this out a long time ago. Lacking the Force to guide us, it took us a bit longer. Merleau-Ponty and more recent thinkers, such as the biologist and philosopher Francisco Varela and his colleagues Evan Thompson and Eleanor Rosch, have led us to acknowledge the nagging fact that we are always *embodied*.[3] They explore the importance of the body and its actions, noting that when we perceive a thing, it's always as part of something we're doing. This runs against our usual intuitions. It would be normal to think that, first, we see what's going on around us. We aren't acting yet, just taking in information. Once our minds understand what's happening in the world, we make a decision about what to do next. Finally, once we've decided what to do, our brain sends the right signals to the body and we take appropriate action.[4] Essentially, before thinking starts, perceiving has to finish. Before action starts, thinking has to be complete.

This breakdown of the process makes sense, and it keeps the edges of different concepts – perception, cognition, action – clean and unblurred. But this is not the point of view you're looking for. The Jedi know better. What the Jedi say more than anything else about the Force is that it *flows*. Deliberate, intellectual thought might have some of that stop-start character – first seeing, then thinking, then acting – but both phenomenology and the Jedi resist that kind of overthinking.

So our normal intuitions suggest that the mind is buffered from reality by perception on one side and action on the other. Jedi let go of such precious illusions and feel the Force flow *within* what they're doing; their perceptions and actions are part of one unified process.

This is why changing a person's perceptions gets them to do new things and interact with the world in new ways. Obi-Wan doesn't profoundly affect Luke's perception of the world by having him meditate quietly, being inactive and pensive. Instead, he makes Luke dodge lasers from a remote while wearing a helmet with the blast shield down, forcing the young would-be Jedi to let go of his old habits and pay closer attention to the task in which he's presently engaged. He becomes more sensitive to the Force within the flow of what he is doing. Luke takes the first step into a larger world where perception, thinking, and action aren't neatly separated, but *intimately intertwined*. Awareness and understanding of the world around us are not abstract; they involve our bodily selves in the process of getting things done.

Bodily actions don't have to be dramatic, though. One of the differences we often see in bodily movement as a person develops some expertise in an area is that their movements become increasingly efficient, increasingly subtle. Learning to do *less* takes effort and skill. Jedi must be "calm, at peace, passive," but they are living beings. Such quiescence is not our natural state, as though we were droids who can "close down for a while" when not in use. Passivity, rather ironically, requires effort, practice, and discipline. But skillful masters still utilize some kind of bodily activity. There's no more accomplished master of the Force than Yoda, but even he directed the motion of Luke's X-wing with his hand. Likewise, we see several Jedi push against the weak minds of stormtroopers and others with a slight wave of the hand.

"You Must Feel the Force Flowing through You"

Scholars such as Varela, Thompson, and Rosch emphasize not breaking the "perception–action" loop and separating its components. These philosophers and cognitive scientists[5] are often called *enactivists*, because they claim that thinking and experience are *enacted*: they don't exist *except while they are happening*. Running doesn't exist in your legs and get switched on once in a while, and you don't walk around with a handshake in your pocket for whenever you need one. Running and handshakes are something you *do*, not something you *have*. For enactivists, the mind and your experience are, similarly, things you do. This means that you can't separate knowledge, or perception, from action. It's a bit like stopping a spinning wheel to get a better understanding of its motion, or like Luke trying to predict the seeker remote with his conscious self, instead of *feeling* his way, actively, bodily, through the task – just as Qui-Gon exhorted Luke's father Anakin just before the Boonta Eve podrace, "Remember, concentrate on the moment. Feel, don't think."

We normally think about experience as involving us creating it moment by moment. We take in information continuously from the world around us and use it to build a little model for ourselves of what's going on, so that decisions can be made and actions planned. It's as though our bodies are starships with hierarchical command structures, Com-Scan providing data, a captain responding to the information, and a crew implementing the action the captain commands.

If the enactivist appreciation of the perception–action cycle is right, though, it means that experience isn't constantly built, consulted, and then acted on. It's always present, but also always in a process of developing and changing as we interact with the world. Think of it like a dance. At any moment, the dance has a certain progression to it. One step is already going on as the next begins. Each is a continuation and transformation of the last one – there aren't clear lines where one step ends and the next begins. The same is true in a masterful lightsaber duel, as we witness Anakin and Obi-Wan on Mustafar struggling to breach each other's defenses, but being anticipated and blocked before they've even begun their strike. It's the same way with experience: there's never a time when the perceiving bit is "finished" so that the thinking bit can get started, and never a final time when the thinking is "done" so that we can start the action.

Every perception and action carry a certain momentum from what we were already seeing and doing at the time. That natural *flow* helps us get things done. Obi-Wan emphasizes to Luke that a Jedi feels the Force flowing through him. It's a powerful experience, partially controlling their actions. Our normal experience is similar; we're always in some flow of activity and are constrained or limited by that to some extent.

"A Jedi's Strength Flows from the Force"

The constraints the world places upon us often limit what we can do, but they also enable us to achieve great things when we work *with* them rather than resist or try to ignore them. When we learn to use a new tool, it may restrict us, forcing us to act in a strange or different way. But once we become disciplined in its use, coordinating our actions within its constraints, we can achieve much more with it than without. Be clumsy or random with a lightsaber, and you'll likely lose a few limbs, but once you've taken the time to master the weapon, to discipline your actions with it, you will make a formidable opponent – even more formidable are the few Jedi or Sith who've mastered the double-bladed lightsaber, such as Darth Maul and Exar Kun, which introduces novel constraints but even greater fighting abilities. The sheer energy being swung around with a lightsaber makes it heavy to wield, and Luke is forced early in his training to use both hands to keep the weapon under control. A Jedi can learn to use the weight and momentum of a lightsaber to almost move itself, just as we might learn to use the weight of a hammer as a benefit to its swing, rather than an obstacle to its use. Similarly, as a Jedi's proficiency improves, we see more fluid, one-handed use.

The flow of the Force partially controls a Jedi's actions, but as they become more disciplined, it enables them to achieve truly remarkable things. This is what Yoda means when he says that a Jedi's strength flows from the Force. Jedi who are able to coordinate their actions with that flow can work with the full potency of the universal relationship between all things. Of course, there's a certain appeal in ignoring the effort and patience required for such discipline. The ease of acting in a careless and brutal manner is certainly seductive, but let's not start down that dark path.

"A Certain [Bodily] Point of View"

Being alive simultaneously puts demands on you and makes things possible. You have a body that you have to keep in working order and that allows the world to affect you – things can bang into you, trip you, cut your hands off, and so on. But your body also enables you to do things – eat, drink, buy droids, and fly starships. Varela, Thompson, and Rosch argue that having to cope with the world around us is what gives rise to consciousness and experience in the first place. The world isn't full of abstract, neutral stuff; it's full of things *meaningful* to us, things that affect us and can help or threaten us. Your world depends on your point of view, and it is always experienced in terms of what you need to do and can do – as Qui-Gon instructs Anakin, "Always remember, your focus determines your reality."

When you look around you, you'll see flat bits of ground you can walk on, or drops over which you might fall. You might see things coming at you to be dodged or things you could lift, throw, or catch. When holding a hammer, you'll start seeing things in terms of whether they can be hit, driven, or broken. Hold a lightsaber and things look much more *cuttable*.

The Jedi's sensitivity to the Force makes a host of special actions available to them, but they still perceive the world in terms of those actions, from their bodily perspective. For us non-Jedi, an object has to be within arm's reach to be perceived as immediately *liftable*. Not so for Jedi, who can pick things up at a great distance; but that "liftability" will still be part of how they see objects. The more they live in the Force, the more their actions are coordinated with the Force, and the more different their perceptions will be from ours.

Think of the difference between Luke's and Yoda's perceptions of the sunken X-wing. Luke still sees the world more in terms of his old habits and so doesn't perceive the ship as liftable. He's unable to interact with the ship in that way, and, as a result, the action is inconceivable for him. He thinks his master wants the impossible. For Yoda, the ship is just one more object embedded in the flow of the Force. Size matters not.

The more we know, the more we become aware and become capable of; though we could just as well say that the more we're capable of, the more we become aware, and so the more we know – these things aren't cleanly separated. The character of our experience owes as much to the kinds of skills we have as to anything else. This is a particularly important point, because philosophers who emphasize embodiment and bodily experience are certainly not saying that we are *just* bodies, merely "this crude matter."

"The Way of the Force"

We tend to think about our experience feeling the way it does because of the influence or nature of the sensory organs involved. Things look like they do because of how our eyes work. Things have sounds because of our ears. If that's the case, to experience the Force we're going to need a special Force-organ, right? Well, things are much more complicated. Skin, for instance, has many different kinds of receptors – for texture, pressure, temperature, and more than one kind of pain. We also have a plethora of other kinds of sensory systems – a sense of balance, the position of our own limbs (*proprioception*), various visceral systems associated with things like hunger and thirst, and so on.[6]

These various sensory systems also interact; there's no simple one-to-one relationship between a sensory organ and a perceptual experience. None of our normal ways of perceiving the world are *only* supported by their supposed sensory organ. Normal vision owes a surprising amount to our sense of balance – one marvels at how well Luke and Han kept their visual focus on the incoming TIE fighters while spinning around in the *Millennium Falcon*'s gun turrets.

Psychologists have also studied a host of what are called *cross-modal illusions* involving more than one sensory system.[7] One example is seeing two flashes where there was only one because you either *hear* two beeps at the same time or *feel* two taps on your arm. Another is hearing some spoken sounds differently depending on what you *see* a person's lips doing. We tend to perceive the *whole* of what's happening, not its different parts. It actually takes some skill to pay attention to just one isolated aspect of what we're experiencing. On Dagobah, Luke's first brush with the dark side in the bog tree causes him to feel "cold, death," something not quite right. The experience is a mishmash of senses that he's aware of as a whole, but can't clearly understand or perceive yet as different elements.

So it isn't just the kind of sensory organ involved that matters to how we experience things. But can the way you're *acting* really make such a difference? Yes. The Tactile-Visual-Substitution-System (TVSS) is a piece of technology originally developed in the 1960s by psychologist Paul Bach-y-Rita to help blind people.[8] It consists of an array of vibrating pins, normally worn on the back, controlled by a small computer connected to a camera. The person wears the camera on a pair of glasses. The patterns of light picked up by the camera drive the patterns of vibrations on the person's skin. With practice, the person can learn to do elementary things, such as move around a room without bumping into furniture, or spot when something is moving toward them. Users of the device don't pay much attention to the sensation on their skin, though. They don't speak as though they're touching things, but rather talk about objects around them almost as if they can see them. What the TVSS tells us is that what matters for the flavor of our experience isn't which sensory organ is involved. What matters is how we can interact with the world around us.

So Jedi don't need a special Force-organ to perceive the Force – midi-chlorians are kind of redundant. The Force's influential flow is present everywhere – between every tree, rock, and spaceship, and even between proton torpedoes and exhaust ports. If you can be sensitive to those kinds of patterns, ready to pick up on the influence of the Force, you can learn to perceive as the Jedi do with any (and probably all) of your sensory organs. The Force isn't something Jedi just see, or hear, or taste, or touch, but rather it is something they experience on its own terms, probably using their whole body to do it.

Our experience of the world around us isn't determined by what sensory organs we have, but about the kinds of *things that we can do*.[9] The body matters, so we can't get away from that. But the body isn't *all* that matters. What the body is *doing*, the flow of skilled action as an embodied person interacts with their world – that's where experience happens.

"Be Mindful of the Living Force"

In Obi-Wan's succinct description, "The Force is an energy field created by all living things. It surrounds us. It penetrates us. It binds the galaxy together." Everything that happens exists within its flow, creating relationships between all things – from people and their thoughts to other living beings, objects, and even worlds. Jedi discipline, their skill, enables them to feel the flow of the Force, through which they can perceive how all things are related. By acting in coordination with it, at one with it, they can achieve marvels.

Merleau-Ponty, Varela, Thompson, and Rosch aren't so mystical about it, but for them, it is the same with human perceivers. We don't exist outside of our worlds, like someone receiving information remotely through a droid, able to send commands back to move the droid's limbs. We are living beings embedded in the flow of what's happening, dealing in a continuous way with various demands, influences, and opportunities in the world around us. We always see the world in terms of the demands it's making upon us and possible actions we might take. It's our lot as physical, bodily beings to have to face those demands, but as *capable* beings to be sensitive to what we might do in order to cope with them. To that extent, our reality depends greatly on our own *bodily* point of view. Our experience of reality emerges in the flow of our actions, and continuously changes as we interact with the world and as we learn new skills. Experience, like the Force, isn't static; it *flows*. Though ever present, it's also always changing, always different.

You are a living being – not just "crude matter" – always bodily but never *just* a body. You live in a Force of habits, skills, and abilities, of environmental pressure and social influence. You know what it's like to be a Jedi because you experience and act within a field of pervasive forces already. Your life creates it, and your increasing skills make it grow. You have spent your life becoming attuned to this field of forces, more sensitive to it, able to do more, and continuously taking another step into a larger world. And it will be with you, always.

Notes

1. Although Merleau-Ponty is not always the easiest philosopher to read, a good place to start is probably the relatively short and accessible *The Structure of Behavior* (Boston: Beacon Press, 1967). Have a look at *The Phenomenology of Perception* (London: Routledge & Kegan Paul, 1996) if you get *really* interested.

2. The notion that mind and body are separate things is most famously associated with another French philosophy, René Descartes (1596–1650); see his *Discourse on Method and the Meditations*, trans. F. E. Sutcliffe (Harmondsworth, UK: Penguin Books, 1968). Descartes claimed that we could doubt everything except the fact that we have experiences. That includes doubting the existence of our own bodies! Descartes concludes that the mind must be something independent of the body. Merleau-Ponty argued that, to doubt something, you have to give reason to doubt, and in giving reasons Descartes would have to refer to the very world he was doubting. So there's no reason to ignore the fact that we exist in our bodies as part of the world.

3. See Francisco J. Varela, Evan Thompson, and Eleanor Rosch, *The Embodied Mind* (Cambridge, MA: MIT Press, 1991); and Evan

Thompson, *Mind in Life: Biology, Phenomenology and the Sciences of Mind* (Cambridge, MA: Harvard University Press, 2007).

4. The philosopher Susan Hurley refers to this way of thinking as "the classical sandwich" – cognition (the mind) is sandwiched between perception (as input) and action (as output); see her *Consciousness in Action* (Cambridge, MA: Harvard University Press, 1998). But Hurley, Merleau-Ponty, and others would argue that this is a mistake. Thinking can happen in the action itself – acting is part and parcel of how we think. An example is when you rotate a jigsaw piece while deciding whether it fits. The physical action of rotating the piece is part of how you go about making the decision – the behavior is part of the cognitive process.

5. Cognitive science is a scientific area that studies the mind. It is interdisciplinary, involving philosophy, psychology, computer science, robotics, linguistics, anthropology – basically, any field of inquiry that might add to our understanding of the mind and how it works.

6. See Mohan Matthen, "The Individuation of the Senses," in *The Oxford Handbook of the Philosophy of Perception*, ed. Mohan Matthen (Oxford: Oxford University Press, 2013).

7. For a nice overview of several such illusions and their implications, have a look at Shinsuke Shimojo and Ladan Shams, "Sensory Modalities Are Not Separate Modalities: Plasticity and Interactions," *Current Opinion in Neurobiology* 11 (2001): 505–9.

8. See Paul Bach-y-Rita, "Tactile Vision Substitution: Past and Future," *International Journal of Neuroscience* 19, no. 1 (1983): 29.

9. I explore these ideas in some detail in Marek McGann, "Perceptual Modalities: Modes of Presentation or Modes of Interaction?" *Journal of Consciousness Studies* 17 (2010): 72–94.

19

"Never Tell Me the Odds": An Inquiry Concerning Jedi Understanding

Andrew Zimmerman Jones

Han Solo gives the Force no credit when he first discusses it with Luke and Obi-Wan on the way to Alderaan. When Luke blocks the training remote's blaster bolts with his lightsaber, Han dismisses it as *luck*. He is, without a doubt, wrong. Or is he?

As an audience, we know that Han Solo's belief about the Force is an *untrue* belief. It doesn't conform to the reality of how the *Star Wars* universe operates. But does this mean that Han is actually *wrong* to hold that belief, at that time, given the evidence he has at his disposal?

A Long Time Ago, in a City-State Far, Far Away

In our galaxy, in a time much more recent than the Battle of Endor, Greek philosophers came up with the idea that orderly causal laws regulate the universe. One of the earliest thinkers credited with this notion is the philosopher Thales (620–546 BCE). Much like ancient Jedi Masters after the fall of the Republic (about whom information is scattered in rare Jedi holocrons), little is known of Thales, though he is referenced by other, better-known Greek philosophers, such as Aristotle (384–322 BCE):

The Ultimate Star Wars and Philosophy: You Must Unlearn What You Have Learned, First Edition. Edited by Jason T. Eberl and Kevin S. Decker.
© 2016 John Wiley & Sons, Ltd. Published 2016 by John Wiley & Sons, Ltd.

Thales, too, to judge from what is recorded about him, seems to have held soul to be a motive force, since he says that the magnet has a soul because it moves the iron.[1]

Certain thinkers say that the soul is intermingled in the whole universe, and it is perhaps for that reason that Thales came to the opinion that all things are full of gods.[2]

Here, at the very dawn of Western philosophy, we find that the first attempts to make sense of the universe are eerily similar to the concept of the Force. Perhaps someday a historian will unearth some of Thales's actual writings – prequels to Aristotle, if you will – and find that he called these "gods" *midi-chlorians*.

The ancient Greeks established a philosophical standard for what *knowledge* is, a standard that remains heavily endorsed today: "justified true belief." It is somewhat (though not completely) trivial to say that knowledge must consist of things that I believe and that are also true. If I have a belief that Yoda is a Sith Lord, it is hard to legitimately classify that view as knowledge. In fact, even if *Episode VII* were to reveal that Yoda had indeed been a Sith Lord all along, making the statement "Yoda is a Sith Lord" true, it *still* wouldn't classify as knowledge, because I don't *believe* it now as I'm writing it.

However, let's assume that I *did* believe firmly that Yoda was a Sith Lord and it was revealed that Yoda was indeed a Sith Lord. Could this "true belief" be classified as knowledge? Socrates argued against the view that "true judgment" alone is enough for knowledge:

Suppose a jury, none of whom are eyewitnesses to a crime, listen to testimony and come to the same judgment an eyewitness would have made. It turns out that their judgment is true, though only by coincidence; but it's not real knowledge – only the eyewitness has that. So true judgment is not the same as knowledge.[3]

Socrates argues that some sort of justification beyond the mere holding of a true belief is required for knowledge. If I hold a belief for a good reason, and that belief is in fact true, it's considered knowledge. And, indeed, Socrates ultimately argues that right opinions can be trusted only because they are inspired by something divine ... an argument that continues to resonate in some quarters today.[4]

These days, the average third-grader probably holds more true beliefs about the physical world than Thales, Socrates, or even Aristotle did. Philosophers love to debate the nature of truth, while scientists love trying to find it. Scientists have shown us that theories based on belief in "souls" or "gods" that cause movements within inanimate objects – such as a magnet moving toward a piece of iron – are neither justified nor true. But let's set aside the question of *truth*. We know, after all, that Han's belief is false. The more interesting question is whether Han's belief is *justified*.

Hume Shot First

A scruffy-looking Corellian smuggler may seem an odd choice to embody the philosophical value of *skepticism*, but pickings are slim in the *Star Wars* galaxy if we're to find someone who embraces a rational, scientific worldview. The only other evident example is Admiral Motti, who foolishly taunts Darth Vader about his "sad devotion to that ancient religion." For his part, Han's default skepticism is established early on:

HAN SOLO: Hokey religions and ancient weapons are no match for a good blaster at your side, kid.
LUKE SKYWALKER: You don't believe in the Force, do you?
HAN SOLO: Kid, I've flown from one side of this galaxy to the other. I've seen a lot of strange stuff, but I've never seen *anything* to make me believe there's one all-powerful Force controlling everything. There's no mystical energy field controls *my* destiny. It's all a lot of simple tricks and nonsense.

In a sense, calling a lightsaber "ancient" is like calling a Sony Walkman "ancient."[5] Only twenty years earlier, when Solo was a boy on Corellia, the Jedi were prominent warriors during the Clone Wars and celebrated heroes of the Republic. Young Anakin Skywalker instantly recognizes Qui-Gon Jinn's lightsaber, identifying him as a Jedi, even on backwater Tatooine. So we should interpret Han's dismissal of the Force not as merely a rejection of the unknown, but as a considered rejection of an explanation that he's heard before. Still, why would Han dismiss something like the Force without any direct knowledge of it?

To answer these questions, we turn to the philosopher David Hume (1711–1776), who sought to understand how humans gain knowledge and understanding without any appeal to a deity. More specifically, Hume argued against belief in *miracles* based on human testimony – precisely the sort of testimony Han Solo would need in order to believe that miracles supposedly arise from the Force. As Hume explains, we believe human testimony because, in our experience, people – or at least some people – are *trustworthy*. Our experience also tells us that the universe operates by *consistent laws of nature*. If someone is describing a genuine miracle – something that occurs outside of, or in direct violation of, the laws of nature – then these two sources of experiences are in conflict. And for Hume, there's no contest as to which should win, as established by his general maxim, "That no testimony is sufficient to establish a miracle, unless the testimony be of such a kind, that its falsehood would be more miraculous, than the fact, which it endeavors to establish."[6] For Han Solo, who has lived among pirates, con artists, and smugglers, the scales should tip *against* the trustworthiness of human testimony. Han's experience offers no alternative *other* than the idea that alleged "miracles" are the result of "simple tricks and nonsense."

At the time of Han's glib dismissal of "hokey religions," Luke's own experience with the Force consists of exactly two pieces of evidence: Obi-Wan's "These aren't the droids you're looking for" mind-trick and his literal disarming of a Mos Eisley ruffian with his lightsaber. The second of these, though impressive for a man of Obi-Wan's age, doesn't require any miraculous powers.[7] So, Luke's initial belief in the Force is based on little more than a great deal of faith in the claims of a reclusive hermit who's been lying about his name and who his Uncle Owen called a "crazy old man." Luke's beliefs could just as easily be a result of his moisture-farm-boy gullibility as of his future destiny as a Jedi … and even Socrates would argue that such a belief is unjustified.

Though Han eventually befriends Luke, it's not clear that he ever truly adopts a belief in the Force. Han knows an accomplished pilot could've made the shot that destroyed the Death Star. Indeed, Luke himself claimed to have previously "bulls-eyed" womp rats of the same size. He isn't present when Luke telekinetically summons his lightsaber to escape the Wampa on Hoth. When Han's unfrozen from carbonite in Jabba's palace, he responds to Chewbacca's claim that

Luke is a Jedi Knight as a "delusion of grandeur." He's fatalistic and sarcastic when Luke tells him his friends have a rescue plan in place. Essentially blind during the battle at the Sarlacc pit, Han doesn't directly witness the full scope of Luke's growing abilities. Han isn't present for either of Luke's confrontations with Vader, so he never witnesses the telekinetic battle on Cloud City or the Emperor throwing around Sith lightning. When Luke senses Vader on the *Executor* as the Rebels approach Endor and claims he's endangering their mission, Han says dismissively, "It's your imagination, kid." Han has every reason to believe that Luke is an unparalleled pilot and an exceptional soldier, but he isn't compelled to believe the Force actually exists.

Han does have some direct experience that's difficult to challenge, though. On Bespin, Darth Vader absorbs several blaster bolts into his gauntlet and then telekinetically rips Solo's blaster from his hand. Though these are manifestations of Vader's Force powers, they *could* be explained through some form of advanced technology built into Vader's cybernetic suit. Nevertheless, in the decades following the Battle of Endor, having married a woman who grows to become a powerful Jedi herself, and having produced three Jedi children, Han witnesses sufficient evidence of the Force to acknowledge that it has real power, that there *is* an invisible energy field flowing through the universe that some people can learn to manipulate. How should he interpret such new evidence? Must one resort to *mysticism*, or is there a role for *scientific* inquiry within the *Star Wars* universe?

The Jedi as Scientist

There must be recurring natural laws at work in the universe for devices as complex as starships, droids, and Death Stars to function in predictable ways. Though we see technicians and mechanics in the *Star Wars* films, no characters actively conduct scientific research. Presumably, the Kaminoans have scientists working on the clone army project, but they get no screen time.

The *products* of science have a role in *Star Wars*, but there's no indication that the *process* of science does. Science isn't merely about creating stuff, but also about providing explanatory frameworks that make sense of physical phenomena. Science plays an explanatory role only twice in the films, when the plot advances through direct appeals to scientific reasoning:

1. Midi-chlorians are offered in *The Phantom Menace* as an explanation for Anakin's virginal conception.
2. Yoda, Obi-Wan, and the padawans in *Attack of the Clones* use the evidence of the pull of gravity to discern the location of the planet Kamino.

The Jedi—and, presumably, the larger society of the Republic—have a general grasp on scientific reasoning. They understand that nature behaves in ways that make sense by following repeated patterns.

In fact, the very act of wielding the Force requires this understanding. Yoda uses the Force to levitate an X-wing because he knows with certainty that he can. When Luke expresses disbelief, Yoda explains that is why he failed in his own attempt to do so. Though this statement appears to be an appeal to the importance of *faith* prior to evidence, Yoda's *own* belief is not at all prior to evidence. Though Yoda doesn't adopt Han's skeptical view of the Force, his belief in his own abilities to manipulate the Force is based on the same justification as Han's dismissal of it: *inference from past experience.*

Darth Vader applies his reliance on the power of the Force in a particularly deft way when he structures his plan to capture Luke on Bespin by first capturing Han and Leia. Vader tortures them, not to extract information, but for the express purpose of sending a message to distant Luke through the Force. It's a bold plan, but is based firmly on Vader's own experience. His major steps toward the dark side were triggered by prophetic visions of his mother's torture and his wife's death in childbirth. So he had every reason to think that similar visions would lead Luke into a rash response. He must've believed that his son would be powerful enough to sense not just his friends' suffering, but also their location on Bespin, or else the trap couldn't possibly have worked.

Compare this to the cloudiness that Yoda and Mace Windu experience in foretelling anything through the Force in the final years before the fall of the Jedi. During this time, they openly declare that their ability to wield the Force is "diminished," and a Sith Lord is allowed to gain power while sitting right across the table from them. It's clear that Vader and Luke retain some sort of consistent clarity in the Force that eluded the more disciplined Jedi Masters at a time when "the dark side clouds everything."

Though wielding the Force is based upon willpower, and belief plays a role in this, the Force itself seems to follow rules, even if those rules may be difficult to discern. The Jedi are able to grow and thrive precisely because training to perceive, manipulate, and flow with the Force is an activity with repeatable patterns. Find young kids with high midi-chlorian counts, put them through a thousand-year tested training regimen, and you'll end up with accomplished Jedi. This isn't mysticism; it's science.

Shut Up, Threepio!

The process of inferring a general rule or prediction from individual experiences is known as *induction*, and the fact that it works so well is the cornerstone of our scientific understanding of the world. Though this process is often called *inductive reasoning*, Hume claims that induction itself isn't actually reasoning at all. There is no line of reasoning, he says, that can take a person from seeing one, two, or even a dozen examples to creating a general rule that applies in all similar situations.

Hume doesn't say that inferences from individual cases to a general rule are always unjustified. Indeed, all evidence seems to suggest that they *are* justified: using induction actually seems to work! But Hume's grand question is: *why* does it work? The answer that Hume offers is the principle of *custom* or *habit*: "Custom, then, is the great guide of human life. It is that principle alone which renders our experience useful to us, and which makes us expect, for the future, a similar train of events with those which have appeared in the past."[8] It's force of habit that justifies Han's opinion about Luke's first success with the training remote being mere luck, but custom also justifies Obi-Wan's observation, "In my experience, there's no such thing as luck." Custom justifies Luke's disbelief in his own ability to levitate large objects, but also justifies Yoda's conviction that "size matters not."

As these examples demonstrate, it's possible for beliefs justified by custom to be true in some respects and yet false in others. Hume is aware of this, recognizing that we experience specific events in a specific time and place; although we must generalize these experiences to function as predictions in the world, we can't guarantee these generalizations will hold. The mere observation of events that seem connected together can't lead directly to a generalization, however. We can observe a great many connections and see that *probability* increases as the number of observed connections increases, but this isn't the same as identifying a connection with any degree of *certainty*. If Luke were to watch the twin suns rising on Tatooine day after day for a year, he'd be justified in his belief that the twin suns would rise the following day, but there's no certainty that this is the case – particularly if Tarkin's Sun Crusher project had succeeded![9]

There's no "tipping point" where the probability or number of examples is so great that it becomes *one hundred percent*. There's always the possibility of an outlier coming along that defies all odds. Indeed, it's precisely with this in mind that Han Solo declares, "Never tell me the odds," as he plans to act in defiance of them.

Always in Motion Is the Truth

The lack of a clear, precise, and logically sure path between individual events and general rules or explanations is a big problem for the school of thought that holds that "knowledge is justified true belief." This has become known as the *problem of induction*.

One way around this problem is to not merely rely on connections between events, but also focus on our understanding of the *process* by which certain causes trigger certain effects. If we know that two things happen in connection by time and space, but don't know the causal relationship between them, then we don't understand them.

This is where inductive reasoning comes into play. It allows the scientist (or philosopher, or Jedi) to move from discrete observations of events connected together to an explanatory framework of *why* these events are connected together. Vader doesn't just observe passively that when he holds up his hand, Imperial Admirals happen to choke to death. Rather, he has an understanding of how he *causes* these deaths. In just the way that Vader cannot fully explain his understanding of the Force – beyond warning that it shouldn't be "underestimated" – so we humans are unable to explain induction. The best we can do is to test whether our explanations hold up as we attempt to apply them in various experiments. This constitutes the *scientific method*.

But the ancient Greeks, like Dark Lords of the Sith, spring up to cause problems. If scientific knowledge is built on induction, and the problem of induction is real, then this knowledge isn't actually justified. And if it's not justified, then it isn't actually knowledge, according to the *justified true belief criterion*. This would seem to lead to *skepticism*: the idea that truth or knowledge either doesn't exist or can't be known at all. A strict philosophical skeptic is forced to refrain from holding any belief or claiming any true knowledge.

One attempt to resolve this dilemma is *fallibilism*. An outgrowth of the pragmatic skepticism suggested by Hume himself, it was given a name by the American scientist and philosopher Charles Sanders Peirce (1839–1914):

> We cannot in any way reach perfect certitude nor exactitude. We can never be absolutely sure of anything, nor can we with any probability ascertain the exact value of any measure or general ratio.... Indeed, most everybody will admit it until they begin to see what is involved in the admission – and then most people will draw back. It will not be admitted by persons utterly incapable of philosophical reflection.... The doctrine of fallibilism will also be denied by those who fear its consequences for science, for religion, and for morality.... It is precisely among those animated by a spirit of science that the doctrine of fallibilism should find its supporters.[10]

Fallibilism is not so much a distinct philosophy as a claim about how to approach knowledge, claiming that no belief is infallible. We can hold a belief, and call it knowledge, even without certainty (or *conclusive* justification), because certainty doesn't exist for knowledge claims.

This doesn't, however, mean that we're wrong in holding such beliefs. As the contemporary philosopher Hilary Putnam puts it, "[F]*allibilism does not entail skepticism* ... *real* doubt, as opposed to paper doubt, requires a context-specific *reason for doubting* – a reason with practical bearing – and the general fact that we are not infallible is, in any normal context, not such a reason."[11]

From the perspective of fallibilism, Han Solo can claim he knows that no "mystical energy field" controls his destiny, while Obi-Wan knows that such a field does exist. There's a disagreement here and, in the *Star Wars* universe, Obi-Wan is right and Han is wrong. Neither of them is being inherently unreasonable, however.

Fallibilism teaches an important lesson: the truths that we understand about the universe can only be the truths available to us at that specific time. This is one way of interpreting Obi-Wan's statement to Luke, "You're going to find that many of the truths we cling to depend greatly on our own point of view." In this case, truth isn't reduced to my subjective evaluation of the facts at hand, but rather my subjective experience of certain *facts* that really are relevant in shaping what I believe or claim to know. Failure to acknowledge the *conditional nature* of our beliefs and knowledge can be a dangerous thing. Therein lies the path to the dark side.

Notes

1. Aristotle, *On the Soul (De Anima)*, trans. J. A. Smith, in *The Basic Works of Aristotle*, ed. Richard McKeon (New York: Modern Library, 2001), 541. A translation is also available online at http://classics.mit.edu/Aristotle/soul.1.i.html (accessed February 23, 2015).
2. Ibid., 553.
3. Keith Quincy, *Plato Unmasked* (Spokane, WA: Eastern Washington University Press, 2003), 355. Quotation is from Plato's *Theaetetus*.
4. Ibid., 105. Quotation is from Plato's *Meno*.
5. For younger readers, a Sony Walkman is a portable device from the 1980s used to play cassette tapes. The subsequent Sony Discman was used to play CDs. With the existence of the iPod, iPhone, and other MP3 players, in the words of Grand Moff Tarkin, "their fire has gone out of the universe."
6. David Hume, *An Enquiry Concerning Human Understanding* (Boston: Simon & Brown, 2011), 100.
7. In the Expanded Universe literature, droids (with no connection to the Force) have been programmed to effectively wield lightsabers.
8. Hume, *Enquiry*, 39–40.
9. The Sun Crusher is another Imperial superweapon, like the Death Star, but designed to destroy suns rather than planets. It is described in Kevin J. Anderson's 1994 *The Jedi Academy* trilogy.
10. C. S. Peirce, "The Scientific Attitude and Fallibilism," in *The Philosophical Writings of C. S. Peirce*, ed. Justus Buchler (New York: Dover, 1955), 42–59.
11. Hilary Putnam. *Philosophy in an Age of Science* (Cambridge, MA: Harvard University Press, 2013), 319.

Episode VI

RETURN OF THE NON-HUMAN

20

Mindless Philosophers and Overweight Globs of Grease: Are Droids Capable of Thought?

Dan Burkett

I think, therefore I am. These are the words that flow through the neural pathways of IG-88 as it powers up for the very first time. The IG assassin droid is the crowning achievement of Holowan Laboratories – the very first "sentient machine." But is such a thing even possible? Are droids capable of *thought*?

The mechanical occupants of the *Star Wars* galaxy certainly exhibit many human-like characteristics. C-3PO claims to have all manner of feelings – a great number of them *bad*. Like many of us, he worries incessantly about his own fate. When Princess Leia's ship is captured by Imperials, he laments that he's most assuredly "doomed" and will be "sent to the spice mines of Kessel or smashed into who-knows-what." This constant state of anxiety makes Threepio an incredibly cautious individual. He mistrusts the safety of escape pods, hates flying, and strongly warns against angering a Wookiee during a game of holochess. But Threepio's fears might be entirely justified, because if the helpless cries of that little GNK power droid in Jabba's torture chamber are anything to go by, then it seems that droids are capable of feeling something like *pain*. Fortunately, droids also appear capable of enjoying the good things in life – Threepio expresses *pleasure* when he announces that his oil bath "is going to feel *so* good." His similarities with humans don't stop there. He shows *embarrassment* at being "naked," *guilt* when hiding from Luke after R2-D2's escape,

The Ultimate Star Wars and Philosophy: You Must Unlearn What You Have Learned,
First Edition. Edited by Jason T. Eberl and Kevin S. Decker.

and even the more flawed attribute of *forgetfulness* when he neglects to contact his companions via comlink on the Death Star.

Artoo also expresses some uniquely human features. He's stubborn – fighting over a flashlight with Yoda in the swamps of Dagobah and refusing to show Luke's message to anyone but Jabba the Hutt on Tatooine. He also engages in startling acts of heroism – risking life and (mechanical) limb to save the Queen's starship in *The Phantom Menace*, rescuing Padmé from the depths of the droid factory, delivering Leia's plea for help to Obi-Wan Kenobi, and attempting to open the doors to the shield generator bunker on Endor. These are only a sample of the many times that Artoo saves his friends, and his heroism seems to stem from a very real concern he shows for his companions. He worries about Anakin as he departs for Mustafar, and about Luke when he goes missing on Hoth. Furthermore, this concern is coupled with the visible relief both he and Threepio display upon seeing their master "fully functional again."

Even the interactions that occur *between* droids share many of the features that are common in human relationships. Artoo and Threepio bicker incessantly. Artoo once calls Threepio a "mindless philosopher," to which Threepio responds by calling Artoo an "overweight glob of grease" and later a "near-sighted scrap pile." The two droids fall out while trudging across the Dune Sea on Tatooine, but then – in typical human fashion – appear genuinely relieved to see each other on the Jawa sandcrawler. Despite their differences, they also display a real interest in each other's wellbeing. Threepio quietly tells Artoo to "hang on" before he launches into the Battle of Yavin, and then quickly hides this momentary display of affection by asking, "You wouldn't want my life to get boring, would you?" After the battle, Threepio once again expresses concern for his counterpart, offering to donate any of his circuits and gears if they'll help in Artoo's recovery. On occasion, the two droids even go so far as to praise one another – Threepio uncharacteristically exclaiming, "Wonderful!" after Artoo helps them escape from Cloud City.

Despite these behaviors, droids occasionally provide us with a jarring glimpse of their true mechanical natures. Threepio initially refuses to pretend to be an Ewok god, claiming that "it just wouldn't be proper." This is an incredibly human response – implicitly appealing to some idea of etiquette or morality. But in the very next breath, Threepio explains what he really means by this, noting that it is merely *against his programming* to impersonate a deity. So, even though droids certainly exhibit a great number of human-like characteristics, they are also programmed machines. The question remains: are droids capable of what we call *thought*?

"We Seem to Be Made to Suffer. It's Our Lot in Life"

It's worth considering why this question of droid intelligence is so important for the denizens of the *Star Wars* galaxy. Truth is, the treatment of droids is very different from that of humans and other sentient creatures. Mechanical beings are bought and sold, owned and abused. They are overworked, unpaid, and imprisoned with restraining bolts. When a droid knows too much – as in the case of Threepio – the solution is simply to wipe its memory, thus destroying any sense of identity and individuality it possessed. We would recoil in horror if we saw humans treated in this way, but this treatment of droids largely fails to move us. Even Padmé Amidala – a champion of justice who's disgusted to find that slavery still exists in the galaxy – shows little concern for the maltreatment of droids all around her.

Not only are droids treated as property, but also they're the victims of extreme prejudice. They're banned from many establishments, the owner of the Mos Eisley cantina gruffly declaring, "We don't serve their kind here," despite happily catering to a menagerie of other beings. This disregard for droids can even be seen among the Jedi who – while doing all they can to respect human and alien life – think nothing of laying waste to thousands of battle droids. They dispatch the Separatist droid forces – armed, unarmed, and noncombatant alike – without the slightest hint of remorse. Indeed, their prejudice against mechanical beings seems to run deep. When Obi-Wan argues that Vader is beyond redemption, he cites as evidence the fact that his former apprentice is "more machine now than man," as though it disqualifies him from any sort of moral consideration.

Clearly, the Jedi – along with most of the occupants of the *Star Wars* galaxy – believe that there is some important moral difference between the mechanical and the biological. The assumption, it seems, is that while droids may be capable of acting just like us, what's actually going on inside their heads is very different.

"Do You Speak Bocce?"

Threepio claims that, for a mechanic, Artoo seems to do "an excessive amount of thinking." But are droids really capable of *thought*? For contemporary philosopher John Searle, thought requires *understanding* – something that he claims no machine, no matter how advanced, could ever be capable of.[1] He builds his argument upon the assumption that all "intelligent" machines operate according to the same basic process: they take an input of symbols, run these through a program, and then give some appropriate output of symbols. Consider the search engine currently open in my Internet browser. Suppose I want to ask it what species Chewbacca is. I type out my question and hit "Enter." The search engine now has its input – a string of symbols in the form "WHAT SPECIES IS CHEWBACCA?" The search engine then takes these symbols and manipulates them via an algorithm that makes up its search program. After a fraction of a second, it provides an output of symbols on my screen: "WOOKIEE."

Despite my search engine's incredible ability to answer this question, most of us would be reluctant to claim that it had any *understanding* of what it did. Consider the very different process you would go through in answering this same question. You would no doubt picture the loveable sidekick in your mind's eye, recalling his appearance and comparing it against your knowledge of the many creatures that inhabit the *Star Wars* galaxy. You would make a match with the Wookiees – a brave and loyal race of beings who valiantly defended their home world against an invasion by Separatist forces. Along the way, you'd also pause to consider precisely what we mean by the concept of a *species*. The search engine does none of this. It doesn't understand who Chewbacca is or what Wookiees are. It merely responds to my input of symbols by providing an appropriate output of symbols. According to Searle, it's this absence of understanding that precludes something like a search engine from being capable of "thought."

Obviously droids – particularly those as complex as Artoo and Threepio – are far more advanced than any search engine we've created. But Searle asserts that this lack of understanding holds true for *all* machines. In order to demonstrate this, Searle uses the famous "Chinese Room" thought-experiment.

As a variation, let's consider the "Bocce Room." Bocce is, of course, the interplanetary trade language Threepio describes as "like a second language" to him – which is saying something, given that he's fluent in over six million forms of communication. Suppose that you're placed alone in a small room. There's a slot at each end of the room: one labeled "Input," and the other "Output." On the shelves around you are many books. Within those books are a set of rules containing every conceivable phrase that can be said in Bocce, along with the appropriate response to each phrase. The rules all have the following format: "If you receive input 'X,' then give output 'Y.'" No English translations of either the questions or the answers are provided.

Suppose then, that someone fluent in Bocce – someone who *understands* Bocce very well – is outside the room. She has no idea how the room works, nor what's contained within. She writes a question in Bocce on a slip of paper and feeds it through the "Input" slot. In the interior of the room, you receive her query. Imagine that the slip of paper says, "Keez meeza foy wunclaz?" You look along the shelves, finding the appropriate volume for phrases that begin with the word "Keez." After flicking through the pages, you find the following rule:

> "If you receive input 'Keez meeza foy wunclaz?,' then give output 'Nokeezx.'"

You studiously obey the rule, writing your answer on a slip of paper and feeding it through the "Output" slot. A number of further inputs and outputs occur in exactly the same way. Searle argues that this exchange models the process common to all forms of artificial intelligence – be they search engines, human-made robots, or droids. An input of symbols is given and run through a "program" – the series of rules contained within the books – and an appropriate output is provided. Assuming that the volumes are comprehensive enough, and that your ability to look up the phrases is relatively time-efficient, we can imagine the individual outside the room being completely convinced that she's conversing with someone who's fluent in Bocce.

This, however, is far from the truth. As Qui-Gon astutely notes, "[T]he ability to speak does not make you intelligent." While you may be able to very effectively *imitate* a fluent Bocce speaker, you're not actually fluent in the language. You don't *understand* Bocce. You have no idea, for example, that the first question asked of you is "Can I upgrade to first class?" to which you replied with a curt and emphatic "No." The way in which you answer this question is very different from the way in which it would be answered by someone who *actually understood Bocce.*

The same, argues Searle, is true of all artificial intelligence. While advanced robots like droids might be capable of providing convincing imitations of human behaviors and emotions, they'll still be operating according to the same input–program–output process. They may *act* anxious or concerned, or *behave* as though they're experiencing pain or pleasure – but these are merely expressions of rules contained within their programming: appropriate outputs for particular inputs. Since droids are machines, and machines necessarily operate according to this process, they will never – according to Searle – be capable of understanding, nor of thought. This, it seems, may be the very intuition that underpins the terrible treatment of droids. But is it correct?

"He's Quite Clever, You Know, for a Human Being"

There's a good chance that Searle's argument stems from an inflated sense of the way our own minds work. What if *we* operate according to the input–program–output process just described? Would this alter our perspective on whether machines have the ability to think? Might it change the way we think droids should be treated?

The suggestion that our brains merely run programs might seem improbable, but consider the way in which we learn language. As children, we make simple associations between certain sounds and certain things that we experience out in the world. The repeated use of the word *father* to refer to a particular older male gives us reason to connect that term with that individual. In this way, our early use of language is very much like that of machines. We take certain inputs ("Where is my father?"), run them through a program (our recollections of the person with whom the term *father* is usually associated), and provide an appropriate output (gesturing toward the specific individual with whom we associate the word *father*).[2]

Our deeper understanding of precisely what the term *father* means – that it is a relational concept that can be either genetic or social – doesn't come until much later. It's only with this understanding that we can fully grasp the implications of a statement like "Darth Vader is Luke Skywalker's father." But, somehow, this understanding is built upon a system of language that begins with the simple input–program–output process. Given this, it may very well turn out that "understanding" is simply an intricate arrangement of *many* of these three-step processes working in tandem. If this is the case, then there's no reason to think that sufficiently complex machines (like droids) couldn't be capable of developing understanding in the very same way.

There's another problem with Searle's argument that's worth noting. It's very clear to us that the person inside the room doesn't understand Bocce. We need only try to talk to him in Bocce when he's outside the room to show this. But it's not the *person* inside the room who represents the machine in this thought-experiment; *it is the room as a whole*. The question is not, then, whether the *individual* understands Bocce, but rather whether *the entire system* understands Bocce. The difference is subtle, but important. The answer to the first question is clearly "no." The answer to the second question remains a little more uncertain.

There may, therefore, be space for understanding in the Bocce Room, and thus the possibility of droids possessing understanding and thought. But there's one last concern that's difficult to shake – the nagging intuition that there's still a fundamental hurdle that will forever disqualify droids from possessing minds quite like ours: namely, *the fact that they're made of different material* than living creatures.

It may seem a trivial point, but it does a surprising amount of work in dictating the way in which we interact with the world around us. It explains, for example, why we think it's entirely acceptable to use physical force on an uncooperative printer, but would never think of treating a misbehaving pet in the same way. It's why we barely bat an eyelid when we see dozens of battle droids cut down with a lightsaber, yet cringe in sympathy as we watch Luke lose his hand. We are biological beings, and we identify most easily with things made of the same "stuff" as us. But the idea that *only* biological beings should be capable of thought has little basis. Philosophers often like to illustrate the problem with this position by considering what might happen if an advanced silicon-based alien race were ever to visit Earth. [3] It's possible that they would compare their robust, intricate mechanical minds to the delicate, fleshy lumps in our own craniums and quickly come to the very same conclusions that we tend to make about mechanical life forms. "They're so primitive," they would say, "understanding can't possibly occur inside that *mush*."

Ultimately, our favoritism toward the biological seems ill-founded. Consider another thought-experiment. Within the *Star Wars* galaxy, it's common for limbs and body parts to be replaced by incredibly advanced mechanical substitutes. But imagine if, in our own world, we took this one step further – developing a mechanical device that was capable of perfectly replicating the entire function of a human brain. We'd no doubt be hard-pressed to convince people to swap their natural brain outright for a fully mechanical upgrade – even if we could guarantee a flawless transfer of all of a person's character traits and memories. But suppose this transition took place little by little. Suppose that you began by merely swapping out a tiny part that represented only around 1 percent of your brain. You'd be completely unaware of this change – and your mind would continue to function as it always had. You would be just as capable of thought and understanding as always.

What if you were to swap out a little more? Perhaps another 5 percent? It seems that the difference would still be negligible – there are, after all, quite a few individuals who have undergone a brain hemispherectomy and continued to live very normal lives with only *half* a brain. In light of this, it seems that we should be able to replace at least 50 percent of our own brain while still retaining our capability for thought. But is this the limit? Do we stop thinking and understanding as soon as we become 51 percent mechanical? This doesn't seem plausible. It's unclear how that extra 1 percent of mechanical brain could cause such a significant change in our mental processes. Even if it could, there's no principled reason to think that this should occur at 51 percent any more than at 75 or 99 percent.

In fact, it seems we could continue to swap out our brain piece by piece until all that lay within our cranium was mechanical. Furthermore, we could do this without losing any of our capability for thought or understanding. But if this is possible, then the distinction between the biological and the mechanical is irrelevant. Thought, it would seem, relies on far more than just physical operation.

Dignity for Droids

While it's hard to clearly prove that droids are capable of thought, there's enough doubt to make us seriously consider the way in which they're treated. The biological–mechanical distinction isn't as relevant as we might first assume, and the fact that droids run on programs doesn't necessarily prohibit them from possessing understanding. There's a real possibility that the human-like behaviors they exhibit – fear and pain, hope and pleasure – are indeed genuine. If this is the case, they should not be treated as second-class citizens. They should be afforded the same rights and dignities so easily granted to humans and other sentient creatures. Suffering should not be their lot in life.[4]

Notes

1. John Searle, "Minds, Brains and Programs," *Behavioral and Brain Sciences* 3 (1980): 417–57.
2. For further discussion of the way in which we come to learn concepts, see Paul Churchland, *A Neurocomputational Perspective* (Cambridge, MA: MIT Press, 1992).
3. For further discussion of this argument, see Steven Pinker, *How the Mind Works* (New York: Norton, 1997).
4. For another argument that droids should not be treated as slaves, see Robert Arp, "'If Droids Could Think ... ': Droids as Slaves and as Persons," in *Star Wars and Philosophy*, ed. Kevin S. Decker and Jason T. Eberl (Chicago: Open Court, 2005), 120–31. See also James F. McGrath, "Robots, Rights, and Religion," in *Religion and Science Fiction*, ed. James F. McGrath (Eugene, OR: Wipf and Stock, 2011), 118–53.

21

Can Chewie Speak? Wittgenstein and the Philosophy of Language

Rhiannon Grant and Myfanwy Reynolds

Some of the dialogue in the *Star Wars* films has become deservedly iconic, instantly recognizable even to people unfamiliar with the series – such as "May the Force be with you." Plenty more has fallen into obscurity, often equally well deserved – can you recall any of Anakin and Padmé's romantic dialogue from *Attack of the Clones*? Fan discussions of dialogue tend to focus on either the truly great or the truly terrible, but there's a great deal of dialogue that we can't evaluate as either great or terrible because it's untranslated – and maybe untranslat*able*.

The "galaxy far, far away" in which *Star Wars* takes place is home to thousands or even millions of species and cultures that mix freely across many planets. Several human characters speak two or more languages.[1] On top of that, there are droids with noises of their own, some comprehensible to organic speakers, others requiring a "human/cyborg relations" specialist like C-3PO to translate. *Star Wars* is full of beeps, growls, screeches, and burbles. Are they instances of *language*? How about Chewbacca? Can Chewie speak?

Does "Rrwwwgg" Count as Speaking?

Fans well versed in the wider *Star Wars* universe may wish to interrupt us here. As the Expanded Universe expanded, the alien cultures of *Star*

The Ultimate Star Wars and Philosophy: You Must Unlearn What You Have Learned, First Edition. Edited by Jason T. Eberl and Kevin S. Decker.

Wars got fleshed out, and it's canonical that Wookiee noises are a language – Shyriiwook. So why are we asking this question? Ultimately, it has to do with *meaning*. Calling something a language doesn't mean it actually *works* as a language, any more than calling yourself a Jedi means you have Force powers. So, do Chewbacca's noises work like a language?

As viewers, it seems instinctively obvious to us that Chewbacca *is* speaking; he's expressing his thoughts for others to hear. Yet we also know that he doesn't communicate in any language we understand, and perhaps not in any way that fulfils the usual criteria for language at all.

Consider a typical exchange between Chewbacca and Han Solo. Han and Chewie's dialogues follow a basic pattern. Han speaks, asking a question or making a point, in English (representing Basic, the most prevalent language in the *Star Wars* galaxy); Chewbacca then makes a noise. Without context, we'd have no reason to assume this is speech,[2] because his noises don't resemble the form of any language that humans speak. They *do* resemble animal sounds, which aren't usually classified as speech: wampas and rancors both make growling, howling noises that wouldn't be out of place coming from Chewbacca. If we're going to count Chewbacca's noises as talking – as language – why don't we do the same for these others?

We've run into a problem: there is no single definition of what language is. However, linguist Noam Chomsky has advanced the idea that an utterance must have a *syntax* (or structure) determined by a *grammar* (or set of rules) in order to be part of a true language. Taken by themselves, Chewie's utterances don't seem to have enough structure for natural language. For one thing, Chewie usually makes only one noise at a time (although the noises may be lengthy). For another thing, Chewie's noises don't generally have identifiable gaps, breaks, significant variations in tone, or anything else that might suggest the internal structures that Chomsky requires.

Of course, it's always immensely difficult to imagine what a truly alien language would be like (would it be based on sounds at all?), but there are sounds that usually don't change much between languages – sounds that correspond to names of a person, planet, or group of people, for example – which Chewie manages to convey without making any of the sounds we recognize as making up those names[3] or speaking for the length of time required to deliver them. The first objection isn't significant: it's entirely possible Chewbacca can't physically articulate the sounds needed to produce, say, "Luke Skywalker," and so he's substituting others. However, unless Wookiees have perfected some kind of super-abbreviated speech, it's unlikely that Chewie's sounds can contain all the information implied by the surrounding dialogue.

Chewie's noises, then, have neither the content (information) nor the form (length, structure) we expect of speech, and Chomsky probably wouldn't hesitate to file them firmly under "not speech." The nail in the coffin is that Chewie's dialogue wasn't scripted. On set, Peter Mayhew just made appropriate-sounding noises at the right moment; in post-production, these were replaced with roars based on animal noises. The conclusion that these noises aren't real language is so obvious as to be unnecessary: Chewbacca doesn't speak.

Chomsky's theory of the nature of language, though, concentrates on structures, and doesn't touch at all on one of the most important topics in the philosophy of language: *meaning*. The organized complexity Chomsky identifies in human language is distinct from animal noises chiefly because it permits the expression of conceptual meanings that are inaccessible to animals. A wampa can tell another wampa where its latest catch is, but it probably can't have a reasoned discussion about, say, the ethics of eating meat. The question "Does Chewbacca use language?" is thus equivalent to "Do Chewbacca's noises convey meaning?" The next question would be, given that none of us speak Shyriiwook, "How could we tell?"

Wrenches and Hydrospanners: Meaning through Use

How does language convey complex meanings? How do we derive meaning from a string of sounds or signs that aren't *individually* significant out of context? There've been many theories about what exactly constitutes meaning and how it's produced, and the Austrian-born philosopher Ludwig Wittgenstein (1889–1951) contributed significantly to two of these theories.

Wittgenstein once (allegedly) threatened the eminent philosopher Karl Popper with a poker. A lifelong eccentric, he spent three years as a Ben Kenobi–like recluse in a Norwegian village before serving in

World War I. His most substantial work, *Philosophical Investigations*, was published after his death and soon became a classic in the field of philosophy of language. In *Philosophical Investigations*, Wittgenstein took an outright U-turn from the viewpoint of the only complete book he published in his own lifetime, the *Tractatus Logico-Philosophicus*.[4]

In the *Tractatus*, Wittgenstein developed the so-called "picture theory" of language. The idea is that language works by creating a series of "pictures" of the world – so the sentence "Yoda is on Dagobah" tells us how one thing (Yoda) is arranged in relation to another (Dagobah). Similarly, "Han Solo is a scruffy-looking nerf herder" tells us how a thing (Han) relates to a category (scruffy-looking nerf herders). Language is complex, of course, and this theory has room for examples like "It's a trap!" as long as the object named by "it" has been previously identified. Within this theory, a statement is meaningful if it creates a valid picture of part of the world – one that is or could be true.

However, it soon becomes clear that many uses of language are unaccounted for. "Use the Force," for example, is an instruction, not a description. Beyond this, some uses of language *change* the picture of the world – certain acts are actually performed simply by saying that you are doing them, as when Palpatine renames his new apprentice by saying, "Henceforth, you shall be known as Darth … *Vader*." In order to correct the omissions in the "picture theory," Wittgenstein later turned his attention away from truth-as-description as the measure of what makes language meaningful. Instead, in the *Investigations* Wittgenstein focused on language's *context*.

Wittgenstein argues in the *Investigations* that instead of focusing on whether a statement is true or not – whether it matches the world – we need to look at how a remark is *used*. To show this, he invents a very simple language, with only two or three words, which can't be explained by the picture theory. We can imagine such a language existing in the galaxy far, far away, too. Imagine Han is fixing the *Falcon*'s engine and Chewbacca is handing him tools: if he says "wrench," he gets handed a wrench; if he says "hydrospanner," he gets a hydrospanner.[5]

In this very simple language, the words aren't descriptions but *instructions*. In a more complex language, it'd be necessary to say more ("Can I have a … please") or to use nonverbal elements, like holding out your hand, in order to show it's a request. Otherwise, your friend might be overcome with an attack of wit and reply to "hydrospanner" by saying something like "Yes, that's a hydrospanner, well spotted!"[6]

Wittgenstein calls each of the specific ways and circumstances in which we use language *language-games*. Each game has its own rules and can be learned by itself; although we can also take words and phrases across from one language-game to another. Giving orders, as in the example above, is a language-game – you can give orders with single words, like "Fire!" if everyone knows that each word is an *order* (and not, say, an *instruction* to bring the speaker a source of fire, or a *warning* that something nearby is on fire). Other language-games Wittgenstein mentions include describing an event, such as Threepio telling a fireside story to the Ewoks; speculating about events ("Do you think they'll melt us down?"); making up stories – as Lucas has wonderfully done; telling jokes ("How many Gungans does it take to screw in a light bulb?"); and thanking someone, as when Han tells Luke after his rescue from Jabba's clutches, "Thanks for coming after me, I owe *you* one!"[7]

Other philosophers have debated about the application of what counts as a language-game, tending to think of larger things like whole religions as single games. For our purposes, though, it's more useful to think of language-games as small units. "Being a Jedi" or "being a pilot" is too big and complex a practice to be a useful concept here – games, both in our world and in *Star Wars*, are actually quite restricted. The rules of holochess, for example, only apply when the board is in front of you. Likewise, telling a story has rules that differ depending on whether the tale is the terrible legend of Darth Plagueis the Wise or something funny that happened at the Mos Eisley cantina.

One of the most important effects of Wittgenstein's turn away from truth and toward use as a measure of the meaning of words is that it leads us to think about the *social aspects* of language. We use words with other people; we learn words from them; we use words to communicate and coordinate actions with them; and, Wittgenstein argues, we can't even have meaningful words *without* other people. This section of Wittgenstein's work has been called the *private language argument* – a misleading name, because his claim is actually that a truly private language, a language for one speaker only, is *impossible*.

How to Describe a Disturbance in the Force

If Obi-Wan Kenobi is out in the desert with not even a droid or Qui-Gon Jinn's Force-ghost for company, could he create a meaningful word? Suppose that Obi-Wan senses a disturbance in the Force, and to record this he invents a symbol – Wittgenstein uses the example "S" – and marks it in his diary. A few days later, Obi-Wan senses something in the Force that seems to him to be the same sensation as before, and so he marks S at another place in his diary. In the second instance, is he using S correctly? How would he know?

There are problems here that may not be immediately apparent. One is about memory: is Obi-Wan recalling the previous sensation S accurately enough to compare it with the later sensation, which may or may not be the same? There's also a problem about the definition of S: without an independent way of checking for the correct use of S, how can Obi-Wan tell the difference between *thinking* that he's using S correctly and *actually* using S correctly?

Wittgenstein's answer is that he can't. At any particular time, he might *think* that he's using S correctly (i.e., it always stands for the same sensation), but he might *actually* be using S to refer to two different sensations. A language that is entirely and privately the possession of one individual can't have the kind of checking procedure that a real language needs. If Obi-Wan wants to invent a new word, he needs someone else with whom to use it, someone who can also use the word and whose use can be compared with Obi-Wan's. There will always be the possibility for disagreement – Obi-Wan and his friend can argue about what's a table, about what's funny, about what counts as S – but without the kind of community that creates those arguments, he can't really use a word at all.

When asked how many languages he speaks, C-3PO's answer is "over six million forms of communication." So far as *quantity* is concerned, he could well have a far more complete knowledge of these languages than any organic speakers raised with them. It doesn't matter how well he "knows" a language, though, if it doesn't work – that is, if he tries to communicate with a speaker of that language and fails. It's not the completeness of his vocabulary and grammar databases that tells us, for example, that C-3PO can speak Ewok, but rather the fact that he can talk to Ewoks.

Learning the *Lingua Galactica*

The *Star Wars* films and Expanded Universe materials teem with processes, objects, and entities that are unique to their fictional setting, are without counterparts in real life, and would need to be learned by someone encountering them for the first time. Each of these new concepts is named and described to us in the films with either a wholly new term – like *lightsaber*, which didn't exist before Lucas coined it (although the script still uses the generic "laser sword" in places) – or an existing term used in a new way, like *Force*. In some cases, the audience learns the words at the same time as the protagonist on screen: when Ben Kenobi produces Anakin Skywalker's lightsaber for the first time, Luke's incredulous "What is it?" prompts Ben to explain directly: "Your father's lightsaber. This is the weapon of a Jedi Knight." Ben next explains to Luke what the "Force" is – a much preferable explanation to Qui-Gon's explanation to Anakin of what "midi-chlorians" are.

Most of the time, however, the audience works out what new terms mean without ever getting a direct explanation. Instead, they just observe how the characters use them. For example, the backstory of the Sith Order is never explained in the films (though it is in Expanded Universe sources), nor does anyone ever define a "Sith" outright. Still, someone watching only the films can construct a perfectly *workable* definition of "Sith-ness" by observing the term in use.

This is the way you learn how to use words in any situation: you hear how someone else uses a word, and from there you get cues for how to use it yourself. Where Wittgenstein's theory is revolutionary, though, is in arguing that this process of communal use, understanding, and feedback is the *only* way language gains meaning. As we saw, you can't create a new word by yourself, since you need others to use it with you. Furthermore, you can't just make a word mean whatever you personally like simply by redefining it – despite Ben Kenobi's contention that his description of Vader having "murdered" Luke's father is a true description of events "from a certain point of view," Luke is having none of it. If a word is going to change its meaning, several people, at least, need to use it in a new way, because a private language for one person isn't a language at all.

Conversely, if more and more people *do* start to use a word in a new way, eventually the newer usage will become its accepted meaning – either coexisting with an older meaning or superseding it. *Handy* meant something very different to Chaucer than to a modern Anglophone, and ditto for *naughty* in Shakespeare's day; and there's no doubt at least one word in this very sentence will appear strange to someone reading a century from now.

"Let the Wookiee Win"

Earlier, we said that Chewie's speech doesn't meet the requirements laid down by Chomsky for being a language: his utterances are too short and unstructured. For Wittgenstein's "meaning is use" theory, though, these shortcomings become less relevant. Chewie is *communicating:* however it's happening, he clearly passes on information and opinions (sometimes very strongly expressed) to Han and others.

In storytelling terms, the trick is simple, since it's just a matter of ensuring that Han's dialogue tells us just enough about the content of Chewie's utterances without simply repeating them in English. In Wittgenstein's terms, this trick not only maintains the sense of being in an alien world we don't fully understand, but also provides us with sufficient information that we can be confident Chewie really is using language without this ever being stated explicitly. Like Han and Leia, Chewie is a *person*, not a mere brute like a wampa, or a dumb machine.[8] Despite this, Shyriiwook isn't a language in the world in which we live. Unlike, for example, the Elvish of Tolkien's Middle-Earth, Shyriiwook isn't a fully constructed language;[9] it doesn't have an internal grammar, stable vocabulary, or consistent transcription.[10]

What it *does* have is the conversational behavior of a language within the script of the films. Because it allows Chewie to take full turns in a conversation, it serves the function of a language within the setting. Just as we learn the names of new objects by hearing and seeing them used by characters, we learn that Chewie is speaking a language by watching others respond to Chewie's utterances in ways we expect people to respond to language in our world. We have to be wary, though, of overgeneralizing conclusions based on a fictional world. We must acknowledge that the script, visuals, and soundscape of the films have been carefully crafted both to tell us that other characters understand them (inside the film) as well as to ensure that the *audience* understands what's happening (outside the film). This provides a high degree of context that the real world often conspicuously lacks.

To delve too deeply into surveying syntax, grammar, information content, and prosody to determine what makes language *language* is perhaps to miss the point. Wittgenstein shows how a pared-down language consisting only of commands – or beeps, or growls – can be perfectly workable as long as it's understood, while a more nuanced language would be functionally useless if there's nobody else to use it with: imagine if Marc Okrand's Klingon language – the foundation for all spoken or written Klingon in the *Star Trek* universe[11] – had been lost, or Tolkien's carefully crafted Middle-Earth linguasphere had remained an unpublished, unseen "secret vice"?[12] What defines language should not be *what is said* but *whether it is understood*, and *Star Wars* provides a case study of galactic proportions to show that understanding is happily possible without decipherable words. In what's still one of the most iconic images in the saga, the medal ceremony in *A New Hope*, the only dialogue comes from Chewbacca and R2-D2 – and we know without a doubt that it *is* dialogue. We have tuned into Artoo and Chewie's speech, their languages, sufficiently to understand the feelings they're expressing – joy from Artoo and undoubtedly frustration from Chewie for his lack of a medal – despite the lack of words in any language an Earthling could understand.[13]

Notes

1. It possibly says something about modern, mass-market, English-language film that sci-fi movies are often the only ones where bilingualism is common or normal amongst the characters and multiple languages are spoken onscreen. Exactly what it says is a matter for our colleagues in the sociology department.
2. There are other pairs of characters who behave in a similar way – this analysis could be applied almost without change to C-3PO and R2-D2, for example.
3. On this point, it's interesting to compare a stage direction in the script of *Return of the Jedi*, when C-3PO is relating the group's adventures to the Ewoks. Most of the story is in the Ewok language of squeaks and growls, but "[t]hroughout the long account, certain familiar names are distinguishable in English: Princess Leia, Artoo, Darth Vader, Death Star, Jedi, Obi-Wan Kenobi" (Laurent Bouzereau, *Star Wars: The Annotated Screenplays* [London: Titan, 1998], 289).

4. Ludwig Wittgenstein, *Tractatus Logico-Philosophicus*, trans. D. F. Pears and B. F. McGuinness (New York: Routledge, 2001).

5. Ludwig Wittgenstein, *Philosophical Investigations*, ed. G. E. M. Anscombe, P. M. S. Hacker, and Joachim Schulte (Chichester, UK: Blackwell, 2009), §2.

6. For discussion – albeit involving a different sci-fi genre – of how difficult linguistic communication may be between individuals embedded in different cultural contexts, see Paul A. Cantor, "From Shakespeare to Wittgenstein: 'Darmok' and Cultural Literacy," in *Star Trek and Philosophy*, ed. Jason T. Eberl and Kevin S. Decker (Chicago: Open Court, 2008), 3–18.

7. Wittgenstein, *Philosophical Investigations*, §23.

8. Although the line between thinking and nonthinking entities in the *Star Wars* universe seems blurry. For example, Qui-Gon tells Jar-Jar that ability to speak doesn't make him "intelligent," with it being unclear whether by *intelligent* he means *sentient* or *not stupid*. The *Millennium Falcon*, meanwhile, isn't treated as a person by the characters, but Threepio does communicate with it and complains vociferously about the *Falcon*'s "most peculiar dialect." For further discussion of Threepio and other droids' ability to communicate and what this might mean for whether they have *minds*, see Dan Burkett's essay in this volume (chapter 20), as well as Robert Arp, "'If Droids Could Think … ': Droids as Slaves and Persons," in *Star Wars and Philosophy*, ed. Kevin S. Decker and Jason T. Eberl (Chicago: Open Court, 2005), 120–31.

9. See Ruth S. Noel, *The Languages of Tolkien's Middle-Earth: A Complete Guide to All Fourteen of the Languages Tolkien Invented* (Boston: Houghton Mifflin, 1980).

10. Indeed, in the scripts as published, it isn't transcribed at all: Chewie doesn't have dialogue headers, and his speech is variously described as "yelling," as "growling," or as a "roar," "howl," or "bark." Bouzereau, *Annotated Screenplays,* 58, 138, 178–9, 248, and throughout.

11. See Marc Okrand, *The Klingon Dictionary* (New York: Pocket Books, 1985); Marc Okrand, and *Klingon for the Galactic Traveler* (New York: Pocket Books, 1997). The only exception is the Klingon actor Mark Lenard's speech in *Star Trek: The Motion Picture*, which he made up himself.

12. Giving the title to the lecture in which Tolkien first talked at length about the process of constructing language. J. R. R. Tolkien, "A Secret Vice," in *The Monsters and the Critics and Other Essays*, ed. Christopher Tolkien (London: George Allen and Unwin, 1983), 198–223.

13. And it thereby avoids some of the common criticisms of George Lucas's English-language dialogue as well.

Can the Zillo Beast Strike Back? Cloning, De-extinction, and the Species Problem

Leonard Finkelman

It is a time of discovery.
Using new technologies, human
scientists stand on the verge of cloning
extinct organisms.

Meanwhile, in a distant galaxy, the last of the
ZILLO BEASTS has died at the hands of the Jedi.
In an effort to harness the beasts' terrifying power, the evil
Sith Lord Darth Sidious has ordered that the species be resurrected
through cloning.

Against these attempts at DE-EXTINCTION, rational thinkers urge caution,
turning to philosophy to restore order to both galaxies....

A long time ago, on the far, far away planet of Malastare, legends were told of humongous monsters known as the Zillo Beasts. With a massive, snake-like body covered in protective horns, five dexterous limbs, a spiked tail, and a mouth filled with razor-sharp teeth, a single Zillo Beast had the capacity to level an entire city by itself. The planet's children would be warned: don't wake the Zillo Beast! They needn't have worried. All the Zillo Beasts were supposed to be dead.

The Ultimate Star Wars and Philosophy: You Must Unlearn What You Have Learned,
First Edition. Edited by Jason T. Eberl and Kevin S. Decker.
© 2016 John Wiley & Sons, Ltd. Published 2016 by John Wiley & Sons, Ltd.

That was before the Clone Wars, when Republic forces awoke a very much alive and angry Zillo Beast – the last of its kind.[1] It was before that last Zillo Beast caught the attention of Darth Sidious, who wanted to harness the monster's terrible destructive power. It was before Lord Sidious, in his guise as Supreme Chancellor Palpatine, ordered his top scientists to clone the beast after it was killed and the species was finally driven to extinction.[2] The Zillo Beasts had gone extinct – really, this time – but might they awaken again?

Cloning was a common practice in that distant galaxy, where entire clone armies were grown and trained to fight wars across star systems. A young clone named Boba Fett gained notoriety as the galaxy's most feared bounty hunter.[3] In the Unknown Regions beyond the galaxy's outer rim, the Chiss tactical genius Mitth'raw'nuruodo – who would later become Imperial Grand Admiral Thrawn – hatched a plan to clone himself so that his legacy might live on beyond his potential death.[4] One might wonder if the Zillo Beasts could be cloned, but it seems more appropriate to wonder why the Zillo Beasts hadn't been cloned yet.

On our planet, the question of whether or not an organism can be cloned is more difficult to answer. Cloning technology remains in its infancy; nevertheless, success seems inevitable. Following the production of the first viable engineered clones, scientists are already asking: can we resurrect Earth's extinct species? Might the woolly mammoths wake again? The reawakening of extinct species, or "de-extinction," has gained massive popular appeal. Tens of millions of dollars have already been spent on attempts to clone extinct organisms, but it's not yet clear that this has been money well spent.

Julian Baggini has said that philosophy is what we have left to discuss after we agree on all of the facts.[5] Imagine, then, that Republic scientists succeed in cloning a Zillo Beast: what questions would be left to ask? It might be a fact that the clone *looks like* or *behaves like* a Zillo Beast, but it turns out that neither of those facts can tell us if the clone actually *is* a Zillo Beast. It takes a scientist to say whether we can clone extinct organisms, but it takes a philosopher to say whether cloning can actually reawaken extinct species.

Philosophers sometimes use far-fetched examples to answer the questions that are left after we agree on all the facts. These "thought experiments" are meant to show us what we really believe: that is, which ideas we're willing to hold on to when we push those ideas to their logical limits. So let's take the idea of de-extinction to a galaxy far, far away: when the stars are already overrun with clones, are we still willing to defend the idea that extinct species can be reawakened? Some astro-droids may think that philosophers are mindless, but we'll show those overweight globs of grease how philosophy can contribute to the development and understanding of science and technology.

How De-extinct Species Strike Back

We need to agree on some facts before delving into the philosophical debate over de-extinction. Let's start with the obvious: what is a *clone*? Very simply, a clone is any organism that's genetically identical to another organism. Technically, the first clones we encountered in the *Star Wars* galaxy were the Tonnika Sisters – a pair of identical twins who were in the Mos Eisley cantina when Luke Skywalker and Obi-Wan Kenobi first met Han Solo and Chewbacca.[6] But technicalities are rarely satisfying, as anyone who's dealt with a protocol droid can attest. When we talk about clones, we normally don't have naturally born identical twins in mind.

Human scientists generally claim that the most famous clone on Earth is a sheep named Dolly, created by Scottish geneticists in 1996,[7] but *Star Wars* fans know better. The most famous clone on this or any other world is the bounty hunter Boba Fett, created by the skilled cloners of Kamino to be an exact genetic duplicate of Boba's "father," Jango Fett. Boba and Dolly are clear examples of what really comes to mind when we think of clones: not just genetic duplicates, but *genetically engineered* duplicates.

Both the Scots and the Kaminoans engineered their clones in the same way. They used a method known as *somatic cell nuclear transfer* (SCNT). All vertebrate organisms have two fundamentally different kinds of cell in their bodies. *Germ* cells (sperm and eggs) have nuclei containing half of the organism's genetic code: these cells combine with another organism's germ cells to create a new, genetically distinct embryo during sexual reproduction. Once it has a full complement of genetic material, the embryo starts to create *somatic* (body) cells. All somatic cells are descended from an original collection of *stem* cells. Stem cells in different parts of a developing embryo will use different parts of the same genetic code, such that a stem cell in one part of the developing body becomes skin while another in a different part of the body becomes hair. Since they all start with the same full set of genetic instructions, each somatic cell has a nucleus containing *all* of the organism's genetic code.

Suppose that we take a nucleus from one of these somatic cells and microsurgically implant it, with its full complement of genetic material, into an egg whose nucleus' original genetic material had been removed. This transfer creates an embryo similar to one created by sexual reproduction. The embryo will eventually grow into a genetically identical twin of the somatic cell's original owner. That's how SCNT creates clones. In principle, SCNT should work with a nucleus taken from just about any of a body's somatic cells.[8] But no one ever said that the body had to be *living* or from a living *species*. Darth Sidious knew this when the last Zillo Beast died and left a heap of somatic cells lying outside the Republic Senate chambers. Human scientists know this as well and are recovering genetic material from extinct species, as they did from a mammoth carcass found frozen in the Siberian tundra in 2013.[9]

Patience, my young padawan cloner: there are obstacles that make de-extinction more difficult than cloning from living species. The somatic cells from which we take genetic material don't have to come from living bodies, but the egg cells into which we implant that genetic material have to be alive. Even if we could find living egg cells ready to receive genetic material from long-dead organisms, embryos don't simply grow up into mammoths, Zillo Beasts, or bounty hunters on their own. An embryo will only grow into a fully viable organism when it develops in the right environment, which is normally provided by the womb of a member of its own species. Dolly developed in the womb of another sheep. But where can we find a mammoth womb to clone a mammoth?

A tour of Kamino's cloning facilities reveals one possible solution. Boba Fett and his millions of cloned brethren in the Grand Army of the Republic were grown in *artificial wombs*. Grand Admiral Thrawn later found Spaarti "cloning cylinders" that served the same purpose: to create a developmental environment that resembles a living womb closely enough to produce a viable organism from an embryo.[10] The success of Darth Sidious's plan to clone the Zillo Beast depended on his scientists' ability to create an artificial womb for that species. Human scientists haven't yet created an artificial womb. But rest assured: our finest Scottish geneticists and others around the world are working on it. We'll catch up with the Kaminoans soon enough. Once we do, it won't be long before the first clone of a mammoth trumpets its presence to the world.

The Species Problem: Biology's Phantom Menace

Earth's scientists will probably create a woolly mammoth clone in the not-too-distant future, but will the clone *be* a woolly mammoth? This may seem like a silly question. After all, if an animal walks like a duck and talks like a duck, then it must be a duck. But don't forget the question posed by Luke Skywalker in the novelization of *A New Hope*: "What's a duck?"

What makes a duck a duck, a mammoth a mammoth, or a Zillo Beast a Zillo Beast? This is called the *species problem*, and it's one of the oldest in the philosophy of biology. It happens all the time: two biologists agree on all the observable facts about an organism, but still disagree about how to *categorize* that organism. The *Star Wars* galaxy has seen its share of these disputes, such as when the Encyclopedia Galactica controversially asserted that the Neimodian and Duros species were one and the same.[11] One might point to the differences between the two – coloration, temperament, and so on – but the question of whether or not these add up to a difference in species remains open. What's a Neimoidian? That's a philosophical question.

It's commonly believed that organisms within different species have distinctive traits. Tigers have stripes, cheetahs have spots, Wookiees are tall, and Ewoks are short. Popular understanding of genetics holds that a species has a unique genetic code, which explains why humans have human babies and Ewoks have woklings. This way of defining species – by specifying some trait or set of traits unique to all and only members of the species – is called *species essentialism*, and it traces at least as far back as the famed Greek philosopher Aristotle (384–322 BCE).

Essentialism is the view that permits us to say that the Zillo Beast's clone would be a member of the Zillo Beast species. Since clones should be identical, the two organisms would have to share the same trait or set of traits unique to the Zillo Beast species. It's tempting to accept essentialism – if you've seen one Zillo Beast, you've seen 'em all – but biologists generally aren't essentialists these days. Instead, the predominant view in contemporary biology is that species *evolve* by *natural selection*, which is a view that conflicts with essentialism.

Evolution is any change in a species over time. Natural selection causes evolution by preserving beneficial *variations* within a species. In order for natural selection to work, the organisms within a species must vary from one another, they must be able to pass their variations on to subsequent generations, and some variations must give the organisms bearing them a better chance to reproduce than others. Ever since Charles Darwin (1809–1882) first proposed the theory, biologists have found that natural selection works so well because variability is a fundamental fact that is true of all species. If a species has evolved by natural selection – and it seems that all species have – then the species can't have an essence because there's no one trait or single set of traits common to all of its members. If natural selection is true, then species essentialism must be false.

Biologists now accept that species rise and species fall. They are born, they grow, and they die. In that sense, a species is like an individual organism. Individuals don't have essential traits because they grow and change throughout their lives. Consider Anakin Skywalker, who was by turns a precocious child, an obnoxious teen, a heroic young man, a terrifying human–machine hybrid, and an immaterial Force ghost. What makes Anakin the same individual through all that? Perhaps nothing more than the fact that Shmi Skywalker gave a name to her child at his birth and others continued to apply that name throughout his existence. As long as there is some connection to that origin, Anakin is Anakin. Contemporary philosopher Michael Ghiselin proposes that we should think of species in the same way: as individuals identified by their origins.[12] This view is called *species nominalism.*

What makes a duck a duck, a mammoth a mammoth, and a Zillo Beast a Zillo Beast? Here's the nominalist answer: if each of those species has evolved by natural selection, then it can only be that ducks are connected to the particular origin of ducks, mammoths to the particular origin of mammoths, and Zillo Beasts to the particular origin of Zillo Beasts. There's no trait or set of traits – nothing we can point to or measure – that's common to all members of the species. There are only relations to other members of the species.

If Once a Species Starts Down the Dark Path …

Perhaps you're wondering why any of this should be a problem for the prospects of de-extinction. Perhaps you see how Darth Sidious's Zillo Beast clone would be connected to the origin of all Zillo Beasts. This is one case in which your eyes can deceive you. Don't trust them. The species nominalist sees species as individuals. De-extinction is therefore *resurrection*, from a certain point of view. The tragedy of Darth Plagueis the Wise, when recounted by his apprentice Darth Sidious, implies that dead organisms could be resurrected through the dark side of the Force. Does the tragedy of the Zillo Beast imply that extinct species can be resurrected through cloning?

Species and organisms alike are born and grow and change, and so biologists consider species and organisms alike to be individuals. If cloning can resurrect extinct species – if SCNT can bring one kind of individual back from oblivion – then cloning should also be able to resurrect dead organisms. To see how effective a tool cloning can be for waking the dead, we can turn our attention to the Unknown Regions beyond the *Star Wars* galaxy's Outer Rim, to a planet in the Nirauan system. There's an outpost there whose five buildings resemble the fingers of a hand grasping for the stars. This outpost, called the "Hand of Thrawn" complex, is a cloning facility. The work done there has one goal: to bring Mitth'raw'nuruodo, also known as Grand Admiral Thrawn – heir to the Empire following the defeat of Darth Sidious – back from the dead.

Thrawn, ever the brilliant tactician, devised a plan to maintain control of the Empire even after meeting his proverbial destiny. He openly prophesied his return ten years after his apparent death, and then established the Hand of Thrawn complex to grow his own clone. The clone was programmed to wake one decade after the Grand Admiral's reported demise, and Grand Admiral Thrawn would be returned to life. If the scheme had worked, then it might be true, from a certain point of view, that Thrawn had been resurrected, but not from a point of view shared by any biologist. To understand why not, let's return to the cloning facilities on Kamino.

Forty years before Thrawn's clone prepared to awaken on Nirauan, the Kaminoans created Boba Fett through SCNT using Jango Fett's DNA. We can clearly see that Boba and Jango were different people. One could be on Kamino while the other stalked bounties on

Coruscant. One sat in the passenger's seat of *Slave I* while the other sat in the pilot's seat. Boba watched as Jango was decapitated during the Battle of Geonosis. The experience scarred the young clone for life, and none of us need a degree in psychology to understand why: he watched his "father" die. There could be little comfort in the idea that Boba carried his father's entire DNA sequence. Jango Fett would remain dead and Boba Fett would remain alive because each was a unique person with a unique birth and subsequent life. The two, while *qualitatively identical* at the genetic level, were nonetheless *numerically distinct* as living organisms.

There really isn't much difference between Jango and Boba, on the one hand, and Thrawn and his clone, on the other. In both cases, one individual was the clone of the other. Yes, Boba lived at the same time as Jango, and no, Thrawn's clone didn't live at the same time as Thrawn, but this isn't a relevant difference. Thrawn's clone could've easily awoken too early, or Thrawn's death could've been mistakenly reported. Thrawn and his clone are clearly numerically distinct individuals in these cases. It's really only an historical accident that Thrawn did in fact die before his clone awoke, and so the clone should still be considered a numerically distinct organism – that is, someone *other* than Thrawn himself.

Resurrection requires more than the creation of an individual that bears a very strong, or even precise, *resemblance* to another individual that had previously died. An individual is only resurrected if that *very same* individual is somehow returned to life from death. This is what occurs when Emperor Palpatine returns, after his apparent death near Endor, in a younger cloned body.[13] In this case, however, Palpatine *survived* his original body's death as a spectral form of dark side energy that comes to inhabit a cloned body. Thus, Palpatine remains the same *person* even though his cloned body is numerically distinct from the *body* Vader threw down the Death Star's reactor shaft. In Palpatine's case, cloning isn't what enabled his resurrection; it was dark side magic, which is a power that (thankfully) remains beyond the reach of any human science.

The comparison between the Fetts and the Thrawns shows that, in the case of organisms, cloning doesn't – and *can't* – resurrect anyone. Clones of an organism are always numerically distinct from the original organism, regardless of whether that organism is alive or dead at the time. This shouldn't come as too great a surprise since the original and its clone always have different births. Such is the case with organisms. What about species? Can the Zillo Beasts awake again?

Remember: organisms are considered individuals because they're identified by their births and subsequent life stories. An organism's death is a part of its unique life story, and so death is part of what identifies an individual organism. This is one the reasons that Jango, Boba, Thrawn, and Thrawn's clone are all numerically distinct individuals. Each has a unique origin, unique life story, and unique death. Remember also: species are considered individuals because they evolve by natural selection. They have origins, they grow, and they go extinct. The extinction of the Zillo Beasts is therefore a part of the species' unique "life story."

If Darth Sidious were to succeed in cloning the last Zillo Beast, it would mark the origin of a *new* individual. What makes a Zillo Beast a Zillo Beast? From the biological point of view, it would be the organism's place in a sequence of events that starts with the species' birth on Malastare and ends with its extinction on Coruscant. Since the clone would be created after the extinction event, it must be that the clone falls outside the sequence that identifies the Zillo Beasts. Cloning can't resurrect extinct species because the philosophy of biology holds that extinct species stay extinct *by definition*. It's unknown whether Darth Sidious's plan to clone the last Zillo Beast ever succeeded. The Zillo Beast *clone* might have awoken. Nevertheless, the Zillo Beast *species* remains at rest, forever asleep.

A New Hope for Extinct Species?

Scientists on Earth currently debate whether the mammoth, an extinct species of elephant, can be resurrected through cloning. After pushing the idea of de-extinction to its limits in a galaxy far, far away, we now have an answer: *no*, not if the woolly mammoth species is an individual.

This doesn't mean we've philosophically disproven the possibility of cloning mammoths; nor does it mean that we've philosophically disproven that SCNT is a viable technology. All it means is that a mammoth clone wouldn't be a part of the same species as earlier, expired woolly mammoths, just as a Zillo Beast clone wouldn't be part of the same species as the last Zillo Beast who died on Coruscant. We'd therefore have to come up with new names for the species to which these clones belong.

The purpose of philosophy's far-fetched examples is to show which beliefs we want to keep and which we're willing to discard when those beliefs are carried to extremes. When we carry the idea of de-extinction to its logical extremes, we're forced to accept one of two mutually exclusive points of view. One is that de-extinction *can't* work because species are individuals. This point of view is determined by one's unwillingness to discard belief in the theory of natural selection. After all, it's a theory with an incredible amount of supporting evidence, not least of all the apparent genetic relation between Neimoidians and Duros.

The other point of view is that de-extinction *can* work. If one is unwilling to discard this belief, then species must be defined by unique traits. This requires seriously reconsidering one's understanding of the theory of natural selection. Following the works of contemporary philosophers Hilary Putnam and Saul Kripke, a group of philosophers calling themselves the "New Essentialists" recommend taking this route. The New Essentialists argue that essentialism can be compatible with natural selection if one looks beyond organisms' traits for species essences. Their work is gaining traction among philosophers, but hasn't convinced many biologists.[14]

Philosophical reflection leaves the choice of reconsidering de-extinction or reconsidering biological theory. You are free to make this choice, but you must do it alone. I cannot interfere. Can anyone help the mammoths or the Zillo Beasts? You must choose, but choose wisely.[15]

Notes

1. "The Zillo Beast," *Star Wars – The Clone Wars.*
2. "The Zillo Beast Strikes Back," *Star Wars – The Clone Wars.*
3. For further discussion of Boba Fett, see David LaRocca's chapter in this volume (chapter 7).
4. Timothy Zahn, *Star Wars: Vision of the Future* (New York: Bantam Spectra, 1998).
5. Julian Baggini, *The Pig That Wants to Be Eaten* (New York: Penguin Group, 2006).

6. Fraternal twins, like Luke and Leia, don't count as clones because they're not genetically identical (e.g., Luke has a Y chromosome and Leia doesn't). Luke's initial attraction to Leia may have been incestuous, but at least it wasn't narcissistic.

7. Ian Wilmut et al., "Viable Offspring Derived from Fetal and Adult Mammalian Cells," *Nature* 385 (February 27, 1997): 810–13.

8. Cells from the body's immune system wouldn't work because those cells don't have a full complement of genetic material.

9. The discovery was announced in the popular press at http://siberiantimes.com/science/casestudy/news/exclusive-the-first-pictures-of-blood-from-a-10000-year-old-siberian-woolly-mammoth (accessed February 21, 2015).

10. Timothy Zahn, *Star Wars: Dark Force Rising* (New York: Bantam Spectra, 1992).

11. Visit the archived Holonet News page at http://archive.today/9LzS7 (accessed February 21, 2015).

12. For more on the concept of biological individuality, take a look at my essay, "All for One and One for All: Mogo, the Collective, and Biological Unity," in *Green Lantern and Philosophy*, ed. Jane Dryden and Mark D. White (Malden, MA: Wiley, 2011).

13. Tom Veitch et al., *Star Wars: Dark Empire Trilogy* (Milwaukie, OR: Dark Horse, 2010).

14. Marc Ereshefsky, "Species," *Stanford Online Encyclopedia of Philosophy* (Spring 2010), http://plato.stanford.edu/archives/spr2010/entries/species (accessed February 21, 2015).

15. For additional discussion of the metaphysical and ethical implications of cloning, see Richard Hanley, "Send in the Clones: The Ethics of Future Wars," in *Star Wars and Philosophy*, ed. Kevin S. Decker and Jason T. Eberl (Chicago: Open Court, 2005), 93–104.

Episode VII
THE FANDOM AWAKENS

"In That Time ... " in a Galaxy Far, Far Away: Epic Myth-Understandings and Myth-Appropriation in *Star Wars*

John Thompson

Jaws was never my scene
And I don't like *Star Wars*.

– Freddie Mercury, "Bicycle Race"

Aside from the late Freddie Mercury, most folks like *Star Wars* an awful lot. After all, it's got spaceships, droids, aliens, lightsabers, laser guns, mysticism, and a gang of misfits who save the day against all odds. Many of its fans are even more fascinated by the way that creator George Lucas used ideas from mythologist Joseph Campbell (1904–1987) to structure his epic saga. Examinations of *Star Wars* in the context of Campbell's *The Hero with a Thousand Faces* are a staple of PBS discussions of popular culture. I still recall reading a mythic *Star Wars* analysis in an anthropology class as a college freshman; and Bill Moyers's *The Power of Myth*, a series of six interviews with Campbell in 1988 filmed at Lucas's Skywalker Ranch, still gets resurrected on many stations during their annual pledge drive. There's no doubt the enduring popularity of *Star Wars* has much to do with its mythic dimensions. However, there are problems with Campbell's work on myth and Lucas's use of Campbell's ideas in *Star Wars*. Both

The Ultimate Star Wars and Philosophy: You Must Unlearn What You Have Learned,
First Edition. Edited by Jason T. Eberl and Kevin S. Decker.
© 2016 John Wiley & Sons, Ltd. Published 2016 by John Wiley & Sons, Ltd.

Campbell and Lucas promote a simplistic view that encourages fans to avoid some darker, more unsettling ideas in *Star Wars*, which may obscure myth's true power.

I'm well aware that suggesting this may be more perilous than attacking the Death Star. Criticizing such a beloved fixture of popular culture can provoke a surprisingly deep emotional reaction, and I know several people who regard all things *Star Wars* as "sacred."[1] In this instance, I feel like Moses drawing near the burning bush only to hear God command, "Put off your shoes from your feet, for the place on which you are standing is holy ground" (Exodus 3:5, RSV). So as I go bare-footin' along here, bear in mind that, as a teacher of religion and philosophy, my role isn't to be just a caretaker of culture but also a *critic*.

Myth: It's More than Hokey Religions and Ancient Weapons, Han

Few words are as fraught with misunderstanding as *myth*. While, for most people, *myth* means something like "falsehood" or an old tale about a bunch of gods no one believes in anymore, it's in fact something more complex. One of my seminary professors said that we don't make up myths; myths make *us* up. Myths are ancient stories, typically set "long ago" (*in illo tempore* – Latin for "in that time"), that provide answers to perennial questions: where did we come from? Why are we here? How should we live? These questions don't lend themselves to easy answers. We should also distinguish between *myth in general* and specific individual myths, each of which has a very particular focus. Scholars have wrestled with the notion of myth in general for centuries, but have yet to agree upon a single satisfactory definition.

Myth comes from the Greek *mythos*, which can be translated as "story," but with the implication that it may have divine origins, in contrast with *logos*, which defined everyday discourse. Several early philosophers – such as Xenophanes and Plato – were highly critical of myth for its fantastic features, turning to *logos* as the way to truth. Furthering this trend of reliance on *reason*, Aristotle narrowed down myth to its purely literary dimension, defining it simply as "plot." Despite Aristotle's critical attitude, he's correct that *myth* denotes a story or narrative of a particular sort – mysterious in origin, demanding attention, yet concealing a deeper meaning than first meets the eye. In this sense, myth is like poetry, painting, or music. Myth in general defies a neat summary and points to something beyond any specific tale. In addition, the connection to the divine – as what defies rational understanding – suggests that myth contains multiple meanings. In fact, specific myths often have various versions, depending on the context.

While comparative studies of myth focusing on origins and "true" meanings began in earnest during the nineteenth century, the rise of the social sciences – anthropology and sociology – in the twentieth century deepened our understanding of how myth functions. Bronislaw Malinowski (1884–1942) was an anthropologist whose fieldwork in Melanesia convinced him that myth isn't merely a story carrying symbolic meaning but is, in fact, a "living reality":

> Studied alive, myth, as we shall see, is not symbolic, but a direct expression of its subject matter. . . . Myth fulfills in primitive culture an indispensable function: it expresses, enhances, and codifies belief; it safeguards and enforces morality; it vouches for the efficiency of ritual and contains practical rules for the guidance of man. Myth is thus a vital ingredient of human civilization; it is not an idle tale, but a hard-worked active force; it is not an intellectual explanation or an artistic imagery, but a pragmatic charter of primitive faith and moral wisdom.[2]

Despite the now-controversial claim that myth is located in "primitive" cultures, what Malinowski says is basically sound: myth isn't trivial, it's foundational to society, and its force shouldn't be confined to any specific story. Myth is a human universal because it establishes parameters for living in a meaningful world; it defines reality as we know it. Beyond this, myth isn't irrational, since it often includes genuine empirical observations and even certain "scientific truths."[3] However, myth also affords little room for critical questioning or dissent. We could say that myth is *ideology* – or a comprehensive body of ideas and beliefs, conscious or unconscious, that guides an individual or society in story guise.

As human universals, myths are stories pointing to a people's highest values and most sacred beliefs; for example, the great scriptures of the world's religions can be studied as mythic material. As a vital cultural force, myth is fundamental to how we understand ourselves and reality. Myth is all encompassing, defining a worldview, yet different societies will have different myths based upon their different environments and histories. Since there are many myths around the globe, encountering a new culture often leads to a clash of mythic worldviews. Despite this, some argue that beneath such surface differences lies a universally shared mythic core.

Joseph Campbell: "Man of the Monomyth"

Campbell remains one of the most famous mythologists, but he was by no means the first. Unlike earlier students of myth, Campbell was not interested in myth's ultimate origins, nor was he interested in denouncing myths as simplistic explanations of the world now surpassed by modern science. Rather, Campbell investigated myth as a source of timeless human truths still relevant for contemporary life. He drew on a variety of approaches to myth, especially psychoanalysis and the work of Carl Jung (1875–1961).

Campbell contended that there's a single "monomyth," sometimes dubbed the "Hero's Journey," underlying all the world's mythologies. In its full form, this journey entails seventeen stages, but here's a summary:

> The basic monomyth informs us that the mythological hero, setting out from an everyday home, is lured or carried away or proceeds to the threshold of adventure. He defeats a shadowy presence that guards the gateway, enters a dark passageway or even death, meets many unfamiliar forces, some of which give him threatening "tests," some of which offer magical aid. At the climax of the quest he undergoes a supreme ordeal and gains his reward: sacred marriage or sexual union with the goddess of the world, reconciliation with the father, his own divinization, or a mighty gift to bring back to the world. He then undertakes the final work of return, in which, transformed, he reenters the place from which he set out.[4]

Campbell thought that this heroic quest provided the fundamental mythic structure of all cultures, and there are numerous examples in the world's mythologies: Hercules, the Buddha, Moses, even Jesus.

More importantly, according to Campbell, the Hero's Journey traces the psychological and spiritual path to which each individual is called.

Campbell's theory is compelling and testifies to his amazing ability to synthesize findings from various fields. His monomyth allows us to see patterns in, and make connections between, different tales across widely divergent cultures. Moreover, by highlighting what he considered universal human truths, Campbell's ideas continue to resonate with a wide audience hungering for common ground in an increasingly fragmented society. Ironically, Campbell's scheme has achieved an almost mythic status of its own. Small wonder, then, that Campbell's monomyth would appeal to young filmmaker George Lucas.

Lucas's Campbell Soupçon

Campbell's influence on *Star Wars* seems obvious, but the details are difficult to determine, partly because Lucas himself gives different accounts of it. The standard story is that Lucas had written two drafts of *Star Wars* when in 1975 he rediscovered *The Hero with a Thousand Faces*, a book he'd read years before in college. Campbell's Hero's Journey provided a perfect focus for Lucas' sprawling epic. In a later interview, though, Lucas said that soon after completing *American Graffiti* in 1973, while immersed in other projects,

> It came to me that there really was no modern use of mythology ... so that's when I started doing more strenuous research on fairy tales, folklore and mythology, and I started reading Joe's books. Before that I hadn't read any of Joe's books.... It was very eerie because in reading *The Hero with A Thousand Faces* I began to realize that my first draft of *Star Wars* was following classical motifs.[5]

Despite this, it may be that other pop culture sources, such as John Ford's *The Searchers*, the films of Akira Kurosawa, and the obscure French comic series *Valerian and Laureline* provided more commonplace inspirations for Lucas, and that he concocted the story of Campbell's influence later on.[6]

Yet *Star Wars* includes nearly every stage of the Hero's Journey. Luke Skywalker, a simple farm boy on the planet Tatooine (Campbell's "the ordinary world"), seeks out the enigmatic hermit Obi-Wan

Kenobi ("meeting the mentor"), who introduces him to the mystical wisdom of the Force. With Obi-Wan's guidance, Luke then leaves home on a quest to save Princess Leia ("answering the call to adventure"). Along the way, he's helped by the androids C-3PO and R2-D2 ("meeting companions"), encounters shady characters and danger at a cantina in Mos Eisely ("crossing the threshold"), only narrowly escaping from stormtroopers into space. On the way, he begins his Jedi training ("undergoing trials"), frees the Princess ("encountering the goddess"), and escapes with the plans to the Death Star ("the magical elixir/ultimate boon" that will save the people). Luke then joins the Rebels in the assault on the Death Star, during which Darth Vader pursues him ("Dark Father," his nemesis with whom he'll eventually reconcile) as he's seeking to make the kill-shot ("magic flight/pursuit"). After destroying the Death Star, Luke reunites with his friends at the Rebel base, where he receives a medal for his heroism ("crossing the return threshold," "master of two worlds," and "freedom to live").

It'd be difficult to conclude that *Star Wars* was *not* tailor-made to Campbell's specifications – a perfect example of the Hero's Journey, something Campbell himself notes in *The Power of Myth*. However, this all begs a larger question: does Campbell's heroic monomyth *really* explain all the world's mythologies?

"Great, Kid! Don't Get Cocky!"

Most criticisms of Campbell's view have to do with its overreach. Campbell sought to give us *the* theory of myth, and such a grand narrative will almost invariably have holes. Campbell's monomyth leads us to see similarities between tales and, in so doing, overlooks many significant differences. To gain genuine understanding, it's just as important to note *contrasts* between myths, especially when they reflect very distinct cultures: "It is just as important to stress differences as similarities, to avoid creating a Joseph Campbell soup of myths that loses all local flavor."[7]

A related point has to do with Campbell's psychological approach to myth. While valid, this approach assumes certain things about myth and the human psyche. These assumptions might be explained by the fact that Campbell worked closely with Carl Jung and Mircea Eliade (1907–1986), both of whom also proposed theories of myth with universal scope that relied on psychoanalytic theories. All three were members of the Eranos Circle, a group of influential scholars who met regularly to discuss topics focusing on the comparative study of religion, spirituality, and psychology.[8] Campbell, however, tends to overlook the social dimensions of Jung's "collective unconscious," and virtually ignores the larger political and cultural contexts of mythic narratives.

Campbell's theory is also exceedingly conservative and founded on a deep nostalgia: for him, the cure for modern problems is found by returning to earlier notions of spirituality and moral virtue. In promoting a "living mythology," Campbell harkens back to a lost "golden age" from which we've fallen, but to which we can return with effort and the guidance of a "sage" (Campbell himself? Lucas? Now Abrams?). Beyond this, feminists have pointed out that Campbell's heroic monomyth is male centered. Not only are nearly all of his examples male, but also the very structure of the monomyth puts female figures in secondary roles like seductive temptresses or maternal/erotic "goddesses."[9] A related point is that the heroic monomyth is permeated with violence: the hero must engage in a series of violent struggles to reach his goal, for which he's amply rewarded. Campbell can say that violence is symbolic as a necessary aspect of personal growth that "requires a death and a resurrection," but this is beside the point.[10] Campbell's theory is untroubled by problematic dimensions of human nature and condones destructive force as an essential part of our development.

Campbell's theory has proven quite influential; as mentioned, it has attained quasi-mythic status itself. Thanks in no small part to *Star Wars*, the monomyth has become *the* hidden, sacred knowledge pervading our pop culture, revealed for our salvation by the archetypal "Wise Man." It's so prevalent in television and movies that a veritable cottage industry of studies focused on various elements of his monomyth in dozens of films has developed.[11] From a scholarly perspective, it seems Campbell has crafted *the* master narrative of myth. Yet his work has flaws, and Lucas's adaptation suffers some of the same shortcomings.

"And You Said It Was Pretty Here!"

Tensions between *mythos* and *logos* date back to ancient Greek philosophers, if not earlier. Most societies require their members to accept the worldview informing their fundamental mythic narratives. This kind of indoctrination – *socialization* or *enculturation* – is inevitable if we're to live in community. As Dr. Dysart, the pensive psychiatrist in Peter Schaffer's play *Equus*, observes, "We need a story to see in the dark." But myth brooks no dissent from its version of reality. To question myth (or at least a particular authorized version) is to question the very foundation of a culture. In mythic terms, critically examining myth seems like a decidedly Promethean, even Luciferian, project, involving just the sort of heroism Campbell extols!

Earlier, I stated that myth is ideology in story guise, and unquestioned ideology often has very bad repercussions. There are many historical examples of myth's destructive power: the Hindu creation myth from the *Rig Veda* regarding the sacrifice of Purusha, the cosmic person, provides divine justification for India's traditional social caste system; the Teutonic myth of the "Master Race" grounded Nazi ideology; and the widespread myth of the "divine right of kings" legitimated brutal despotism across Europe for centuries. In the United States, one myth is the all-too-familiar "rags to riches" story, suggests Robert Segal. Other critical studies that unmask particularly powerful, harmful myths in the contemporary United States include Justin Fox's *The Myth of the Rational Market* and Richard Hughes's *Myths America Lives By*.[12]

As with these examples, the mythic structure of *Star Wars* has immense hidden power, and this power (like the Force itself) has a dark side. The epic embraces a cosmic dualism of essential conflict ("forces of light" vs. "forces of darkness") in which certain groups or individuals are clearly superior ("chosen ones"). This heroic tale puts in the foreground the male protagonist in his struggles, ignoring the larger communal, economic, and institutional forces at work. Most disturbing of all, *Star Wars* cavalierly accepts, and even celebrates, violence as integral to the heroic life. The fates of ordinary people are ignored except when they affect the hero or a few others among the "chosen." We don't have to delve too deeply to see these same themes informing the presentation of U.S. history; there's a solid mythic line in the popular imagination running all the way from Plymouth Rock through Valley Forge, the Alamo, Custer's Last Stand, and the American "victory" over the Soviet Union in the Cold War. Moreover, consider this: given a little tweaking, couldn't *Star Wars* also serve as an inspiration for terrorist groups such as al Qaeda? Because this heroic tale obscures the much larger background picture of that galaxy far, far away so long ago, can't we ask what's *really* going on with the Empire and the Rebellion? Might we more accurately call the Rebels "insurgents," like the Iraqis who resisted U.S. occupation during the ill-conceived Iraq War of 2003–2011? This would make Luke, Leia, and their compatriots terrorists, at least from the Empire's perspective.[13]

We could also ask about the political and market forces that informed *Star Wars* and have, in turn, been shaped by it. In the 1980s, critics of Ronald Reagan derided his logistically unfeasible S.D.I. (Strategic Defense Initiative) as "Star Wars," yet a large portion of the American public believed this fanciful missile shield would be effective despite its technical flaws and staggering costs. The United States is now even more bedazzled by costly military technological gadgetry of dubious value. Perhaps even more disquieting, *Star Wars* itself has grown far beyond anyone's expectations to now include six movies (with a new trilogy and additional spinoff movies on the way); several television series; a veritable library of books, comics, and video games; and a monumental mass of merchandise (clothing, action figures, accessories, etc.). How much energy and capital have gone into all this, to say nothing of the enormous use of resources? *Star Wars*, despite its mythic aspects, never was a pure artistic or spiritual creation so much as it is *Star Wars*™, a product packaged, marketed, and delivered to a mass audience as part of a global commercial enterprise. This fact, curiously, is hidden in plain sight to most fans, many of whom are entranced by Lucas's superficial use of Campbell's monomyth and don't see how we're all held captive by the mythic imperatives of global capitalism. The few remaining Jedi may sense a sinister irony here: *Star Wars*™ is the real Empire, and the fans are its legions of consumer-subjects.[14]

A Final Word

Fans, this chapter may have been something of a buzzkill, but let me assure you that, unlike Freddie Mercury, I *do* like *Star Wars*. Nevertheless, we must explore and critique *our own* society's values, practices, and products. To do so isn't necessarily to deride or denigrate them. There's nothing wrong with enjoying a truly ripping yarn (and *Star Wars* rips the heck out of most popular sagas), and we don't need to be ashamed about yearning for our own lightsabers. Everyday life can be sometimes rather drab; who wouldn't want the occasional space adventure in the company of a couple of funky droids, a major babe, and a loyal Wookiee? I only ask that we pause to think about what else might be at work in all this.

It turns out that *Star Wars*, like real life, has its troubling aspects. At the very least, it makes sense to ask whether members of the Lucas Inc. Billionaire Entertainers Boys' Club, while undeniably successful, might not have any deeper insight than the rest of us; certainly, they don't appear to be aware of what "myth" actually is or how it functions. While they grasp enough about myth to see *some* of its power and significance, they don't grasp enough to see its darker, potentially destructive aspects, or even how modern myths hold them in their sway. Still, these folks are richer and more powerful than you and me, which means it's up to us to "speak truth to power" even if they may not always notice or even care. Because, like it or not, *their* force is most definitely with us.

Notes

1. I'm leaving aside here the fact that "Jedi Knight" is an officially recognized religion, with its own rites, sacred texts, and various sects.
2. Bronislaw Malinowski, "The Role of Myth in Life," in *Magic, Science and Religion and Other Essays* (Westport, CT: Greenwood Press, 1984), 98.
3. Native American myths often include accurate descriptions of the natural world. Creation myths in Genesis faithfully depict the basic view of the world shared by peoples throughout the Middle East during the Bronze Age: a three-tiered universe (heaven, earth, and underworld) bounded by primordial waters.
4. Robert Ellwood, *The Politics of Myth: A Study of C. G. Jung, Mircea Eliade, and Joseph Campbell* (Albany: State University of New York Press, 1999), 144.
5. Stephen and Robin Larsen, *Joseph Campbell: A Fire in the Mind* (Rochester, VT: Inner Traditions, 2002), 541.
6. For details of these different accounts, see "Star Wars Origins – Joseph Campbell and the Hero's Journey," www.moongadget.com/origins/myth.html (accessed December 2, 2014); as well as Michael Heileman, "The Ancestry of Star Wars," www.kitbashed.com/blog/fairytales-and-the-heros-journey (accessed December 2, 2014).

7. Donald J. Constentino, "African Oral Narrative Traditions," in *Teaching Oral Traditions*, ed. John Miles Foley (New York: Modern Language Association, 1998), 183.

8. Members of Eranos also included theologian Rudolf Otto, scholar of Jewish mysticism Gershom Scholem, and the Islamicist Henry Corbin. The Bollingen Foundation, a wealthy sponsor of Eranos, also aided the publication of Eranos scholarship via Princeton University Press's Bollingen Series, which first published Campbell's *Hero with a Thousand Faces*. For details, see Steven M. Wasserstrom, *Religion after Religion: Gershom Scholem, Mircea Eliade, and Henry Corbin at Eranos* (Princeton, NJ: Princeton University Press, 1999).

9. To see problems with the gender roles of *Star Wars* from the feminist perspective, see Cole Bowman's chapter in this volume (chapter 14).

10. Joseph Campbell and Bill Moyers, *The Power of Myth*, ed. Betty Sue Flowers (New York: Doubleday, 1988), 152.

11. The most extreme example is Stuart Voytilla's *Myth and the Movies: Discovering the Myth Structure of 50 Unforgettable Films* (Studio City, CA: Michael Wiese Productions, 1999).

12. See Robert A. Segal, *Myth: A Very Short Introduction* (New York: Oxford University Press, 2004), 139–40; Justin Fox, *The Myth of the Rational Market: A History of Risk, Reward, and Delusion on Wall Street* (New York: HarperCollins, 2009); and Richard T. Hughes, *Myths America Lives By* (Urbana: University of Illinois Press, 2003).

13. To see why filmmaker Kevin Smith would agree with this, but may be wrong to do so, see Charles Camosy's chapter in this volume (chapter 6).

14. To extend the irony, Lucas himself explored how mythologically supported consumerism could come to dominate a near-future society in his pre–*Star Wars* film, *THX-1138* (1971).

Star Wars, Emotions, and the Paradox of Fiction

Lance Belluomini

HAN:	What's going on … buddy?
LANDO:	You're being put into carbon freeze.
FETT:	What if he doesn't survive? He's worth a lot to me.
	(While Han and Leia gaze into one another's eyes in the foreground.…)
VADER:	The Empire will compensate you if he dies. Put him in!

The carbon-freezing chamber scene from *The Empire Strikes Back* never fails to send chills down my back. It's the most powerful, dramatic, romantic, and emotional scene in the entire *Star Wars* saga.[1] We feel emotionally stirred when we witness the intense romantic moments between Han and Leia. We can't help but feel the sadness and anguish that Leia and Chewie are going through when Han is lowered into the pit, and we feel sorry for Chewie with each wild howl he lets out. We're fearful of what will happen to Han. We're angry at Vader for using Han as a test subject. And we're anxious when Fett takes off in *Slave I* with Han's carbonite-encased body. Why? Because we care about Han and worry about his fate.

But our strong emotional reactions to these scenes raise intriguing philosophical questions: why should we care about what happens to Han, Leia, or anyone in the *Star Wars* universe when we know they don't exist? Isn't there something irrational about having an emotional

The Ultimate Star Wars and Philosophy: You Must Unlearn What You Have Learned, First Edition. Edited by Jason T. Eberl and Kevin S. Decker.
© 2016 John Wiley & Sons, Ltd. Published 2016 by John Wiley & Sons, Ltd.

response to fictional characters? Philosophers call this the *paradox of fiction*.

Let's lay out this paradox as it relates to the *Star Wars* films in three claims:

1. We have genuine and rational emotional responses to the fictional characters and events in *Star Wars*.
2. In order to have genuine and rational emotional responses, we must believe these characters and events really exist.
3. Nobody believes these fictional characters and events in *Star Wars* exist.

Claim 1 seems true for many of us who, when we watch *Star Wars*, experience genuine and rational emotional responses to Han and Leia during the carbon-freezing scene. We're joyful when they share a passionate kiss and Leia says, "I love you," while Han famously responds, "I know." We're sad when they're separated from one another and Han is lowered into the pit. Claim 2 challenges this, because it says that in order to have these genuine and rational emotional responses to Han and Leia, the responses must be properly supported by our beliefs about what should provoke such responses. But our emotional responses to Han and Leia aren't properly aligned with what we actually believe. Claim 3 states the belief we have concerning the fictional universe of *Star Wars*: Han and Leia are purely fictional characters. Interestingly, each of the three claims seems correct when viewed separately, but the claims conflict when viewed together. Hence the paradox.

Three main theories attempt to solve the paradox of fiction: the *illusion theory*, the *thought theory*, and the *pretend theory*. Because all three claims can't be jointly true, each theory rejects or changes one of the three claims. Let's consider each to see if any of them can plausibly explain our emotional reactions to *Star Wars* and bring order to the galaxy we cherish!

"You Know, I Did Feel Something"

The English poet and philosopher, Samuel Taylor Coleridge (1772–1834), said that our proper engagement with fiction involves a "willing suspension of disbelief,"[2] and we seem to do precisely this when we watch *Star Wars*. Just as Luke feels something real when he blocks the bolts from the seeker remote with his blast shield down, we too seem to feel something real when we watch Obi-Wan teaching Luke about the Force. While engrossed in the films, we believe in the characters, the ships, and the situations depicted. The *illusion theory* claims that the fictional work creates in us the illusion that the characters and situations depicted actually exist. Those who support this view don't see a problem with our emotional responses to *Star Wars*.[3] Illusion theorists attempt to solve the paradox of fiction by denying claim 3 and replacing it with the claim that a special type of belief about the existence of characters and events arises in the course of our engagement with fiction.

This theory is appealing. When we watch the lightsaber duel between Vader and Obi-Wan in *A New Hope*, we feel they are real people, and when we hear them speak, we sense that they've known one another for a lifetime. Who can forget Vader's taunting remarks: "I've been waiting for you Obi-Wan. We meet again at last. The circle is now complete. When I left you, I was but the learner, now I am the master." Moments later, Vader adds: "You should not have come back!" We're absorbed and emotionally engaged – we experience fear, wonder, and sadness when Obi-Wan is struck down. We tend to talk about these characters as if they're real people who have a real history with one another, and we wonder what really happened between them "before the dark times, before the Empire."[4]

There is a tension here: while many fans like to talk as if the characters and events in *Star Wars* are real, none of us *actually believe* that Luke's heroic journey is real. We don't really believe that Darth Vader exists, or that he really has twin children named Leia and Luke who were separated at birth. We don't really believe the *Millennium Falcon* is a real ship that can make the jump to hyperspace, no matter how much we wish it were true. Philosopher Gregory Currie underscores this point in his dismissal of the illusion theory: "Hardly anyone ever literally believes the content of a fiction when he knows it to be a fiction; if it happens at moments of forgetfulness or intense realism in the story (which I doubt), such moments are too brief to underwrite our sustained responses to fictional events and characters."[5]

The other problem with the illusion theory is that we don't fully *act* as if we think the characters and events depicted are really before our eyes. If we believed in the real existence of these fictions, then these beliefs would be manifested in our behavior. When Luke confronts Vader on Bespin, Vader welcomes him: "The Force is with you, young Skywalker. But you are not a Jedi yet." This scene chills many of us to the bone. But while we may feel scared, we don't feel threatened by Vader, nor do we believe we're in danger. If we believed Vader was real, even temporarily, we'd likely run from our house in fear of Vader showing up with his 501st Legion of stormtroopers. But we don't. Instead, we watch *The Empire Strikes Back* over and over despite being scared by Vader. Our lack of action precludes the explanation that we're under the illusion that Vader is real. Given that the illusion theory can't successfully deny claim 3, it can't solve the paradox of fiction.

"Be Mindful of Your Thoughts"

According to the *thought theory*, our emotional responses to fictional characters and events are caused by our thoughts, replacing claim 2 with an amended claim: in order to have genuine and rational emotional responses to the characters and events in *Star Wars*, we don't need to believe they exist; we just need to form *mental representations* of them.[6] When we take in the image of Vader using the Force to choke Captain Needa for having lost track of the *Millennium Falcon*, it isn't these images that cause the emotional responses. Instead, our emotional responses are triggered by our thoughts, which mirror or represent the fictions.

One observation that the thought theory makes is that we often have emotional reactions to imaginary situations: imagine standing on a precipice where you then entertain the thought of falling over the edge.[7] There's no real danger because there's no one around to push you over, and you certainly don't intend to jump. But if you vividly imagine falling over the edge of the steep cliff and hitting the ground, you can genuinely scare yourself. You're not scared by a belief that you're actually in danger. Instead, you're scared by the content of your thought – the mental image of something bad happening. This, according to the thought theory, is what happens when we're engaged in fiction. Think of when the wampa approaches Luke right as the lightsaber jumps into his hand. He ignites it, frees himself, and cuts off the attacking wampa's arm. This immediately triggers emotional responses within us. We feel a range of emotions such as anxiety, fear, and surprise. Just as the mere thought of falling over the edge of a dangerous cliff scares us, the mere thought of the wampa moving in to attack Luke scares us. We don't need to believe that the wampa or Luke exist in order to have genuine and rational emotional responses.

But isn't there a more direct connection between the behavior of the fictional characters and our emotions? When we hear Han's screams of agony in the torture room on Cloud City and we witness his torture, there's no time to reflect and form any conscious thoughts or mental representations – while this may work in a book or at the edge of a precipice, there's no time to do this in a movie. Thought theorists disagree. They would argue that no reflection is needed. The visual and auditory stimuli we take in can certainly cause an immediate mental representation that can then trigger emotional responses in us.

However, in order to produce emotional responses in us, the mental representation of Han must be something that's connected in the right way to our affections. For instance, thinking about C-3PO calculating the odds of surviving an attack on an Imperial Star Destroyer evokes nothing in me. I need to be able to relate to the fictional situation and individuals in order to produce an emotional reaction. Han needs to represent either myself or someone I care about. The "falling over the cliff" example illustrates this point. You get scared when you recognize that it is *you* who's falling. Notice that Han's torture scene is different than the "falling" example. You can't imagine yourself in the situation Han is in because Han isn't you and Han doesn't represent you. And you can't imagine anyone you know in his situation. To actually feel bad for Han, you must construct a situation where you can relate to him. And the only way would be to say you think that he is real or resembles someone you know. But this isn't plausible. We can therefore draw a parallel between the "falling" example and Han's torture case: in both situations, we hold a background belief that the person in the situation (the one falling, the one being tortured) is real. We represent Han in the same way that we conceive of someone we witness being tortured on the news: as a real person. So the thought theory assumes that the things we have thoughts about are real. But thought theorists aren't illusion theorists: they don't think we're under the illusion that fictional characters and scenarios are real.

To further undermine the thought theory, consider the pity we feel for Han when we watch him being tortured, and how Vader strikes fear into us. We instantly have real emotional responses as the rack tilts forward onto the torture device and Vader activates the mechanism. But our emotional responses don't seem to be caused by any immediate "thoughts" or "mental representations" of Han being tortured by Vader because the thoughts don't correspond to any existing objects. Hence, those thoughts don't seem to be the real objects of our emotions. Our experience also doesn't feel like a fear of an immediate thought. It doesn't feel like we pity a thought. Rather, we experience fear and pity *directly* because Vader is torturing Han. We don't have pity for our *thought* of Han. Instead, we pity *Han himself*. The thought theory struggles with providing a satisfying answer as to *what* we fear and *whom* we pity. Ultimately, the thought theory can't adequately explain why we have emotional reactions to fiction.

"You're Imagining Things"

The *pretend theory* attempts to dissolve the paradox of fiction by describing the emotions we have as audiences of fiction as different from the real-world emotions we experience. This involves a denial of claim 1. The *pretend theory* says that the emotions we experience while watching *Star Wars* are not *genuine* emotions. Rather, they're *quasi-emotions*.

Consider the feeling of awe we experience during the "Binary Sunset" scene in which Luke stands on the desert ridge outside his homestead, framed by the setting twin suns of Tatooine with the moving Force theme music. We feel for Luke as he momentarily looks down in sadness and frustration – his hopes of joining the Imperial Academy on hold for "a whole 'nother year." But Luke finds the inner strength to look back up, and we relate to his hope for a better future.

The philosopher Kendall Walton says that when we watch a fictional scene such as this, we not only pretend that what we're seeing is happening, we also pretend to have certain feelings. He draws an analogy with children playing "make-believe," pretending to be all kinds of things: pilots, astronauts, even characters from their favorite sci-fi movies:

Children do not peer into worlds apart, nor do they merely engage in a clinical intellectual exercise, entertaining thoughts about cops and robbers, or whatever. The children are in the thick of things; they participate in the worlds of their games. We appreciators also participate in games of make-believe, using works as props. Participation involves imagining about ourselves as well as about the characters and situations of the fiction – but not just imagining that such and such is true of ourselves. We imagine doing things, experiencing things, feeling in certain ways.[8]

My 4-year-old son likes to pretend he's Darth Maul. He enjoys putting on performances when we're entertaining guests, twirling his double-bladed retractable lightsaber toy around, to "Duel of the Fates." My son is participating in a game of make-believe, and the lightsaber is the prop he uses to play this game. Similarly, we completely immerse ourselves in the characters and events depicted in *Star Wars*. But while my son's plastic lightsaber is a physical prop in his game, the films themselves are props for our imaginings.

The pretend theory says that when we feel scared while Vader interrogates and chokes Captain Antilles in *A New Hope*, we're just imagining that we're terrified of Vader. Our apparent fear is only a "quasi-fear," which is less intense than the real emotion. Since we're interacting with Vader in make-believe, we pretend to fear him. We imagine having emotions as opposed to actually experiencing real emotions. Put differently, we simulate situations and emotional states – particularly the kind we wouldn't want to endure in our daily lives.

"Luke, Trust Your Feelings"

What can we say for the pretend theory? Are we prepared to commit to the idea that the emotions we experience while watching *Star Wars* aren't real but rather quasi-emotions? Well, let's take Obi-Wan's advice in *A New Hope*: "Trust your feelings."

First, we *do* seem to be in touch with our emotions much of the time. We're unable to control the positive emotions we feel when Yoda lifts Luke's X-wing out of the Dagobah swamp. We feel triumph, joy, surprise, and amazement. When Luke attempts to lift his X-wing but gives up in defeat, we feel sad as we witness his despair and dejection. Yoda's lesson on the power and nature of the Force also adds to our emotional engagement. His speech is full of optimism. The music also moves us: the scene starts with a somber version of the Force theme and ends with the triumphant version of Yoda's theme. We're left with a triumphant feeling that certainly feels like real-world triumph.

Walton would point out, though, that we lack the ability to tell the difference between "quasi-triumph" and real triumph, adding that there's a behavioral difference between real emotion and quasi-emotion. If I experience quasi-triumph when Yoda lifts Luke's X-wing from the swamp, it stays with me only a short time and doesn't cause me to act; but real triumph would stay with me longer and motivate me to act, perhaps letting out a roar and raising my arms. We must admit, though, that a real-world emotional reaction doesn't always motivate behavior. We often feel real triumph and joy without expressing it outwardly. Experiencing real-world triumphant feelings can also come in varying intensities. So, the triumph a viewer feels when Yoda lifts the X-wing is likely to be less intense than the triumph she felt when *Apollo 11* landed on the moon in 1969, but maybe more intense than the feeling of solving a jigsaw puzzle.

The analogy to games of make-believe raises another objection to Walton's pretend theory. If we're merely pretending to be scared and angry at Vader for torturing Han, then we should be able to control when we pretend and when we don't, since pretending is a *voluntary* activity. But it doesn't make sense to say we can stop pretending to be emotionally moved when Vader tortures Han: the feelings we experience happen involuntarily. We have no choice but to fear the dianoga that lives in the Death Star trash compactor, and to delight when Han swoops in to Luke's aid and gives him a clear shot at the Death Star's exhaust port.

There's a clear difference between watching a fictional film and playing children's games of make-believe. When my son pretends his lightsaber is real, he does this by choice, for he could've pretended it's a pirate sword, imagining he's Captain Hook. He has freedom in his pretend-play and can decide to use his prop in a variety of ways. And because he can, he has a degree of control over his emotional responses to the use of props. We, on the other hand, don't have this degree of freedom to pretend when we watch *Star Wars*. As onlookers, we experience involuntary emotional states in response to the images and sounds. We don't pretend to have the emotions we do.[9] So it's not looking like the pretend theory can solve the paradox.

"It's Like Something out of a Dream"

Fictional worlds like the *Star Wars* galaxy allow us to experience a range of positive and negative emotions.[10] Similarly, when we dream, we experience an imagined world that elicits all kinds of emotional reactions. A fictional film is therefore like a dream – the only difference being that our mind both creates and experiences a dream, whereas a fictional film is a manufactured experience created for us. While we dream, our experience in the dream is real. The emotions we experience in dreams are certainly as real as the emotions we experience when awake.[11] The same is true of fiction. Whether we watch the climactic lightsaber duel in *The Empire Strikes Back* in which Vader suddenly attacks Luke from hiding or whether we have a dream about it, we can still experience real fear and surprise in the same intensity.

So where does this leave us with the paradox of fiction and emotions in relation to *Star Wars*? Let's review the competing three claims that result in the paradox:

1. We have genuine and rational emotional responses to the fictional characters and events in *Star Wars*.
2. In order to have genuine and rational emotional responses, we must believe these characters and events really exist.
3. Nobody believes these fictional characters and events in *Star Wars* exist.

None of the three theories we've considered can solve the apparent puzzle.[12] We don't fear any real threat of Vader and his stormtroopers invading our homes, and we certainly don't act in ways that suggest we believe in Vader's existence, so the *illusion theory* must be wrong in saying that we temporarily but mistakenly think characters like Vader really exist and might be dangerous. We're frightened of Vader *himself* on the screen, and not at the mental representations we form of Vader, so the *thought theory* can't resolve the paradox. And if our fear of Han being lowered into the carbon-freezing pit feels like real fear, given that we're involuntarily moved by what happens to Han, the *pretend theory* can't help us. Considering the shortcomings of these theories, where do we stand with the paradox of fiction? Perhaps we need to focus on an important word in the first claim about emotions: that they are "rational." Are the emotional responses we have to *Star Wars* rational?

"There. You See, Lord Vader. She Can Be Reasonable"

To this last question, Colin Radford (1939–2001) replies, "No." While we experience genuine and unavoidable emotions in response to fiction, Radford doesn't think they're rational.[13] Our emotional reactions must be "reasonable responses" to our cognitive state to be rational. But with any work of fiction, our emotional reactions to the fictional characters don't meet the "reasonable response" condition. When we see Han lowered into the carbon-freezing pit, the pity we feel for him is not a reasonable response, given that we're just imagining that Han is in an unfortunate situation. Neither Han, since he's not real, nor Harrison Ford, in portraying Han, is in any real danger.

The same is true for all the emotions we experience while watching *Star Wars*. When we witness Emperor Palpatine electrocuting Luke, there's no denying we're fearful of Palpatine and feel compassion for Luke. While Radford would agree that our feelings are real and unavoidable, he'd add that these emotional reactions are not reasonable responses to fictional scenarios. But couldn't we argue that our fearful reactions to Palpatine are not unreasonable by pointing out that he's a truly terrifying and evil figure? We have good reason to fear him when Vader says to Moff Jerjerrod, "The Emperor is not as forgiving as I am," or says to Luke, "The Emperor will show you the true nature of the Force. He is your master now." Radford would reply that even though we're moved by the images of Palpatine, and by the fictional things we hear Vader say about him, our reactions aren't made rational because of those things, for we don't believe we're in any danger given our correct belief that Palpatine doesn't exist.

Nevertheless, there's no doubt we're moved by the images we see and the sounds we hear in well-made films – which is part of the reason why *Star Wars* continues to be a major part of our popular culture. We care about the fictional characters and events taking place in this fairy tale world. We feel pity for Luke when he returns to his homestead only to find the charred remains of his aunt and uncle. We instantly feel tense and uneasy when C-3PO gets shot on Cloud City. We're left in a state of wonder when Luke takes off from Dagobah and Yoda says, "No. There is another."[14] We feel relief and satisfaction when Vader throws Palpatine down the reactor shaft. And we derive pleasure from the positive and negative emotions we experience.

But our reactions to *Star Wars* highlight an important puzzle: why do we have the same emotional responses to things that are real that we have toward things that are not? Radford's view of emotions provoked by fiction as irrational provides us with a persuasive and plausible way to solve the paradox of fiction, defend the truth of central claims like 2 and 3, while denying the "rational" component of claim 1. This suggests we should accept our mysterious ability to be moved by fiction and recognize this is part of our nature.[15] While it may seem counterintuitive to say our genuine emotional reactions to *Star Wars* are irrational, accepting that it's part of our nature to react irrationally to characters like Han and Leia will enable us to take that "first step into a larger world."[16]

Notes

1. Irvin Kershner (1923–2010), the director of *The Empire Strikes Back*, would agree: "The Carbon Freezing Chamber is complex technically and dramatically. It's truly one of the few drama scenes in the picture. It has to do with love, hate, extreme fear; it has to do with anger. It has many emotions, plus the complexity of steam, sparks, lasers, of all kinds of effects." J. W. Rinzler, *The Making of The Empire Strikes Back* (New York: Random House, 2010), 175.
2. Samuel Taylor Coleridge, *Biographia Literaria: Selected Poetry and Prose of Coleridge* (New York: Random House, 1951), 264.
3. See David Suits, "Really Believing in Fiction," *Pacific Philosophical Quarterly* 87, no. 3 (2006): 369–86.
4. George Lucas also speaks as if the *Star Wars* characters he created are real. *Star Wars* historian J. W. Rinzler told fans he's had conversations where Lucas told him that Boba Fett survived the events of *Return of the Jedi*: "I've been in meetings with George where he confirms that Fett survived. If it comes from George, then it's true!" http://redd.it/2avk5i (accessed October 29, 2014).

5. Gregory Currie, *The Nature of Fiction* (Cambridge: Cambridge University Press, 1990), 189–90.

6. See Robert Yanal, *Paradoxes of Emotion and Fiction* (University Park: The Pennsylvania State University Press, 1999); and Peter Lamarque, "How Can We Fear and Pity Fictions," *British Journal of Aesthetics* 21, no. 4 (1981): 296.

7. Noël Carroll, *The Philosophy of Horror* (New York: Routledge, 1990), 80.

8. Kendall Walton, "Spelunking, Simulation, and Slime: On Being Moved by Fiction," in *Emotion and the Arts*, ed. Mette Hjort and Sue Laver (New York: Oxford University Press, 1997), 38.

9. The analogy to children playing make-believe also doesn't hold because, when a child engages in a game of make-believe, the child is the protagonist. When we watch *A New Hope*, we're just onlookers. As onlookers, we feel for the characters (our protagonists), not ourselves.

10. At times, we even purge certain suppressed emotions and achieve a cathartic release – not something we normally get to do in our ordinary lives. In his *Poetics*, Aristotle discusses the knowledge and consolation we can gain from fictional tragedies.

11. Director Christopher Nolan thinks that dream emotion is as real as waking emotion. In the 2010 *Inception* Blu-ray documentary *Dreams: Cinema of the Subconscious*, Nolan says, "It's clear to me that the dream is an experience of the mind but it's not possible to dismiss an experience of the mind as unreal. When you dream or when you imagine things, there's reality to that. If you're dreaming about your relationship with a person – the emotions of the experience are real – they're as real as the emotions experienced in the real world. There's no more proof for these things in the real world than there are in the state of the mind – that is where emotion takes place." For further philosophical analysis of *Inception* and other films written or directed by Nolan, see *The Philosophy of Christopher Nolan*, ed. Jason T. Eberl and George A. Dunn (Lanham, MD: Lexington Books, forthcoming).

12. This isn't a complete list of theories that try to dissolve the paradox of fiction. For example, Gregory Currie defends the *counterpart theory* – the view that fictional stories actually provoke thoughts about real people and situations. While it's possible for some fictional characters and situations to cause an emotion that has a real-life counterpart as its object, in most cases, the objects of our emotions are the characters in the images we see. When we feel pity for Luke after he finds the smoldering remains of his aunt and uncle, we don't necessarily reflect on what we see and then relate it to someone we know who's gone through a

similar loss or our own such loss. See Gregory Currie, *The Nature of Fiction* (Cambridge: Cambridge University Press, 1990).

13. See Colin Radford, "How Can We Be Moved by the Fate of Anna Karenina?" *Proceedings of the Aristotelian Society* 49, no. 1 (1975): 67–80.

14. This moment works on so many levels. Not only is it visually dazzling with the shifting light and shadow on Yoda, but it's also narratively revealing. We're instantly sent into a state of wonder, and we ask ourselves, who is this "other" to whom Yoda is referring? *Star Wars* makes us wonder, and we become so engaged in this fictional world that we even wonder what happens after certain scenes end. In the Cloud City dining room, we wonder what happens after they sit down with Vader. Do they eat? What do they talk about?

15. For a discussion on the idea that our emotional response to fiction is natural and biologically rooted, see William Irwin and David Kyle Johnson, "What Would Dutton Say about the Paradox of Fiction?" *Philosophy and Literature* 38, no. 1A (2014): A144–7.

16. I wish to thank Kevin Decker, Jason Eberl, Bill Irwin, and Jonathan Evans for their helpful comments on earlier versions of this chapter.

25

The Mind of Blue Snaggletooth: The Intentional Stance, Vintage *Star Wars* Action Figures, and the Origins of Religion

Dennis Knepp

Aside from providing hours of fun, *Star Wars* action figures can help illuminate some theories about the science of the mind and how religious thinking originated. This may sound weird, since action figures don't have minds. Nevertheless, the different ways we play with action figures reveal what the philosopher Daniel Dennett identifies as three stances we can take in understanding something.[1] From a *physical stance*, we understand the figures as molded pieces of plastic. From a *design stance*, we understand the figures to be molded such that their hands can hold weapons. And from an *intentional stance*, we think of the figures as having plans and projects of their own, like Han's intention to shoot Greedo before Greedo has a chance to shoot him. Playing with action figures involves all three stances in interesting ways. Since playing with action figures involves treating things that don't have intentions as if they did, we can also learn something, according to Dennett, about the origins of religion in terms of superstitious minds ascribing intentions to things that don't have them. Playing with action figures illustrates how a science of the mind is possible and what can go wrong in the religious mind.

The Ultimate Star Wars and Philosophy: You Must Unlearn What You Have Learned, First Edition. Edited by Jason T. Eberl and Kevin S. Decker.
© 2016 John Wiley & Sons, Ltd. Published 2016 by John Wiley & Sons, Ltd.

Introspection in Jabba's Palace

You'd think it would be easy to study the mind, since we all have one: you, me, J. J. Abrams ... everybody. Understanding the mind should be as easy as lounging like a Hutt and eating a Klatooine paddy frog. "Your Jedi mind tricks don't work here because I'm the master of my own mind," so would say a Huttese or Toydarian version of René Descartes (1596–1650). In his *Meditations*, Descartes tells about how he sat in a stove-heated room in November 1619 thinking about his mind.[2] "I am my mind and I know my mind better than anything else": this is the method of *introspection*. Descartes sat and thought about his mind, concluding that his mind was completely distinct from his body. It sure feels that way to me as well. My experience of my mind is very different than that of my stomach or my feet. Descartes's *dualist* theory of mind and body has been influential for centuries, but the method of introspection isn't very *scientific*. Science is all about verifying observations in *objective* ways, and a person can't objectively verify *personal* experiences about his own mind. Nor could I look into your mind to see if you're having the same experience as me because our mental lives are entirely personal. It would, of course, be cool if our mental life were like Darth Vader's helmet and could be removed so that someone else could look through the same eyes. But it's not. One's *first-person perspective* is not a mask that can be removed and shared. No one else can look through my eyes. I know you don't want to hear the odds, but a dualist theory of the mind doesn't fly as a true science. If the only way to study the mind is from the first-person perspective, there can be no verification: you're better off trying to fly through an asteroid belt.

In the twentieth century, philosophers began to think of new ways to study the mind. The key is to switch from a first-person (introspective) view to a third-person (objective) perspective. Instead of studying my own personal mind, I can study how someone else uses her mind. This investigation can be scientific since other people can verify the conclusions I draw. In short, give up the Hutt's lounger and instead think about what the other killers in Jabba's hideout are thinking. At first, this seems impossible. After all, didn't we agree that we can't have access to other minds? The mind is not like Vader's mask – we can't look through someone else's eyes. But actually, we do it all the time, as shown by how we play with *Star Wars* action figures.

Blue Snaggletooth

Daniel Dennett is one of the most famous philosophers in America today and one of "The Four Horsemen" (as in the Apocalypse) alongside Richard Dawkins, Sam Harris, and Christopher Hitchens – part of the "New Atheists" movement.[3] Maybe Dennett's not as famous as Mark Hamill, but he represents philosophers who study how the mind works without appealing to a mysterious "ghost in the machine." Dennett also doesn't believe in "hokey religions" that postulate supernatural spirits with mental lives. As we'll see, playing with *Star Wars* action figures illustrates Dennett's theory of how a science of the mind is possible.

To illustrate, I have a vintage Blue Snaggletooth action figure that sells for hundreds of dollars on eBay.[4] His name is Zutton or Zutmore (depending on the source), but everyone knows him as "Snaggletooth" because he has a single sharp tooth pointing up the left side of his mouth. Zutton is described by one source as a "Snivvian artist," as well as a bounty hunter who has "a reputation in the Outer Rim as an efficient, decent hunter, whom even his targets and law enforcement could respect."[5] But, according to another source, his name is "Zutmore" and he's based on a character from the infamous *Star Wars Holiday Special*.[6] Zutmore is a short character in a red jumpsuit sitting in the cantina. Apparently, Kenner tried to make his action figure based upon a black-and-white photo, resulting in a figure as tall as other *Star Wars* figures and wearing a blue jumpsuit with silver boots and gloves. This "Blue Snaggletooth" was sold exclusively through Sears in 1978 in the Cantina Scene collection with three other figures: Walrus Man, Greedo, and Hammerhead.[7] The Blue Snaggletooth figure is rare because the following year his form was corrected: short with red clothing and furry feet. Mistakes from the manufacturer are always more valuable to the collector; so the tall Blue Snaggletooth with silver boots is more valuable than the corrected short Red Snaggletooth with furry feet.

At the most basic level of understanding, Blue Snaggletooth is a piece of molded plastic. This is the level of physics and chemistry: what Dennett calls the *physical stance*.[8] We can understand that Blue Snaggletooth was created with a certain kind of plastic in a certain shape through use of a mold. Notably, some of the Blue Snaggletooths (Snaggleteeth?) have a little dent on the big toe of the right boot while others don't – mine doesn't have this dent.

Understanding Blue Snaggletooth from the physical stance also includes understanding how it would perform in physical situations. If I launch him with enough force from my homemade catapult, he'll land safely on a cushion; if not, he'll crash on the floor. That's physics. It would pain collectors to know that, in my childhood, I did such things with my Blue Snaggletooth and my other action figures. Many days of play involved some sort of combat between *Star Wars* characters in which action figures were smashed together. As a result, my action figures show signs of wear and tear. Rare vintage action figure buyers commonly use the AFA Action Figure Authority scale, from 10 to 100, to grade the wear and tear of toys.[9] I'd be surprised if my Blue Snaggletooth is beyond the "very good" scale at AFA 50. This estimation involves looking at Blue Snaggletooth as a physical thing with physical marks that would bring his grading lower on the AFA scale and thereby cause him to have less value on the collector's market. This is the physical stance.

Designed for Action

Of course, Blue Snaggletooth is more than just a physical piece of plastic. It has a *design*. Blue Snaggletooth has more value on the collector's market because its design is rare among other Snaggleteeth out there. Coin collectors always value mistakes over exact copies, and so it is among vintage action figure collectors. For starters, Blue Snaggletooth is designed to look like a character from the notorious *Star Wars Holiday Special* – itself a rarity given that it was broadcast only once (November 17, 1978, on CBS) in the United States.[10] There's a good reason for this. The *Holiday Special* is so bad that George Lucas has said that he'd like to smash every copy of it with a sledgehammer; and Carrie Fisher has said that she plays it at parties "mainly at the end of the night when I want people to leave."[11] So an action figure from the

Holiday Special is even rarer given its unpopularity and the difficulty in obtaining a copy of it – at least before the advent of YouTube.[12] This is compounded by the fact that, as we've seen, Blue Snaggletooth was a mistake that was replaced by the shorter Red Snaggletooth the following year. The action figure's increased value is explained by its faulty design. Understanding Blue Snaggletooth from what Dennett calls the *design stance* gives us information about it that's not available from the purely physical stance.[13]

Other elements of design are common to most other vintage *Star Wars* action figures. They typically have five movement points: the head swivels, the pairs of legs and arms move, while the arms and legs themselves stay straight. Many have hands designed to grip weapons that could be mixed and matched: you could put a Jawa's ionization blaster in the hands of Boba Fett because their hands are generically designed to hold nearly any type of weapon. They also have holes on the bottom of their feet so they can be put onto pegs in various action sets to reenact important scenes. In the Kenner *Land of the Jawas* playset, you can sit your R2-D2 on a spot that will allow the Jawa to shoot him with an ionization blaster and make him fall over. Since all the action figures have peg holes, I could put any figure on these pegs, pull the lever, and make them fall down. This level of understanding is only available if we consider the *design* of the action figures. Other rare designs include the retractable telescoping light saber in the 1978 Luke, Ben Kenobi, and Darth Vader; the 1978 Jawa with a vinyl cape; the 1980 rocket-firing Boba Fett; and the 1985 Yak Face.[14] The design stance allows us to understand why these figures are rare and valuable to the collector, an understanding not available from a purely physical stance.

Blue Snaggletooth Says, "A Parsec Is a Unit of Distance, Not Time"

The physical stance covers looking at an action figure as a piece of molded plastic, with all its colors and abrasions. The design stance includes identifying which character the plastic is supposed to represent, as well as how the shape of its hands allows it to hold weapons, how the peg holes enable it to stand on various playsets, and how its legs bend to sit in vehicles like a landspeeder or through the saddle of a dewback. But that's not enough to fully understand and appreciate the playtime value of this action figure. When you play, you don't just put the designed plastic figure in the pilot's seat of the *Millennium Falcon*. When the *Falcon* takes off, you pretend the figure is brave enough to fly that "hunk of junk." Sometimes you reenact famous scenes like in the Mos Eisley cantina when Han Solo brags, "It's the ship that made the Kessel run is less than 12 parsecs." Sometimes you modify or create your own scenes, such as using Blue Snaggletooth to call Han's goof and say with a know-it-all chortle, "A parsec is a unit of distance, not time." What would Han say or do in response? Would Han shoot Blue Snaggletooth for embarrassing him? Or would Han out-geek him by responding that "he was referring to the shorter route he was able to travel by skirting the nearby Maw black hole cluster, thus making the run in under the standard distance"?[15]

Playing with action figures gets us to think about what someone else would think. You think about their *intentions*: what will Han do or say to Blue Snaggletooth? And you decide based upon your understanding of Han's character, his beliefs, and the situation in the Mos Eisley cantina as you've set it up. In short, you do exactly what Descartes said was impossible to do: you imagine *being* Han Solo and think about what Han Solo would think. You think about someone else's mind. Instead of being a rare and exotic experience, this turns out to be a common practice. This is the third level of understanding, which Dennett calls the *intentional stance*. A science of the mind thus seems possible because we think about the thoughts of others all the time; and since this is a *third-person* perspective, we can verify when others do this as well. Here's Dennett's description of how it works:

> First you decide to treat the object whose behavior is to be predicted as a rational agent; then you figure out what beliefs that agent ought to have, given its place in the world and its purpose. Then you figure out what desires it ought to have, on the same considerations, and finally you predict that this rational agent will act to further its goals in the light of its beliefs. A little practical reasoning from the chosen set of beliefs and desires will in many – but not all – instances yield a decision about what the agent ought to do; that is what you predict the agent *will* do.[16]

So first we decide to treat Han as a rational agent. He's not an idiot. Then we figure out Han's beliefs given the evidence, and his desires, and then what he would do to further his goals. We can now ask, in the Mos Eisley cantina, would Han Solo shoot a bounty hunter like Blue Snaggletooth first without provocation? Or would he shoot only in self-defense after the bounty hunter had shot first? If Descartes is right, then maybe only Han Solo could know the mind of Han Solo. But from a third-person perspective, different people can think about this and discuss what Han would do. For example, I disagree with George Lucas on this issue: the Han Solo I know would shoot first rather than give a nerdy lecture on the Kessel Run. So in my play-acting, Han shoots first. He's a scoundrel.

But Action Figures Don't Have Thoughts

You might think it goes too far to attribute goals and rational agency to Han Solo or Blue Snaggletooth because plastic action figures clearly don't have intentions. When you play with an action figure, *you give it intentions*. You decide what it will do in the circumstances in which you've chosen for it to act; and this is completely different than *predicting* what a real person would do in similar circumstances. Thinking about how Harrison Ford will act in *Episode VII* to portray an older, grizzled Han Solo is different than playing with an *Episode VII* Han Solo action figure. The action figure can't and won't do anything without you initiating things, because they have no intentions of their own. Unlike you or Harrison Ford, they aren't "intentional systems."[17]

In discussing superstitious beliefs, Dennett warns about wrongly projecting intentions onto intention-less objects.[18] If, like Han Solo, you've ever begged your vehicle to "hold together," then you've done this. Cars and starships don't respond to begging, and yet people beg their cars to start and Han begs the *Falcon* to hold together under fire – even affectionately calling it "baby" – because they attribute intentions to these machines as if they could act in certain ways if only they felt like it. Dennett thinks that superstitious beliefs are like this. Lightning strikes because Zeus is angry; corn grows in the spring because Demeter is pleased; the sun makes it across the sky because Apollo carries it in his chariot. In each case, intentions are projected upon intention-less objects: lightning, corn, and the sun are not thinking things that have moods or minds. But by attributing their actions to Zeus, Demeter, and Apollo, the superstitious mind projects intentions onto these natural things and then tries to appease the gods. Dennett, however, rejects the reality of supernatural forces and understands religion as a "natural phenomenon" – just as Han Solo expresses his disbelief in "an all-powerful Force controlling everything." Dennett rejects supernatural beliefs as wrongheaded uses of the intentional stance. Projecting intentions onto intention-less systems betrays a "sad devotion" to "ancient religion."

Playing with action figures is different, however, because we *know* that we're projecting intentions onto things without minds. That's the crucial difference. The superstitious mind thinks that lightning really does act with intention; whereas playing with action figures involves *pretending* that the designed piece of molded plastic has intentions. As kids, we practice using the intentional stance and so get better at it. We know that we're using the intentional stance *creatively* in a context where it wouldn't work without our creative input. We can play with action figures by giving them beliefs and having them act accordingly, yet still understand that it's *we* who are giving them those beliefs. I thus think that understanding what happens when we play with action figures can reveal how a science of mind is possible and illuminate a theory of the origins of the religious mind. That's pretty good for a group of characters from a "wretched hive of scum and villainy."[19]

Notes

1. Daniel Dennett, *The Intentional Stance* (Cambridge, MA: Bradford/MIT, 1987), 13–35.
2. "Descartes," in *Stanford Encyclopedia of Philosophy*, http://plato.stanford.edu/entries/descartes/ (accessed September 28, 2014).
3. "Four Horsemen Discussion Full Unedited Video," https://www.youtube.com/watch?v=rRLYL1Q9x9g (accessed September 28, 2014).
4. Thank you to my cousin Mike Knepp, who first brought the value of Blue Snaggletooth to my attention. In researching for this chapter, I also came across a rock band from Ann Arbor, Michigan, called Blue Snaggletooth.
5. "Zutton," http://starwars.wikia.com/wiki/Zutton (accessed September 28, 2014). Searching for "Snaggletooth" redirects to "Zutton."
6. "What Is a Blue Snaggletooth?" http://www.youtube.com/watch?v=CaqV7u4o09E (accessed September 28, 2014).

7. "Cantina Adventure Set (1978 Sears Exclusive)," http://www.rebelscum.com/vintCantinaAdventure.asp (accessed September 28, 2014). Thanks, Mom and Dad!

8. Dennett, *The Intentional Stance*, 16.

9. AFA Action Figure Authority, "Modern Grading Scale," http://www.toygrader.com/grading_scales.aspx (accessed September 28, 2014).

10. "Star Wars Holiday Special," http://en.wikipedia.org/wiki/Star_Wars_Holiday_Special (accessed September 28, 2014).

11. Ibid.

12. http://www.youtube.com/watch?v=6c3B18gAJyc&list=PLaJhh0k4dkH0v5g_kxxLLApyffIHEn4bR (accessed October 15, 2014).

13. Dennett, *The Intentional Stance*, 16–17.

14. "Top 5 Most Valuable Star Wars Action Figures," http://actionfigures.about.com/od/historyofactionfigures/tp/top_5_starwars.htm (accessed September 28, 2014).

15. "Kessel Run," http://starwars.wikia.com/wiki/Kessel_Run (accessed September 28, 2014).

16. Dennett, *The Intentional Stance*, 17.

17. Ibid., 22–3.

18. Daniel Dennett, *Breaking the Spell: Religion as a Natural Phenomenon* (New York: Viking Penguin, 2006), 116–25.

19. Thank you to my wife, Jen McCarthy, for her helpful comments. No Bothans died to bring you this information.

26

Gospel, Gossip, and Ghent: How Should We Understand the New *Star Wars*?

Roy T. Cook and Nathan Kellen

On April 25, 2014, Lucasfilm announced that the entirety of the *Star Wars Expanded Universe* (EU) would no longer be *canonical* – that is, it would no longer count as a part of the "official" story told in the feature films and two animated television shows:

> While Lucasfilm always strived to keep the stories created for the EU consistent with our film and television content as well as internally consistent, Lucas always made it clear that he was not beholden to the EU. He set the films he created as the canon. This includes the six *Star Wars* episodes, and the many hours of content he developed and produced in *Star Wars: The Clone Wars*. These stories are the immovable objects of *Star Wars* history, the characters and events to which all other tales must align. . . .
>
> While the universe that readers knew is changing, it is not being discarded. Creators of new *Star Wars* entertainment have full access to the rich content of the Expanded Universe. For example, elements of the EU are included in *Star Wars: Rebels*. The Inquisitor, the Imperial Security Bureau, and Sienar Fleet Systems are story elements in the new animated series, and all these ideas find their origins in roleplaying game material published in the 1980s.[1]

This announcement raises deep questions about the nature of fiction and the degree of control that the authors of fiction – George Lucas and Lucasfilm – have over what counts as true within the fictions that

The Ultimate Star Wars and Philosophy: You Must Unlearn What You Have Learned, First Edition. Edited by Jason T. Eberl and Kevin S. Decker.

they create – the canonical *Star Wars* universe. Lucasfilm has, in effect, decreed that the stories told in the EU no longer count as genuine parts of the *Star Wars* story, stipulating that fans should no longer take the information found in these stories to be relevant to interpreting and understanding the stories, characters, and events in the movies and television shows – unless the creators re-canonize portions of the EU via their inclusion within future installments of the canonical films and television shows. In short, in this press release Lucasfilm is attempting to tell fans how they *should* understand and interpret the *Star Wars* fiction.

This question – how we actually do and, perhaps more importantly, how we *should* understand a particular fiction – is a deep question in the philosophy of art. Three particular aspects of this question are important here:

- What external information is relevant to how we understand a particular story?
- How much control do the creators of a fiction have over how fans should interpret the fiction?
- How much control do the fans/consumers of a fiction have over how the fiction should be interpreted?

Lucasfilm's press release suggests that their view of the matter is pretty simple:

- The only external sources relevant to how we understand the *Star Wars* fiction are the views of George Lucas and Lucasfilm.
- The creators of *Star Wars* have almost total control over how fans should interpret the fiction.
- Fans of *Star Wars* have very little control over how the fiction should be interpreted.

The idea that authors have this sort of absolute control over how their works should be understood has been challenged by critics and philosophers – most notably by French theorist Roland Barthes (1915–1980). In "The Death of the Author,"[2] Barthes challenges the idea that authorial intention and authorial biography are essential ingredients for interpreting fictions, arguing that literary and cinematic works, once completed and made public, can and should be understood and assessed independently of the details of their creation. Barthes does not claim that intentions of the author *must* be ignored. Instead, he challenges the privileged role traditionally accorded to the author's intentions and biography. Barthes says that what the reader brings to a text is of equal importance with what an author puts into that text, and any interpretation that ignores other factors (including the beliefs, desires, and attitudes of the audience) is flawed.[3]

Barthes's challenge to the control that authors have over the meaning of their creations raises doubts about whether Lucasfilm can and should tell us how to understand the *Star Wars* fiction, and which stories we should count as official, canonical parts of that fiction. In addition, the way in which the canon/noncanon distinction plays out in huge fictional universes such as *Star Wars* suggests that the way the distinction is drawn is *dynamic, negotiated,* and *participatory.*[4] What counts as an official, fictionally true, part of the story in such massive serial fictions is, contrary to what Lucasfilm suggests, not something that can or should be legislated by the creators of such fictions, but instead involves a complex (often implicit) interaction between those who create fictions and those who enjoy them.

The Mechanics of Canon in the *Star Wars* Universe

The first *Star Wars* film was released in 1977. Two more films followed, along with comics, novels, roleplaying games, television shows, toys, trading cards, video games, and much else. Prior to the early 1990s, there was little official guidance about what parts of this increasingly immense body of material should count as canonical, that is, which material we should treat as reliably telling us what (fictionally) happens to Luke, Leia, Han, Chewie, and the rest.[5] The most we were given was the oft-repeated pronouncement attributed to George Lucas: "The movies are Gospel, and everything else is Gossip!"[6]

This changed in 1994, when Lucasfilm released its first official statement regarding canon:

> "Gospel," or canon as we refer to it, includes the screenplays, the films, the radio dramas and the novelizations. These works spin out of George Lucas' original stories, the rest are written by other writers. However, between us, we've read everything, and much of it is taken into account

in the overall continuity. The entire catalogue of published works comprises a vast history with many offshoots, variations and tangents like any other well-developed mythology.[7]

This division of the massive *Star Wars* saga eventually developed into a multileveled hierarchy of degrees of canonicity that governed our understanding of the *Star Wars* fiction up to the 2014 press release:

> *G (George Lucas) Canon*
> Anything created, at least in terms of overall story, by Lucas himself, including the six (soon to be more) films, scripts, and unpublished notes.
> *T (Television) Canon*
> The *Clone Wars* animated theatrical film and television show.[8]
> *C (Continuity) Canon*
> All recent works, and some older works, released under the *Star Wars* title.
> *S (Secondary) Canon*
> Those works (usually older) that authors and fans are free to attend to or ignore as they see fit. Includes works that conflict with, or don't quite fit with, the G, T, and C Canon.
> *N (Non) Canon*
> Anything in direct conflict with G, T, C, and S canon, including intentionally imaginary stories, such as the "What if?" *Infinities* comics.[9]

As a general rule of thumb, a particular story in a particular category listed above was taken to reliably report what really (fictionally) happened in the *Star Wars* universe to the extent that it does not contradict anything in any higher level of continuity.

One interesting aspect of this hierarchical approach to canonicity – unique to the *Star Wars* universe, and much more complicated than canon/noncanon distinctions drawn elsewhere, such as the Marvel or DC Comics universes – is its apparent *pluralism*. Pluralism is the idea that there might be more than one equally legitimate interpretation of a particular fiction. In interpreting the *Star Wars* fiction, stories that fall into G, T, or C Canon seem nonnegotiably true. If my understanding of the events in the *Star Wars* universe contradicts a story that falls into one of these three categories, then I've made a mistake or I'm unaware of the relevant facts. Similarly, stories in N Canon are nonnegotiably false, since these explicitly contradict stories in the nonnegotiably true G, C, or T Canon. Stories in S Canon are much more flexible, however: prior to the April 2014 press release, both creators and fans were free to pick and choose which S Canon stories they wished to incorporate into their understanding of the *Star Wars* fiction. In particular, there might be two distinct S Canon stories that conflict with each other, but neither of which conflicts with G, C, or T Canon. As a result, one fan could incorporate one of the stories into his understanding of the *Star Wars* fiction, while another fan could equally legitimately incorporate the other story into her understanding. Thus, S Canon opens up the possibility for a rich pluralism with regard to interpreting the *Star Wars* fiction by allowing different understandings of the story based on different incorporations of S Canon material.[10]

The practice of dividing a fiction into canonical and noncanonical parts – or into three or more grades of canonicity, as is the case here – isn't merely an exercise in fanboy/girl esoterica. Once a fiction is massive enough – and the *Star Wars* fiction is certainly quite massive – the canon/noncanon divide can play a practical role in pointing to which portions of the story are required knowledge for understanding and interpreting the overall universe. Consider a hypothetical couple: Anne and Bob. Anne has seen all six of the live-action films, but hasn't seen or read any other *Star Wars* material. Bob has never seen any of the films or television shows, but has read all of the *Star Wars* novels and comics, except those that retell the stories shown in the films. Even though Bob has *much* more information at his disposal, Anne is in a better position to authoritatively describe and understand the main characters and events in the *Star Wars* universe in virtue of the fact that her base of evidence, while much smaller than Bob's, is privileged in its canonicity. In short, canon/noncanon distinctions make massive fictions like *Star Wars* accessible: familiarity with the smaller substory – the canon, or central parts of it – is both necessary and sufficient for understanding the overall story as a whole.

There are a number of other useful observations we can make about canon.[11] First, noncanonical works are often relevant to interpretation, even if they don't describe events we are to understand to have actually occurred in the *Star Wars* universe. For example, the *Star Wars: Infinities* graphic novels tell a series of "What If?" stories – one for each of the original trilogy films. The first imagines what would've happened if Luke's torpedoes had failed to destroy the original Death Star. The second imagines what would've happened if Luke had frozen to death on Hoth. The third imagines what would've happened if C-3PO had malfunctioned during the exchange between Jabba the Hutt and Princess Leia (disguised as Boussh). None of these stories provide any information regarding what (fictionally) happened in the *Star Wars* universe. But they do provide contrary-to-the-fact information regarding what these characters would have done in different circumstances. Such information can be important in forming our impressions of the characters' personalities. For example, in the first *Infinities* graphic novel, we learn that Luke's heroic drive to stop the Empire is not quelled by the failure to destroy the Death Star, while, as we might suspect, Han Solo quickly returns to smuggling work (although he returns to fight the Empire five years later).

Second, and as we noted above, canonicity practices are:

Dynamic
The location of the canon/noncanon distinction – the criteria determining what counts as Gospel versus gossip – varies over time.
Negotiable
The canon/noncanon distinction is not an inherent property of the fiction(s), but is the result of complex, ongoing, implicit agreements regarding what is to count as Gospel and what is to count as gossip.
Participatory
Determination of the canon/noncanon distinction – the negotiation that determines what stories count as Gospel and which count merely as gossip – involves fans of the fiction in essential ways.

Thus, a particular work will not be eternally canonical or eternally noncanonical. Rather, a work can be taken to be canonical at a time, but its status is always up for revision, with certain works that were once noncanonical later receiving canonical status, and former parts of the canon later becoming noncanonical. The latter, Gospel-to-gossip category is exemplified by the *Star Wars Holiday Special*, which was presumably meant to be part of the canonical story at the time it was produced.[12] The former, gossip-to-Gospel category includes appearances of Aayla Secura in the *Star Wars Tales* comics (beginning with issue #19), which were explicitly noncanon due to the *Infinities* imprint appearing on the cover (they were also explicitly framed as not totally reliable holo rentals). Once Lucas decided to have Aayla Secura appear in *Attack of the Clones* – a last-minute decision[13] and likely due in part to the extreme popularity of the character – her backstory as depicted in these comics was raised from N Canon to C Canon.[14] Another key example is the city-planet Coruscant, which first appeared in Timothy Zahn's *Thrawn Trilogy*, was then digitally inserted into the 1997 Special Edition of *Return of the Jedi*, and featured prominently in Episodes I through III.

Examples of the influence that fan participation can have on canon include:

- Admiral Firmus Piett reappeared in *Return of the Jedi* due to fan mail received by George Lucas.
- The color of droid R4-G9, who appeared in *Revenge of the Sith*, was decided by a fan club poll.
- Cartoon Network had an online poll to determine which Jedi would be featured in future episodes of *Star Wars: Clone Wars*.[15]

Thus, canon/noncanon distinctions usually come about via a complex, holistic interaction between the creators of a fiction and the consumers (fans) of that fiction, and there are numerous instances of this in the history of the *Star Wars* universe; at least, this is how it was prior to the April 2014 press release. But Lucasfilm has now drawn a new line, with what was formerly G Canon and T Canon counting as Gospel, and the rest being irrelevant gossip – unless the creators explicitly incorporate formerly noncanonical material into new installments of the franchise. The question remains: is it in Lucasfilm's power to tell us which stories we should, and should not, take into account when understanding and interpreting the *Star Wars* universe?

Canon and the Erasure of Ghent

When reading or viewing fictions, such as the stories told about *Star Wars*, we are meant to imagine that certain things are (fictionally) true of characters and other things aren't (fictionally) true of them. We're clearly meant to imagine that Princess Leia is Luke Skywalker's sister, and we're clearly not meant to imagine that she lives in San Francisco. This much is right regardless of whether we use the old five-part, negotiable, and participatory hierarchy of canon categories, or accept the new, sharp, and presumably nondynamic divide.

But there are other aspects of our interpretation of the fiction that are deeply affected by the differences between the G, T, C, S, and N Canon hierarchy, and the new criterion implicit in Lucafilm's press release. Consider Zakarisz Ghent, who first appears in the *Thrawn Trilogy* as a "slicer" associated with the smuggler Talon Karrde. These novels were originally C Canon and very relevant to our understanding and interpretation of the *Star Wars* universe as a whole. According to the new scheme laid out by Lucasfilm, however, they are no longer canonical – Ghent never appears, nor is mentioned, in the films and television shows and is thus mere gossip, not Gospel.

What does this mean with regard to how we should understand what really happened (fictionally) in the *Star Wars* universe? Are we to imagine that there's no longer anyone important named "Ghent" in the imaginary galaxy in question? More importantly, perhaps, are we supposed to now *forget* about Ghent's interactions with Princess Leia in the Zahn novels? Are these episodes no longer relevant to our understanding of what sort of a person Leia is?

This last question is critical to our understanding of the *Star Wars* Universe. Labeling all EU material as noncanonical doesn't just erase the existence of beloved characters such as Ghent. It also erases many of the important elements of stories that fans have relied on to form their own complex understandings of the central characters who do remain. While many fans balked at the death of Chewbacca in the first novel of the *New Jedi Order* series, *Vector Prime* – crushed by a falling moon while saving Han and Leia's son, Anakin Solo – the stories that followed, depicting Han's grief, anger, and ultimate recovery from this tragedy, give tremendous insight into Han's character that fans are now deprived of under the new canon/noncanon criterion. Of course, these stories can still be taken to be relevant to our understanding of the *Star Wars* fiction in the indirect way that formerly N Canon works were relevant: they tell us how Han *would* have reacted if Chewbacca had died in this manner. But they no longer tell us how Han *did* react when Chewbacca *in fact* died this way. If these stories no longer count as canonical, then this means that Lucasfilm has changed the nature of the saga's central characters.

Based on our earlier discussion, it's not clear that Lucasfilm *has* the authority to legislate what counts as canonical *Star Wars* content in this manner. The complex canon/noncanon divide has always been something that resulted from a dynamic interaction between fans and creators – as well as being influenced by other factors, such as commercial concerns. While Lucasfilm's announcement might initially reshape the canon in the way they desire, there's no reason to think that fans will suddenly cease to have any influence on what counts as Gospel and what counts as gossip. Nor is there any reason to think that fans shouldn't have partial control over which stories they can legitimately take to be part of the genuine story of the *Star Wars* universe. In short, Lucasfilm's new criterion might change where the line between Gospel and gossip currently lies, but it won't – and in principle can't – change the way that canon/noncanon distinctions work, and so it can't change the fact that the distinction is dynamic, negotiable, and participatory.

The announcement by Lucasfilm outlines what they would now like to treat as canonical, describing those stories that George Lucas himself thinks "count." But where the actual canon/noncanon line lies is a matter that's never settled and is always responsive to a number of pressures, including, but not limited to, both creators' preferences and fan input. There's little reason to think that Lucas can forbid us from taking EU stories into account in the long run. There's even less reason to think that our taking them into account won't have effects on where the distinction between Gospel and gossip resides. While the opinions of George Lucas and Lucasfilm in this matter are important, this doesn't mean that the fan who truly believes that the *Thrawn Trilogy* – or even the *Holiday Special* – should be treated as canon has no say in the matter. Lucasfilm told us their view on the matter. Now, fans should continue to fight for their favorite stories and continue to influence what happens in the *Star Wars* universe in various ways.[16]

One prominent author of EU materials has already suggested that he will understand the situation in roughly this manner. Timothy Zahn cleverly describes his position as compatible with Lucasfilm's new criterion, although the view he describes clearly is not:

> [A]s far as I can tell from the announcement, LFL [LucasFilm] is **not** erasing the EU, but simply making it clear that nothing there is official canon. That's **not** necessarily a bad thing, nor does it immediately send everything into alternative-universe status. If nothing from the Thrawn Trilogy, say, is used in future movies (and if there's nothing in the movies that contradicts it), then we can reasonably continue to assume that those events **did** happen. It looks to me like the Legends banner is going to be used mainly to distinguish Story-Group-Approved canon books from those that aren't officially canon but might still exist....

[E]ven if something from the *Thrawn Trilogy* **does** show up in a movie in a different form, we authors are masters of spackle, back-fill, and hand-waving. For example, if Ghent appears in the movies but never mentions Thrawn, I can argue that he simply doesn't want to talk about that era, or else has completely forgotten about it (which for Ghent isn't really much of a stretch).[17]

In short, rather than relegating Ghent to mere gossip, Zahn has decided to treat his own novels and other EU works as true in the *Star Wars* fiction until contradicted by future work, rather than false in the *Star Wars* fiction until corroborated by film or television, which is Lucasfilm's official stance. In Zahn's view, Ghent is Gospel until there are reasons to think otherwise. This is, of course, essentially the understanding of canonicity that was codified in the dynamic, negotiable, and participatory G, T, C, S, and N Canon hierarchy at work prior to Lucasfilm's press release. While Zahn has a particularly privileged position from which to negotiate canon matters with Lucasfilm, his comments nicely illustrate the resistance – that is, negotiation and participation – that fans of all sorts can mobilize in attempts to influence canon.

One final observation: the canon/noncanon divide does not merely tell us that some stories count as genuine parts of the *Star Wars* fiction while others do not. It also dictates which *version* of a particular story counts as genuine when there are multiple versions from which to choose. For example, the canon/noncanon distinction determines whether we should take the original releases of Episodes IV through VI to be Gospel, and the later Special Editions to be mere gossip, or vice versa. Lucas altered a number of things in the Special Editions, but the most controversial change is found in the confrontation between Han Solo and Greedo in Episode IV. Han kills Greedo before Greedo can get a shot off in the original version, while in the Special Edition Greedo shoots first, but misses.[18] Clearly Lucas and Lucasfilm would like us to take the most recent variant of this critical scene to be the canonical one, but given what we've said so far, there's no reason why fans can't resist this interpretation, standing up for the canonicity of the original versions of the films via active negotiation of, and participation in, the determination of the canon/noncanon divide. *Star Wars* is, after all, about rebellion.

The conventions and practices that were shaped and encouraged by Lucasfilm themselves with regard to the canon/noncanon divide – in particular, the dynamic, negotiable, and participatory nature of this distinction – throw some doubt onto whether or not Lucasfilm truly has the authority to unilaterally dictate which *Star Wars* stories, or versions of stories, fans should take to be "genuine" parts of the central story. Thus, if you want your favorite story to be Gospel, rather than mere gossip, then keep explaining why it *is* or *should be*. If you're lucky, or your case is particularly compelling, then it might one day become Gospel again. Did Han shoot first? You bet he did!

Notes

1. https://starwars.com/news/the-legendary-star-wars-expanded-universe-turns-a-new-page.html (retrieved August 23, 2014).
2. Roland Barthes, *Image, Music, Text*, trans. Richard Howard (London: Fontana, 1977), 142–8.
3. For a useful overview of the subtleties of Barthes's (evolving) views on authorship, see Sean Burke, *The Death and Return of the Author: Criticism and Subjectivity in Barthes, Foucault, and Derrida* (Edinburgh: Edinburgh University Press, 2010), 39–50.
4. For a more detailed examination of how the canon/noncanon distinction in massive serialized collaborative fictions (MSCFs) such as *Star Wars* is grounded in practices that are dynamic, negotiated, and participatory, see Roy T. Cook, "Canonicity and Normativity in Massive Serialized Collaborative Fictions," *The Journal of Aesthetics and Art Criticism* 71 (2013): 271–6.
5. Informal practices – governed more by fan attitudes than any official proclamation by Lucasfilm – were in place at this time. For example, the *Star Wars* comics published by Marvel Comics were not taken very seriously. But no hard lines existed.
6. B. Hays, "Speculation Concerning the Future History of the Continuing *Star Wars* Saga," *Fantastic Films Collectors Edition* 20 (1980): 45.
7. Sue Rostoni and Allen Kausch, quoted in *Star Wars Insider* 23 (Fall 1994).
8. This category would have included the live action *Star Wars: Underworld* television program, had it not been put on hold, and the upcoming *Star Wars: Rebels* animated show and novel based on it, were it not for the attempted revision to canon that is the subject of this chapter. This category does not contain the *Star Wars Holiday Special*!

9. This taxonomy is adapted from Wookipedia, http://starwars.wikia.com/wiki/Canon#cite_note-D_canon-fb-7 (accessed August 23, 2014). Note that fan fiction and other nonlicensed work does not fall into any category in this taxonomy, despite the fact that such works might influence our understanding of the *Star Wars* fiction as a whole.

10. Note that this picking and choosing amongst S Canon works is exactly how Lucasfilm will be treating *all* noncanonical works now, including works that were previously C Canon. Note, additionally, that it is Lucasfilm, and not the fans, that gets to do the choosing on this new Lucasfilm-endorsed understanding of canonicity.

11. For more in-depth discussion of how canon/noncanon distinctions work in *Star Wars*, see Will Brooker, *Using the Force: Creativity, Community, and Star Wars Fans* (London: Continuum Press, 2003); and Cook, "Canonicity and Normativity in Massive Serialized Collaborative Fictions."

12. Of course, the *Star Wars Holiday Special* aired before the *Star Wars* fiction had grown large enough to warrant a formalized canon/noncanon distinction. Nevertheless, it is clear that the program was originally intended to be an official part of the story (hence the inclusion of our first glimpse of Boba Fett), even if Lucas himself disavowed the program shortly after it aired.

13. See "Interview with Amy Allen," http://www.theforce.net/jedicouncil/interview/amy_allen.shtml (accessed August 23, 2014).

14. Also relevant is the fan petition to ensure her appearance in *Episode III*; see http://boards.theforce.net/threads/aayla-secura-in-epiii.8603503/page-9 (accessed August 23, 2014).

15. There are many other examples of fan activities influencing the canonical content of the *Star Wars* universe: http://starwars.wikia.com/wiki/List_of_fanon_elements_in_continuity (accessed August 23, 2014)

16. Of course, stories that do not contradict definitive central works, such as the six live-action films, will continue to have more claim to canonicity than stories that do conflict with these works, regardless of what fans do.

17. http://makingstarwars.net/2014/04/timothy-zhan-on-star-wars-legends-and-his-future-with-star-wars/ (accessed August 23, 2014).

18. In fact, there are three choices here, since later versions of the Special Edition depict Han and Greedo shooting at almost the same moment.

Contributors
Troopers of the 501st Legion

Don Adams is Professor of Philosophy at Central Connecticut State University. He teaches logic and the history of philosophy. Most of his publications are on ancient Greek philosophy, especially the philosophy of Socrates. When he teaches Plato's theory of censorship, he sometimes uses the following question in class: if a Wookiee and a Luxan got into a fight in the piano bar onboard *Galactica*, how much damage would they do as measured in quatloos? (By the way, "five thousand" is not the correct answer.)

Kyle Alkema is an unaffiliated philosopher who most recently published a chapter in *It's Always Sunny and Philosophy* (Open Court, 2015). The only reason he'd consider taking up chewing tobacco would be to adopt the nickname "Chewbacca."

Adam Barkman is Associate Professor and Chair of the Philosophy Department at Redeemer University College in Canada. He's the co-editor of four books on popular culture and philosophy, including *Manga and Philosophy* (Open Court, 2010), and the author of five books, most recently *Making Sense of Islamic Art & Architecture* (Thames & Hudson, 2015). Although convinced, on the basis of having read nearly every Expanded Universe novel and comic, that the *Star Wars* saga narrates one of the greatest mythologies of our time,

The Ultimate Star Wars and Philosophy: You Must Unlearn What You Have Learned, First Edition. Edited by Jason T. Eberl and Kevin S. Decker.
© 2016 John Wiley & Sons, Ltd. Published 2016 by John Wiley & Sons, Ltd.

Adam swears he'll boycott *Episode VII* if it has another damned Death Star in it!

Annika Beck is a scholar in residence at the Kierkegaard Library, St. Olaf College, but was recalled from her goodwill mission to the Ewok settlements of Endor to write for this volume. She has ongoing research interests in moral psychology, philosophy of religion, and bioethics. When she isn't picketing Jawa sandcrawlers to demand droid freedom, she can be found on her home planet engaged in research and creating art with her galactic glue stick and Imperial embossing gun.

Lance Belluomini did his graduate studies in philosophy at the University of California, Berkeley; San Francisco State University; and the University of Nebraska–Lincoln. He's recently contributed chapters to *Inception and Philosophy* (Wiley, 2011), *The Walking Dead and Philosophy* (Wiley, 2012), and *Ender's Game and Philosophy* (Wiley, 2013). His philosophical interests include ethics and the philosophy of popular culture. Ever since he saw the deleted Anchorhead scenes featuring Luke and Biggs, he's had this strange recurring dream where he goes into Tosche Station, picks up some power converters to repair Luke's T-16 Skyhopper, and then flies it through Beggar's Canyon, where he attempts to "bull's-eye" womp rats.

Cole Bowman is a writer and independent scholar living in Portland, Oregon. She's also a contributor to *Ender's Game and Philosophy* (Wiley, 2013) and is eager to dispel the old rumors that space is a "boys' club." When she's not using the Force against the patriarchy, she attempts to build her own lightsabers and searches the sky for signs that another Death Star has moved into position in the outer atmosphere – both to very limited success.

Dan Burkett is a doctoral student in philosophy at Rice University. He specializes in social and political philosophy, morality, freedom, and the philosophy of time. He's recently contributed chapters to both *Futurama and Philosophy* (Open Court, 2013) and *Homeland and Philosophy* (Open Court, 2014). If there's a bright center to the universe, then his home of New Zealand is the place that it's farthest from.

Charles C. Camosy is Associate Professor of Christian Ethics at Fordham University in New York City. His interests include bioethics, the dialogue between philosophy and theology, and the intersection of ethics and public policy. His fourth book, *Beyond the Abortion Wars: A Way Forward for a New Generation* (Eerdmans, 2015), attempts to move the debate beyond the simplistic and antagonistic life/choice binary. Whether writing a book, teaching his students, or having a Twitter exchange, he tries to both argue for and live out Obi-Wan's great insight: there are alternatives to fighting.

Roy T. Cook is Professor of Philosophy at the University of Minnesota–Twin Cities, a resident fellow of the Minnesota Center for Philosophy of Science, and an associate fellow of the Northern Institute of Philosophy at the University of Aberdeen, Scotland. He's the author of *This Is Philosophy of Logic* (Blackwell, forthcoming), *The Yablo Paradox: An Essay on Circularity* (Oxford, 2014), *Key Concepts in Philosophy: Paradox* (Polity, 2013), and *A Dictionary of Philosophical Logic* (Edinburgh, 2009). He's also the editor or coeditor of *The Routledge Companion to Comics and Graphic Novels* (with Frank Bramlett and Aaron Meskin; Routledge, forthcoming), *The Art of Comics: A Philosophical Approach* (with Aaron Meskin; Wiley, 2012), and *The Arché Papers on the Mathematics of Abstraction* (Springer, 2007). In addition, he's published over fifty academic articles and book chapters on the philosophy of mathematics, the philosophy of logic, mathematical logic, the aesthetics of popular culture (especially film and comics), and related topics. As a child, Roy owned every Kenner *Star Wars* action figure ever produced except Blue Snaggletooth and Vlix.

Kevin S. Decker teaches philosophy at Eastern Washington University, where he often lectures about the phenomenology of peaches and the rights of vampire citizens. He is the editor or coeditor of several anthologies of philosophy and popular culture, including the original *Star Wars and Philosophy* (with Jason T. Eberl; Open Court, 2005). His book, *Who Is Who? The Philosophy of Doctor Who* (I. B. Tauris, 2013), has been popular on the convention circuit, where he's frequently mistaken by fans for Mark Hamill.

George A. Dunn lectures in philosophy and religion at the University of Indianapolis and the Ningbo Institute of Technology in Zhejiang Province, China. He's the editor of *Avatar and Philosophy* (Wiley, 2014) and *Veronica Mars and Philosophy* (Wiley, 2014) and a coeditor of *True Blood and Philosophy* (Wiley, 2010), *The Hunger Games and Philosophy* (Wiley, 2012), *Sons of Anarchy and Philosophy* (Wiley, 2013), and *The Philosophy of Christopher Nolan* (Lexington, forthcoming). He's also contributed to similar books on *Iron Man*, *Mad Men*, *Battlestar Galactica*, *Terminator*, and other pop culture topics. A hopeless romantic, he's spent a lifetime looking for love in Alderaan places.

Jason T. Eberl is the Semler Endowed Chair for Medical Ethics and Professor of Philosophy at Marian University in Indianapolis. He teaches and publishes on bioethics, medieval philosophy, and metaphysics. He's the editor of *Battlestar Galactica and Philosophy* (Wiley, 2008); coeditor (with Kevin S. Decker) of the forthcoming *The Ultimate Star Trek and Philosophy* (Wiley), as well as the original *Star Trek and Philosophy* (Open Court, 2008) and *Star Wars and Philosophy* (Open Court, 2005); and coeditor (with George A. Dunn) of *Sons of Anarchy and Philosophy* (Wiley, 2013) and *The Philosophy of Christopher Nolan* (Lexington, forthcoming). He's also contributed to similar books on Stanley Kubrick, J. J. Abrams, *Harry Potter*, Metallica, *Terminator*, *The Hunger Games*, *The Big Lebowski*, and *Avatar*. A huge fan of J. J. Abrams's work, he nevertheless plans to wear sunglasses to the premiere of *Episode VII* to compensate for lens-flares.

Leonard Finkelman let loose a Tusken Raider howl upon receiving his PhD in Philosophy from the City University of New York Graduate Center. He first demonstrated his commitment to philosophy a long time ago in a dorm room far, far away, when he refused on moral grounds to play as a dark side character in the Jedi Knight series of PC games. He now teaches philosophy of science to the padawans of Linfield College in McMinnville, Oregon.

Rhiannon Grant completed her PhD at the University of Leeds. She works on Wittgenstein, mainly in relation to religious language, with a particular interest in Quaker and feminist theologies. She allows undergraduates to use the Jedi as an example of a religion in class discussions, but doesn't let them use the Force during exams.

Matt Hummel earned a Master of Arts in Liberal Studies with a focus in Ethics and Values from Valparaiso University. His interests include philosophy of law, applied ethics, communications, and humane education. He works in Evansville, Indiana, as a paralegal for the public defender agency, where he confronts the dark side daily, helping smugglers prove they didn't shoot first. He contributed to *Dungeons & Dragons and Philosophy* (Wiley, 2014). He strives to learn the Stoic patience of a Jedi as he awaits the next installment of the *Star Wars* franchise.

Andrew Zimmerman Jones studied physics and philosophy at Wabash College, and earned a Master's Degree in Mathematics Education from Indiana University–Purdue University Indianapolis. He now hashes out a living as a freelance writer/editor. He runs the About.com Physics website and authored *String Theory for Dummies* (Wiley, 2010). He's put his neck on the line to assist the Rebel Alliance in several previous volumes, including *Green Lantern and Philosophy* (Wiley, 2011) and *The Big Bang Theory and Philosophy* (Wiley, 2012). He's married to a lovely princess and father to two Ewok padawans (don't ask!), living with them on the forest moon of Indiana.

Nathan Kellen is a doctoral candidate at the University of Connecticut. His dissertation is on the philosophy of truth and logic, and in his spare time he enjoys working on ethics and the philosophy of mathematics. He hopes to soon pass his Padawan trials to join the ranks of the Jedi Knights of philosophy. Much like some who've skirted alongside the dark side of the Force, he believes philosophy should be brought to the peoples of the galaxy, rather than kept in the Temple and Library.

Dennis Knepp teaches philosophy and religious studies at Big Bend Community College in Moses Lake, Washington. He has chapters in Wiley's Philosophy and Pop Culture books on *Twilight, Alice in Wonderland, The Girl with the Dragon Tattoo, The Hobbit, Superman, Avatar,* and Black Sabbath. He's been a *Star Wars* fan since 1977 at age seven and still has many of the vintage action figures with several spaceships, including the *Millennium Falcon* (Thanks, Mom and Dad!). He dedicates his chapter to his cousin Mike Knepp (currently serving in the U.S. military), who first taught him the value of the collectible Blue Snaggletooth.

David LaRocca is a visiting scholar in the Department of English at Cornell University and a lecturer in the Department of Philosophy at the College at Cortland, State University of New York. Among other works in philosophy and film, he's the author of *Emerson's English Traits and the Natural History of Metaphor* (Bloomsbury, 2013) and editor of Stanley Cavell's *Emerson's Transcendental Etudes* (Stanford, 2003), *The Philosophy of Charlie Kaufman* (University Press of Kentucky, 2011), and *The Philosophy of War Films* (University Press of Kentucky, 2014). His next project on Boba Fett could address the ethics of service to lords and masters in dialogue with Mr. Stevens from *The Remains of the Day* and Mr. Carson from *Downton Abbey*. How odd it would be to discover affinities between a mercenary's brawn and a butler's discerning poise.

William A. Lindenmuth is Associate Professor of Philosophy at Shoreline College. He received his MA in Philosophy in New York City from the New School for Social Research, and his BA in English from Saint Mary's College in California. He's taught in New York, Las Vegas, Seattle, and Rome, Italy. He specializes in normative ethics and moral psychology, particularly through the media of literature and film, arguing that our stories show us both who we are and who we'd like to be. He's contributed to the forthcoming *The Philosophy of Christopher Nolan* (Lexington) and *The Ultimate Star Trek and Philosophy* (Wiley). You can find him online in the MOOC "Philosophy and Film" at Canvas.net. Meanwhile, he keeps searching for a life greater than that of an ordinary philosopher, a life of significance – of conscience.

Greg Littmann is your father and Associate Professor of Philosophy at Southern Illinois University Edwardsville. You were hidden from him when you were born, and he's been biding his time by publishing on philosophy of logic, evolutionary epistemology, and the ethics of professional philosophy, as well as writing many chapters for books relating philosophy to popular culture, including volumes on *The Big Bang Theory*, *Doctor Who*, *Dune*, *Game of Thrones*, *Planet of the Apes*, and *The Walking Dead*. When his troops finally locate you, you will join him, and together you will rule the galaxy. If you've ever had the feeling that you're more special than other people, this is why.

Terrance MacMullan is Professor of Philosophy and Honors at Eastern Washington University. His book, *The Habits of Whiteness: A Pragmatist Reconstruction*, was published by Indiana University Press in 2009, and he's previously published work on popular culture and philosophy in *The Daily Show and Philosophy* (Wiley, 2007, 2013) and *Star Wars and History* (Wiley, 2013). His proudest achievement was winning second place at the 2014 Spokane Comic Convention for his Qui-Gon Jinn costume.

Daniel Malloy is a lecturer in philosophy at Appalachian State University. His research focuses on issues in ethics. He's published numerous chapters on the intersection of popular culture and philosophy, particularly dealing with the illustration of moral questions in movies, comic books, and television shows. He's pretty sure those *were* the droids he's looking for.

Marek McGann is a lecturer in the Department of Psychology at Mary Immaculate College, University of Limerick, Ireland. He teaches and publishes in the areas of cognitive science and the philosophy of mind, and has a particular interest in the issues of embodiment and consciousness. He spends much of his day finding new ways to motivate students he thinks could do with doubling their efforts.

Jennifer L. McMahon is Professor of Philosophy and English at East Central University in Ada, Oklahoma. She has expertise in existentialism, aesthetics, and comparative philosophy. She's published numerous essays on philosophy and popular culture, most recently in *Buddhism and American Cinema* (SUNY, 2014) and *Death in Classic and Contemporary Cinema* (Palgrave, 2013). She's edited collections, including *The Philosophy of Tim Burton* (University Press of Kentucky, 2014) and *The Philosophy of the Western* (University Press of Kentucky, 2010). While she hopes to have shown that her ambivalence toward Leia has a more legitimate foundation, she admits her negativity toward the princess could just be the result of the fact that she ended up with Han.

Nicolas Michaud teaches philosophy in Jacksonville, Florida. His current research and writing focus on marginalization, disabilities studies, and floppy-eared jerks who ruin perfectly awesome Galactic Republics. He *really* hates Jar Jar Binks.

James M. Okapal is Associate Professor of Philosophy at Missouri Western State University. He's published essays on moral value, ethics in film, and free will in *Harry Potter*. He's currently the chair for the Philosophy and Culture Area at the Pop Culture Association/American Culture Association National Conference. Craving neither adventure nor excitement, his ultimate goal is to become Chief Librarian of the Jedi Archives and rediscover all of the knowledge lost during the Great Jedi Purge of 19 BBY.

Myfanwy Reynolds isn't the philosopher you're looking for. She holds a Master's Degree in Medieval English Literatures and is primarily interested in medieval popular romance and other stories of farmboy heroes, long-lost parents, and strange lands.

Charles Taliaferro is the current Chair of the Department of Philosophy at St. Olaf College, and has authored, coauthored, or edited over twenty books, including *Turning Images* (Oxford University Press, 2011). He's contributed to philosophy and popular culture volumes on *Harry Potter*, the Olympics, the Rolling Stones, and other topics. On his campus, he has an awkward robot modeled on R2-D2 that carries books and student papers.

John M. Thompson, when last heard from, was Associate Professor of Philosophy and Religious Studies at Christopher Newport University, having earned his PhD in the Cultural and Historical Study of Religion at the Graduate Theological Union in Berkeley, California. Even as a child growing up in the wilds of suburban Washington, DC, he had broad interests in Asian cultures and religions, as well as myth, symbol, and ritual. Ancient records indicate that he's written two books on Buddhism, edited a volume of essays on the intersection of politics and religion in Asia, and published various articles and reviews in a wide array of journals and books, among them *Psych and Philosophy* (Open Court, 2013) and *The Devil and Philosophy* (Open Court, 2014). Some people say that he has since disappeared into the deserts of Tatooine, where he lives in a cave practicing martial arts, listening to rock and roll, and searching the scriptures for secret instructions on the mysteries of brewing beer. Others say that he lives in Williamsburg, Virginia, with his beautiful wife and daughters along with a motley pack of troublesome cats and dogs.

Index

Abraham, 32–6
Abrams, J.J., 3, 269, 288
Achilles, 42–52, 130
action figures, *Star Wars*, 287–94
Agamemnon, 45, 130
agency, 187, 189–91, 292
Alderaan, 70–72, 101, 129, 138–9, 163, 183, 197, 200, 208
American Graffiti, 267
Amidala, Padmé, 12, 17, 20, 23–7, 29, 34–5, 42–3, 48–51, 54, 83, 90, 94, 96, 103–6, 108–10, 118–23, 141, 149–50, 152–3, 161–71, 198, 204, 232–3, 240
   handmaidens of, 164, 170–171
amoralism, 79–88
Apollo, 46, 293
appetite, 173–4
Aristotle, 60, 122, 133–5, 219, 221, 254, 264–5
artificial intelligence, 236–9
Artoo-Detoo, 75, 185, 188, 231–2, 248, 267, 291
Augustine, 101–10, 198, 204
autonomy, 190
awareness, 21–2, 211

Bach-y-Rita, Paul, 215
Baggini, Julian, 251
Barthes, Roland, 297
beauty, 154, 198
   feminine, 172–80
Beauvoir, Simone de, 164–7
being, 177–9
   being-for-itself, 177–8
   being-in-itself, 177–8, 198
belief, justified, 219–28
Bespin/Cloud City, 9, 32, 37, 68, 123, 128, 130, 132, 139, 145, 223, 232, 276, 278, 284
betrayal, 136–45
Binks, Jar Jar, 1, 50, 90–98, 150, 199
Blue Snaggletooth, 289–94
Bocce, 234–7
body, 172–80, 209–17
   anxiety about, 179–80
   conscious, 177–8
   control of, 176–7
Bordo, Susan, 172, 175–6, 179–80
bounty hunting, 79–88
Brahman, 196
Brie, Shira/Lumiya, 108
Buddha, the, 122, 266

The Ultimate Star Wars and Philosophy: You Must Unlearn What You Have Learned,
First Edition. Edited by Jason T. Eberl and Kevin S. Decker.
© 2016 John Wiley & Sons, Ltd. Published 2016 by John Wiley & Sons, Ltd.

C-3PO, *see* Threepio
Calrissian, Lando, 8–9, 67–8, 137, 144–5, 198, 274
Campbell, Joseph, 3, 263–72
canon/canonicity, 3, 296–306
    hierarchy of in *Star Wars*, 299–302
categorical imperative, 95–6
certainty, 226–7
Chewbacca, 3, 34, 36, 74, 86, 137, 142, 184–5, 222, 234, 240–248, 252, 274, 298, 303
Children of the Jedi, 189–90
Chinese Room, 234, 237
Chomsky, Noam, 241–8
Christianity/Christendom, 33, 100, 106, 122, 195
Civil War, Second Galactic, 143
Clone Wars, 28, 54, 57, 59, 81, 90, 150, 164, 183, 186, 251
cloning, 250–259
cognition, 137–8
Coleridge, Samuel Taylor, 275–6
compassion, 26
conscience, 141
consciousness, 208–9
Confucius/Confucianism, 53, 55, 58–61, 122
Corellia, 139, 143, 221
Coruscant, 25, 41, 48, 61, 139, 185, 257–8, 302
courage, 152
cupidity, 106–7
Currie, Gregory, 276

Dagobah, 123, 128, 132, 134, 139, 146, 155, 188, 215, 232, 243, 280, 284
Dao/Daoism, 53, 56–8, 196, 199–200, 205
Darth Bane, 10, 47, 140, 143–4, 151
Darth Caedus, *see* Solo, Jacen
Darth Maul, 119, 191, 199, 213, 280
Darth Plagueis, 25, 56, 121, 141, 144, 244, 256
Darth Plagueis the Wise, Tragedy of, 7, 121, 244, 256

Darth Sidious, *see* Palpatine
Darth Tenebrous, 144
Darth Tyranus, *see* Dooku, Count
Darth Vader, *see* Skywalker, Anakin
Darth Venamis, 144
Darth Zannah, 144
Darwin, Charles, 255
Dawkins, Richard, 289
de, 55
death, 13, 16–17, 25–6, 70–76, 87–8, 96, 106, 119, 121, 179
Death Star, 8, 36, 86, 129, 131, 151, 183, 197, 222–3, 232, 264, 268, 300–301
Death Star II (Endor), 35, 38, 67–77, 124, 126
de-extinction, 250–259
democracy, 2, 124, 149, 153, 155
Dennett, Daniel, 287–94
Descartes, René, 175, 177, 288, 292–3
design stance, 287, 290–291
Djo, Tenel Ka, 108
DNA, 250–259
Dooku, Count, 27, 40, 47, 51, 91, 124, 150
droids, 74–6, 137–8, 162, 183, 185–6, 189–90, 213, 223, 231–9, 263
    as property, 233
    prejudice against, 233
dualism, 202–3, 205
    mind–body, 175, 209, 288
duty, 96, 107, 137, 142
    civic, 131–5
Dworkin, Andrea, 165

egoism, ethical, 80–82
Eliade, Mircea, 268
emotions, 274–84
    quasi-, 279–81
    rational, 283–4
Empire, Galactic, 32, 53–4, 68, 70–76, 79–80, 82, 84, 86, 90–91, 93, 122–3, 127–8, 131, 133, 137–8, 142, 148, 151, 271, 276
Empire Striketh Back, The, 80

enactivism, 211–17
Endor, Battle of, 72, 75, 198, 219, 223
Epictetus, 20–25
Episode I – The Phantom Menace, 1, 2, 9, 14, 20, 23, 42, 43, 49, 148–9, 165, 224, 232
Episode II – Attack of the Clones, 2, 8, 27, 49, 149, 152, 224, 240, 301
Episode III – Revenge of the Sith, 1, 2, 3, 15, 21, 26–7, 51, 74, 86, 105, 117, 164, 302
Episode IV – A New Hope, 1, 2, 36, 76, 125, 129, 148, 151, 163, 173, 188, 253, 276, 280, 298, 305
Episode V – The Empire Strikes Back, 2, 50, 85, 117, 122–3, 128–9, 166, 173, 274, 277, 282, 305
Episode VI – Return of the Jedi, 2–3, 31, 42, 67, 76, 80, 85, 87, 123–4, 127–8, 156, 172–80, 302, 305
Episode VII – The Force Awakens, 1–2, 29, 156, 220, 293
Equus, 270
ethics, 8, 21, 33, 61, 68, 137
Euthyphro, 135
evil, 2, 7–18, 21, 27–9, 69, 96, 101–10, 131, 196–205
  privation theory of, 198–9
  problem of, 101–10
evolution, 254–5
Ewoks, 183, 232, 244–5, 254
Expanded Universe (EU), 1, 3, 80, 88, 240, 246, 296–306
experience, 219–28
  inference from past, 224

faith, 31–41, 107, 124, 205, 222, 224, 265
fallibility/fallibilism, 154, 227–8
family, 117–27, 135–6, 144
fat, hatred of, 172–80
fatherhood, 117–26
feelings, 137–8
Feminine Mystique, The, 167–8

feminism/feminist, 161–71
  and embodiment, 172–80
  different types of, 162
  Second Wave, 165
Fett, Boba, 3, 79–88, 142, 179, 251–2, 256–8, 274, 291
Fett, Jango, 29, 74, 81, 252, 256–8
fiction, 275–84, 296–306
  illusion theory, 275–7, 282
  paradox of, 275–84
  pretend theory, 275, 279–83
  thought theory, 275, 277–9, 282
Fletcher, George, 138, 142
Force, the, 2–3, 11, 14–15, 21–9, 50, 56–8, 100–110, 136, 143, 155–6, 161, 186, 195–205, 208–17, 219, 223–5, 240–241, 243, 245–6, 270, 276, 294
  dark side of, 3, 7–18, 27–9, 31, 34, 36, 40, 81, 86, 100–101, 103, 118–19, 121, 124, 130, 136, 143, 150–151, 155, 195–205
  light side of, 7–18, 100, 136, 143, 195–205
Ford, John, 267
Foucault, Michel, 172, 176–7
Frankfurt, Harry, 97–8
freedom, 8, 11, 133, 149, 153, 175, 196
free will, 103–10
Friedan, Betty, 167–8
friendship, 127–135

gender, 172, 179
Geonosis, Battle of, 81, 257
Ghent, Zakarisz, 303–6
Ghiselin, Michael, 255
God, 32–6, 100–101, 105–10, 195–6, 198, 203
good/goodness, 2, 21, 102–10, 118–26, 130–131, 154, 196, 198
  eternal vs temporal, 105–7
Greedo, 1, 168, 184, 186, 287, 289, 305
Grievous, General, 29, 184, 191
ground, 204–5
guardians, 13–14, 118, 150–156

habit, 211, 214, 217, 225
Hale, Benjamin, 184
happiness, 105, 134, 156
Harris, Sam, 289
Hector, 43, 45–6, 130
Hegel, G.W.F., 3
heroes, 129–30, 134–5, 263–72
Hero's Journey, 266–7
Hero with a Thousand Faces, The, 263, 267
Hinduism, 270
Hitchens, Christopher, 289
Holocaust, the, 101
Homer, 45, 49–50, 172–3
Hoth, 37, 129, 222, 232, 300–301
Hudorra, Kai, 53, 58, 61–2
Hume, David, 222–7
Hursthouse, Rosalind, 183–4

identity, 172–80
    female, 161–71
ideology, 265, 270
IG-88, 231
Iliad, 42, 45, 49, 50–51, 130
indifference, 22–3, 26
induction, 225–8
    problem of, 226
innocence, 73–5
intentional stance, 287, 292–4
intentions, 22, 69, 70–73, 76, 90–98
interpretation, 44, 297–8
    authorial, 297–306
Isaac, 32–6
Islam, 34, 100, 122

Jabba the Hutt, 36, 74, 80, 82, 86–7, 128–30, 132, 134, 146, 166–7, 172–80, 185, 190, 198, 222, 244, 288, 301
Jawas, 183, 232, 291
Jedi, 2, 9, 12, 17–18, 20–29, 34, 36, 47, 53, 58–9, 61–2, 75, 91, 97, 100–101, 104, 105, 118–21, 132, 143–4, 146, 148–56, 161, 175, 186, 195–6, 200, 203, 208–17, 219, 224–5, 233, 268, 276

Council, 22, 42, 47, 49
    female, 163
Jennir, Dass, 53, 58–62
Jesus Christ, 15, 119, 266
Jettster, Dexter, 8
Jinn, Qui-Gon, 20–21, 24–8, 47, 49, 119, 122, 196, 212, 214, 221, 235, 245–6
Judaism, 34, 100, 122
Jung, Carl, 266, 268
just war theory, 68–77, 84
justice, 9–12, 14, 44, 133, 148–56

Kamino, 81, 223–4, 252–7
Kant, Immanuel, 48–9, 94–8, 190
Karrde, Talon, 137, 303
Keller, Simon, 139–40, 144
Kenobi, Obi-Wan, 8, 22–7, 31–2, 36, 42, 44, 81, 83, 92, 100–101, 104–5, 109, 119–22, 125, 128–9, 135, 138, 141, 146, 148, 155, 167, 173, 186, 195, 197, 200–201, 202, 208–12, 216, 219, 222, 224–5, 227–8, 232–3, 242, 245–6, 252, 267–8, 276, 280, 291
Kierkegaard, Søren, 31–41
Killik Twilight, 197
K'kruhk, 54, 56–8
knowledge, 219–28
Kripke, Saul, 259
Kun, Exar, 213
Kurosawa, Akira, 267

language, 236–9, 240–248
    grammar of, 241, 248
    "meaning is use," 243–7
    picture theory of, 243
    syntax of, 241, 248
    theory of, 243–8
language-games, 244
Laozi, 53, 56–8, 122
Legacy of the Force, 143
Lessing, Gotthold, 33
li, 60
liberty, *see* freedom
life, 186–7

logos, 264, 269
love, 105, 107–8, 118–26, 153, 204–5
loyalty, 130, 134–46
    "loyalty to loyalty itself," 136, 143–4
    voluntary, 138
Lucasfilm, 1, 297–8, 302, 305–6
Lucas, George, 1, 2, 90, 100, 127, 172,
    196, 202–3, 263–72, 290, 293,
    296, 299, 302–4
Lumiya, *see* Brie, Shira

Malastare, 250, 258
Malinowski, Bronislaw, 265
Mandalorians, 82, 88, 142
Mandate of Heaven, 55
Manicheanism, 202–3, 205
marriage, 166–7
meaning, 213–17, 240–248, 265
mental representations, 277, 279
mercenaries, 79–88
Merleau-Ponty, Maurice, 208–10, 216
metaphysics, 100, 201
midi-chlorians, 2, 14, 18, 27, 50, 118,
    121, 216, 220, 224, 246
Mill, John Stuart, 188
Millennium Falcon, 8, 137, 184, 198,
    215, 243, 276–7, 292–3
mind, science of, 289–94
mind-trick, Jedi, 28
miracles, 222
Mitth'raw'nuruodo, *see* Thrawn, Grand
    Admiral
monomyth, 266–72
morality, 15, 18, 102, 141–3, 183–91,
    232
    moral agency, 109–10
    moral considerability, 183–5
    moral law, 94–6
    moral luck, 91
    moral philosophy, 68–77, 79–88
    moral realism, 46–52
    moral relativism, 80–82
    moral relevance, 185–91
    moral responsibility, 75, 102
    moral significance, 184–5
    moral status, 74–5, 183–91

Moran, Caitlin, 170
mother/motherhood, 165, 168
Mothma, Mon, 164, 168, 170
Moyers, Bill, 263
Mozi/Moism, 61–2
Mustafar, 44, 92, 101, 107, 121, 197,
    212, 232–3
mysticism, 223, 263
myth/mythology, 3, 263–72

Naboo, 9, 27, 43–4, 48, 149–50, 163,
    165, 170
Nagel, Thomas, 91–3
Nausea, 177–78
nerf herder, scruffy-looking, 243
Nicomachean Ethics, 133
Nietzsche, Friedrich, 8, 14–18, 43–52
nihilism, 43–52
"noble lie," 13
norms, social, 176

objectification, sexual, 165–8
Odysseus, 130
Odyssey, 130, 172–3
Okrand, Marc, 248
Oldenquist, Andrew, 139, 142
Olié, Ric, 201
Order, 66, 54, 56, 61, 75, 110, 151,
    191, 200
Organa (Solo), Leia, 34, 42, 68, 71,
    86–7, 92, 124, 128–35, 138–9, 141,
    143, 145, 161–80, 224, 231–2,
    247, 267, 271, 274–5, 284, 298,
    301, 302–3

Palpatine, Emperor/Darth Sidious, 2,
    7–18, 21, 27–9, 31–2, 34–6, 38–41,
    44, 47, 50–51, 53, 58, 61, 73–4, 85,
    90–91, 94, 97–8, 101, 103–4, 109,
    121–3, 125, 128–30, 133, 139–42,
    149–50, 161, 164, 170, 187,
    189–91, 196–7, 223, 243, 250–251,
    253, 256–8, 283
panentheism, 195–7
partiality, 141–2
patriarchy, 165

Patroclus, 43, 46, 130
peace, 107, 133, 148, 211
Peirce, Charles Sanders, 227
perception, 210–212, 216–17
Pettit, Philip, 137, 141–2
phenomenology, 208–17
Philosophical Investigations, 243
philosophy, Chinese, 53–62, 100
physical stance, 287, 290–291
Plato, 7–18, 55–6, 60, 122, 132–5, 148–56, 175, 264
pleasure, 36, 68, 187–8
pluralism, 299
Popper, Karl, 242
power, 9, 21–2, 45, 110, 123, 141, 149, 152, 166
Power of Myth, The, 263
Prabhavananda, Swami, 197, 202
Priam, King, 43, 46, 51
private language argument, 244–5
probability, 226
properties, 186–91
    physical, 186–7
    psychological, 187–91
proportionality in war, 68, 70, 73, 75–6
proprioception, 215
psychology, 268–9
Putnam, Hilary, 227, 259

qi, 100, 200, 205

R2-D2, *see* Artoo-Detoo
Radford, Colin, 283–4
Rakata, 15–16
Reagan, Ronald, 271
reason, 11–13, 148–56, 202–3, 264
    inductive, 225
Rebel Alliance, 3, 35–6, 67–77, 80, 82, 84–7, 91, 124, 128–35, 138, 142, 146, 164, 268, 271
"rectification of names," 58–9
religion, 165, 205–6, 265, 293–4
ren, 60
Republic, 11–13, 132, 148–56
Republic, New, 76, 156, 170

Republic, Old Galactic, 10, 13–14, 28, 50, 54, 58–9, 61, 75, 82, 86, 117, 120, 133, 148–56, 163, 188, 224, 251
rights, 165
role models, female, 161–71
Roquentin, 177–8
Rosch, Eleanor, 210, 216
Royce, Josiah, 136–46
Rubens, Peter Paul, 174
"Rule of Two," 47, 140, 151
rule utilitarianism, 68

Sartre, Jean-Paul, 172, 177–80
Schaffer, Peter, 270
Schelling, Friedrich, 201–5
Schweitzer, Albert, 186
science, 221, 223–4, 226, 251–9, 288
Searchers, The, 267
Searle, John, 234–37
Second Sex, The, 164–5
Secura, Aayla, 301–2
See-Threepio, 75, 127, 146, 184, 188, 231–2, 240, 244, 245, 267, 278–9, 284, 301
self, 36, 125
    historical, 138
    self-awareness, 74–5
    self-determination, 177
sensory systems, 215
sentience, 187–91, 197
Separatists, 33, 42, 50–51, 57, 59, 150, 204, 233–4
sexuality, 166–8
shi, 55
Shyriiwook, 241–2, 247
sin, 105, 120
Singer, Peter, 188
Sith, 7, 9–18, 40, 47, 49, 58, 90, 100–101, 104, 107, 140–141, 143–4, 146, 148, 150–151, 196, 204, 213, 220, 224, 246
    Brotherhood of Darkness, 151
skepticism, 221, 227
Skywalker, Anakin/Darth Vader, 1, 2, 7, 11–12, 17, 20–21, 23–9, 31–54, 62,

79–83, 87, 91–2, 94, 96, 101, 103–10, 117–30, 132–4, 140–142, 145, 149, 151–2, 166–9, 173, 184, 191, 196–7, 199–201, 204, 212, 214, 221, 224–5, 232–3, 236, 240, 243, 255, 257, 268, 274, 276–7, 279–80, 282, 288, 291
Skywalker, Ben, 107
Skywalker, Luke, 2, 31–42, 75, 80, 87, 92, 100–102, 117–18, 123–35, 137, 139–41, 145, 148, 154, 156, 166, 170, 173, 175, 177–9, 188, 201, 208–11, 214–15, 219, 221–5, 228, 236, 242, 244, 246, 252, 254, 267–8, 271, 276–84, 291, 298, 300, 302
Skywalker, Mara Jade, 107
Skywalker, Shmi, 12, 25–6, 118–20, 163, 168, 170, 355
slavery, 11, 21, 150
Sleazebaggano, Elan, 104
Smith, Kevin, 3, 67–8, 85
Socrates, 8–9, 17, 130–131, 148–56, 220–222
Solo, Allana Djo, 108
Solo, Anakin, 110
Solo, Han, 1, 8–9, 34, 36, 68, 80, 82, 87–8, 92, 94, 127, 137, 139, 142–3, 145, 166–7, 173, 184–7, 195, 215, 219, 221–5, 227, 241, 243, 247, 252, 274–5, 278, 283–4, 287, 292–4, 301, 303, 305–6
Solo, Jacen/Darth Caedus, 88, 102–3, 107–10, 143
Solo, Jaina, 88, 143
somatic cell nuclear transfer (SCNT), 252–3, 256, 258
Sophists, 9–10
soul, 11, 16–17, 55–6, 106, 148–56
Spaceballs, 100
species, 254–9
    essentialism, 254–5
    nominalism, 255–6
    problem, 254
speech, 241–8
Star Wars and Philosophy, 2–4

Star Wars Holiday Special, 289–91, 301, 304
Star Wars: The Clone Wars, 3, 74, 185, 296
stereotyping, 164–9
Stoics/Stoicism, 2, 20–29, 119–20, 122
suffering, 109, 188, 239

Tano, Ahsoka, 184
Tarkin, Grand Moff, 70, 138, 163, 183, 226
Tatooine, 15, 61, 119–20, 128, 131, 138–9, 162, 170, 172, 221, 232, 267, 279
Telemachus, 130
terrorism, 67–77, 85–6
Thales, 219–21
theodicy, 100–110
thinness, 173–80
Thompson, Evan, 210–211, 213, 216
thought, 231–9
Thrasymachus, 9, 150–151
Thrawn, Grand Admiral, 187, 251, 253, 256–8
Thrawn Trilogy, 137, 302–5
Tolkien, J.R.R., 247–8
torture, 69, 174, 224
Tractatus Logico-Philosophicus, 243
Trade Federation, 9, 43–4, 150, 165
truth, 110, 219–28
Tusken Raiders/Sand People, 12, 26, 35, 42, 46, 120, 183, 205
tyranny, 2, 85, 96, 148–56, 180, 196

understanding, 25–6, 211, 234–5, 247–8, 287–94
utilitarianism, 31, 68–9, 72

Valerian and Laureline, 267
Valorum, Chancellor, 150, 165
Varela, Francisco, 210–211, 213, 216
vice, 21

virtue, 21, 25–6, 60, 93, 120, 130, 133, 137, 152, 198–9

Walton, Kendall, 279–81
Walzer, Michael, 85
war, 79–88
will, 104–10, 203–5
Windu, Mace, 28–9, 91, 124, 152, 186, 190, 224
wisdom, 2, 8, 21, 119, 122, 131, 154
Wittgenstein, Ludwig, 242–8
Wolf, Susan, 93
woman/womanhood, 3, 161–71
    stereotypes of, 164–6
    strong, 162
wu-wei, 57

Xenophanes, 264
xenophobia, 187

Yavin, Battle of, 36, 78, 145, 232
Yoda, 9, 15, 17, 25–6, 29, 31, 35–6, 41, 47, 50–51, 80, 103, 105–7, 109, 118–20, 123, 128, 132, 135, 139, 141, 151, 154, 177, 195, 198–201, 205, 208, 210–214, 220, 224, 232, 243, 280–281, 284
Yuuzhan Vong, 76, 110

Zahn, Timothy, 137, 302–5
Zao, Master, 57, 61
Zarathustra, 15–16
Zeno of Citium, 120
Zeus, 132, 293
Zhou Empire, 53–5, 60
Zhuangzi, 199–201, 205
Zillo Beast, 184–7, 189, 191, 250–251, 253–9
Zutmore/Zutton, *see* Blue Snaggletooth